FIGHTING IN GOD'S LIVING ROOM

WARFARE IN ELYSIUM

Servant of Jesus (Yeshua) Christ

Larry K. Thompson

ISBN 978-1-64468-622-5 (Paperback)
ISBN 978-1-64468-623-2 (Digital)

Covenant Books, Inc.
11661 Hwy 707
Murrells Inlet, SC 29576
www.covenantbooks.com

DEDICATION

This book in its entirety is dedicated to the Living God of Abraham, Isaac and Yacub (Jacob), i.e., Yahweh, Elohim, along with his Holy, Exalted, Only Begotten Son, The Lord and Savior, Yeshua (Jesus) Christ and His Eternal, Divine Holy Spirit who has made all things possible for me. I am eternally grateful, humbled, and indebted to the God of Israel forever! I can never repay God for his abundant mercy that none of us on earth deserve. However, I can, I will, and I do receive it as the unconditional gift of God's love for my soul. I cannot attest to anything that God has done for others because I do not know for that is their responsibility. Yet what I can shout from the top of Mount Sinai is that the God of Jerusalem has without fail sustained, protected, guided, defended, and shielded me from my enemies by his love, whether they be celestial or terrestrial, demon, or man, more times than I can count or dare to remember. God has been a faithful, present help in times of trouble especially during the struggles of life that we all share even when I because of evil pride, rebellion, and disobedience refused to or did not call upon him. His mercy is endless as the sand upon the shores by the seas. God's devotion to love is unparalleled in human history or affairs. No one can ever love you more than God can and does, period! I will forever proclaim the goodness of the Lord, for I am a living witness to his bountiful mercy. Life has so many twists that we try to anticipate or overcome as we navigate upon the sea of life in our little arks. Steering feverishly trying to avoid the shipwrecks, reefs, waves, storms, and dangers of life, while searching for the lighthouse or nearest shoreline for refuge as best we can without drowning in sorrow, self-pity, defeat, sadness, or madness, foolishly thinking that we are the "captains of our ships" or the "masters of our destiny" hah. Go tell that to someone that simply does not know any better.

*We should all know better than that! My God because of his Son, Jesus Christ has given me courage, strength, mercy, intestinal fortitude, help, deliverance, perseverance, hope but most important of all, God Almighty through Jesus Christ, has given me his "unconditional" love. God's love is a commodity that is unpurchaseable, unlimited, unredeemable, unrelenting, unforgettable, untransferable, unimaginable, unbelievable, and unthinkable. However, more powerful than all of this, God's love is... **UNDENIABLE!** If you are ever in need of a reason to keep on going forward or to hold on just one more day regardless to the situation you may find yourself enmeshed, remember, pain is proof that you are still alive. You have another chance... Do not give up! Fight with all of your might and hope in Christ! All of us hurt from time to time, all of us cry at some time in our lives, either silently or loudly. Nevertheless, keep in mind that God has promised that he will wipe away every tear. How can God wipe away a tear if you have not cried any tears? If you are hurting for any reason right now, as all of us do occasionally, let me offer you a recommendation. Do not look to family, friends, lovers, or acquaintances. Albeit God allows them in our lives as supporting cast members. Instead, look to pray to your Creator, God Almighty. For he knows what things you have need of before you ask, as well as the depth of your pain. Trust him with all of your heart and do not depend upon your own understanding and God will abundantly supply all* *of your needs according to his riches in glory through Christ, Our Lord (God's words and promises) found in Proverbs 3:5–6.*

I wanted to say more to expand this dissertation. However, my God has tempered my message to be short, brief, direct, and to the point, but more imperatively to **His Glory! God has stated that he will not share his glory with anyone. He will share his love with everyone who accepts it, but not his sacred glory with anyone period!** *Therefore, my reply to him is I will stop here Lord. I pray for the peace of Jerusalem for it is the City of the Great King. Jerusalem is the **only** city in the world that is in heaven and on the earth simultaneously. To my Father, Avery Thompson Sr. and my Mother, Mary L. Williams, I simply say thank you for all of your love, support and encouragement during the most imperative years of my life. I dearly miss you both. I will dedicate the next book to the two of you God willing, I live and am able to pen another literary prose to his sacred glory by doing so. Therefore, let me humbly request that in the interim period in memoriam that you accept, honorable mention, in lieu of devotion to God first. Therefore, I voluntary humble myself to the Lord God who created me via the two of you. Additionally, to my son, Jason Henderson, Dad loves you always. You have consistently demonstrated exceptional intelligence, tenacity, strength, and independence throughout your experiences way beyond your peers and my high expectations. You have truly made me a proud and joyful Father, you are a true soldier; you are and will always be the apple of my eye! I would also like to thank and express my sincere gratitude to my high school sweetheart, Stephanie Camille Sammons (pictured with author at Detroit Northwestern*

High School 1977 Prom), who prayed for me endlessly as she witnessed to me about Christ. Well, I can honestly say the results of her prayers for me have been my faith and belief in Jesus Christ as the Son of God and the Kingdom of God Almighty world without end! Take Care until we meet again... May God bless, your prodigal son, Larry... Maranatha.

PREFACE

This book is the maiden book in the mini-book series entitled 'Highway of Holiness to Christ' Isaiah 35:8–9 relating to the Kingdom of Almighty God and his Son, Jesus Christ. Specifically, this book is about the origin of all warfare, both in heaven and on earth, which unbelievably, actually started in heaven above, where God dwells supremely atop the pinnacle and hierarchy of all principalities or powers, dominions, thrones, or spheres of his creation. God's sovereignty reigns over all in heaven or on the earth. Whether these domains are visible or invisible, including his divinely created spiritual beings—i.e., angels and mankind. Consequently, all wars occur as a direct result of heavenly rebellion, revolution, and usurpation against God's Divine authority. See Revelation 12:7–9 that states and there was "war in heaven" Michael and his angels fought against the dragon and the dragon fought and his angels. But they did not prevail; neither was there place found in heaven any longer. So the Great Dragon was cast out, that Old Serpent, called the Devil and Satan, which deceives the whole world he was cast out into the earth and his angels were cast out with him. Heaven's War has devastating eternal consequences for humanity. The spiritual forces of good and evil fighting for supremacy…light versus darkness… God versus the Devil…culminating in the final destiny of your soul.

Who will win? Whose side will you be fighting on? Do you **know** for **sure** where you will spend eternity? If not, I invite you to read this short book to help you make the eternal choice to accept Jesus Christ as your personal Savior to guarantee it is in God's Living Room in Heaven. God eternally evicted Satan from his Living Room in heaven so that he could extend an "open invitation" to all willing humanity to be there with him alongside his Son, Jesus (Yeshua)

Christ! See **Deuteronomy 30:19 that says, "I call heaven and earth as witnesses today against you, that I have** *set before you life and death, blessing and cursing; therefore choose life,* **that both you and your descendants may live."** However, the choice remains an individual decision either way to accept or to reject this heavenly invitation…that has eternal consequences no matter which one you choose. Choose wisely for it will be your eternal home!

CONTENTS

INTRODUCTION

Fighting In God's Living Room

This book was written using the Holy Bible, which all God revering Christians (those who by faith believe that Christ is Lord) consider to be the inspired, authoritative word of Almighty God to man. Although some borrowing perspectives or idioms from other books were included, reviewed, sampled and consulted, the Holy Bible will be the primary source for information regarding this inquiry. Obviously, I have never been to Heaven (physically) well then again, all of us have been, allegorically speaking, because we all originated in the mind of God who has always been in heaven...but I am going back either in the rapture or upon the completion of this marathon race that we call life...the Lord willing. The purpose and intent of this book is to explore why, where, how, whom, and when wars originated and why does God "seem" to be silent on the matter. This exploratory narrative is dedicated to ascertaining an overview inquiry via GIP, not GPS—i.e., Global Positioning Satellites. GIP simply means, in this context "God-Inspired Perspective" or God's point of view of divine geo-introspection into this phenomenon as well as to what God is *actually saying* about wars' origins as well as its summation. Wars are a violent, calamitous struggle, pitting one side or group against the other. Negotiations are no longer a part of the dialogue, because war means that all sides have in their perspective, painstakingly exhausted the necessity or ability to resolve their differences peacefully or amicably between or amongst themselves or others through diplomacy. The terminal result leads to a physical confrontation resulting in the decimation, death, and destruction of the other side into total submission involuntarily. Wars are the final end game that will declare which position, which group, which entity will ultimately have its influence as the dominant or sole ruling authority in any struggle.

Here on earth the causation of wars have numerous origins that lead to the inevitability of wars rationality to fight among various entities including. incursions, skirmishes, and battles as they are fought between or among nations, states, countries, races, tribes, and people, clans, or ethnic groups. Review the words of the Lord in **James 4:1–3** that says, *"Where do wars and fights come from among you? Do they not come from your desires for pleasure that war in your members? You lust and do not have. You murder, covet, and cannot obtain. You fight and war yet you do not have because you do not ask. You ask and do not receive because you ask amiss, that you may spend it on your pleasures."*

Powerful aircraft carriers, ships, aircraft, submarines, armadas, and flotillas carrying Marines, sailors, soldiers, and weaponry to various parts of earth's hemispheres to fight other indigenous populations. Furthermore, these well-organized, equipped, armed forces assemblage to fight at all costs in the sanctioned annihilation of the opposing side only to emerge as the victor over the vanquished. Wars are the only place where second place finishes result in the death and humiliation of the losing side. Once the battle begins, there is no turning back, no compromising, no second guesses, or second-place trophies wanted here. Additionally, various and different ethnic groups illustrated by Croats killing Serbians in Slovenia, racial superiority instigated wars (ethnic cleansing) erupt without hesitation to exterminate, subjugate ethnic Muslims or minorities. The Hutus in Africa, fighting violently against the Hottentots without showing mercy as they savagely butcher innocent men, women and children with machetes and machine guns. The Rohingya have witnessed the barbaric atrocities of genocide upon them by the Myanmarian government (state-sanctioned killing) of humans simply because of diverse race or religious persecution identification. The Africans and

Black populations in Western Africa were decimated, enslaved, barbarically butchered, inhumanely captured, murdered, tortured, and sold into slavery as they were chained together only to be carted off like animals to the "New World" during the Middle Passage to the Americas and all other corners of the globe. In addition, it is where their descendants still to this very day (**almost four hundred years later**) bare the scarlet letter of racial bigotry, lynching, police assassination, generational poverty, and ghetto life entombment... All of this despite having, one "black-skinned" president in over two hundred years of the Republic! America the Beautiful. African-Americans are the walking dead, dead while living, a second-class citizen in the land of "*O beautiful for halcyon skies for amber waves of grain*" whereby first-class citizenship is promised to all Americans...*except* us!

Godlessly, amazingly, shamefully, mercilessly, and disgracefully, there is this humongous collective "quietness or silence" by our fellow "white Christian" brethren and sisters here in America when they witness the crimes against their "Christian" brethren. Maybe it is because they benefit from two significant prongs of the same pincer. I am white, so I get all of the benefits of "white privilege" that diabolical, fabricated, Satanic inspired, man-made entitlement in a racist country that attaches an artificial, superficial, subjective, value to my pigmentation (no melanin) which is nothing but a demonic lie from Satan himself regarding "white superiority" and all it <u>costs</u> me is ***my silence***. I benefit from this because I am a member of the privileged group. However, I cannot be condemned because I am a "Christian" and God will grant me all of the benefits of my professed "faith" in Jesus. Well, well, well look'r a here, Uncle Jed, as Jethro Bodine of the Beverly Hillbillies television show would always say (*country slang phrase*) these white Christians get *two* benefits and black Christians and other marginalized people in America get <u>one</u> if Jesus Christ is their Savior in the paradise of God. This is a mysterious paradox, somewhat eerie in a sense. All of this talk, preaching, sermons, singing, prayer and worship about God on Sunday morning. By the way, the Sabbath is Saturday ***not*** Sunday or day of the Sun God. While white racial superiority, entitlement, privilege, bigotry, hatred with demeaning, dehumanizing, atrocious mentality and actions occur (the other six days of the week against blacks) without abatement, whereby people "claim" to be Christian and love Christ.

But obviously forgot or simply ignore some of Jesus Christ words specifically, where Christ says, "**How can a man say he loves God whom he _cannot see_ and hates his brother** (blacks and others) **that _he does see_ he/she is a liar, the _truth is not_ in him! (1 John 4:20)**. Elie Wiesel, an Ashkenazi Jewish holocaust survivor stated it best when he said, I quote, "What hurts the victim the most is not the violence of the oppressor, but **the silence** of the bystander," unquote. Jesus Christ calls it hypocrisy and so do I! However, there is an even more practical question that these "Christians" may want to ask themselves. This question is; if you cannot live with accept or tolerate non Anglo-Saxons on earth how can you live in harmony with them in God's divine paradise? This life and mannerisms are a "dress rehearsal" for the eternal kingdom of God. One final scripture that I would like to leave our white fellow "Christian" "brothers and sisters" with is something else they seemed to have forgotten that the Lord Jesus Christ said, "_The first shall be last and the last shall be first in the Kingdom of God_" (Matthew 20:16). Well, I guess we all know who the first and the last are here in America. Furthermore, the Ashkenazi Jews that were in Western Europe at the time of the Jewish Diaspora were almost completely annihilated without a trace in Europe, by the Germans during World War II as a pogrom of the "final solution" of Adolf Hitler's plan to rid Germany and Western Europe of this Jewish population's existence problem. Adolf Hitler was a sadistic, satanic, maniacal, racist, demon who killed almost 50 percent of the total Ashkenazi Jewish population alive or present in the Western European theater with minimal to no outcry from the rest of the world including _my country tis of thee, sweet land of liberty of thee I sing_ also known as the United States of America! Fact, America _did not_ voluntarily go to war against the Nazis of Germany to degrade or stop the wholesale genocide of the Jewish people. The Americans became involved in the war _after_ being bombed suddenly or unexpectedly then prepared to fight after Japan bombed Pearl Harbor, Hawaii. Japan, Italy, and Germany promptly declared war on the United States since they were allies.

Finally, I would be remiss if I did not acknowledge the unlawful, violent military use of force or conquest against the American Indians, Mayans, and Mexicans who were already here (indigenous, lawful, residents) **of America first, way** before (hundreds of years) Columbus petitioned Queen Isabella and King Ferdinand of Spain for ships, which they sailed to America upon. These "alien" ships were the *Santa Maria*, the *Pinta*, and the *Nina* to cross the seven seas in search of supposedly a promised, quicker trading route to the Far East and India only to either not follow his map, navigator or his misdirected compass to "*discover*" America, hah. THIS SOUNDS LIKE THE FIRST STEPS OF A PLANNED CONQUEST TO ME. The American Indian is the only sovereign people on God's planet whose land taken from their possession and ownership by secular military force. Afterward, all of them, then physically removed from cherished hunting, fishing, worshipping and idea tracts of land for raising their children. Forcibly evicted from their native homeland spaces and relocated inside of a "reservation tract of land" within their own country! Some would dare say or state that so are The Palestinians too. I would respectfully disagree because this is a spiritual issue not a natural one.

God Almighty says that **he gave their land** to his people the Hebrews in **Joshua 24:5 and 8**. Listed here: **And I sent Moses, Aaron, and I plagued Egypt, according to that which I did among them. I brought you into the land of the Amorites, which dwelt on the other side of Jordan, they fought with you, and I gave them into your hand that you might "possess their land" and I destroyed them before you**. I am not a challenger to God's authority but anyone whom willing is more than welcome to take my place can challenge God of their own volition by themselves. I will offer no help or advice to you or anyone else who dares to challenge God. You will receive no encouragement or enticement from me either way period! You are welcome! Neither do I offer any condolences for what God will do unto you. Continuing with the narrative, The Mayans are so far removed from North America to the South American continent in vast numbers to the best of our current knowledge attributed to you guessed it *lebensraum*—i.e., "German" for living space for "white settlers" in North America. The devil was successful in **dividing** holy angels one from the other in heaven or God's Living Room causing a catastrophic war on earth that is still raging today like out of control California wildfires. Some angels now demons fought for Satan and others fought against him with Michael the Archangel on the side of Christ Our Lord. Satan deployed a mathematical formula that Aristotle whom tutored the young Alexander the Great, at his father, King Phillip II of Macedon's behest. Lucifer is still using the same formula today. The formula is divide and conquer. Satan has divided the world along racial superiority lies. **Jesus Christ stated in Mark 3:25 that a house-divided against itself could not stand**. So let us apply this to America. If America continues to remain bitterly divided against each other predicated upon racial, political, financial or any other means, could it survive or will it fall, as did the ancient Roman Empire, which divided against itself while simultaneously fighting external wars.

Christ said no and so do I. Contemporary white Americans today **are not** responsible for the sins of their ancestors of yesterday. Let me make this point perfectly clear to all readers so there is no misunderstanding whatsoever. It is a demonic lie to insist, penalize, accuse, imply, infer, or have malice toward any contemporary white person today for the crimes of their ancestors of yesteryear. Satan is a deceiver and a liar who wants persons of color specifically black or African Americans to hold contemporary white Americans hostage to guilt or shame for crimes (slavery, human trafficking, lynching, murder, rape, generational oppression and impoverishment) **they did not commit**. This is preposterous, evil, deceptive, corrosive, polarizing, toxic, un-Christian-like, and divisive and creates hostility on both sides needlessly. Remember Jesus said that a house divided against itself cannot stand. The Bible tells us as believers, worshippers and adherents of the tenements of Jesus Christ in **Ephesians 6:11** to **put on the whole armor of God that you may be able to withstand the wiles** (or tricks) **of the devil**. This satanic trick creates anger, bitterness, resentment, hostility, and mistrust between the two groups. Lucifer laughs hysterically bellowing demonic undertones aloud-proclaiming mission accomplished. This gives him a hollow victory when this debauchery occurs and a foothold in our lives from where he can mount more debilitating counter-attacks upon our faith and walk with Jesus Christ and each other as mandated in the American Pledge of Allegiance.

Cited here, "*I pledge allegiance to the Flag of the United States of America and to the Republic, for which it stands One Nation under God, Indivisible, with Liberty, and Justice for all.*" The word of God commands us as worshippers of the Invisible God of Israel in **Ephesians 4:27. Neither gives place unto the devil.** Satan surmises I have divided them now I can conquer them all! However, if contemporary white Americans both Christian and non-Christian alike, are not willing to or it appears that they do not or will not acknowledge the grave injustices, sins, crimes and abuses of their forefathers. Who have marginalized and savagely stolen land, resources, people (African slaves) and incalculable wealth or property of indigenous populations worldwide to ensure their own survival at everyone else's expense within America. They will be complicit and magnify the crimes of their ancestors. The word of God cautions all believers in Christ regardless to ethnicity to understand our true enemy is Satan. Not one another as the devil whispers his lies to us and says we are better, superior or more special breed than other ethnic groups. Consequently, we alone are entitled to exclusive privileges that others cannot attain by virtue of inheritance due to "the Master Races Supremacy" evil concept. Satan is the author and conductor of all confusion and evil. Believers in Christ precautionary directive is listed in **Ephesians 6:12** that reads, "**For we do not wrestle against flesh and blood** (*i.e., black nor white*) **but against principalities, against powers, against the rulers of the darkness of this world against spiritual wickedness in heavenly places**." America is not perfect. However, America's greatness comes from its historical ability and willingness positively to redress past injustices. I list a couple of examples for support of this premise. These are slavery, via The Civil Rights Act of 1964, and the Thirteenth and Fourteenth Amendments to United States Constitution. Furthermore, financial incentives, conciliations and allowances to Southern states via civil war reparations to the South during Reconstruction Era and #metoo women movement today as an example of previous blatant, institutional, discriminatory, degrading, and egregious sexual harassment of women in all forums of American lifestyle or venues of association of gender diversification assembly.

Wearing red hats, shouting and demonizing opposing perspectives, spewing hatred does not make America Great. These specific polarizing actions makes America hate. However, recipients or beneficiaries of ill-gotten wealth are in no moral position to demand that descendants, offspring, and others who are victims of their ancestors' crimes—to tell unjustly, generationally enslaved, criminally victimized people to "just pull up" their bootstraps. When their ancestors stole not only their boots, their bodies, their labor, and their bootstraps as well! God declares that there will be a day of reckoning, i.e., Judgment Day. Whereby all shall give complete account of their conduct on this earth. Keep watch. It will not be long now as the End Times are rapidly approaching all humanity. Let us see what saith the Lord when he judges the quick and the dead on this harrowing day. Jesus said, **there will be weeping, wailing and gnashing of teeth (Matthew 13:42).** For the record, I just wonder who will be weeping, walling and gnashing their teeth. Will it be the oppressors or the oppressed on Judgment Day?

Furthermore, the Mexicans are referred to as "illegal aliens" what a joke! They were here **_before_** the white "settlers" from Europe whom the Native American, Mexican and Mayans considered to be "illegal aliens" travelled via the *Mayflower* ship. Just because you possess stolen property by brute, force does not mean that you are the rightful owner of it. Let me provide readers with a simple everyday example just in case someone pretends that he or she does not understand what I am saying here. If someone takes your car at gunpoint, _a.k.a. carjacking_ this is the use of brute force. Afterward, he or she begins driving it all around town even occasionally making repairs, putting gas inside of the gas tank and paying any or all toll fees, registration, or licensing fees, getting the oil changed, rotating the tires, and getting the engine tuned up. Does these voluntary self-serving acts that the person is using to maintain the vehicle in good operational care or status make the carjacker "entitled" to keeping your car? Do these actions all of which are good to enhance the vehicle's performance, drivability, etc., make them the **legitimate owner** of it because they still have their gun in their possession just in case you come to ask for it back without the police? Not!

Therefore, analogously, all the things regarding "improvements" of the modern era that the European settlers did to the North American continent after forcibly taking America from the Natives, then enslaving Africans to build it, all aforementioned, do not make them or their descendants the **rightful owner** of America. I could go on infinitely about the sufferings of racial groups around the world and that would be a laborious task all by itself. However, this will suffice as enough illustrations to depict the crimes against or wars against humanity and barbaric acts of man-to-man under the guise of progressive civilization. I recall the words of Voltaire when he said, "*I want to know the steps that man has taken from Barbarism to civilization.*" Unfortunately, there was a war that occurred many millennia ago that had, is having and will continue to have a devastating impact upon all of us eternally whether we like it or not. This war's impact is the eternal deciding factor between good and evil, light and darkness… God and the devil. This war occurred in the celestial region of our galaxies that we are still wandering around trying to discover or figure out in "outer space." This war occurred in the celestial heaven or the spiritual zip code dimension—i.e., the region known as the Twilight Zone of our universe!

This battle is unique in many aspects. For instance, this battle or war involved celestial beings not terrestrial or earthly ones that we are and that we are accustomed to interacting alongside. Secondly, this war occurred in the *very presence* of God himself. In fact, it occurred in "God's Living Room" if you will. Furthermore, this war decided the eternal fate of the primary actor Lucifer, who along with his co-conspirators (fallen angels not to be confused with Charlie's Angels) whom not only lost the war, but also instigated it all because he wanted to have a hostile takeover of the very Kingdom of God. The War in God's Living Room started with angels who identify now as demons, some are so evil they are reserved in everlasting chains until the Day of Judgment (**Jude 1:6**) This was literally an "out of this world" galactic, monumentally spectacular, dazzling display of heavenly power that was vastly superior in scope, weaponry, power, personalities, casualty rate, etc., to our indiscriminate, inhumane brutality to each other here on earth.

Summarily, all the Satanic-inspired, so-called manufactured World Wars on earth involving men, if amalgamated could not compare to this unique battle even if they occurred simultaneously on earth. Comparatively speaking they would look like a Sunday picnic outing at the park in scope… Now let us focus our attention to the main event. Therefore, allow the Lord Jesus Christ, the Son of the Living God, open your eyes. *Spiritually*, that is so that you can see the revelation of his work, dedicated to examining his kingdom. Subsequently, so that your soul receives the enriching grandeur of his love with all of the wonders of God's bountiful mercy in assisting you in making a decisive eternal decision regarding your salvation or where you choose to spend eternity.

CHAPTER I

Celestial Warfare

The intent of this journey is to take you through the worlds or *realms of reality* although invisible are just as real as our physical, tangible world. See **Hebrews 11:3** that reads; ***through faith we understand that the worlds were framed by the word of God so that the things which are seen were not made by the things which do appear.*** Also, review **2 Corinthians 4:18** that declares**; *while we do not look at the things which are seen but the things which are unseen for the things which are seen are temporary but the things which are not seen are eternal.*** Part of the problem with being human—i.e., both flesh and spirit creates a constant state of war and confusion as to what reality is (**Galatians 5:17**). This is because of the fight that is ongoing between the flesh and the spirit as enumerated in **Galatians 5:17** that states, "***For the flesh lusts against the Spirit and the Spirit against the flesh and these are contrary to one another so that you do not do the things that you wish.***" The flesh says that if the five senses—i.e., touch, taste, smell, hearing or sight cannot thoroughly pierce through the veil (comprehend or understand completely) then the thing does not exist, or it is an allusion or mystical. Look at **Romans 7:23** that says, "**But I see another law in my members 'warring against the law of my mind' and bringing me into captivity to the law of sin, which is in my members.**" However, the reality is just the opposite. The spiritual realm where God dwells Supreme over all creation (visible and invisible) is more real than what we can only partially relate to now. This sphere of reality has all sorts of angelic spirits obeying, doing, completing as well as disobeying God. Some of those angelic beings thought so much of themselves that they even followed Lucifer in a brazenly but foolhardy, heavenly revolution or Civil War in heaven against the Holy God of Jerusalem!

Lucifer is one of only four angels ever mentioned by name in the KJV (King James Version) of the Bible that Protestant Christians use, not the Latin Vulgate of the Roman Catholics, which identifies others for example, Raphael, in a spectacular rebellion against God. The other three angels identified by name are Michael, Gabriel, and Abaddon or Apollyon (Angel King of the bottomless pit) (**Revelation 9:11**). Remember Michael. Some would dare to add Beelzebub as another angel. However, I declined to do so because my understanding of him is that this was just another name for Lucifer. Satan identified, as the angelic/demoniac King of Evil does not require re-mentioning as another angel to me. This fight resulted in the phrase commonly referred to as War in Heaven. See **Revelation 12:7–8**, "**And *war broke out in heaven* Michael and his angels fought with the dragon and the dragon and his angels fought but they did not prevail nor was a place found for them in heaven any longer.**" The stakes were high. The decision was eternal as was the outcome. For if Satan (Lucifer was his original name before the battle) would had been victorious, then all realms spiritual and natural milieus would be subjected to tyranny, eternally without reservation. Fortunately, God Almighty who coincidentally never took any part in this battle won, as we will see. God is so just he does not fight against an inferior subordinate! That is going to change when he comes down from heaven to fight for Israel in a future battle with Russia. This prophetic (future) war against Israel occurs after Israel's invasion in the war to come with Russia. See **Ezekiel chapters 28–32.** Discussed later in detail.

Many people who have little to no understanding of God quickly criticize God unfairly by saying things such as, if God is love, then how can he allow wars, death, disease, murder, famine, et cetera? Well, whether one believes it or not, God did not allow it then nor does he allow it now. All of these things are a direct result of *the curse* upon man and creation after Adam's fall or willful disobedience in the Garden of Eden. After he and his wife, Eve, chose to disobey God Almighty that are just playing themselves out through the natural course of humanity's evolution on earth. **There is no death in Heaven**! Case in point, in the beginning of the creation God established the world as well as man in *harmony with life*. However, God warned man that if he (Adam/man) disobeyed God the *consequences* would be death, spiritually and physically. See **Genesis 2:15–17 here, "Then the Lord God took the man and put him in the Garden of Eden to tend and keep it. And the _Lord commanded_ the man saying of every tree of the garden you may freely eat but of the tree of knowledge of good and evil, you shall not eat. For in the day that you eat of it you shall surely die."** Man previously had the title, deed as well as ownership of God's created *world of life*... planet earth.

Additionally, man had access to eternal life via the tree of life that God planted inside of the Garden of Eden. Most people do not consider that there were many trees in the Garden of Eden. However, two prominent trees lie situated within the midst of God's garden impacting man forever. The tree of life and the tree of the knowledge of good and evil. This simply means that God intended as well as wanted man to live forever because he provided him with the necessary sustenance (tree of life) to make it so. However, as we know Adam chose another path the way of death. See **Genesis 3:22–24** *that reads, **"Then the Lord God said man has become like one of us to know good and evil and now lest he put out his hand, take also of the tree of life, eat, and live forever. Therefore, the Lord God sent him out (eviction) of the Garden of Eden to till the ground from which he was taken so he drove out the man and placed cherubim at the east of the Garden of Eden and a flaming sword, which turned every way to guard the tree of life!"***

Also, review **Deuteronomy 30:19** that states, "**I call heaven and earth to record this day against you that I have set before you** *the way of life* **and the** *way of death*, **blessing and cursing choose life that both you and your seed may live**." Additionally, review **Jeremiah 21:8** cited here; **now you shall say to this people I set before you the <u>way of life</u> and <u>the way of death</u>**. Finally, look at Joshua's brave declaration to serve his God before his death to the people he led into the Promised Land after Moses death. Review **Joshua 24:15** denoted here, "**And if it seems evil to you to serve the Lord <u>choose for yourselves</u> this day whom you will serve. Whether the gods, which your fathers served that, were on the other side of the river or the gods of the Amorites <u>in whose land</u> you dwell but** *as for me and my house, we will serve the Lord.*"

The very fact God Almighty provided two opposite ways—i.e. (life or death), with instructions to make a choice or choose one of them describes for us that man had a choice. Analogously just like then, man has a choice now on earth either to accept Jesus Christ as Savior or reject him as Lord thus assuring one's eternal damnation apart from God forever. Nevertheless, Adam/man voluntarily chose to disobey God, which forfeited man and God's ownership (man's stewardship) over the world of life. Man handed the keys of life and death on earth to Satan that required God in turn to get them back legally. Jesus did! See **Revelation 1:18.** Christ states, "I am he who lives and was dead and behold I am alive forever more. Amen. And *I have the keys of Hades and death*." Christ accomplished this when he "tasted death" for every man and paid the penalty for our sin once forever. Bible proof for this point is discoverable or found in **Hebrews 2:9**, *"but we see Jesus who was made a little lower than the angels (a man as all men are) for <u>the suffering of death</u> crowned with glory and honor that he by the grace of God should <u>taste death</u> for every man."*

It is extremely imperative to remember that prior to Adam and Eve's rebellion, by eating the forbidden fruit *<u>they did not know</u>* of the existence of **any** evil whatsoever! However, just as God told man that there was a penalty for rebellion back in the Garden of Eden, he also notified Lucifer/Satan that there was a penalty too! Specifically, God tells Lucifer in **Isaiah 14:12, "How you are fallen from heaven, O Lucifer 'son of the morning' how you are cut down to the ground!"** Jesus said that **hell was not created for man, but for the devil and his angels.** See **Matthew 25:41** this is the unseen realm of spiritual abode for fallen angels who just like man exercised their freedom of choice to sin against God. This foreboding place identifiable in **Jude 1:6** as it reads, "**And the angels that did not keep their proper domain but left their own abode he has reserved in everlasting chains under darkness for the judgment of the great day.**" Although God created hell for the devil and not man, the devil sinned prior to man's fall. However man followed the devil by choosing to sin after being warned about the consequences of doing so. However, if man chooses to follow Satan's evil ways he will end up in the same lake of fire with Satan and the other fallen angels.

See **Revelation 20:10** that says, "*The devil, which deceived them, was cast into the lake of fire and brimstone where the beast and the false prophet are and they will be tormented day and night forever and ever.*"

Given the enormous magnitude of the potential punishment (eternally) for willful rebellion against God, one would be quick to irrationally consider or indiscriminately judge the evil mindset of Satan. The purpose and intent of this book, is to examine biblically <u>*why*</u> Satan rebelled against God causing warfare to occur in heaven and on the earth. However, more importantly it is to shed some light on the War in Heaven (Fighting in God's Living Room) that occurred just prior to or immediately after the creation of man. I hope that in turn it will cause all of us to examine our relationship to Jesus Christ who is the ***only mediator*** between God and men. See **1 Timothy 2:5** that declares, "**For there is one God and one Mediator between God and men the man Christ Jesus.**"

Acts 4:12 highlights this by saying, "**Nor is there *salvation in any other*, there is *no other name* given under heaven whereby we must be saved!**" Saved from what is a legitimate question hypothetically that can be asked by anyone who is unsaved. This question as it relates to the destiny of one's salvation is vital. Well the answer to the question simply put, saved from the Holy Judgment of God, which is to punish all rebellion by both man and angels. The word of the Lord says, "**As it is appointed unto man once to die, but after this the judgment**" (Hebrews 9:27).

Therefore, I am praying that all readers of this book have already accepted Jesus Christ (or will) as their personal Savior as I have trusted him as mine. If not, I would highly recommend that you do so now or soon if you were to ask me. The word of God, herein after referred to as WOG says, "**Now is the acceptable time**."

Review **2 Corinthians 6:2** that reads, "**For I have heard you in an 'acceptable time' and in the day of salvation, I have helped you behold *now is the accepted time* behold now is the day of salvation**." Humanity is at a distinct disadvantage in this world regarding either the brevity or longevity of our life span individually. For we do not know the date, place, manner or time of our death if it occurs without our involvement—i.e., suicide. Alternately, others who have some idea are those sentenced to death on a specific date upon conviction of any capital offense against the State in which it occurred, etc.

Furthermore anyone given a dire prognosis by a medical practitioner diagnosis predicated upon any life threatening mortal disease such as cancer, inoperable brain tumor, etc. That is why "now" is considered to be the acceptable time. Right now. One month, one day, one hour or one minute for that matter may be too late. Salvation through faith in Jesus Christ acted upon now will deliver one's soul from eternal damnation but after one's death occurs, to the individual or once judgment starts, it is too late. This is one reason I am not a fan of prayers for the dead. Their fate is sealed. Nothing you say unto God regarding their fate will change it. You can only hope and pray for the living who still have a chance for forgiveness or redemption through Christ. One has a chance as long as one's spirit is inside of one's body even just and up to the point of the spirit leaving the body. Here is a brief story that provides biblical proof for this perspective.

Occasionally, I would ask sort of a trivia question if you would of either family or friends. The question I would ask them is *who was the very first Christian ever admitted to the kingdom of God?* They would pause, look around with inquisitive stares and provide various answers. Some would say it was Enoch others would say it was Noah and some even dared to say the Lord Jesus Christ himself! Then I would patiently wait for dramatic impact lol, before providing them with the actual answer from God's word for the only correct answer. I would tell them that no Old Testament saints qualify because Christ had not yet been immaculately born in the flesh to the Virgin Mary. Therefore, they are ineligible to be Christians. Other answers proffered that it had to be John the Baptist who believed in Christ's divine ministry as the Son of God. Although a good reply, it is still the incorrect answer. Because Jesus had not yet ascended into heaven, so it cannot be John. Christ has to introduce all believers to his father. Jesus was still on the earth when Herod beheaded John and died. Therefore, he did not introduce John or anyone else for that matter to his Heavenly Father at that time. Jesus said if you are ashamed of me, I will be ashamed of you before my Father and his Holy angels.

Afterward, I would tell them that Christ was not the correct answer simply due to the fact that Christ was not a Christian neither could he ever be… Only the *followers of Christ* could be Christians. Therefore, that answer is incorrect. John the Baptist and other believers who died *before* Christ could not go into heaven as Christians because Christ **had not yet died and risen again** for their justification as believers. Therefore, that makes this answer incorrect as well. I tell them go back to the review the crucifixion of Jesus for the answer. The story summarized here says at Christ's crucifixion Jesus's actual cross-hung or stood situated between two thieves or robbers. One of them goaded him to save himself and both of them, the other replied let him alone he has done nothing. However, he added or replied to the other crook you and I are hanging here on crosses because of our criminal actions and for our sins while he is an innocent man. However, look what he asks of Christ *as he was dying* but more imperatively look at Christ's reply that affirms he was the first Christian. **Jesus died first after his death then the repentant, dying thief followed shortly thereafter as he went into heaven after Jesus as the first Christian.** Review the dialogue below for the answer in **Luke 23:39:**

Then one of the criminals who were hanged
with him saying if you are the Christ save yourself

> *and us but the other answered, rebuked him saying, do you not even fear God seeing you are under the same condemnation? And we indeed justly for we receive the due reward of our deeds but this man has done nothing wrong then he said to Jesus Lord remember me when you come into your kingdom and Jesus said unto him assuredly **I say to you today you will be with me in Paradise.***

Consequently, as you can see prayer and dying repentance was offered *for the living* who was in the process of dying (fortunately, for him crucifixion was a slow death) but he still had retention in the body of his spirit and it allowed a positive outcome. He went to heaven with Jesus that very day after his spirit departed from his body. Subsequently, all of us must appear before the judgment seat of Christ! No EXCEPTIONS! This bold declaration is located in **Romans 14:10** it *says,* ***"But why do you judge your brother? Or why do you set at nothing your brother? For we shall all stand before the judgment seat of Christ."***

Even Satan himself will appear before Jesus on bowed knees before being casted into the eternal Gehanna. As the word declares, **"Every knee shall bow and every tongue shall confess that Jesus Christ is Lord to the glory of God the Father" (Philippians 2:9–11)**. However, those of us who have put our trust in Jesus Christ's sacrificial, atoning death by believing that God the Father sent him to save fallen humanity from the eternal penalty of sin will not face condemnation. Biblical support can be located or listed in **Romans 8:1** that states, **"There is therefore now no condemnation to them, which are in Christ Jesus, who walk not after the flesh but after the Spirit."** Comparatively speaking as these two divergent entities war against each—i.e., the flesh versus the spirit. Allegorically stated along the same lines (divergent entities—i.e., holy angels fighting against demons in heaven) as the title of this book, which is "Fighting in God's Living Room."

Chronologically, for us to examine this subject, we must go back, back in time in the eternal heavens eons ago, before recorded history. Even before God told Moses what occurred in the Septuagint (first five books of the KJV) or Jewish Torah—i.e., before Moses, Noah, or any creation. The Bible will be our primary, foundational platform to launch this inquiry or quest into the past as we search it for specific references, words or illustrations to understand the current deadly global events shaping our world in a cataclysmic way with powerful far-reaching devastation, wars, suffering, as well as other horrible impact upon humanity. This feat is accomplishable by using some common sense as well piecing together the puzzles of the word of God as we unite it with dynamic events of our time that are making world headlines daily. One must use God's word as well as one's own imagery or vivid description of eternity in the dateless past in order to understand the events of the dated present. This is actually easier to do than you may think. Actually, let the Lord guide you, as I attempt to set the stage up in your mind as you read the pages of this book. All that is required is that you use some imagination, as well as some sound reason or common sense. Now that we have laid the rudimentary, foundational requirements let's begin this journey back in time so that we can grasp a greater comprehension of the current time, that is to be eclipsed by the return of the Son of God at his Second Coming in due time.

CHAPTER II

Origin

Imagine if you will, God the Father, God the Son Jesus Christ, and God the Holy Spirit in eternity alone in the Heavens before the creation of anything. There is absolutely nothing but the Godhead! There are no atmospheric heavens, no stars, no celestial bodies, no moons, no sun, no earth, no seas, **no angels, and no man**. Again, nothing but God in all of his glory as eternity sits silently before the Lord. God thinks to himself, I will create something other than myself. If you will think about it for a moment, God Almighty is alone! However, he is <u>not lonely</u>. The other two members of the Godhead, Christ the Son and The Holy Spirit are there beside him. The Supreme Being in the galaxy has no one (created beings) to share his mercy and love with or among although he owns the entire galaxy. It is just God. Remember, Jesus said in **Revelation 1:8**, *"I am Alpha (first) and Omega (last) the beginning and the ending said the Lord which is and which was and which is to come the Almighty."*

This is an awesome spectacle! The eternal God has *no subjects* although he possesses ***all power*** (Almighty) throughout the universe. Yet, God is actually alone, possibly if God will pardon me here, *I speak as a foolish man* reciting the Apostle Paul's words... God's empire has **no subjects**. This is probably why God said in **Genesis 2:18** that "it was ***not good*** **for man to be alone**." God knew from personal experience of being alone himself. I emphasize here God ***is*** <u>***not lonely***</u> just alone. There is a major difference between these two idioms. Consequently, I will explain the difference since this will be the continuing theme throughout this section of this narrative so the reader can fully appreciate the context of God's rationale for creating beings without being lonely per se from my perspective. When a person is alone that simply means they are by themselves there is no one near or around or close in proximity to them they are alone. A person can be alone mentally, physically or emotionally.

Contrastingly, when a person is lonely that means they may be near or surrounded by dozens of people physically, yet emotionally or psychologically they are saddened, disconnected or depressed because they are "lonely." They are detached from emotional connectivity with anyone other than themselves. Therefore, they are unable or unwilling to express their internal depression to external people albeit there are many people in their immediate presence they could if they choose to attempt to narrate ones since of isolation or despair. Again, I reiterate, God was not sad because he was lonely or isolated. God was just alone (no beings to share his awesome love, power or kingdom with) at that exact moment in eternity past prior to the creation of his subjects including man, angels, et cetera. I hope that this cements the perspective that I wanted to convey to the readers that I am referencing when I utilize these terms contextually herein this book. Therefore, I now continue pursuing our goal—i.e., to explain how all of this began which is the mission.

God makes a decision. I will create other life forms that can share my love and the glory of my kingdom with me. See **Colossians 1:16** *that states,* **"For by him _were all things created_ that are in heaven and that are in earth, visible and invisible whether they be thrones, or dominions or principalities or powers all things were created by him and for him."** Yes, that is what I will do. God's enthusiasm reaches a Heavenly glow as he decides to make other life forms. God unilaterally decides to create beings with no counselors, advisors, boards or commissions to provide him with insight regarding these futuristic created beings. Although we have no biblical knowledge of "when" God created angels, we know that God did create them. Furthermore, we know via deduction that God created angels _before_ God created men. Deductively we know this because

33

the war in heaven—i.e., God's Living Room occurred *before* the sin in the garden. Therefore, the angels already existed via their creation to revolt in heaven before Satan slipped into the Garden of Eden and deceived Eve. This is where the exclusive title Creator comes into being relating to God. God alone is the Creator of all things and beings. God decided to create many, various or differing kinds of life forms or beings both in heaven where he dwells and on earth where man resides. However, God has to decide many things about these other life forms. For example, where will they live, how will they survive, will they be co-dependent or completely autonomous of me, which ones will live in heaven and which ones will live on earth, what will they look like, in whose image will they be created, what purposes will they serve, what will they do, how will they relate to him et cetera?

Now, for emphasis sake I reiterate, when I speak of God, I am referring to the Godhead—i.e., Father, Son, and Holy Spirit. God is not pluralistic, which some people may refer to as three Gods. It is not one, plus one, and one equals three. Rather, it is one times one, times one, which equals one! Jesus said, **"My Father and I are one. Hear O Israel the Lord Thy God is one."** Consider **Deuteronomy 6:4,** here as biblical proof. Each member of the Godhead is in agreement with this collaborative project obviously. How do we know this, scriptural support (**Genesis 1:26**) *Here is where God says…let us make man in our image, after our likeness…* Logically, God the Father was in agreement with Jesus Christ and the Holy Spirit. Otherwise, there would have been confusion. God is not the author of confusion as enunciated in **1 Corinthians 14:33** that says: **"For God *is not* the author of confusion but of peace as in all the churches of the saints."**

However, God is also, omniscient, or all knowing, meaning that he knows what the result will be from the beginning. This critical point is not to be passively over looked, or casually ignored lightly. Consequently, this critical point is to be from time to time mentally reviewable or considered as we sojourn throughout the travel of this odyssey while we seek answers to questions regarding the motive for Satan's rebellion as well as its impact upon our eternal destiny.

Our quest will involve our thinking imaginatively, laboriously, tirelessly, consistently and occasionally challenging long held beliefs as we crisscross epochs of time to ascertain common sense answers to resolving our inquisitiveness. God "predestinates" each individual whether man or angel into a specific role to play in his kingdom. Oh my predestination is intriguing let's see why. Bible proof is discoverable in **Ephesians 1:3–5,** which reads as follows: "**Blessed *be the God and Father of our Lord Jesus Christ, who has <u>blessed us with all spiritual blessings</u> in heavenly places in Christ. According as he has chosen us in him 'before' the foundation of the world that we should be holy and without blame before him in love <u>having predestined</u> us unto <u>the adoption of children</u> by Jesus Christ to himself according to the good pleasure of his will*."

These roles or duties will detail the activity as well as the responsibility each has as each relates to God or each other in a specific manner albeit it differently yet in unison if you will. Additionally, God's Kingdom extends far beyond any relegated, artificial, geographical boundary in heaven above or earth below. God's Kingdom encompasses all of the domains or realms of his creation that he created by his sovereign will and spoken word. This includes unoccupied planets, territories, oceans, islands, galaxies, dominions, lunar atmospheres or any other place both visible and invisible. God's Kingdom is vast, well beyond the comprehension of mere mortal man's ability to fully comprehend or understand. Remember **all things created are for him and by him exclusively (Colossians 1:16)**. God decides to create a group of beings in the heavens (angels) whose primary role is to serve and worship him.

Read **Psalm 103:20** as biblical proof for it says, "***Bless the Lord you his angels <u>who excel in strength</u> <u>who do his word</u> heeding the voice of his word*.**" God gives them many attributes among them, are abilities and capabilities that man does not possess. This is how they *excel in strength* in comparison to man. Also he grants angels restricted free will. More importantly, angels **have direct, personal, face-to-face and immediate access** to God, his throne, his holy presence within God's Living Room. Angels can visibly behold God in all his heavenly glory that man does not have the ability to quite comprehend or see currently. God can see us, but right now, we cannot see him by divine decree. This is analogous to a two-way mirror. The people behind it can see you although you cannot see them. This may be another reason for Lucifer's arrogance over fallen man. He saw God's power on full majestic display that man has yet to see. I will discuss more on this issue later. However, because God is omniscient he was already aware of Lucifer's sinister schemes, plots, plans as well as his feeling of "superiority" to man. Do not get jealous or feel unloved saints of the Most High God or any other mortal reading this book. For you possess something that Angels can never attain, have or unequivocally proclaim. All of us—i.e. (humankind) have the DNA/RNA image of our God! Man's likeness during his formation, was created in the exact image of God! Created angels on the other hand come from the imagination of God's desire unlike man. Man is the **only** being God chose to be in his own image! This my friend is divine exclusivity predestination! Man holds a sacred, special breed of being or creation much higher, more than and vastly different from angels, animals, fowl, fish, insects, etc.

See **Genesis 1:26–27** as it states, "*God said **let us <u>make man</u> in <u>our image</u>**, after <u>our likeness</u>… So **<u>God created</u> man <u>in his own</u> <u>image</u>** in **<u>the image of God</u> created he them both male and female created he them!*" This should make us all get on our knees to glorify our God who dwells in the third and highest heaven openly, publicly consistently with a loud voice to proclaim that GOD IS GREAT AND GREATLY TO BE PRAISED! Hallelujah to the Lord God of Israel!

God assigns to all angels certain or specific roles, intellect, appearance, duties, etc. God's intent is that each will fulfill their role accordingly. Lucifer, which means the "morning star," was the name that God had originally given to Satan *prior* to his rebellion in heaven. See **Isaiah 14:12**, which says, "***How are you fallen from heaven <u>Lucifer</u> 'son of the morning' how you are cut down to the ground?***" Soon we will see or discover how Lucifer cast himself down to the ground as we proceed on our journey through God's word. However, I will give you a sneak preview; it was because of one of the sins 100 percent of all of us are plagued with too. This is the indelible sin mark of pride. The word of the Lord says that **pride** goes **before** a fall (**Proverbs 16:18).** This is why we must be watchful not careful. For the WOG says in **Philippians 4:6,** *"Be careful for nothing but in everything by prayer and supplication with thanksgiving let your requests be made known to God."*

However, now I will continue with our current theme here more on Lucifer's fall later. Each angel possessed similar attributes, levels of reasoning pretty much like we as humans do. Although similar, there are varying degrees of individual characteristics that comprise each one. Some people are taller, shorter, smarter, and attractive than others. Analogously, angels differ in intellect, rank, wisdom, beauty, talents, et cetera…et cetera. This is one reason why angels just like all of us react to stimuli differently. No matter the milieu, no matter the issue, no two angels or no two people will respond exactly the same way to the same stimulus synonymously. Therefore, each makes a decision on how to reply predicated upon one's own self-interest, thoughts, desires, motives that best aligns with their overall interest intuitively. This will explain why some angels chose to follow Lucifer's Rebellion in heaven against God and other angels chose not to join in this High Treasonous Act against God Almighty. Nevertheless, some of us will follow the Lord and some of us on earth will not follow the Lord God via Jesus Christ until the day we die just as some of the angels did in their estates. Consequently, understand that the outcome will be vastly different for each class as well to say the least. Initially, when God created Lucifer, he was one of the most physically beautiful angels among God's created beings.

Review here God's description of Satan's creation. God describes some of Lucifer's attributes or qualities in **Ezekiel 28:14–15,** cited here, *"**Thou art the 'anointed cherub' that covers and I have set you so. Thou was upon the Holy mountain of God, thou have walked up and down in the mist of the stones of fire, and thou were perfect in your ways <u>from the day you were created</u> till iniquity was found in you.**"* Nevertheless, just like most physically attractive people, Lucifer became filled with pride because of his beauty and "let it go to his head" if you will. God hates pride feverishly.

See **Proverbs 6:16–17**, referenced sequentially numerically here via italics citation which says these six things doth the Lord hate. Yea seven are an abomination to him; (1) *__a proud look__*, (2) *a lying tongue, and* (3) *hands that shed innocent blood*, (4) *a heart that devises wicked imaginations*, (5) *feet that be swift in running into mischief*, (6) *a false witness that speaks lies and* (7) *he that sows discord among brethren*. However there is more identified in **1 Timothy 3:6** that reads, "**N**ot *a novice lest being lifted up __with pride__ he falls into the trap of the devil,*" and **Proverbs 14:3** that states, "*In the mouth of the foolish there is the __rod of pride__.*" The word of God states that *pride goes before destruction and a haughty spirit before a fall* in **Proverbs 16:18**. Lucifer was the "anointed cherub" that covered the mountain of God, walked in the Garden of God [Eden] as he strutted so majestically in the stones of fire (**Ezekiel 28:13–14**). This was the heavenly equivalent of a "cat walk" by runway models. Yet it was much more radiant because of God's orchestration and design. Obviously, the radiance and glare of his presence was captivating to other angels as it dazzled the eyes as well as the mind with such awe inspiring, shimmering glow. No wonder God originally named him "the morning star" or Lucifer prior to him leading, causing and instigating an angelic rebellion against God's grace.

Lucifer was only one of many incredibly beautiful angels created by God. Yet God established an entire hierarchy of angels. Their purpose was twofold. One was to worship God and the second was to be ministering spirits to man. Hebrews 1:13–14 reads, "But to which of the angels said he at any time sit on my right hand until I make thine enemies thy footstool? Are they not all ministering spirits sent forth to minister for them who shall be heirs of salvation?" However, we must understand the entire organizational ranking structure of angels to pierce behind the veil as to why this monumental blunder by Lucifer occurred.

CHAPTER III

Angelic Ranks

Essentially angelic classifications is divisible into four (4) distinct categories or ranks from my finite understanding of the reading within God's words. They are in order of prominence: (1) Archangel, (2) Cherubim, (3) Seraphim, and (4) Cherub. This categorical ranking system of identification is extremely important! Simply because, not only does it identify their ranks or simply clarify the duties of each but, it also provides us with some understanding of God's angelic hierarchy, ranks, respective duties, responsibilities and assignments. Additionally, it gives us our first glimpse into eternity past—i.e., why this war in heaven developed. How does it do this one may ask? It does so by displaying the usurpation against authority or rebellion from designated assignment by God. This is a very imperative point to reflect upon because by doing so we can see the biggest problem man has on earth was also the biggest problem angels had in heaven. This problem was following orders or accepting designated authority over one's station regardless to how they obtained that tier of responsibility. Lucifer did not like the fact that God's authority reined over all creation not just a part of it, or most of it, but all of heaven and earth including him too.

Satan could not fathom how one entity (God Almighty) could rule over all creation with its limitless geographical boundaries—i.e., space, earth, outer space, heaven, the heavens of heavens, the oceans, rivers, lakes and streams unilaterally without placing him (Lucifer) in some significant role as a co-ruler. Satan incorrectly concluded that surely, God needs help ruling over these subjects, animals, man and other life forms and naturally, he has chosen me to be his co-ruler because I am so beautiful. Lucifer's covetous conclusion errantly warped in his misguided sinister imagination in that he did not realize that he himself was also a *created* being. Who required supervision even if he was beautiful or physically attractive with some skills sets that God implanted within him for the benefit of all not just himself. Satan did not understand the finiteness of his uniqueness or accept his defined role in the broader scheme of God's empire. Having said that, let us briefly explore the biblical examples of the angelic defined roles.

Our first example will be the highest ranking of all the angels, the Archangel. The Archangel means just that. He is not the Commander in Chief that is Jesus Christ. However, he is the Chief of Staff or the Chairman of the Joint Chiefs of Staff of the angels. The title archangel is not found anywhere in the Old Testament. The title "archangel" is only alluded to in the Old Testament within the book of Daniel, when the angel Gabriel, tells the prophet, Daniel, that he and Michael one of "the chief princes" fought with a demonic prince or evil angel attempting to prevent Daniel from hearing God's answer to his prayer for twenty-one days. This story's narration is in **Daniel 10:13**, *which reads as follows,* **"But the prince of the kingdom of Persia withstood me one and twenty days but lo, Michael one of the chief princes came to help me and I remained there with the kings of Persia."** This can be a little confusing because he says one of the "chief princes" Michael came to help him. Logically, by reasoning he is implying that there are more than one chief or archangels. I will divide the word of truth more on this later for clarity. Nevertheless, Michael demonstrably identified as the **only** Archangel in the book of Jude.

See **Jude 1:9** that states, **"Yet, Michael 'the Archangel' when contending with the devil he disputed about the body of Moses dared not bring against him a railing accusation but said the Lord rebuke you."** This emphasis is intentional! Simply because it does not say Archangel**s** plural, rather it says the Archangel singular. Another scriptural proof found in the book of Thessalonians, whereby the apostle Paul specifically states...*for the Lord himself shall descend from heaven with a shout, with the voice of the Archangel, and with the trump of God, and the dead in Christ shall rise first* (**1 Thessalonians 4:16**). There is no mention of *archangels* plural. Neither is there any mention of voices of other chief princes or archangels or blowing of *trumps* of God plural but singular. This is because there is **only one** Archangel. The Archangel has the unique distinction of blowing the shofar (trump of God) to announce the coming of the King of Kings to the world in which he created upon his triumphant return at his Second Coming. *All things are/were created by him and for him.* See **Colossians 1:16.** Therefore, Jesus Christ is coming again to reclaim his Fathers ownership! Get ready saints of the Most High God your redemption is drawing nearer! Another place where Michael the Archangel prominently identified is in the book of Revelation. This specific scripture for our purposes will have repeated occurrences numerously considerate readers so please endure the repetitious recitations. It is Revelation 12:7; verse whereby John tells us that, "***And there was war in heaven Michael and his angels** fought against the dragon {Satan} and the dragon fought and his angels. Note it doesn't say the 'chief angels' fought against the dragon it says that Michael and his angels fought against the devil and his angels in a side by side comparison.*"

Additionally, Michaels's positive identification listed in the Old Testament as well in another chapter of the Lord's word—i.e., in the book of Daniel. Michael again is specifically identified even here as the ***great prince*** *who defends the nation of Israel.* Let's review **Daniel 12:1** together in its entirety denoted here it reads; ***And at that time shall Michael stand up the great prince, which stand for the children of thy people and there shall be a time of trouble such as never was since there was a nation, even to that same time. Moreover, at that time thy people shall be delivered everyone that shall be found written in the book.*** Written in the book's meaning is referencing the book of life that contains the entire names of all those who accept Jesus Christ as Lord and Savior discussed in the book of Revelation. Review **Revelation 20:15,** noted here that says, "***And*** *anyone not found written in the 'Book of Life' was cast into the lake of fire."* Now again there is **no mention** of **great princes** plural, just the great prince singular. Therefore, as the only Archangel, among Michael's many duties is the awesome responsibility of fighting for the Kingdom of God in heaven as we saw in **Revelation12:7**. Which if you think about it for a moment it makes sense.

The Archangel fights against God's archenemy Satan. This is another key point to bear in mind. Simply because it shows the sovereignty of Yahweh God Almighty, in that, the Lord never actually engages in a physical battle with the dragon (Satan) or his accomplices. Michael does. God is colossally superior to Satan and all other created beings that he does not fight physically against them. God allows another angel, his own equal to fight against him. God does not fight Satan because God knows that is not a "fair" fight. Satan has no chance of winning at all against God Almighty, nor does any other creature in heaven above or earth below! Zilch. However, I do have some ominous news saints of the Most High God to share with you. This will not always be the case. God says that in the future war-involving Israel against Russia, that he will come down in person to fight against the Russians and their hordes himself. Oh My Lord! Read all of **Ezekiel 38 and 39** for the harrowing nightmare that is to strike Russia. I did not outline it here given the enormity of length it requires to cover the subject matter sufficiently, which will tediously, as well as unnecessarily, interrupt upon our focus on our current topic. However, I denoted it in a subsequent chapter in its entire narrative form for analysis and review. I summarized it for you in bullet point form for quicker and simpler reading and comprehension in upcoming chapters so stay tuned. Do recall considerate reader that our journey is to discover the reasons for Satan instigating war and fighting in God's Living Room. However, this specific chapter outlining or appertaining to the future war between Russia and Israel is so imperative that it must be included and has a collateral nexus to our joint venture.

However, continuing with the primary theme of the book, this action undertaken by God displays his holy justice as well not just his since of fairness. It does so by showing conclusively that God is just, that he allows this fight to occur among or fought between peer angelic beings as opposed to becoming personally involved himself. As aforementioned, this is crucial because it shows that God does not enmesh or involve himself unnecessarily in matters of his estate. Nor does he become personally involved in a dispute that he routinely delegates to subordinates, such as the Archangel, Michael and his angels in heaven above or earth beneath. Satan has masterfully deceived many of us into thinking that he was "God's equal" that is why the war in heaven occurred. When the truth of the matter is, neither he nor any other creature **will ever** amount to God's equal. God says in **Isaiah 40:25** *to whom, will you liken me or (compare me)* **unto or whom shall I be equal?** In fact, we see that Satan was not even an Archangel. We will go more in depth on this later. However, now I will summarize the duties of the Archangel. Summarily, we see that among the various duties of the only Archangel are physically fighting against the Lord's enemy (**Revelation 12:7**). To assist other angels engaged in battle with demonic forces, who are attempting to delay God's answer to prayer (**Daniel 10:13**, **Daniel 9:21**). Furthermore, the Archangel is responsible for defending the nation of Israel against its enemies. The specific delegation or duty to protect the Nation of Israel, by the Archangel, is reviewable in **Daniel 12:1**.

Cited here, "**And at that time *shall Michael* stand up *the 'great prince'*, which *stand for the children of thy people.* And there shall be a time of trouble such as never was since there was a nation, even to that same time and at that time thy people shall be delivered every one that is found written in the book.**" Additionally, the Archangel will announce the coming of the Lord by blowing the heavenly shofar (ram's horn) trump of God at Christ's Second Advent. Furthermore, the Archangel will do this by accompanying him, being alongside the Lord Jesus Christ while standing on the edge of space on the periphery of the earth's atmospheric heaven. See **1 Thessalonians 4:16** that reads, "**For the Lord himself shall descend from heaven with a shout *with the voice of the archangel* and with the trump of God and the dead in Christ shall rise first.**" The Archangel is the heavenly Pretorian. The Archangel serves as Chief of Staff to Christ the Son of God, while he rides behind Jesus

Christ, as Christ leads the legions of holy angels and redeemed people of the Lord toward earth. This heavenly parade of forces occur during the Second Advent of Christ's triumphant return to earth to reclaim it for his Father, Almighty God, when he comes back to the earth to battle the forces of evil. All of the minions of hell will be on earth at this time—i.e., Satan, the Antichrist, the Beast and the False Prophet as Satan's crumbling empire is receding ending Satan's self-imposed, despotic, dictatorial, artificial rule over the people of the earth.

See Revelation 19:11–19 cited below that describes the _combined armies_ of holy angels and all redeemed mankind of the Lord, both Old and New Testament saints descending from heaven toward earth following The Lord Jesus Christ and Michael the Archangel to cleanse the earth of all evil beings regardless to classification as man or fallen angels. Consequently, destroying forever both the despicable rule of Satanic inspired, lopsided, one-dimensional rule of man's law and the sphere of influence by demonic personalities including Lucifer himself as well as all principalities and rulers of the darkness of this world, demons or entities and finally people who reject Jesus Christ as Lord. Review the scriptures below that are located in **Revelation 19:11–19** versus which depict this awesome spectacle.

Revelation 19:11–19

*And I saw heaven opened, and behold a white horse and he that sat upon him was called Faithful and True. And in righteousness, he doth both judge and make war. His eyes were as a flame of fire and on his head were many crowns and he had a name written that no man knew but himself and he was clothed with a vesture dipped in blood and his name is called the Word of God. **And the armies, which were in heaven, followed him upon white horses, clothed in fine linen white and clean**. And out of his mouth goes a sharp sword that with it he should smite the nations. And he shall rule them*

44

with a rod of iron. And he treads the winepress of the fierceness and wrath of Almighty God. And he hath on his vesture and on his thigh a name written KING OF KINGS AND LORD OF LORDS. And I saw an angel standing in the sun and he cried with a loud voice saying to all the fowls that fly in the midst of heaven. Come gather yourselves together unto the supper of the Great God. That you may eat the flesh of kings and the flesh of captains and the flesh of mighty men and the flesh of horses and of them that sit on them. And the flesh of all men both free and bond both small and great. And I saw the beast and the kings of the earth and their armies gathered together to make war against him that sat on the horse and against his army.

Nevertheless, returning to the primary theme of this section, which is to identify or specify some of the awesome duties of the Archangel Michael, he is to stand up for the Hebrew people as the divinely chosen people of God whom they are forever! Read here **Daniel 12:1** *that states, "And at that time, shall Michael stand up the great prince, which standeth for the children of thy people. And there shall be a time of trouble, such as never was since there was a nation, even to that same time and at that time, thy people shall be delivered every one that shall be found written in the book."*

Also, read here Isaiah 41:9 that states you *"Whom I have taken from the ends of the earth, called from its farthest regions, and said to you, you are my servant I have chosen you and have not cast you away."* God made a nation of people out of Abraham descendants, prior to this there were no Hebrew people. The original inhabitants of Jerusalem are identifiable as Jebusites. Read **Genesis 17:1–8** listed here, **"And when Abram was ninety years old and nine (99) the Lord appeared to Abram and said unto him I am the Almighty God walk before me and be perfect and I will make my covenant between me and you and will multiply you exceedingly.**

And Abram fell on his face and God talked with him saying as for me my covenant is with you and you shall be a father of many nations. Neither shall your name be called anymore Abram, but your name shall be Abraham, for a father of many nations have, I made you. And I will make you exceeding fruitful. And I will make nations of you. And kings shall come out of you, and I will establish my covenant between you, and me and to your seed after you. And I will give unto you and your seed after you in their generations for an everlasting covenant _to be a God unto you_ and to your seed after you. And I will give unto you and to your seed after you 'the land wherein you are 'a stranger' (all) the land of Canaan for an everlasting possession and I will be their God." Now that God has proclaimed that he is the God of Israel—i.e., Abraham's descendants he will fulfill his role as their God and their divine protector forever.

Yahweh has stated repeatedly that he is the God of Israel, and any such adverse attacks upon Israel are violation of God's glory significantly—e.g., in **Zechariah 2:8**, *"**For thus said the Lord of Hosts, after the glory. He sent me unto the nations, which spoiled you, for he who touches you _touches the apple of his eye..._"** Simply means when translated that he who "touches Israel" touches "the apple" of God's eye.* This area of the eye is an extremely sensitive area given its direct centered locale within the eyeball. Have you ever had an insect or anyone touch the apple of your eye? Then, if so, you know how painful, irritating or upset God is with any Nation or people given the sensitivity of the "apple" of the eye's location or its placement within the socket of the eyes. Any nation or people who come against the Hebrew State of Israel or the divinely chosen people are poking their finger directly into the apple of God's eye! May God have mercy upon your soul for doing such an atrocity to your own existence? Many Gentile nations (all of humankind that are non (Hebrew Jewish) people deeply resent the fact that the Hebrew people are the divinely chosen people of Almighty God. I do not, I am glad for them. I love the Hebrew people. Do you remember God's promise to Abraham? **I will bless those who bless you and I will curse those who curse you (Genesis 12:3).** _This promise_ *is still in effect today*. There is no "statute of limitations" regarding God's warning or promises unless God himself imposes one upon any promise or warning. Well if they will just keep that same tone of resentment on judgment day, the Lord himself will explain it to them. He will do so not that he has to but, because he wants them to understand, his choices are sovereign, non-appealable to any other authority other than himself. God will chastise and provide a direct consequence to any being, be they human or angel that challenges his sovereignty, solitary, exclusive rights when making a decision to choose as he decides to do. Remember when God told Moses the prophet in **Exodus 33:19**, **"I will have mercy upon whom I will have mercy; I will have compassion upon whom I will have compassion."** This power's exhibition occurred in an incident involving Moses's sister Miriam. Miriam, Moses' elder sister scolded Moses for his choice (as a wife) a black woman, to become his bride named Zipporah. Let us examine this issue further below.

Miriam, if you are unfamiliar with the narrative, was the older sister of Moses, who witnessed him sail off in the makeshift ark made by his mother, Jochebed, who did not want to see her infant son, Moses slaughtered in the genocide/infanticide attack by Pharaoh, set Moses adrift on the Nile River. Pharaoh began killing all male, Hebrew children for fear that the Hebrews would eventually outnumber the Egyptians in any future war or join in an alliance with any potential adversaries if their child (male) bearing was not restricted. *This demonic practice is Reminiscent of the current government control of children allotted to parents in China. Two per household mandatory restriction limits. Unfortunately, this infanticide practice has resulted in the deaths of numerous females at birth because families desire a male heir.* The word of God says there is nothing new under the sun. See **Ecclesiastes 1:9 that cites, "That which has been is what will be. That which is done is what will be done, and there is nothing new under the sun."** Now back to the storyline.

Review **Exodus 1:15–16**. That I have listed here. **"Then the King of Egypt, spoke to the Hebrew midwives, of whom the name of one was Shiprah, and the name of the other was Puah. And he said when you do the duties of a midwife to the Hebrew women**

and see them on the birth stools, if it is a son, then you shall kill him, but if it is, a daughter then she shall live." The Nile River had man-eating crocodiles, serpents, large fish and other dangerous predators lurking in its waters. In addition, it has underwater tides that would quickly drown anyone unfamiliar with the waters strength of navigation at the time his mother let him sail alone in this "ark." Yet God led him safely as he did Noah (Noah's Ark) his family and all the animals in the Ark of God without any helmsman ship by Noah or Moses. God led Noah to Mount Ararat and Moses to a safe harbor, in fact into the arms of Pharaoh's sister of all people, who legally adopted Moses according to Egyptian law. However, Miriam made a mistake as all of us do. She challenged and argued with Moses the Prophet of God **who God ordained** or chose to deliver the Hebrews from Egypt after he married Jethro's **black daughter Zipporah**.

See **Numbers 12:1 that states, "*Miriam and Aaron spoke against Moses because of the Ethiopian woman whom he had married for he had married an Ethiopian woman*." Also** *See* **Exodus 3:18** *that reads; So Moses went and returned to Jethro his father in law and said to him please let me return to my brethren who are in Egypt and see whether they are still alive and Jethro said to Moses go in peace.* Two critical points should be readily observable in this narration. Point 1, there would be no need for either of his siblings to speak against Moses marriage if they—i.e., Moses and Zipporah are of the same racial heritage and Point 2, neither of them had authority to say anything against God's anointed hand-picked Prophet's decision by God who chose Moses to deliver his people. Now, I can tell you many people do not want to hear that detailed in the word of God. There is no way around or white washing that! *It states it twice that she was an **Ethiopian woman**.* God did not want the record tampered with so he emphasized the record where Zipporah's Moses wife DNA ancestry spawned. God wanted all of us to know that Zipporah was black. Ethiopia is located in **only one** continent on earth, **the African Continent** from which **all black people** originated. Black people were the only original inhabitants of Africa all others arrived via caravans, incursions or as conquering invaders to pillage the land and enslave the indigenous black people to extract the vast minerals, gold, diamonds and other invaluable resources embedded in the continents earthen crust. No exceptions! Miriam's behavior toward Moses caused God to act directly against her. Consequentially, God caused Miriam's skin to become "white as snow" with leprosy.

*See **Numbers 12:10**, recited here, "And **when the cloud departed from above the tabernacle 'suddenly' Miriam became as <u>white as snow</u>. Then Aaron turned toward Miriam and there <u>she was a leper</u>. "** Immediately, Moses prayed after Aaron asked for intercession in **Numbers 12:13** listed here; **so Moses cried out to the Lord saying please heal her O God I pray! White (non-melanin) pigmented skin** was considered a **<u>leprous curse</u>** in the Old Testament **<u>not black</u>** skin. What happened to this curse in the New Testament?

Pardon me here readers for this momentary digression, which requires elaboration on something that is contextually relevant, annexed to this current subject briefly before returning to our expeditionary mission purposes. Historically, black people; have been told lies, after lies, after lies for eons regarding their skin pigmentation is **a curse** by false teachers and false preachers especially here in America. African descendants, since the 1600s, in America and Black people from the Africa Continent whom have been trafficked all over the world by enslavers, killers and kidnappers from various Nations. White Europeans were not the only ones who enslaved black people. The Arab and the Middle East Indians also traded in black people—i.e., human trafficking, kidnapping, murdering, raping and forced involuntary servitude of African people and barbarity as well. Although we hear more about the white European enslavements and atrocities than we do the others. However, those others acts of debauchery were equally repugnant as an affront to God Almighty! None will be guiltless before Christ on Judgment Day. Stay tuned.

African people and their successive generations of offspring to this very day (enslavement is not just physical but mental, financial and mass incarceration/imprisonment) enslaved globally, including the USA during the **African Diaspora, <u>because</u> the black Pharaohs of Egypt** <u>enslaved</u> the Hebrew people for over four hundred years. This prophecy foretold to Abraham by God, this was **not** because of the fact that Ham told his brothers Shem and Japheth about Noah (their father) being drunk and naked in the tent (then Noah cursed him and his descendants is a lie) as the reason for our barbaric treatment to this very day in America.

Review **Genesis 15:12–14**, listed here, "**Now when the sun was going down, a deep sleep fell upon Abram. And behold horror and great darkness fell upon him, then he said to him know with certainty that <u>your descendants</u> will be '<u>strangers in a land</u>' <u>that is not theirs</u> and <u>will serve them</u> and <u>they will afflict them</u> <u>four hundred years</u> and also the nation <u>whom they serve I will</u> <u>judge,</u> afterward they shall come out with great possessions. God's divine judgment upon the Black Pharaohs of Egypt "before" the Arabian invasions into Northern Africa—i.e., Egypt thus claiming Egypt as "Arabian" is the reason for African-American, black descendants of the Pharaohs and all successive generations of African Americans as it were is the causation of constant marginalization, dehumanization and maltreatment of the Black American descendants/children of Pharaoh.**"

Furthermore, can someone please help me understand how does a ***curse cure itself*** and become a blessing without divine intervention unilaterally? Somebody somewhere is lying! I just do not know whom right now! Sarcasm intended. However, I am sure Satan is instigating it, since he is the father of lies is involved. Satan is a liar and the Father of Lies. Jesus said that the devil is a liar (**John 8:44**). Furthermore, Christ stated*; you are of **your father the devil** and the lusts of your father you will do, he was a murderer from the beginning and abode not in the truth, and because there is **no truth** in him when he speaks a lie, he speaks of his own for **he is a liar and the father of it**!* Logically, if Miriam became **white as snow** as the word of God tells us here she did, as part of God's chastisement for her speaking against his prophet Moses because of his interracial marriage with the **Black woman Zipporah**. Naturally, that means that **she wasn't white originally** right? If she were white, then it would had stated that she became even "*whiter* than snow" right. Did the curse change and heal on its own? Hmmm… something is amiss. God orders Miriam placed outside of the nucleus of the camp via an allegorical comparison when discussing the situation with Moses, which is, if her father had spit in her face she were considered unclean for seven days. Therefore, they placed her outside the camp for this period before receiving her back again. As denoted in **Numbers 12:14–15. Then the Lord said to Moses if her father had spit in her face, would she not be shamed seven days. Let her be shut out of the camp seven days and afterward she may be received again.** Ultimately, the point being is although chastised by God himself he *had mercy* upon Miriam as Moses' sister and allowed her to recover from her bout with leprosy. The subject matter of the curse of leprosy and its effect upon skin pigmentation may require further discussion, research, investigation and analysis in another book. Therefore, I redirect our attention back to current topic here of this book—i.e., the duties of the Archangel. Summarily, we have biblically examined the duties of the Archangel. Although in the book of Daniel, the angel Gabriel tells him that Michael is one of the "chief princes" who did assist him, we must stop to think shortly. If this is the case, then why are not any of these other *chief angelic princes* ever identified? Not even just one of them! I propose reader that the reason that none is identifiable is that although there are other high-ranking angels; none is equal to Michael the Archangel. However, there is another place within the word of God that should solidify this role of Michael as the only Archangel forever in our vernacular or lexicon, which is in the OT.

*Specifically, it is in the book of **Joshua 5:13–15** which reads, "**And it came to pass when Joshua was by Jericho that he lifted up his eyes, looked, and behold a Man stood opposite him with a sword drawn in his hand and Joshua went to him and said to him are you for us or for our adversaries? So he said no but as <u>Commander of the Army of the Lord</u>, I have now come and Joshua fell on his face and worshipped and said to him what does my Lord say to his servant? Then <u>the Commander </u>of the Lord's Army said***

> *to Joshua take your sandal off your foot for the place where you stand is holy ground and Joshua did so."*

Let us analyze this segment briefly here; Joshua was leading the army of Israel into the City of Jericho. Therefore, Joshua is not the Commander of the Lord's army. He was the Commander of the Israeli Army on earth. Otherwise, Joshua would have been talking to himself, which he was not. Therefore, as he was conversing with this angel when he inquired of whose side was the angel fighting on, Israel or their foes. The angel (Michael) tells him that as **Commander of the Lord's army** (angelic hosts) he has come—i.e., **as Protector of the Nation of Israel.** Simply put he is telling Joshua that he is on the scene ready to fight with his sword already drawn out of its protective sheath for Joshua and the Israelis or Hebrews! However, more importantly the Commanding Angel/Archangel (Michael) tells Joshua to take his sandals off his feet because he was standing on holy ground. My Lord! The ground was not holy because Joshua or the Archangel was there it was holy because **Yahweh, the Lord** came to that spot to speak directly to Joshua.

See **Joshua 6:2**, that reads, *"And the Lord said to Joshua see I have given into thine hand Jericho, and the king thereof and the mighty men thereof."* Michael the Archangel accompanied the Lord as the Commander of his angelic Host! Much like the Joint Military Chiefs and the Chairman of the Joint Chiefs of Staff accompany the President of The United States of America wherever he goes anywhere in the world. The reason being because World War III can break out anytime and they must be with the President at all times while travelling to advise him on all military options including strategic and tactical implementation, deployment use of conventional, chemical, biological and or nuclear weapon usage if the need arises to protect the National Security interests of the United States. Additionally, the Secret Service accompanies the President of the United States on diplomatic missions around the country and world to protect his person at all times. Another way of understanding this simple principle is to look at some basic human organizational hierarchies as illustrations. For example, there are many school principals, but there is **only one** Superintendent of the School District. Analogously, just as there are nine justices on the US Supreme Court and all are Justices in their own right. However, there is *only one,* Chief Justice, whose functions are equivalent as well as diverse to the other eight Justices. Now, one must stop to think if man can structure organizations to a relative degree of centralized power or leadership and have **one leader** among the group **can't GOD** who created all do more than that? Next, we focus our attention upon the Cherubim.

Coincidentally, we get our very first mention of cherubim's from the first book of the Bible, Genesis. Unfortunately, these heavenly beings are performing an ominous duty when introduced to the world or us per se. They are actually protecting the tree of life from two renegades… Adam and Eve, after their eviction from the Garden of Eden by God for their sin. See **Genesis 3:24**, that reads, "*So he drove out the man (eviction) and he placed at the East of the Garden of Eden, Cherubims and a flaming sword which turned every way to keep the way of the tree of life.*" Notice there was only one way into the paradise of God on earth—i.e., the eastern partition. Analogously, there is only one way into God's paradise in heaven via Jesus Christ the Son of the Living God. Jesus said in **John 14:6, "*I am the way* the truth and the life. No one comes unto the Father except through me.**"

God used Cherubim and a flaming sword to keep these two rebels away, accessing or from eating of the tree of life. For if they would had eaten from this tree (which they should had been doing anyway) as opposed to the tree of knowledge of good and evil, they would have had eternal life. However, now that they are rebels (fallen man/ sinners) God would not allow them to get near it or do so because the world would had forever been filled with living sinful people. Access to the tree of life is forever reserved or restricted to those and only those who by faith in Jesus Christ, The Son of God grants access in the New Heaven, New Earth and New Jerusalem. See **Revelation 22:1–2**, cited here, "*And he showed me a pure river of water of life, clear as crystal, proceeding from the throne of God and of the*

Lamb, in the middle of the street and on either side of the river _was the tree of life_ which bore twelve fruits each tree yielding its fruit every month. The leaves of the tree were for the healing of the nations. " Cherubim are simply holy angels who do as God has directed them to do. We see them again in the book of Genesis. This time an angel of the Lord calls Hagar, Abraham's concubine/mistress to notify her that God will provide water for her thirsty child (Ishmael) fathered by Abraham. Review **Genesis 21:14–21** outlined below to see how this story unfolds.

And Abraham rose up early in the morning, took bread and a bottle of water, gave it unto Hagar putting it on her shoulder and the child, and sent her away and she departed and wandered in the wilderness of Beersheba. And the water was spent in the bottle and she cast the child under one of the shrubs and she went and sat her down over against him a good way off at it were a bow shot for she said let me not see the death of the child. Moreover, she sat over against him, lifted up her voice, and wept, and God heard the voice of the lad and the angel of God _called to Hagar_ out of heaven _and said unto her what ails you Hagar? Fear not, for_ **God has heard** _the voice of the lad where he is arise lift up the lad and hold him in thine hand for I will make him a great nation and God opened her eyes and she saw a well of water and she went and filled the bottle with water and gave the lad drink. And God was with the lad and he grew and dwelt in the wilderness and became an archer and dwelt in the wilderness of Paran and his mother took him a wife out of the land of Egypt._

This is another reason why Jews and Arabs whether they like it or not are related. Abraham had two sons initially, Ishmael and Isaac. However, that is another story for another book and another day. Provided God willing and I live and am able to pen it to his glory someday. Since I alluded to this being, another reason why Hebrews and Arabs are relatives at the beginning of this paragraph let me provide additional support. I will list a companion reason before proceeding with this premise. Rebekah, Isaac's wife had fraternal twin sons Esau and Jacob—i.e., she had two nations in her womb. Therefore, any children produced among them would be ***cousins*** since their ancestors'—i.e., Jacob and Esau ***were brothers***. God said that the older would serve the younger and that the younger would be stronger than the elder would.

Review **Genesis 25:21–23** cited here, "***And Isaac entreated the Lord for his wife because she was barren, the Lord was entreated of him, Rebekah his wife conceived, the children struggled together within her, and she said if it be so why am I thus? And she went to enquire of the Lord and the Lord said unto her two nations are in your womb and two manner of people shall be separated from thy bowels and the one people shall be stronger than the other shall and the elder shall serve the younger.*** *" My Lord the Arab-Israeli conflict intensified originally within the womb of their common ancestor Rebekah's womb. Consequently, it should not be a surprise or astonishment to any of us why this horrible conflict continues amongst them today. Afterward, it has evolved between their shared bloodline of Abraham's two sons Ishmael and Isaac to an all-out public warfare. Nevertheless, I return to our story which is the narrative outlining the roles and identity of the Cherubim.*

However, Cherubim figures mentioned throughout scripture are performing God's will. Another place where they are noted doing God's will is when the prophet Elijah is summoned by the King Ahaziah who coincidently, who is the son of King Ahab and Queen Jezebel, two notorious villains' wielding authority ruthlessly, corruptly, unjustly and ungodly to his court. In fact, Queen Jezebel was so evil that God allows wild dogs to have Jezebel for lunch because of her wickedness. Gruesome details listed here in **2 Kings 9:30–36**. It says, *"When Jehu was come to Jezreel, Jezebel heard of it and she painted her face and tired her head and looked out at the window and as Jehu entered in at the gate she said Had Zimri peace who slew his master? And he lifted up his face to the window and said who is on my side? Who? And there looked out to him two or three eunuchs. And he said throw her down, so they threw her down. And some of her blood was sprinkled on the wall and on the horses. And he trode her under foot and when he was come in he did eat and drink and said go see now this cursed woman and bury her. For she is a king's daughter. And they went to bury her but they found no more of her than the skull and the feet and the palms of her hands. Wherefore they came again and he said this is the word of the Lord which he spoke by his servant Elijah the Tishbite saying in the portion of Jezreel shall dogs eat the flesh of Jezebel."*

Also, God allowed dogs to do the exact same thing her unto her wicked husband, King Ahab, who consulted with familiar spirits (Devils in disguise) who was killed in battle although camouflaged due to the fact that God wanted him dead for his transgressions. Review **1 Kings 22:19–20** cited here, by Micaiah the prophet of God. *And he said hear thou the word, therefore the word of the Lord, I saw the Lord sitting on his throne and all the host of heaven standing beside him on his right hand and on his left and the Lord said who will persuade Ahab that he <u>may go up and fall</u> at Ramoth-Gilead? And one said on this matter and another said on that manner.* Interestingly, God decides here during this assembly that he will allow dogs to drink of Jezebels's husband, King Ahab's blood as well since he refuses to call upon the God of Israel and wants the gods of foreign neighbors to proclaim healing for him.

Full details are vividly displayed in **1 Kings 22:34–38** described here. *"And a certain man drew a bow at a venture, and smote the king of Israel between the joints of the harness. Wherefore, he said unto the driver of the chariot, turn your hand and carry me out of the host for I am wounded. And the battle increased that day and the king was stayed up in his chariot against the Syrians. <u>And died at even and the blood ran out of the wound</u> into the midst of the chariot..., one washed the chariot in the pool of Samaria, the* *dogs licked up his blood, and they washed his armor according to the word of the Lord, which he spoke."* Therefore, it becomes easier to comprehend the evil behavior of the son since we have the stories regarding his wicked heritage and his perverse familial lineage. Now back to the story regarding the renegade son, Ahaziah of these two wicked rulers in Israel. King Ahab and Queen Jezebel's son, Ahaziah, commanded the prophet of God, Elijah, to appear before him so that the king can arrogantly display his rule over the man of God.

Yet God wants him to realize that his authority (not power only God has power everyone else uses proxy authority from God's power) is strictly limited to secular matters only. Therefore, a showdown develops. Pseudo-clairvoyantly, it is amazing how the fruit falls so close to the tree? Like father, like son…like mother, so is the daughter as detailed in **Ezekiel 16:44**. One's family DNA is some powerful stuff…It can be good or alternately bad, beautiful or ugly, blessed or cursed. The next time your child does anything that you disapprove of, pause momentarily to consider *where and from whom* they "inherited" this "unbelievable" behavior from first before you go flying all around out of control like a cosmonaut off the wall. Railing your hands in the air like you just do not care or shrugging your hunched shoulders over like you are completely dumbfounded, astonished or shocked as to how or why they could have done such a thing. You know where they inherited this mindset from or got it from, or if you do not, take a quick peek in the mirror it will instantaneously reveal your source of intrigue. However, do not be surprised at whom you see in the mirror's reflection in real time looking back at you, **yes you**… The **both of you**—i.e., mom and dad! All of us who have a child or children must be aware that our offspring have "our genetic" DNA/RNA strands that they "inherited" from us that causes them to behave as they do. No exceptions! Therefore, one should be a little more understanding at times of youthful indiscretion if it is not extremely outrageous or hurtful to others, you or themselves.

Remember the word of the Lord commands us as fathers not to "provoke our children to anger" cited here from **Ephesian 6:4, "And fathers do not provoke your children to anger but bring them up in the training and admonition of the Lord."**

Continuing with our story, King Ahaziah to enforce his decree, orders a captain of his army to take fifty soldiers with him and *forcibly* arrest/escort Elijah before him. Now this has to be insulting toward God. First, Ahaziah's evil mother, Jezebel wanted the prophet of God Elijah dead. Now, her godless son wants him shamelessly brought before him for interfering with his healthcare plan after his fall described here in **2 Kings 1:2**. *And Ahazaih **fell down through a lattice in his upper chamber that was in Samaria and <u>was sick</u> and sent messengers and said unto them go enquire of Beelzebub (Satan) the god of Ekron whether I shall recover of <u>this disease</u>**.* The God of Israel is shamefully ignored and insulted by this miscreant's actions and decides that he will not recover from this illness because he did not ask Almighty God first. A single angel/ Cherubim is present with Elijah as this confrontation is about to occur. This Cherubim can easily be "overlooked" in this dramatic scene if a careful reading is not implemented. Therefore, one must focus very closely otherwise, you may miss the angel's actual presence because the content is so powerful. We pick up the story whereby the prophet Elijah while sitting atop a mountain summit with his young protégé, Elisha, encounters the encroaching Syrian army encircling their current position. Subsequently, here is where the Cherubim/ angel's actual presence is initially mentioned cited specifically in 2 Kings 1:3, "**<u>But the angel/Cherubim</u> of the Lord said to Elijah the Tishbite arise go up to meet the messengers of the king of Samaria and say to him, Is it because there is no God in Israel that you are going to enquire of Beelzebub, the god of Ekron?**" However, it wasn't Elijah's doing it was God's because King Ahaziah wanted the god Beelzebub/Satan consulted regarding his fall as opposed to the God of Israel who could have healed him immediately without the Affordable Health Care Act, a.k.a. Obamacare, without using either BlueCross or BlueShield. This by the way (AHCA) recently ruled "unconstitutional" by a federal judge in The Lone Star State of Texas. Yee-haw ya'll come back and see us now ya hear? Ultimately, this battle will somehow end up in the United States Supreme Court… again. **Stay tuned**.

The King sends messengers to Ekron to ascertain from their god Beelzebub/Satan, whether his health care insurance plan is up to date. Additionally he desires to know when his healing will occur expeditiously since his premiums with his medical provider to ascertain prognosis, diagnosis and treatment success probability for his current ailment or condition without a "referral" from his primary care physician (the Lord God of Israel) are all accounted for in his feeble cerebellum. Even though right now at that very moment (if you will) he is going "out of network" for a supplemental diagnosis and prognosis for services regarding his fall through the lattice at his palace to a **different health care provider** "Beelzebub/Satan" other than his **Primary Care Physician**—i.e., The Lord God of Israel. Now all of us know what happens when you seek "out-of-care network" treatment as opposed to "in network care," which simply is you pay **a substantial penalty** or way much more than if you would had stayed 'in network' according to your insurance plan provision for your treatment. This is no different, as we shall see shortly. King Ahazaiah wanted to know whether he must linger in bed languishing in pain for a longer period. Even though he has consumed the prescription medication provided by his medicine men or was he going to make a speedy recovery as opposed to the drastic alternative…death, resulting from his injuries sustained in the fall. Our current prose continues with the encounter approaching a critical turning point. The messenger's trip to Ekron is abruptly interrupted or halted as they encounter a stranger on the route which brings some terrifying news back to the King's court, simply because the messengers returned back so quickly after being confronted by Elijah the prophet of God Almighty while on their way to Ekron. The news they give King Ahaziah is grim. He receives information that he will die because of a "second opinion" by his **"in care network health care provider"**—i.e., The Great Physician a.k.a. The Holy God of Jerusalem, as told by his post injury medical assistant, the Prophet Elijah. King Ahaziah asks who told them this as they described Elijah so the King issues a royal warrant on the spot to arrest or bring Elijah back to his palace immediately!

Subsequently, Ahaiziah sends a large contingency of troops to arrest Elijah, specifically fifty-one of them to confront Elijah. Listed here in **2 Kings 1:9–10**, "*Then the King sent unto him a captain of fifty with his fifty and he went up to him and behold he sat on top of a hill and he spoke unto him thou man of God, <u>the king has said come down</u>. And Elijah answered and said if I be a man of God, then let fire come down from heaven and consume you and your fifty and there came down fire from heaven and consumed him and his fifty.*" Although Ahaziah, knew his fate, because Elijah has already told his court that he will die because he sought healing or prognosis out of network relating to his fall. Ahaziah undeterred though persists in or with his demand for Elijah to come before him. This child of darkness orders another captain to take another fifty soldiers with him to bring this prophet of God before him. Unfortunately, these soldiers meet the same demise—i.e., they are roasted and burned to their death in a cinder of fire as outlined in **2 Kings 1:11–12**. "*Again, also, he sent unto <u>him another</u> captain of fifty with his fifty and he answered and said unto him. O man of God thus has the <u>king said</u> come down quickly. And Elijah answered him, If I be a man of God, let fire come down from heaven and consume you and your fifty. And the fire of God came down from heaven and consumed him and his fifty.*"

This royal scientist was not about to be outdone by this man of God, so **he orders another captain**, for those of you who are counting this is the third one, and the score is God and Elijah 102 dead; King Ahaziah 0 arrest made. However, this third captain is the smartest of them all. He recognizes that Elijah is truly a man of God, so he pleads with Elijah for his life as well as the lives of the fifty soldiers under his command as told here **2 Kings 1:13**. "*And he sent a captain of <u>the third fifty</u>, with his fifty and the third captain of the fifty went up, came, and <u>fell on his knees before Elijah.</u> And besought him and said unto him, O man of God, I pray thee, let my life and the life of these fifty thy servants be precious in your sight. Behold there came fire down from heaven and burnt up two captains of the former fifties with their fifties therefore let my life be now precious in your sight and the <u>angel of the Lord</u> said unto*" *him go down with him be not afraid of him and he arose and went down with him unto the king."* The Cherubim/angel is specifically mentioned *again* the *second time* in **2 Kings 1:15** cited here. **And the Cherubim/angel** of the Lord who was there to protect Elijah **with his heavenly blow torch directed and escorted the prophet** to go with the soldiers voluntarily to deliver God's message to this soon to be dead man cited in **2 Kings 1:16**. That says, *"And he said unto him thus saith the Lord forasmuch you have sent messengers to enquire of Beelzebub the god of Ekron is it not because there is no God in Israel to enquire of his word? Therefore, you shall not come down off that bed which you have gone up but shall surely die so he died according to the word of the Lord which Elijah had spoken and Jehoram reigned in his stead in the second year of Jehoram the son of Jehoshaphat king of Judah because he had no son."*

The **cherubim/angel** is mentioned in both scriptures specifically to ensure that we all know where the heat and fire was coming from (i.e., 2 **Kings 1:3** and 2 **Kings 1:15**). Here is additional proof that the heat was coming from the blowtorch or trumpet of the Angel/Cherubim assigned to protect the Prophet of God Elijah. Review in your Bible at your convenience, **Revelation 8:6–8** cited here. **"And the seven angels, which had the seven trumpets prepared, themselves to sound, the first angel, sounded and there followed hail and fire mingled with blood. And they were cast upon the earth and the third part of the** *trees was burnt up* **and all** *green grass was burnt up* **and the second angel sounded and as it were a great mountain burning with fire was cast into the sea and the third part of the sea became blood."** Did you notice what happened when the very *first two* angels of the seven angels present blew there trumpets respectively? I hope so, because in both events *fire* was present in each instance or occurrence just like the Cherubim who blew his trumpet to cause fire to come down from heaven to roast alive the 102 Syrian soldiers who came to arrest Elijah for King Ahaziah! King Ahaziah wanted a Health Care Plan from Beelzebub/Satan and not the Lord of Hosts. Unfortunately, for this child of darkness he got an exit plan from God Almighty stage left.

The Holy God of Israel does not wait for a congressional vote between Republicans, Democrats or Independents of both houses of the US Senate or a committee, tribunal or delegation to repeal or replace his heath care plan. He acts swiftly and decisively to let you know whether he has approved or disapproved of one's medical application for services right on the spot! Watch out now. This error could cost someone his or her very life as it did King Ahaziah. Naturally, we should know that God could heal. Look at some examples where Christ healed lepers, crippled, lame, restored sight to blind and impotent folk and Jesus even raised the widow of Nain's son from the dead **Luke 7:11–17**, he raised Jairus's daughter from the dead. **Mark 5:21–43**. In addition, Jesus Christ resurrected Lazarus whom he cared for deeply back to life (**John 11:43**). Christ loved him so much in fact, he wept at his tomb where they buried him before retuning him back to life. These are some of the reasons why Jesus Christ is referenced as the Great Physician! All of these illustrations are enclosed in **John 11:1–46**. Saints of the Most High God your God is currently still in the healing business in contemporaneous times right now too! The word of God provides all of us with a road map to recovery right now regardless to the specific circumstances. Look at **James 5:14–15** cited here. **"Is anyone among you sick? Let him call for the elders of the church and let them pray over him anointing him with oil in the name of the Lord and the prayer of faith will save the sick and the Lord will raise him up and if he has committed sins he will be forgiven."**

God isn't limited to doing miracles in the Old or New Testament eras he can, will and still does it right now via the prayer of faith. God declares in **Hebrews 13:8. Jesus Christ, the same yesterday, today and forever!** However, God isn't just saving eternal souls. He is repairing and restoring back to health now the wholesome quality of life to those who have been injured, inflicted with sickness or disease which has negatively impacted their lives with reduced or marginalized abilities of their life styles as a result of their infirmities this side of the eternal divide too.

There is another encounter where the Cherubim are mentioned this time involving the Prophet Elisha, who was an understudy for the ministry of the raptured Prophet Elijah who has now ascended into heaven itself. Research **2 Kings 2:11**. Now Elisha has his own young understudy to mentor for the work of the Lord whom he was mentoring for the ministry just as he received mentorship when he was an understudy. This particular story involves the King of Syria wanting to fight the Israeli nation as they are struggling to organize their footprint of their kingdom in the land flowing with *milk and honey* promised to them by the Lord God. Essentially, what happens is the King of Syria goes to make war with Israel but all of his plans revealed his sinister plot in advance mysteriously told unto the King of Israel **before** the Syrian King can ever act with any hostile aggression toward the Hebrews. The Syrian king becomes frustrated and thinks that he has a spy among his camp that is telling the Israelites all of his evil intentions. Therefore, he seeks to discover this person's identity. See **2 Kings 6:11–12** cited here: "**Therefore, the heart of the king of Syria was greatly troubled by this thing and he called his servants and said will you not show me which of us is for the king of Israel. And one of his servants said, None my lord, O king, but Elisha the prophet who is in Israel tells the king in Israel the words that you speak in your bedroom so he said go and see where he is that I may send and get him and it was told him surely he is in Dothan.**"

Therefore, the Syrian king quickly assembles a quick reactionary force of his soldiers to surround the city of Dothan where Elisha is with his young prophet in training. Elisha's understudy a young unnamed God-fearing man panics as he sees the encroaching army. He asks Elisha what we can do. God's people are finicky sometimes are we not? Although God displays miracle after miracle we quickly return to our ways of doubting even just a little bit sometimes. This is the flesh lusting or fighting against the spirit. Elisha tells him not to worry *because "they that are with us* are more" than they who are with the Syrians. Now the youth is concerned! This unquestionably is attributed to the fact that the young man believed that his vision in his mind is closer to 20/20 than is the elder statesman Elisha's. However, he cannot see anyone but the two of them. The child understudy must have thought to himself albeit this is a "man of God" this cannot be possible. He is a delirious old man. Thank God, I am here to assist this little senile old man. He sees people who are not here (at least I cannot see them) yet he is talking about "they who are with us are more than they who are with them." What in the world is wrong with him? He must have been saying unto himself. All I see right now is the vast Syrian army and the two of us. Elisha requests that God supernaturally multiply the acuity of the eyes of this impetus youth so that he can really "see" what is about to happen.

Review **2 Kings 6:17** as it reads, *"And Elisha prayed and said Lord I pray you open his eyes that he may see and the Lord opens the eyes of the young man and he saw and behold the mountain was full of horses and chariots of fire round about Elisha!"* Afterward, God supernaturally opens the "spiritual eyes" translation, allows him to see "supernaturally" of this youth into the spiritual dimension and the sight is spectacular and breathtaking to say the least! This child servant is looking directly into the spiritual dimension as it is criss-crossing time zones of celestial and terrestrial boundaries while it is intersecting with the natural hemisphere. Elisha's young understudy was seeing in the natural realm all along previously while Elisha was looking unto the spiritual realm. The unnamed youth's natural eyes were open while his spiritual eyes remained closed. Now that they are, open. The young man sees chariots of fire surrounding Elisha. Hallelujah to the Lord! This kid must have shouted. Thank God Almighty this senile, little old man is here to "open my eyes" and help me to know the truth of the living God of Israel's magnificent power. This little old fella is outstanding, as well as awesome. Who would have known the upcoming child prophet must have reasoned to himself besides me and the Lord God after changing his tune based upon his new sight! Yeah right! Sometimes as believers in Jesus Christ, we easily vacillate between our faith and our sight by seesawing up and down and up and down. Maybe this can be attributed to the fact, that we are too consumed with or busy trying to figure out what or how is God going to do what we need or petition him to do to resolve the issue because we see no way out.

But we must keep in mind, what God stated in **Isaiah 55:8–11** verses cited here: *"For my thoughts are not your thoughts nei-*

ther are your ways my ways said the Lord. For as the heavens are higher than the earth so are my ways higher than your ways and my thoughts than your thoughts." We need to let go, so God can get started. I will digress here a little bit longer shortly to illustrate the point. Years ago, there was an old Greyhound Bus commercial; it said, if I can recount it accurately here; you have a trip to take, get on board, let go, relax and ***leave the driving*** to us. Bam! This is exactly what God is saying to all of us. Have faith in me (believe what I say) ***let go, relax and leave the driving to me***! Hallelujah to the Lord!

Finally, angels of the Cherubim rank prominently discussed in the book of Revelation blowing trumpets, dispensing the last plagues of God, worshipping Christ the Lord, holding back the four winds of the earth, sealing the servants of Jesus, etc. See **Revelation chapters 6–20**, in short, they are completing God's cleansing program for all eternity. The battalions of *holy angels* or *Cherubim* although finite (they do not reproduce in heaven) obey God. Contrastingly we will see evil angels or fallen angels activity who do not obey God in the upcoming chapter on the Nephilim, i.e., evil or "Lucifer's angels" mating with women. This was a companion reason as to why they were casted from heaven and banished to darkness forever. Cherubim are as vast and mighty as the glorious God who created them. Next, we will learn about the third rank of angels identified as Seraphim. Seraphim are obviously some of the most fortunate of all created beings among angels or men. For they have the distinction of being around the throne of God almost incessantly. We get our first glimpse of them performing their sacred duties worshipping the Lord in the book of Isaiah (**Isaiah 6:1–6**) outlined here below:

*In the year that King Uzziah died, I saw the Lord sitting on a throne high and lifted up and the train of his robe filled the temple. Above it stood **seraphim**, each one had six wings with two he covered his face, with two he covered his feet, and with two, he flew. And one cried to another, and said, "Holy, Holy, Holy, is The Lord of Hosts, the whole earth is* *full of his glory. And he who cried out shook the posts of the door and the house was filled with smoke. So I said woe is me for I am undone because I am a man of unclean lips, for my eyes have seen The King, the Lord of Hosts, then one of the* **seraphim** *flew to me having in his hand a live coal which he had taken with the tongs from the altar."*

Coincidentally, this specific scriptural reference has a lot of meaning for me as a believer in Jesus Christ as the Son of God Almighty. The reason is quite simple, which is, this is the **exact same dream or vision** I had "before" I accepted Christ, as my personal Savior/Redeemer. This dream caused me quickly to arise out of bed, get on my knees, confess my sin to God and believe that Jesus Christ is Lord forever! I humbly report this to all of you contextually because nothing to me is more irritating than to hear "believers" talk about their unique experiences in a *boastful manner* as though they *are closer* to God than other believers are. Sometimes, I must confess that when I hear some believers tell some of their testimonies or visions, dreams, et cetera. I become a lit bit annoyed. The reason is because, that to me, it sounds as though they are attempting to say that "I am closer" to God than you. I am God's favorite child here on earth, which places me alongside God and Christ than are any of you. I have emblazoned on my chest a capital "S" and a capital "C" that stands for "Super Christian," like Superman of comic book fame who had a capital "S" on his chest. I propose they should have emblazoned on their chest the capitals "SN" for "SuperNut." God **has no favorites** he loves all of us just the same!

Therefore, with humility I report this to all of you I am not bragging or trying to boast that I am closer to Christ than are any of you. **For I am not any closer than anybody else is!** If readers who have faith will recall the story of John and James story. For new readers to the gospel I will outline it here from their mothers perspective. See the full narrative in **Matthew 20:20–28. "Then the mother of Zebeedee sons came to him with her sons kneeling down and ask-**

ing something from him. And he said to her, what do you wish? She said to him grant that these two sons of mine may sit, one on your right hand and the other on your left in your kingdom. But Jesus answered and said you do not know what you ask. Are you able to drink the cup that I am about to drink and be baptized with the baptism that I am about to be baptized with? They said that to him we are able. So he said to them you will indeed drink the cup and be baptized with the baptism that I am baptized with but to sit on my right hand and on my left is not mine to give. But it is for those for whom it is prepared by my Father! And when the ten heard it they were displeased with the two brothers. But Jesus called them unto himself and said you know that the rulers of the Gentiles lord it over them and those who are great exercise authority over them. Yet it shall not be so among you but whoever desires to become great among you let him be your servant and whoever desires to be first among you let him be your slave. Just as the Son of Man did not come to be served but to serve and to give his life a ransom for many."

Summarily, translated in nonprofessional terms she wanted both of them to sit next to Christ in his kingdom. Jesus told her that it was not his to give but to whomever his Father in heaven wanted to sit on Christ right and left hand positions in heaven. Subsequently, this is just my relateable testimony and that is all it is period in the context of the storyline as a connecting perspective. I love the Apostle Paul because he would always say or preface his remarks with "I am the Chief of all sinners." See **1 Timothy 1:15 whereby Paul says, "This is a faithful saying and worthy of all acceptance that Christ Jesus came into the world to <u>save sinners of whom I am chief</u>."** Therefore, I will borrow from Paul and say the same of myself to all of you with humbleness of spirit and mind. Nevertheless, so when I saw this scriptural reference in the word of God later, as I began reading the Bible (upon my conversion). I got back on my knees for the verification and authentication of God's awesome power, for I had seen this eerily identical vision **<u>before</u>** I ever read it in the scriptures of God.

Therefore, I knew God had a divine calling on my life. God sealed the deal. This was my divine introduction to Jesus Christ as Savior of the world! I knew for sure via seeing or having this dream/vision revelation before my conversion. Afterward, then the exact words detailing the vision/dream, that God was displaying to me his awesome power (omniscience—i.e., all knowing) as well as the necessity for me to have my sin on being eternally covered—i.e. (forgiven) via the shed blood (atonement) of His Son, Jesus Christ. Otherwise, I would have been lost for all eternity without Jesus Christ, as my personal Savior like other unsaved souls who have already passed away. (**My high school sweetheart, Stephanie Sammons prayers for my soul answered**). Naturally, this blew me away! Otherwise, how could anyone explain with preciseness, that I, as a **_nonbeliever initially_** without any reference or knowledge that this scripture existed. For I did not read the Bible, neither did I attend church or believed in Christ as a High school teenager. Have the exact same dream or vision of its existence, prior to conversion, without it emanating from the throne of God sent directly to me from God's Living Room. I proffer a challenge to anyone to explain this to me logically, not with make believe fairy tales or mind numbing, insidious rankling or senseless babbling. However, to do so simplistically, rationally or sanely with spiritual enlightenment or understanding rooted in common sense. I know this feat is highly improbable or unattainable by any mortal this side of the eternal vortex that exists, between heaven and earth due to humanity's finite understanding.

Also, because it is the exclusive divine providence of God alone! The word of God says that the hidden things are _God's alone_. See **Deuteronomy 29:29** here that reads, **"The _secret things_ belong to The Lord our God but those things that are revealed belong to us and to our children forever that we may do all the words of this law."** Reverting to the narrative section at hand. Interestingly, the prophet Isaiah expresses that these Seraphim angels have six wings, not the two that Hollywood is always trying to tell us about in its renditions or fairy tales. Neither are they the two-winged angels depicted in Victoria Secrets "angels" catalogs. Contrastingly, Victoria Secrets models depicted as female, semi-nude, models, attired in sensual clothing, lingerie, bras, etc. with highly orchestrated and choreographed seductive movements on catwalks via slick TV marketing campaigns. Meanwhile, cleverly disguised advertising movements depicting sensuality and sexual seduction during the prime hours when young boys with high out of control, raging testosterone levels or hormones and old boys (men) whose hormones levels are declining who are now using artificial means of medicine and science to maintain virility are watching television for "educational purposes." Allow me to digress for a moment here. Violence of any kind toward anyone is always reprehensible, without justifiable cause such as self-defense or defense of others. Especially, when directed toward or involves girls or women. It is criminal, unacceptable and violates the laws of any civilized society of Homo sapiens in the world.

This type of crime requires punishment proportionately in accordance with due process for the accused, as constitutional law mandates period! However, some of the violence toward women generally speaking, has some causation or gestation in the constant overkill, bombardment of supplanted images of objectification of women. This is certainly attributable to the incessant, day in, day out images, pictures or shows with attractive women scantily or dressed in see through sheer clothing. This includes but is not limited to dresses, bikinis, underwear, panties, leggings, garters, bras and seminude photos, digital imprints or billboards while displaying playful, teasing attitudes, exuding sensuality and sexuality during advertisements. All having the intent of commercially selling cars, boats, motorcycles, cigarettes, and now flirtatious undergarments or any other disposal commodity, etc. However, the marketing advertising intent notwithstanding, it objectifies women with sexual innuendoes that may lead to some violence against women. Question, who comes up with these misogynistic ideals anyway? I dare say I do not believe any woman sits up and contemplates hmmm let me see how many ways I can marginalize my own image and that of all other women via naked caricatures plastered everywhere for the world to see... Then again, I could be wrong. Recently there has been an overabundance of "celebrity" females in their 50's showing off their bodies in scantily clad bikinis, underwear, or other lingerie apparel in selfies, photos while on vacations, atop boats, walking on beaches and just hanging out leisurely just so happens with their cellphones cameras in unimaginable places nowadays. Including but not limited to the bathrooms publicly and privately all in an attempt to "keep up with the Kardashians." Americas favorite go to mascot divas who love to show off their bodies in compromising attire almost but not quite naked. Do any of them want to show off their "brains" and not simply portray women as sexy divas on the prowl for intimate interludes or poses while not once trying to ever say or display her as an intelligent, smart, idealistic, innovative, problem solving and sometimes causing (lol) nurturing, supportive as well as financially independent human being?

Some recent examples are Elizabeth Hurley, Heidi Klum, Jennifer Lopez, and Christy Brinkley. All of them are beautiful but really is it necessary, becoming or healthy example setting for young women who want to emulate them to display their bodies at this age in sexy attire publicly? Review **Titus 2:3–5** here, "**The _older women_ likewise that they '_be reverent in behavior_' not slanderers, not given to much wine, teacher of good things that _they admonish the young women_ to love their husbands to love their children _to be discreet_, chaste, homemakers good, obedient to their own husbands that the word of God may not be blasphemed.**" Good luck with this! The deceased, genius, singer and songwriter, Prince, in his Song aptly entitled "Kiss" has a lyric that said, "Act your age, woman, not your shoe size" and maybe we could do the twirl. Generically speaking, some women are God respecting, decent persons that have their independent perspectives that is overlooked many times by male counterparts who quickly seek to exploit their sexuality, femininity, attractiveness or sensuality as he undresses her publicly almost always first. Let me be the first to say for the record, there are some absolutely, gorgeous and incredibly beautiful women on God's planet earth! Thank you Lord for taking that rib from Adam's body to create the female species! Thank God, it only took him one rib because I would gladly offered up three or four if that what it would have taken to create women! Women in general, are so lovely or beautiful that they caused **unholy angels** to leave their estate and divine relationship with Almighty God to intermingle with humanity creating a hybrid of human/angel species—i.e., Nephilim or Giants, etc. More on them later in an upcoming chapter entitled Nephilim-fallen angels. However, limitations or boundaries must exist, balancing between appreciating the exquisite beauty, loveliness, sexiness and adoration for women proportionally. While simultaneously with having respect, appreciation and holding women in higher esteem.

Rather than limiting women to misogynistic, sexy undertones always discarding or disrobing her clothing without ever attempting to panoramically, explore the vastness, complexity and kaleidoscopic power of her cerebral cortex. Which contains a cadre or smorgasbord of exponential wide-ranging intellectual depth that we as men lack. This is the reason why we (men and women) constantly battle with each other. We as men generally reduce everything appertaining to the woman physically not intellectually. Contrastingly, women attempt to make a connection emotionally or cerebrally with a man to ascertain if there is any brainwave activity. Unfortunately, for her, the prognosis is, there is little to no contact made on that elevated level. Therefore, the lack of communicability is fragmented at best and nonexistent at all at worse.

Women are attempting to converse with men on a vastly different, deep hybrid combination of both emotional and intellectual basis from their complex lexicon withdrawing from the repertoire of their plethora or oceans of perspectives. Whereas men, we are like little tadpoles conversing with them from our little ponds or fishbowls of no emotions, simplistic Dr. Spock, logic only rationale or reasoning with the lack of sensitivity or emotion whatsoever of thoughts! We as males, rarely attempt to disrobe or uncover the nakedness of the female's mental acumen to discover her true inner beauty first—i.e., the beauty of her multifaceted mind. I believe this is the direct result concluded by Satan's cunning, diabolical, ongoing scheming that originated in heaven then inside of the Paradise of God with Adam/Eve on earth. Satan decided that sensuality, seduction and sexual innuendo overtones of allurement, enchantment, tantalizing, rampant sexuality, promiscuity or indiscreet sexuality imaging worked in the Garden of Eden on Adam with Eve why in the world it will not work now. We all know that this caused rebellious Adam to begin eating the fruit of the forbidden tree. Adam totally disregarded what God commanded him to do as the guardian/caretaker/gardener of the Garden of Eden. Satan then says, then why bother with all of the rest. Therefore, Satan has concluded, as he has gambled/forfeited his evil life on it. That this same sexual allurement will work in prime time TV hours, when it is displayed in vivid color on flat screen televisions of various dimensions, with multi-dimensional pixels, with zoom in capabilities on screens ranging from thirty-two-inch TVs all the way to large flat, wall-size TVs too.

Satan decided I would utilize beautiful women in all my schemes to cause men to rebel against God. The vast majority of them half-naked or clothed to entice or entrap and stir up the natural lust and stimulate the male testosterone levels so high these people will not have a clue what is happening to them. Lust is natural (inside man) all things evil do not come of Satan. Ninety-nine percent does! Man is the other one per cent for the total 100 percent of **evil too** now after the fall in the Garden of Eden. Review **James 1:13–15,** cited here that reads, **"Let no man say when he is tempted, I am tempted of God, for God cannot be tempted by evil nor does he himself tempt anyone. But each one is tempted when he is drawn away by his _own lust_ and enticed. Then when lust has conceived it gives birth to sin and sin when it is full-grown brings forth death."** Males all (except homosexuals) we are just ripe for full bombardment of tantalizing fantasies of romantic interlude with these lovely women. The word of God calls this the lust of the flesh and the lust of the eyes. Review **1 John 2:16–17,** _as it states,_ _**"For all that is in the world, the lust of the flesh, the lust of the eyes, and the pride of life—is not of the Father but is of the world. And the world is passing away and the lust of it but he who does the will of God abides forever."**_ Nevertheless, the prophet Isaiah describes for us that the Seraphim covered their feet with two wings, their faces with two wings and used the other two to fly. By my math, that appears to be just right. Three times two is six.

This particular group of angels cry aloud one to the other as narrated in **Isaiah 6:3** they say, **"Holy, Holy, Holy is the Lord of**

Hosts the whole world is full of his glory." This group of angels appears to be the Praetorian Honor guards surrounding the throne of the Lord. Naturally, God does not need any "bodyguards" but they are celestial beings who are "ceremonially" carrying out various tasks near the throne of the Lord. Obviously, God's radiance is so blazingly florescent that they must cover their faces in God's presence with two of their wings. Do you remember how Moses face shined so bright after forty days and forty nights in God's presence on Mount Sinai when God delivered the Ten Commandments to him? His face was so bright that he had to wear a veil when talking to the children of Israel for a temporal period because they were scared of this magnificent sight. See **Exodus 34:30** listed here, "*So when Aaron and all of the children of Israel saw Moses behold the skin of his face shone and they were afraid to come near him*." Holiness to the Lord God's florescent glory whereby his face imaged upon Moses skin causing it to be bright and shinning! In addition, Seraphim appear to be more responsible for ceremonial service before the Lord's throne than any other angels are. They are the "honor guard" if you will of heaven. We see them again crisscrossing the New Testament in the illustration narrated to us by John the Revelator. Coincidentally, John **confirms** the prophet Isaiah's vision of these particular angels by the exact same number of wings and status of surrounding the throne of the Lord. Review **Revelation 4:2–9** that I have denoted here following this sentence to see some of the work these holy angels are carrying out around the throne of God. In accordance to the divine direction for their duties delegated to them by the Lord Our God.

Revelation 4:2–9

And immediately, I was in the spirit. And behold a throne was set in heaven and one sat on the throne and he that sat was to look upon like a jasper and a sardine stone. And there was a rainbow about the throne in sight like unto an emerald, and round about the throne were four and twenty seats. I saw four and twenty elders sitting clothed in white *raiment and they had on their heads crowns of gold and out of the throne proceeded lightings, thundering, and voices. And there was seven lamps of fire burning before the throne which were the seven spirits of God. And before the throne was a sea of glass like unto crystal and in the midst of the throne and around about the throne were four beasts full of eyes before and behind. And the first beast was like a lion and the second beast was like a calf. And the third beast had the face of a man and the fourth beast was like a flying eagle. And the four beasts **had each six wings** about him. And they were full of eyes within and they rest not day and night saying Holy, holy, holy Lord God Almighty which was and is and is to come. And when those beast give glory and honor and thanks to him that sat on the throne who lives forever and ever. The four and twenty elders fall down before him that sat on the throne and worship him that lives forever and ever and cast their crowns before the throne saying Thou art worthy O Lord to receive glory, honor, and power for thou hast created all things and for thy pleasure, they are and were created.*

What one must bear in mind is that John the Revelator, was not born **until** approximately *seven hundred years* **after** the prophet Isaiah! Try that with today's psychic predictions. Not even, close! Seraphim, whom infrequently described, neither mentioned consistently throughout the scriptures of God, as some of the other angels whom receive more notation of actions or discussions receive. Naturally, this is understandably so though. I believe that it is because of their unique role of performing duties directly relating to the altar and throne of the Lord. The Lord intentionally wants this to be so because God is not drawing attention to his throne. He is much too busy trying to rescue fallen man, so that he may be able to approach it. See **Hebrew 4:16** that directs us as follows: "***Let us therefore come boldly unto the throne** of grace that we may obtain mercy and find grace to help in time of need.*" God does not want us approaching his throne timidly. Rather confidently, that he through his Son Jesus Christ, will do, all that we ask for to assist us in our sojourning toward his kingdom, as our ultimate destination in our time of need of God's grace according to his riches in glory in Christ the Lord. Summarily, we can see why the Seraphim class of angels exists as uniquely blessed among angels or men in God's divine hierarchy of eternal life. Upon exiting the conclusion of the narration of the Seraphim, class of divine angels, we inevitably are ushered to the last category of angels that we will discuss. Although examined last, are among the most important ones that we will discuss because this is the division of angels which spawned the most sinister, diabolical, as well as evil mind ever… Satan! This is the group of angels identified as Cherubs. The most infamous of them all is Lucifer. Whom now identifiable by The Lord God as an enemy. How do we know this someone rationally may ask? We do so because of the new name God gives him describes or says it all—i.e., Satan. Satan in the original Aramaic language means enemy, nemesis, or foe. Satan is a unique character in many ways. I say so because, this fellow had to be the greatest ***created*** mind (**God has the greatest mind ever <u>no exceptions period</u>!**) that ever was, is or will be **forever exclusively**! Alternatively, he was the biggest fool there ever was. Also, God (***was not created***) I believe that he is the latter myself, but I will let you decide for yourself after reviewing the biblical track record of Satan's actions.

God tells the story of Lucifer's original creation in the book of Ezekiel (**Ezekiel 28:1–19**). God metaphorically uses the prince of Tyrus as his chief antagonist, but we can deduct from the record that God was actually referring to someone else. Without any further ado let me introduce all of you to the most infamous of all God's created beings… Satan himself. Satan thought of himself as a god. Review **Ezekiel 28:2** cited here, for closer inspection, to discover his mindset. It says, "***Son of man say unto the prince of Tyrus,*** **Thus** *said the Lord God, because thine heart is lifted up and thou hast said, <u>I am a god,</u> I sit in the <u>seat of god,</u> in the midst of the* *seas. **Yet you are a man and not God thou you set your heart as the heart of God**.*" Satan's hypnotic, delusional ambition rooted in self-deception causes him to believe his own lies. Deceiving himself that he is god, he devises a plan to takeover heaven, God's kingdom. So much so, in fact he was the creator of the hostile mergers and acquisitions that we see so vividly in our business world contemporaneously leaving chaos, misery and despair in the commercial world today. Satan called this the hostile takeover program (HTP) if you will—i.e., Heaven Takeover Plan. Satan thought to himself, I got it going on! Just look at me baby. I am a bad motor scooter. Satan with evil pride reflects upon his wisdom as well as his beauty verse 12. He then thinks about being able to walk so proudly with a peacock's flair into the Garden of Eden, God's majestic paradise, verse 13. However, wait! Satan is not finished,…well yes, he is, but I am referring to his bragging. He is covered with at least ten of the most precious jewels in the world that would make any professional gemologist salivate with greed if he could appraise its actual net worth, verse 13 as well as its actual value. Read all of Ezekiel 28:13–19, that I have listed here for your reading convenience that illustrates whom God Almighty is talking about as his nemesis.

*Thou hast been in **Eden, the garden of God**. Every precious stone was your covering the sardius, the topaz, and the diamond, the beryl, the onyx and the jasper, the sapphire, the emerald and the carbuncle and gold, the workmanship of your tabrets and of thy pipes was prepared, In you. In the day that **you were created** you are the **anointed cherub** that covereths. And I have set you so. Thou was upon the holy mountain of God, thou hast walked up and down in the midst of the stones of fire thou was perfect, in your ways from the day that thou was created. Till iniquity was found in thee by the multitude of thy merchandise, they have filled the midst of thee with violence and thou hast* *sinned. Therefore, I will cast thee as profane out of the mountain of God, and I will destroy you O cov-ering cherub, from the midst of the stones of fire. Thine heart was lifted up because of thy beauty. Thou hast corrupted thy wisdom by reason of thy brightness. I will cast you to the ground. I will lay you before kings that they may behold you. Thou hast defiled thy sanctuaries by the multitude of thy iniquities by the iniquity of your traffic. Therefore will I bring forth a fire from the midst of you it shall devour you and I will bring you to the ashes upon the earth in the sight of all of them that behold you. All they that know you among the people shall be astonished at you thou shall be a terror and never shalt thou be anymore.*

God describes Lucifer as the "anointed cherub" that covered God's mountain, verse 14. Actually, God tells us that Lucifer was flawless or **perfect** in his original, created state of being—i.e., perfect in wisdom and beauty (**Ezekiel 28:12, 15**). Nevertheless, God continues by specifically identifying Satan's sins in **Ezekiel 28:16**. God says that the devil became filled with violence, **verse 17**, Satan's heart was lifted up because of his beauty, same verse, that his wisdom was corrupted because of his splendor, **verse 18**, that Lucifer defiled his sanctuaries (designated places assigned to hold his musical gifts) see **Ezek. 28:13**, i.e., the workmanship of your timbrels and pipes. Finally, The Lord tells us that Satan becomes *a horror or terror!* See **Ezekiel 28:19: "All who knew you among the people are aston-ished at you for you have become a horror**." This verse describes how all of the angelic ranks and hosts were shocked by Satan's rebellion given his previous highly regarded status/position within God's Living Room realm occupied by angelic hosts. Nevertheless, we all know now that something inside of this perfect being went spiraling out of control in his self-exalted, spiritual cerebellum. Satan stitch weaved a web of lies into his quilt of conscience by masquerading himself as a god (**Isaiah 14:12**) However, what motivated Satan was his ambition, greed and lust. Satan wanted all other angels and men to worship him as a god just as God Almighty is, was and should be forever. Biblical proof, located in **Matthew 4:9** during the temptation of Christ. Now for those of you who are unfamiliar with this particular chapter it refers to the temptation of Christ. Jesus has just completed his forty-day/forty night fasting when Satan approaches him. Biblical fasting is **no food/no water** period. (The other stuff you hear from some impostor false teachers or lukewarm ministers is rubbish). Satan knows that Christ is vulnerable because the flesh is the only part he has to make an appeal unto in order to cause Christ to sin. Satan tells Christ to turn the stones into bread "if" he was the Son of God. Simply because the flesh is, pardon the phrase "the weakest link" in the composition of man. Jesus's reply stuns Satan. *Jesus said that man does not live by bread alone but by every word that proceeds out of the mouth of God (**Matthew 4:4**).* This is what fasting actually demonstrates. Simply put fasting demonstrates that man does not live be bread (food) alone but by every word that proceeds out of the mouth of God Almighty. Additionally, Jesus said *the spirit is willing but the flesh is weak* (Matthew 26:41). The flesh is weak for many reasons. Among some of the reasons is, the flesh ruled only by fleshly satisfaction, it requires energy to do it tasks, whatever that maybe and it tires if it is not fed or nourished. The flesh wars or fights against the spirit. And the spirit fights against the flesh. **The carnal (fleshly desires) mind of man is not subject to the law of God, neither indeed can it be (Romans 8:7).**

Summarily, Satan tells our Savior that he will give Christ the glory of all the kingdoms of the world if Jesus would _worship him_. **Matthew 4:8–9** listed here; *again the devil took him up on an exceedingly high mountain and showed him all the kingdoms of the world and their glory and he said to him all these things I will give you if you will fall down and worship me.* See, this is a clear example of what I meant about Satan being the dumbest being ever. Satan is dumb in **_comparison_** to our God only is my point! Let me provide a word of caution to all readers including myself, before continuing with this theme. Satan is **much smarter** than _you_ *are or I will ever be*. Let me provide some reasons I say this, among them are Satan has seen the very face of God, he has walked in the very Paradise of God's Heavenly Sanctuary—i.e., God's Living Room and in the Garden of Eden, Satan has seen the very throne of God. Satan lives in the spiritual dimension as God does, yet he has access to the natural dimension. So let us compare this to ourselves just a bit by asking; when have any of us ever seen the face of our Creator? When have you or I ever walked in the Garden of God in Eden? When have you or I ever lived in heaven among God once upon a time? Therefore, I caution us to be humble before Christ, knowing that although Satan is a fallen angel, he knows way more about God than any of us do combined. For all we have to do is look at one aspect of our lives to understand or know this. For example, humans are inside or bound within the natural dimensions of this world. Thereby subject to or contained by the laws of gravity and the body of flesh. Satan lives in the spiritual realm but has access to both spheres—i.e., natural and spiritual milieus physically. Enough said about that. I now rejoin the earlier narrative after Satan offers Christ the kingdoms of the world. My answer to this is that he is dumb for believing something so asinine or stupid i.e... That he can *give* Jesus the world. How can he give Christ something that **already belongs** to Jesus? The word of God declares **that the earth is the Lord's and the fullness thereof (Psalm 24:1)**. Satan continues his temptation of Christ, attempting to get him to commit suicide by jumping from the top of the perched pinnacle so that God's angel could catch Jesus "if" he was truly the Son of God. See **Psalms 91:11–12** that reads, "*For he shall give his angels charge over thee to keep you in all your ways they shall bear you up in their hands lest you dash your foot against a stone.*" Jesus rebuked him by telling him the proper balance, application and interpretation of God's words in scripture by informing the deceiver *that one shall not test or tempt God* (**Matthew 4:7**). Another rudimentary way of looking at this perspective via an everyday application would be like someone telling a Christian police officer, that you do not have to take your duty issued firearm to work with you because you are a "Christian" and Christ will protect you on or off duty per se. Albeit the basic premise here is true, one still has to properly balance, as well as apply the proper scripture and common sense. Furthermore, although that is true regarding God's divine protection generally speaking, yet when applied in the mannerism described that would be tantamount to tempting or testing God (**which none of us will ever be worthy to do**) and it is fool hearty. Furthermore, most police officers, per departmental policy are **required** to carry his/her firearm at all times "on or off duty." Regardless to whether they are a Christian or not. Because they may need to use it to protect their life, as well as the life of another officer or the public as peace officers twenty-four hours a day. Nevertheless, I redirect our attention back to the narrative. Ah ha, Satan knew something that we generally overlook—i.e., God did not "legally regain ownership" rights back over man and the earth **until** *after the crucifixion of Christ*. Therefore, Satan reasoned to himself. If he could get Jesus to stumble anywhere along the road leading up to his propitiation/substitutionary death for our sins just before or *prior* to his, death (our sanctification by faith in him) his resurrection (our justification in the eyes of God) seated at the right hand of God the Father (ensuring our pending glorification) Satan would win eternally. ***The earth temporarily "legally" belonged to Satan during the intermittent time period between the falls of Adam/ Eve all the way until the resurrection of Christ into heaven during his divine ascension back to heaven from where he came from and had always had been!*** This is a long time when measured in human years of using our calendars as the measuring rod. It is vital for us completely to understand, that Jesus had to get the keys back from Satan that Adam/Eve "voluntarily deeded" over to him in the Garden of Eden. Although God evicted Adam and Eve, they forfeited the ownership property rights to earth to Lucifer. Furthermore, we must bear in mind at all times there were ***two different*** acts of rebellion in the Garden of Eden. I alluded to this earlier whereby I said **falls plural with an "s"** as opposed to **fall** singular and no's. Eve, she alone, committed Eve's disobedience inside the Garden of Eden, by partaking of the fruit, then eating it independently. This was a divisible, severable, and independent act of rebellion apart from Adam. Specifically she took the fruit, and then ate it by herself away from the presence of Adam. This is *one act* of rebellion or disobedience then after she sinned, she gave the **_unnamed fruit_** (so please quit saying it was an apple) to Adam. Adam, Eve's coconspirator a.k.a. "el Dumbo," chose voluntarily disobedience to God and ate the very same fruit from the tree of the knowledge of good and evil. This was the **_second act_** of defiance of Almighty God. We generally think of them as a singular action, because we have listened to some well-meaning messengers during sermons who have not thoroughly explained this to us as I just aforementioned. They are separate and divisible acts committed by separate and different individuals. Two different individuals unilaterally did them both over a span of time not *definitively* mentioned in the word of God as to whether or not when it occurred immediately—i.e., within a few minutes after Eve's action or hours or what. Naturally, to God Almighty the time when it occurs is actually irrelevant per se. The fact of the matter is that it occurred at all is the problem period! Many implications or inferences exist in God's words without direct association. We need not pretend as though we have all the answers to God's words, thoughts, ways, et cetera. It is okay occasionally, to say that I simply do not know as we attempt to explain biblical truisms. Like here, I do not know exactly when it happened. Additionally, neither do I know either what type or kind of fruit it was that they ate. This is why the word of God tells us to **study to show ourselves approved unto God a workman that need not be ashamed _rightly_ dividing the word of truth in 2 Timothy 2:15**. The translation here is, so that we will not be talking dogmatically, errantly or in an uninformed manner about stuff we either heard or do not understand or just making things up as we go along the way. Deceiving ourselves or other innocent souls seeking God's truth. Alternately, even worse yet, as it states in **1 Timothy 4:1**: **"Giving heed to deceiving or seducing spirits and doctrines of demons."** This is woefully worse than the first act of negligence on our part if done in such a heinous "Slick Willie" style.

Continuing with our mission, which is to discover why all of this happened or occurred with Lucifer's instigation. Lucifer was so physically attractive as well as appealing that it drowned out another attribute of his at the time—i.e., his wisdom. Look at **Ezekiel 28:17**, that states, "***Thine heart was lifted up <u>because of thine beauty</u>, you have <u>corrupted your wisdom</u> because of thy brightness, I will cast you to the ground. I will lay you before kings and they shall behold you***." Lucifer saw himself as many others see themselves when lifted up with evil pride. He envisioned a world where he reigns supreme and subordinate angels and humanity were worshipping him as opposed to worshipping God. Lucifer coveted a throne higher than God's throne. Review **Isaiah 14:13**, that says, "***For you have said in your heart, I will ascend into heaven, I will exalt my throne 'above' the stars of God. I will sit also upon the mount of the congregation in the sides of the north.***"This deviant did not wait one moment! As soon as he had the opportunity, he seized the moment! Satan exercised via action the Latin phrase "Veni, vidi, vici" way before Alexander the Great did so. The phrase which when translated into English says, "I came, I saw, and I conquered!" Satan has forever marred the class of Angelic Cherub blemishing their ranks via his murderous self-indulgent behavior. Now Lucifer has become a demon. Satan is the High Priest of Hell forever of demonic angels. Here is further proof. Do you recall or remember the Ark of the Covenant? For those of you who are unfamiliar with this special Hebrew artifact or symbol. It rose to Hollywood fame during Harrison Ford as Indiana Jones in Raiders of the Lost Ark. However, to the Hebrews and God Almighty it was famous way before then and its symbolism remains the archetype of heavenly worship to the Living God of Israel! Even today! The Ark had two angels kneeling atop of it in the design that God told Moses to do when fashioning it. These angels faced each other. Symbolically, it appears that they surrounded the throne of the Lord just as they do in heaven (**Exodus 25:18–21**). These angels identified as Cherubs and Cherubim. However, earlier we saw that it is actually the Seraphim class whom are the angels surrounding the Lord's throne. How do we reconcile this scripture with those earlier statements? We can simply do so by carefully evaluating the scripture. A closer look at the scripture in **Exodus 25:18–21** says that "***And you shall make <u>two cherubim</u> of gold of hammered work you shall make them at the two ends of the mercy seat. Make one <u>cherub</u> at one end and the <u>other cherub</u> at the other end you shall make the <u>cherubim</u> at*** *the two ends of it at the two ends of it of one piece with the mercy seat. And the cherubim shall stretch forth their wings on high covering the mercy seat with their wings, and their faces shall look one to another, toward the mercy seat shall the faces of the cherubim be"* *(verse 20)*. Naturally, these were not the Cherubim angels but these were Seraphim as we have clearly seen explained in our narrative regarding angelic classes earlier. However, God Almighty for simplicity at that specific time or era seeing no need to go in to specific detail regarding the classification or ranks of angels during Moses lifetime or at the time of the Ark of the Covenant's construction. Moses received instructions from God simply to describe them as Cherubim or angels not necessarily the class or category of angels. Moses lived centuries before the Prophet Isaiah ever came upon the landscape of life. Nevertheless, during Isaiah's lifetime or ministry, God Almighty, deemed it essential for us to understand that there is a distinction amongst angels and specifies that it was Seraphim surrounding his throne. Another way of looking or reviewing this fact or at this issue is to do so via a different prism. This prism illustration is observable in the names of Lucifer versus the name of Satan. Throughout scripture the names, Lucifer and Satan usage appears interchangeably referring to the same evil persona without going into detail as to their respective or actual meaning. However, as we now know, Lucifer means "bright" or "morning star" this is very positive. Yet, Satan means enemy or nemesis this is vastly diverse than the positive name of Lucifer originally. Nevertheless, although the names have different meanings, both are associated with the same demon. It is a different class altogether with diametrically opposed names of identification. However, both names refer to the same person. Likewise, albeit cherubim and angels refer to the same species as does seraphim—i.e., both are classes or ranks of angels. Seraphim simply is a different category or class of angels altogether versus cherubim within angelic celestial ranks. Analogously, the Cherubim construction atop the Ark of the Covenant are angels just like the Seraphim whom it is symbolically portraying around the throne of God. Yet, both names refer to angels regardless to their classification or group affiliations as a whole.

All of the items that God instructed Moses to replicate on earth are simply duplicates or copies of things in heaven. Cited here in **Hebrews 9:23** as it states, "*Therefore it was necessary that the 'copies of the things in heaven' should be purified with these, but the heavenly things themselves with better sacrifices than these.*" See **Hebrews 10:1** cited here, "*For the law having a shadow of good things to come and not the very image of the things can never with these same sacrifices which they offer continually year-by-year make those who approach perfect.*" God told Moses to put the mercy seat above upon the ark verse 21. However, God says that he will meet with him and talk to him from *above* **the mercy seat**… verse 22. Get it! God did not say that he would talk to Moses or the High Priests **from** the mercy seat but from **above it**. Furthermore, the symbolism shows that God the Father is *above* all. Additionally, this is attributable to fact that the earthly images do not have the exact glory of their heavenly originals! Now watch this. Paul tells us in the book of Hebrews, that the **sanctuary in heaven** was **setup or pitched** by the Lord and *not man* (**Hebrews 8:2**). Therefore, the one on earth **does not** have the **same glory**. Furthermore, Paul tells us that it serves as an example and *shadow* **of heavenly** things (**Hebrews 8:5**). However, since Jesus has entered directly into heaven itself for us, **Christ and has become our mercy seat**. This is the reason why the angels atop the Ark of The Covenant angels were depicted in the way they were on this holy artifact because it was a "foreshadowing" that Christ would become our mercy seat. Therefore, angels because of their inferiority to Jesus Christ cannot be displayed "over" Jesus, not even "symbolically" on the Ark due to his authority over all of God's created beings. Review **Hebrews 7:22** denoted here, "*By so much more Jesus has become a surety of a better covenant.*" *Also see Hebrew 9:24 cited herein,* "*For Christ has not entered the holy places made with hands which are 'copies' of the true but into heaven itself now to appear in the presence of God for us.*" Consequently, Jesus now seated at the right hand of the Father, neither beneath him nor over him. Look at **Hebrews 10:12** that states, "*But this man (Jesus) after he had offered one sacrifice for sins forever sat down at the right hand of God.*" *Also, review*

Hebrew 8:1–2, denoted here, "Now this is the main point of the things we are saying, we have such a High Priest who is seated at the right hand of the throne of the Majesty in the heavens, a minister of the sanctuary and of the true tabernacle, which the Lord erected, and not man. **Thus, God's mercy seat is Christ himself!"** *This simply* means that God speaks directly to us through Christ. We have biblical support located at **Hebrews 1:1–4, which** says, "*God who at various times and in various ways spoke in times past to the fathers by the prophets, has in these last days spoken to us by his Son. Whom he has appointed heir of all things through whom also he made the worlds who being the brightness of his glory and the express image of his person and upholding all things by the word of his power. When he had by himself purged our sins sat down at the right hand of the Majesty on high having become so much better than the angels as he by inheritance obtained a more excellent name than they.*" Obviously, angels are not covering the face of Christ in heaven as they hovered near the mercy seat upon the ark! Angels cover *their* faces in the presence of Christ as they bow their knees saying **Holy, Holy, Holy is the Lord God Almighty, which was, is, and is to come.** This we saw earlier in **Isaiah 6:1–3.** Repeated here again, *in the year that King Uzziah died. "I saw The Lord sitting on a throne, high and lifted up and the train of his robe filled the temple, above it stood Seraphim. Each one had six wings with two he covered his face, with two he covered his feet, and with two he flew as they cried aloud to each other Holy, holy, holy is the Lord of Host, the whole earth is full of his glory!"*

Finally, Jesus referred to this group of angels when talking about children. Christ said take heed that you do not despise one of these little ones (children) for I say unto you **that in heaven their angels do always behold my Father's face**, which *is in heaven {Matthew 18:10}.* Cherubs appear to be the largest group of angels for many reasons. Primarily, because if we deduct from scripture that we partially already examined, documented, shown and provided scriptural support for, that there is only one Archangel. Therefore, that settles that. Secondly, Cherubim performed specific missions as directed by the Lord that seemingly suggest this is a smaller corps as well as have been described and Seraphim assignments appear to be ceremonial tasks directly relating to the altar and throne of God. Naturally, this is a finite group of celestial beings designated specific roles by Almighty God. Their mission is to accomplish his holy will in heaven and on earth. Thus, Cherubs appear to be the largest group of them all. Another reason is that many of them followed Lucifer in his failed attempt to overthrow God's kingdom after eviction from and out of heaven with him. I will explain more of about this here as follows. Historically, Bible scholars have consistently cited **Revelation 12:4** to illustrate that approximately _one-third_ of the Cherubs/angels joined in the rebellion against God Almighty. Mathematically this equates to 33 1/3 per centile of these cherubs/angels followed Lucifer in this specular display of outright treason as it states, "***His tail** (red dragon/Lucifer influences)* ***drew** (guided or misdirected)* **the *third part of the stars* of heaven and did *cast them* to the earth**." Logically, this verse is not referring to the celestial stars that govern the skies as shinning lights. How do we know this for certain someone may ask? Well primarily or naturally, we can deduce and know this because that would have caused the complete annihilation or destruction of planet earth! If one star, meteorite or asteroid collides with earth (which they will due in the near future) as part of The Lord of Hosts divine judgment says, they will strike earth as part of God's earth cleansing program. When these stars make contact with earth, the outcome is devastating. **See Mark 13:25 that reads, "And *the stars of heaven* shall fall and the powers that are in heaven will be shaken."** This scripture shows us that it was not the celestial stars of heaven per se as well. For these stars will fall at a futuristic date only known or determined by God Almighty himself. Furthermore, these celestial bodies of stars and comets move at a lightning speed beyond our imagination that such an event would wipe out all humanity and life forms on the earth, as we know it today. Additionally, earth would suffer a tremendous upheaval in all sorts of cataclysmic activity e.g. tidal waves, the size of skyscrapers, oceans burning with the heat of a thousand suns, artic winters so cold life on earth would be impossible, ocean waters rising far beyond the ability of natural barriers to contain them. All seasons of the year are alterable—i.e., winter, spring, summer and fall of the seasonal calendar year with horrendous implications for humankind are out of season. This entire point means is that it will be cold when it should be hot and vice versa, it will rain when it should be dry vice versa, etc. This is a result of drastic weather pattern changes and interference from atmospheric, cosmic physics and elemental forces such as summer to winter overnight. The expected weather patterns for farming, planting, harvesting, cultivating grains, fruit and vegetables within arid landscapes suddenly impacted by droughts or famine causing devastation to vital sources of food supply. Tornadoes, firestorms, blizzards, hailstorms, etc. would blast across earth's geography or landscape with blinding speed destroying fertile crops, fragile forestation and delicate plants, insects required for pollination, animals, fish and other food life chain cycle sustaining nutrients humankind requires for survival. Life on earth would be unsustainable if just one star fell on earth, yet alone, a *third of the stars* affecting earth's delicate membrane, which symphonically requires balancing by the word of God's power, would become tipsy turvy. Earth's atmosphere, geological crust, topography, air, oxygen supply as well as all other life forms on earth experience simultaneous obliteration! All life would instantaneously become extinct and there would be no more earth. Furthermore, as we review Satan's original name, which was Lucifer. Which when translated, means bright and morning star, we can rationally assume that the other fallen angels albeit they are unnamed in the scriptures regarding salvation, had names that associated them in some form with the "stars of God' too or celestial names like each of us have names that help identify us. Obviously, no one on earth knows the number, names or how many angels originally created by God Almighty, in heaven that existed before their descent into utter tyranny other than the divine Godhead comprised of Father, Son and Holy Spirit. Herein after referred to as FSH. However, we know there was a lot or plenty of them originally prior to some of them joining the Luciferian Rebellion abandoning their holy habitation (**Jude 1:6**). Additional scriptural proof that there are many angels is documented in the words of Jesus Christ when he was in the Garden of Gethsemane facing arrest by the Sanhedrin Council for blasphemy according to their self-serving judgment of guilt of Christ alleged sacrilege or blasphemy determination against (i.e., Kangaroo Court decision) God. Let us pick up the story, as Christ just prior to his arrest, after the traitor, Judas Iscariot, led the way of the mob arrestors to one of Christ's favorite praying gardens. The entire narrative is located in **Matthew 26:46–67**. However, for brevity we will zero in on the specific words of Christ in **Matthew 26:52–53**. Peter assaulted Malchus, one of the arresting mob members with his sword, causing a significant injury to his ear. Actually, Peter cuts it off. Coincidentally, Christ heals his ear right there on the spot. Malchus, a servant of the High Priest of the Sanhedrin Council stunned by both events—i.e., the sword blow on the right ear when he reached out to arrest Jesus in the Garden of Gethsemane after Judas kissed Christ on the cheek. However, more importantly by Christ's immediate action of healing him right afterward. This act alone should have cleared him of any crimes against God had they really been concerned about the kingdom of God. Jesus inquires after this assault as well as insult, by asking Judas if he was betraying the Son of Man with a Kiss. This has now become a discoverable moment for all of us. Now we know where the phrase euphemistically coined the "kiss of death" similar to the one that Brutus did with Julius Caesar as he led the assassins who all in a choreographed manner violently stabbed him to death on the steps of the Roman Senate palladium originates. Nevertheless, Christ tells Peter to put his sword back into *the sheath. Because **all who live by the sword shall perish by the sword** or <u>**do you think that I cannot now pray unto my Father and he will provide me with more than twelve legions of angels**</u>? (Matthew 26:52).* My God, this is amazing! Christ tells us that God would have provided him with **more than twelve legions of angels** even at this precise moment or the twelfth hour, if you will, if Jesus wanted it to occur. However, Christ had already prayed that *God the Father's **will*** be done and not ***his own*** will. Here it is imperative for us to understand the precise meaning of what Jesus was telling them as well as us by contrast and comparison. Simply put, by comparison of the Roman Legion's soldier assemblage or numerical troop membership during the zenith of the Roman Empire's power was vast. One legion of centurions, could contain anywhere between three thousand to six thousand battle hardened troops who were veterans of numerous, blood thirsty conquests and campaigns under the leadership of the various Roman Generals, Emperors or Caesars of Rome. Viva la Roma!

Therefore, if one were to apply that number as a modest baseline or a conservative comparison—i.e., 3k–6k to **the multiple of twelve** that Jesus referred to in this specific verse comparatively to the basic legion meaning of the Caesars warriors or troops. Christ could have prayed to save his fleshly "human life" and his Heavenly Father would had sent anywhere from 36,000 to 72,000 Holy Angels with flaming swords drawn on a 911 emergency response mission flight to fight on Christ's behalf. These angels would be against an easily defeasible self-righteous mob of religious zealots, with torches, clubs and swords. Who were loosely organized, self-righteous, untrained in warfare and men. Who would be fighting against divine, celestial angelic beings who were veterans of the heavenly war in Heaven or God's Living Room instigated by Lucifer to wipe them off the face of the earth permanently! Translation here, it would be the equivalent to you or I using a sledgehammer to swat or kill an annoying fly! Simply because they were oblivious or did not know, what they were doing or with whom they were violating. Trust me, they would have found out very fast had Jesus prayed that God send him help immediately to get rid of these trivial little "toy soldiers." These men were plastic little imps comparable to mosquitoes to divine angels who are much more powerful. Therefore, all of us should be thanking God on bended knees to celebrate the fact, that Christ refrained himself for asking for help, clearly denoting that Christ wanted to do God's will and not his own. Jesus Christ is Lord to the glory of God the Father forever! Consequently, we can celebrate that Christ **did not** ask his Father to send those angels. Otherwise, all of humanity would have been lost for all eternity no exceptions! Remember the word of God specifically says, **without the shedding of blood** there is no forgiveness for sins. Jesus came **after** he **was sent** by God the Father to die for "our sins" **not to save his human body** from death. Review

Matthew 26:38–39 here, for it says, ***then he said to them my soul is exceedingly sorrowful unto to death. Stay here and watch with me. He went a little farther and fell on his face and prayed saying Father, if it is possible let this cup pass from me, nevertheless <u>not</u> as I will</u>*** *but* ***<u>as you will</u>****. Jesus was not sorry that he was going to **physically "taste death for everyman"** as it says in **Hebrews 2:9** for that is the reason why he arrived. Jesus was sorry that he was going to experience *separation temporarily* from his Father and the Holy Spirit. **This had never occurred** before in the annals of the Godhead—i.e. (FSH), The Father, The Son, Jesus Christ and The Holy Ghost. Here is Bible support; Christ asks his Father as he was dying on the cross: outlined here in **Matthew 27:46**, *"And about the ninth hour Eli Eli lama sabachthani"—i.e., My God, My God <u>why have you forsaken</u> me?* This riveting statement causes the heart to shriek. The Son of God is asking his Father why (what is the reason) have you forsaken me. Christ was asking in other words, what I have done that that has offended you at all that in fact it has caused you to turn away from me! Father, I as you know have done nothing, yet, I feel internally the full measure of aloofness, isolation and abandonment from you at this exact moment in eternity present! I repeat, this **has never occurred** where any member of the Holy Trinity (FSH) felt forsaken or abandoned by any of the other two members of the eternal, sacred Godhead! Also, this is the first time in all of eternity that the Godhead had one of its eternal, non-severable, divine, members "outside the loop" of its **holy radius** commonly referred to in military terms as "***missing in action***" or MIA for short. Jesus Christ at this precise moment as he suffered for our sins was <u>Missing In Action</u> from the Holy Trinity. This must be what death is like. I don't think that any of us could imagine the utter abominable feeling of rejection, internally ripping the foundation of one's spirit from the anchor of one's soul, as the soul, wrenching, writhing with the feeling of total forsakenness or lack of the presence of God anywhere near the departing soul. The emotional toll this could and will take upon any who dies without Christ, as Lord will experience this overwhelming sense of the lack of the awareness or presence of God Almighty or his Son or his Spirit forever. Daily we take this feeling of God's omnipresence for granted. Some of the reasons we do relates to the fact, we can feel the warmth of the rays of the sun on our faces or bodies, or the cool of the air breeze as it flows effortlessly across our torso or our legs. Additionally, we can feel the winter blast freeze that makes us shudder to find warmth wherever and sometimes with whomever. However, not to be outdone, we hear the sounds of birds tweeting in the trees as if they have never tweeted before and it was only 24 hours ago since their last tweet session. Furthermore, we listen to the sound of cascading waterfalls or ponds, while watching lakes, rivers, streams or ocean water as it flows seamlessly where the wind or water current circuits leads it. Furthermore, when looking out into the sky we see the limitless nature of God's divine hand and presence. The word of God says **the heavens declare the glory of God** in **Psalms 19:1.** All of these things are witnesses to the existence as well as the very presence of God in our lives. Therefore, we errantly presume, so we think, they (evidence of God's omnipresence) will also accompany us in the next world or as we are dying *__without__* Christ in our lives. Ahh that isn't true my friend, as we witnessed in the sentence above, where Christ had to experience this dreadful feeling of despair or monumental despondency in our place (only those who accept Christ won't experience this) because he **tasted death** for Christians (believers who accept) exclusively. Nevertheless, for **everyman** generally who is willing to believe that he is the Son of God and their Savior. All this means is that Christ has tasted death for "everyman" that *__will accept him__* as their Redeemer. God had to intentionally, briefly turn his back to Jesus (during his crucifixion) from heaven to allow the full weight of the consequences of sin's penalty imposition upon Jesus not in a watered down version or in an abbreviated fashion. Jesus had to have the full death experience' without God's presence just like Jesus Christ had the full "life experience" of man, from birth to adolescence, to young man to mature adult to death as God's sacrificial lamb. Jesus had to drink from the dregs of death's cup (recall what he said to John, James and their mother) to pay for the full penalty not just a part, a portion or some of it but all of it! God had to turn his face away temporally from his Only Begotten Son so that he would not witness the horror imposed upon **him who knew no sin but**

became sin for us as denoted in **2 Corinthians 5:21**. Simply because only God knows, what he may have done if he continued painstakingly watch his Son suffer for others (fallen man) that **he did not** do. The entire T3 Heaven's audience, including holy angels and the unholy demons too, derived from all of the aforementioned classes or ranks of angels. Each one individually and all of them collectively had to stand by silently without uttering a single sound to witness the most unbelievable, shocking, heavenly foundation shaking, epic and colossal miscarriage of justice event in the entire cosmos since God created the worlds with Jesus and his Holy Spirit. The most devastating spectacle ever on display i.e…**the crucifixion of Christ**! Although he created the world and the world was created for him and by him. (See **Colossians 1:15–19**) listed here, **He is the image of the invisible God, the first born over all creation. For <u>he created all things that are in heaven and that are on</u> the earth, visible and invisible, whether thrones, dominions, principalities, or powers. All things were created through him and for him. And he is before all things and in him all things consist and he is the head of the body the church who is the beginning the firstborn from the dead that in all things he may have the preeminence. For it pleased the Father that in him all fullness should dwell. And by him <u>to reconcile all things on earth to himself</u> by him, whether things on earth or things in heaven having made peace through the blood of his cross.** Now unbelievably during Christ's crucifixion, "the man" that "*he created*" within the world to take care of it for him as a steward in the Garden of Eden, is **taking his life** from him in an act of total debauchery to atone for the sin of man. This was so monumentally repugnant, that God Almighty turned away from this spectacle along with his holy angels, all with tilted halos, bowed heads, broken hearts, upon bended knees, crying with weeping eyes while kneeling beside God's throne witnessing this heinous crime. Their God was painfully suffering on a wooden cross at Calvary's Gate, albeit voluntarily, knowing as Jesus himself knew that Jesus ***did not commit any sins*** against his Heavenly Father! My God! Tearfully, from my heart, soul and every cell, atom or molecule that comprises my life I want say **Thank you Lord Jesus Christ**! We are truly unworthy of God's love, mercy, grace or forgiveness each of us period. No exceptions! Cautiously added, for anyone who may want to claim self-righteousness. I include this sentence intentionally here. The word of God says **all have sinned and come short of the glory of God (Romans 3:23).** This unselfish act of sacrifice by Jesus Christ on behalf of fallen man has to rip one's soul away from its foundation with sorrow of heart!

Summarily, we can see via scriptural support, that there are four (4) categories or ranks of angels, which I will recap here. They are Archangel, Seraphim, Cherubim and Cherub. Nevertheless, simply illustrating the rank does not explain for us this diabolical strategy to overthrow the Kingdom of God or the motive for this evil incident in heaven's ecclesiastical courtyard of divine serenity. For me, this is a major paradox. That I will briefly attempt to explain before continuing on with our quest to thoroughly examine the biblical record to understand why Satan instigated this war against God or for causing these "high crimes and misdemeanors" against the Holy Lord God of Israel and his divine Heavenly Constitution. Simply put, we are trying to repent of our sins, accept Jesus Christ as our Savior, expand our views to eat, be among or risen within the very presence of God and Jesus Christ, at the last trump on Resurrection/Judgment Day after this life on earth has ended. However, contrastingly Satan, who was *originally already* in heaven as well within the very presence of God, is fighting against God causing his complete banishment and separation from God's presence for all eternity. This is a baffling paradox or mystery to me. However, I am not alone. The Apostle Paul called this "the mystery of iniquity" too way before I contemplated it. Review **2 Thessalonians 2:7–8,** cited here that says, *for the **mystery of iniquity** is already at work only he who now let's will until he be taken out of the way and then shall that Wicked be revealed whom the Lord shall consume with the spirit of his mouth and shall destroy with the brightness of his coming.* Satan is going all out to wage war against man in this final conflict between him and Yahweh, God Almighty, until the very end. He is unwilling to stop. Therefore, God has to stop him. There is no turning back now. The cast for the dye has been set. *The War in Heaven will become the War* *on Earth!* All of God's created beings will be involved in it one way or another. Some of you may recall that Switzerland claimed neutrality in World War 2 between Nazi Germany and the rest of the world. Hah. Now we find out they had kept many stolen European Jewish treasures for the Nazis. God declares that there is no such thing as neutrality. The Swiss proclamation of "neutrality" was much ado about nothing. It was all lies. The Swiss had been lying all along while they as well as other financers of Germany's systematic, methodical, maniacal, murderous genocide as well as debauchery against the European Jewish people was occurring, they were profiteering on the backs of plundered Ashkenazi Jewish treasures, paintings, cash, artifacts, heirlooms, priceless family possessions, wealth, gold, art, etc. The Swiss and their German cohorts were nothing more than a den of thieves, murderers and liars. Also, their country in exchange for a neutral posture publicly while (privately) they sequestered European Jewish accounts for the Germans they weren't attacked in a quid pro quo for maintaining encrypted accounts by the Germans for eons all *under the cover* of neutrality. Remember what the Lord Jesus Christ said, "***He that is not with me is against me***" (**Matthew 12:30**). Switzerland was not with the Jewish people, they were with the Nazis in Germany while lying feverishly to the rest of the world that they were neutral bah humbug! I have some unfortunate news for the country of Switzerland predicated upon the word of God here that simply is, your country will not escape the judgment of the Holy God of Israel as easily as you desire or anyone else for that matter may think. God has recorded every single scintilla of your criminal acts. He is well aware of all of your complicit deeds, actions or role in the subjugation of the Israeli people in the conspiracy of tyranny against them. Although Adolf Hitler, himself and those who aided him (Switzerland) is personally accountable and responsible for this diabolical attempt to annihilate God's Hebrew people, while simultaneously stealing their property, belongings, wealth or hard earned possessions will not be allowed to evade Judgment. Although God is the Creator of all countries, the worlds, cosmos and the God of all countries (**Hebrews 1:1**), God only identifies himself as the God of Israel! Rest assured you have it on the credibility of God's word.

Stay tuned Switzerland the God of Israel has an interview with you soon as he does with the whole world that comes against the Hebrew people!

The Cherub division of angels that remained loyal to The God of Israel and Jesus Christ can only imagine what the Lord is thinking about them as a group. God loves them all just as he does you and me. Here is biblical proof See **Revelation 22:8–9** that states, "**And I John saw these things and heard them and when I had heard and saw them I fell down to worship before the feet of <u>the angel</u> that showed me these things. Then he said to me See that you do not do that,** *I am your fellow servant and of your brethren the prophets and of those who keep the words of this book <u>Worship God</u>!*" John should have known better since he was with Jesus Christ on many occasions as a disciple prior to his forced exile to the Isle of Patmos. However, he was human too and as such entitled to a mistake, which was correctable by the Cherub/angel who talked with him. The angelic class of Cherub do not have to be concerned about their future with God or Christ realistically just because or since Satan came from their rank or group. Naturally, they must be asking themselves is there another evil one in our midst that has been undiscovered? However, they can rest assured that the Lord knows that there is not another evil angel among them because he is omniscient—i.e., all knowing and would have dealt with that individual a long time ago.

See **Hebrews 4:13**, it reads, "*<u>Neither is there any creature</u> that <u>is not manifest</u> in his sight <u>but all things</u> are <u>naked and open</u> unto the eyes of him with whom we have to do*." The Lord did not spare Satan and those angels who joined him in a devious rebellion. Logically, he would not allow another evil angel to rest among the Cherub class or any other rank as an "evil sleeper" agent (to be revealed later his true evil intent) to remain hidden in disguise among them only to unleash terror all over again in heaven. Trust me the Lord is saying and wants all to know including holy cherubic angels. I am not going to go thru this again for my son's sacrifice is once for all eternity. Next, I shift our focus of our quest upon the landscape or region/location where this motivation for this heinous treachery against God and Satan's real motive for instigating the greatest crime occurrence in the pantheon of heaven.

The next chapter's theme is designed as a biblically based review of the approximate landscape of heaven—i.e., the layers or dimensions of heaven. I hope that this will allow us to comprehend the arena, topography or geography of its milieu to provide a clearer understanding to the war's transition from heaven to earth within this narrative. Clarifications of the foundation of heaven will assist us with knowing where this war started and where this war will end unambiguously.

CHAPTER IV

T3 Heavens

There has always been some misunderstanding or confusion in Christendom about Heaven, the atmospheric heavens and Heaven where God dwells divinely overseeing all of his creation. Therefore, I want to expand our insight into this controversy by biblically examining this irksome matter in order to continue our quest or search into the War inside of the Kingdom of heaven, specifically within God's Living Room. The Apostle Paul tells us in 2 **Corinthians 12:1–7** that he was "caught up" to the *third heaven*. Here are the actual cited words of **2 Corinthians 12:1–7**: "**It is doubtless not profitable for me to boast. I will come to visions and revelations of the Lord. I know a man in Christ who fourteen years ago whether in the body or out of the body I do not know-God knows such a one was <u>caught up</u> to <u>the third heaven</u>. And I know such a man how he was 'caught up into Paradise' and heard <u>inexpressible words.</u> Which it is <u>not lawful for a man to speak,</u> of such a one I will boast yet of myself, I will not boast except in my infirmities for though I might desire to boast I will not be a fool, for I will speak the truth. But I refrain lest anyone should think of me above what he sees me to be or hears from me and lest I should be exalted above measure by the abundance of the revelations *a thorn in the flesh* was given me a <u>messenger of Satan to beat me</u> *lest I should be exalted above measure*.**"

My Lord! Wow, that was awesome! Obviously, Paul could count and he assumed that so could or so would any prospective reader of the Holy Scriptures be able to do as well. He stated that he was caught up to the **third heaven** which means by consistent symbolization there must be **two heavens** before or preceding the third heaven that he pierced through enroute to God's throne in Paradise before his arrival at the final heaven where God dwells. Paul sees the revelations of the Lord that are *unlawful and not permitted* by God in some instances for a man to even utter or discuss Verse 4. The entire scripture actually reads; *how that he was **caught up** into paradise and heard **unspeakable words**, which it is **not lawful for a man to utter**.* T3 simply means in the context of this book, the Three Heavens. There is (1) the atmospheric heaven or sky, (2) outer space heaven and (3) the third heaven where God sits exalted far above all principality and authority ruling over both visible and invisible domains simultaneously. See **Colossians 1:16** listed here, "**For he created all things that are in heaven and that are on earth, visible and invisible whether thrones, dominions, principalities, or powers. All things were created through him and for him.**" However, the Apostle Paul was not the only one to have such a glimpse of the third heaven. John while exiled on Patmos Island, while banished for preaching the words of Christ to a dying world, went there as well. This is why we refer to him as John the Revelator. John was allowed to see holy revelations of the apocalyptic world that will occur in our lifetime and not his own. Let us explore his contact with heaven now. John tells us in **Revelation 4:1** the following *after these things (his initial encounter with Christ)...*"*A door was open in heaven, and the first voice which I heard was like a trumpet speaking with me, saying come up here (third heaven) and I will show you things which must take place after this. Immediately I was in the Spirit and behold a throne set in heaven...*"

Clearly, John the Revelator, whisked into the third heaven from the earth supernaturally—i.e., raptured and allowed to have a vision of the future from Christ. From this point onward as he vividly details in the entire book of Revelation of futuristic events, including those in our current time. Wow! This scriptural reference establishes where

God has temporarily situated his throne. Until he brings it down to become the new heaven and new earth that he will create with Christ (**Revelation 21:1**). God will do this so that man, as Christ promised, can be where I am. Review **Ephesians 1:10** that reads as follows, "*that in the dispensation of the fullness of times, he might gather together in one, all things in Christ, both which are in heaven and which are on earth even in him.*" And **John 14:2–4**, "*Where Jesus cites, in my Father's house are many mansions, if it were not so, I would have told you. I go to prepare a place for you and if I go and prepare a place for you. I will come again and receive you unto myself that where I am there you may be also!*" Praise the Lord Hallelujah! The Apostle Paul tells us *in 1 Corinthians 2:9 that eye has not seen, nor has ear heard neither can it enter into the heart of man what God has prepared for those who love him.*

God is simply telling us that it is unimaginable to conceive what he has in store with his plans to celebrate, welcome and present to all believers in Christ Jesus at the welcoming home or homecoming extravaganza ceremony. This will occur during the First Supper in heaven at the Lord's Table. Hollywood, with all of its lights, red carpets, pizzazz and showbiz wizardry cannot even come close to this heavenly majestic display, draw-dropping regalia. That God Almighty with his Holy Spirit will highlight at the Inaugural Festival Banquet to Honor his Only Begotten Son Jesus (Yeshua) Christ on the day of our arrival. This is the fulfillment of promises God made eons ago regarding his truly united family at the Lord's Harvest during the ingathering or assembly of Saints worldwide including Old and New Testament and Tribulation saints. Stay Tuned God is coming to get you (believers) to take you to heaven your new and final home to be with him and Christ forever and ever! The word of God commands us in **Luke 21:28 when we began to see such things** (the End Time Signs occurring) *to look up* **your redemption draws near!** Cheer up, stand up and shout out from your belly to give God the Glory due unto his sacred name!

The Bible commands believers in Christ in **Psalms 107:2, "Let the redeemed of the Lord say so!"** Well I am just saying so here. JESUS HAS REDEEMED ME! Do not be shy now. We praise simple minded, over paid, self-indulgent athletes running down across a field with a football; or who shoots a basketball into a hoop rim or smashes a tennis ball across a feeble net or that hits little white balls into a hole in the ground. Unabashedly. However, we want to praise God with a stiff upper lip. We appear to be scared or to be embarrassed in "public" with such adoration or exultation of Christ where others see us. Therefore, we encourage "silent" praise to the one who has saved our souls from suffering destruction and damnation forever. Additionally, he wants us to live with him and Christ in eternal bliss in Paradise so how dare we timidly praise him like a little mouse. **NO WAY! GOD the Father, CHRIST and the HOLY SPIRIT** are *much more worthy* of our praise than any of these athletes could ever be. So let's show it! Therefore, I right now am asking or better yet challenging you right now wherever you are reading this book to shout out to the Lord and tell this dying world that you are redeemed with or by the blood of Jesus Christ and **not ashamed** to say it! Remember Jesus said in **Mark 8:38, "For whoever is ashamed of me and my words in this adulterous and sinful generation of him the Son of Man will be ashamed when he comes in the glory of his Father with the holy angels."** I just did my shout! Therefore, do yours as you so choose to do? Feel free to use this one if you do not have one already. **Lord God, I do not care who sees me, hears me or whom is looking at me right now. I am not ashamed to publicly, openly as well as voluntarily worship, praise, glorify, magnify and exalt Your Holy Name Yahweh and that of Your Holy Son, Jesus Christ and that of Your Holy Ghost world without end! Amen and Amen.**

The second heaven is just beyond our reach if you will, where Satan dwells temporarily for the time being. Until he is casted out, unto the earth and embodied within the Man of Perdition, the Anti-Christ (**2 Thess. 2:3–4 and 9**). Consider these words of Jesus who said, **"That I beheld Satan as lightning cast from heaven" (Luke 10:18, Isaiah 14:12).** When Satan was cast from heaven that was simply referring to the second heaven from the third heaven where God lives, ruling sovereignly over all his creation visible and invisible. God intends always for the devil to have a constant feeling of spiraling downward, far away from him. Satan temporally still has partial access to God from the second heaven's balcony currently. Bible proof is in the WOG that says Satan is the "accuser" of the brethren (believers in Christ) (**Revelation 12:10**). Lucifer runs and tells God Almighty every, single thing that believers do that violates any laws, commandments, or statutes of God period. He yells aloud from the second floor of his realm to God saying things like; see, look at them, they can't obey you for a second. He continues saying things as he did this and she did that. Yawdy yawdy yaw. He is a little snitch. Satan is constantly whining about our imperfect conduct as believers in Christ. Yet he does not take into account for one second that we are "born sinners" whereby he is a _chosen_ renegade. Since he is the **_accuser of the brethren,_** he has to have an audience or ability to speak directly to God regarding his accusations. Otherwise, it is just senseless babbling aloud about nothing. However, in a way even though God hears it somehow still it is babbling on about nothing because of Christ the Lord's sacrificial death for us. Thus, he does this from the porch of the second heaven's balcony for now. His purpose in doing so is to cause division between our Lord and us. Satan hopes that God will become angry with the individual, State or people and punish them harshly. Similar to the way that all fallen angels such as he is being punished for his usurpation. Jesus just looks at his Father and says **_Father forgive them for they know not what they are doing_** as stated in **Luke 23:34**.

In addition, Father that is why you sent me into the world... to forgive them of their sins. Finally, Christ tells his Father and ours too, that I have paid the penalty for the sins of the whole world excluding Satan and his fallen angels. Satan's chatter does not matter. Even though he is using his Twitter, Gmail or Facebook accounts to text his tweets to you Holy Father. Satan cannot for the love of Christ, understand why man received forgiveness of his sins and he and his demoniac soldiers are not. The answer is quite clear. Jesus died for **our sins** because **God so loved the world (all people will-ing to believe that Christ is Lord) that he gave his only begot-ten son that _whoever believes_ in him should not perish but have everlasting life.** Additionally, the Lord's word says **For God did not**

send his Son into the world <u>to condemn</u> the world but that the world through him (Jesus Christ) might be saved (John 3:16–17). Additionally, **God has <u>no pleasure</u> in him that dies in sin.** See **Ezekiel 18:32.** Satan and all demons **must pay** for their <u>**own**</u> sins. Since they are eternal beings (without souls) but cannot physically die per se, they will receive punishment "within the bodies" they were designed/embodied or inherited during their original created state for all eternity. This is a very unique situation to explain but let me provide more data if I may. Dogs, cats, squirrels, and other animals on earth have bodies but *do not have* spirits or souls. All animals and any other created beings (excluding man who was created in God's image) including angels has no soul. So please quit lying to your children, telling them things about the pet's demise/death that "fluffy" is in heaven. No, he is not. Fluffy, Fido, Felisha and any other family pet that has died is dead. He/she is dead period! Fallen angels or demons have eternal bodies but do not have souls or spirits just like cats, dogs or squirrels, etc. How do we know this with 100 percent accuracy? We do so by simply believing God's word. Review if you will **Genesis 2:7,** that reads, "*And the* **Lord God formed man of the dust of the ground and 'breathed' into his nostrils** *the* <u>**breath of life**</u> **and man became a** <u>*living soul!*</u>" Now watch this, review **Genesis 2:19,** that reads; **and** *out of the ground the Lord God formed* <u>*every beast*</u> *of the field and* <u>*every fowl of the air*</u> **and brought them to Adam to see what he would call them and whatsoever, Adam called every living creature that was the name thereof.**

Here is the most significant difference God <u>**didn't breath**</u> into their nostrils—i.e., animals or fowls orifices at any time the breath of life period! God created them alive with breath from God's divine hand. God had to breathe life "into Adam" whereas beast and fowl or fish created with life breath already inside of them. Furthermore, their *creation is not* **in the image of God.** They do not have souls or eternal spirits… They have temporal bodies after the fall in Eden. Allow me to provide a rudimentary basic example if I may, to illustrate this perspective succinctly. Original pancake recipes—i.e., "made from scratch" require the following basic <u>separate</u> items, pancake or flour mix, water or milk, eggs, butter, salt, and the utensils necessary to fry them. Whereas "premixed pancake" mixes contains all of these items without you having to include any of them individually. You just add water for liquefaction, stir up then fry. Analogously, just as pancake premixes, animals, birds, fish, etc., were "premixed" **_with_** the "breath of life" **already included** during their creation. Man was **without breath** and **lifeless** as his body lay on Eden's dew of grass. God made man if you will, from scratch without the breath of life. Man, was not "premixed" with breath of life as the animals were. This makes man exclusive. God breathed life into Adam and he became a living soul! This is the reason humankind's creation is physically and spiritually the image of God! Herein contains the key difference. Since fallen angels or demons were created in heaven. That makes them "celestial" or of the cosmos **not from** "the dust of the ground" as celestial beings they were intended to live forever in harmony with God and all of his creation in a structured hierarchy of order not superior or inferior to others but alongside them. However, Lucifer created all of this evil illusion and the ideology of "superiority" beginning with the superiority of angels over men and superiority of men over other men, ethnicities, or races. **This is the ruse the devil used to inspire** **_"white superiority" or the "Master race" evil derives its nebulous_** **_creation_ spawned on earth from a demon created in heaven that is going to hell or the lake of fire burning with brimstone forever**. Furthermore, this is the lie that is still being told to this very day. This lie is exploding with exponential negative consequences worldwide but especially for Black American citizenry residing in America. The lie I am referring to is the demon inspired lie of "superiority" of one race of people over the other race of people. Read here in **Acts 17:26–27, "And he has made from 'one blood' <u>every nation of men</u> to dwell on all the face of the earth and has determined their pre-appointed times and the boundaries of their dwelling. So that they should seek the Lord in the hope that they might grope for him and find him though he is not far from each of us."** Animals are of the earth, since they are "terrestrial" meaning being born on, created on or of the earth. Animals created purposes originally as service support intended for man. However, after the fall of man inside the Garden of Eden, the purpose dramatically altered for beasts, fowl and fish to become food, burden bearers and service beasts. This was a major upheaval from the original intended life span cycle causing death. Consequently, because of "***the curse***" upon man and animals, they became carnivores or killers of anything or anyone including humans and other animals that represent "meat" for their palate. Remember God Almighty **cursed all** after the fall in the Garden of Eden—i.e., Adam, Eve, the serpent and nature itself. Here is proof, see **Genesis 3:9–18**, whereby God encounters a sinful Adam who confesses after blaming his wife Eve whom confesses after blaming the serpent (Satan) who beguiled her. Boy, what a trio of cowards. Nevertheless, I sincerely doubt if any of us would have done any better. See their loathing below.

Genesis 3:9–18

And the Lord God called unto Adam and said unto him Adam where are you and he said I heard your voice in the garden, and I was afraid because I was naked and I hid myself and he said who told you that you were naked? Have you eaten of the tree whereof I commanded you not to eat? And the man said The woman who you gave to be with me she gave me of the tree and I did eat and the Lord God said unto the woman what is this that you have done? And the woman said, the serpent beguiled me, and I did eat, and the Lord said unto the serpent because you have done this you are cursed above all cattle and above every beast of the field. Upon your belly shalt you go and dust shall you eat all the days of your life and I will put enmity between you and the woman and between your seed and her seed it shall bruise your head and you shall bruise his heel. Unto the woman, he said I will greatly multiply your sorrow and your conception in sorrow shall you bring forth children. And your desire shall be to your husband and he shall rule over you. And unto Adam *he said, because you have hearkened unto the voice of your wife, and have eaten of, the tree, of which I commanded you saying thou **shall not eat** of it of it cursed,* **is the ground** *for thy sake in sorrow shall, you eat of it all the days of thy life.* **Thorns and thistles shall it bring forth** *to thee and you shall eat the herb of the field.*

However, before any of us become sanctimonious, self-righteous (which we tend to do) quite often, very easily without prompting or holier displaying than thou attitudes. We need reminding that God Almighty sent his Son, Jesus Christ to die for "**our**" sins too! God is asking all of us this very same proverbial question personally, that he asked Adam in the Garden of Eden. Which is simply this, where are you? The vast majority of us have absolutely no idea where we are (spiritually) speaking that is of course. We are staggering through life like a drunken man groping in the darkness of this present evil world until death touches us on our shoulder and tells us it is time to meet our Maker. Our souls are oblivious to the things of God. Because we place such a higher premium on the things of this world, ransoming our souls in a bartered exchange for temporal happiness. Neglecting the spiritual man's need for harmony with Jesus and God because now we do not "see" God. Therefore, we lie to ourselves as we allow the enemy of Jesus Christ to lie to us as well. Therefore, we errantly conclude that it is okay to put God on hold for just a bit longer until our souls long for or need him. Yet, God said the soul that sins against me shall die. Review **Ezekiel 18:4** denoted here reads; ***Behold all souls are mine as the soul of the Father, so also the soul of the son, the soul that sins it shall die.*** This includes the fallen angels, even though their creation was in heaven and not in the image of God, nor of the same organic or cosmopolitan matter—i.e., "dirt" as was man. Therefore, they lack "souls." Essentially, they cannot be *born again* as man can, if he accepts Jesus Christ as his personal Savior. This is another reason why Satan and fallen angels cannot be forgiven or saved **they do not possess a soul for rebirth** as does man. Furthermore, more importantly, Christ the Lord **did not die** for **their sins**. Fallen angels in accordance with divine law for penalty or punishment instituted by God Almighty must die for their own sin. Here is additional biblical support for this premise. There was a man named Nicodemus, whom was a Pharisee (as was the Apostle Paul) who had significant influence with his Jewish peers as a ruler of the synagogues in Israel. However, periodically he came to Jesus at night (publicly ashamed) of asking Jesus salvation questions in public for fear of reprisal by his religious sect. Nevertheless, Nicodemus asked Jesus *how a man* could be born again. Review **John 3:4 listed here**: Nicodemus said to him (Jesus) **how can a man** be born when he is old. Can he enter a <u>second time</u> into his mother's womb? Jesus answers verse 4–5 most assuredly, I say to you <u>unless one is born of water and the Spirit</u> he cannot enter into the kingdom of God.** Therefore, unlike fallen angels man can be born of water (baptism) and of the Spirit (Holy Spirit) indwelling man. Moving right along, consequently, in the new heaven and the new earth animals will not die at all because there is no death, no sorrow, no crying, no pain, and no night at all in heaven period! See **Revelation 21:4.** Angels as aforementioned are comprised of only mind and body. Man bears a unique distinction; he is the only being in heaven or earth that God created his own—i.e., the **image of God**. See **Genesis 1:26–27**, cited here for you; *Then God said, let us create man in <u>our image</u> according to <u>our likeness,</u> let them have dominion over the fish of the sea, the birds of the air, and over the cattle over all the earth and over every creeping thing that creeps on the earth. So God created man in <u>his own image</u> in <u>the image of God</u> he created him male and female he created them.* Before, I go further I humbly request that you notice he **never** said let them **have dominion** of one race or group **over** the other of humanity. So where does this evil ideology of enslavement, superiority, war and murder emanates from? I will give you only one guess. Bingo, you got it, **Lucifer himself!** Consequently, man is born with a mind, a body and a **soul**. Furthermore, man was tempted to sin by Satan against the Lord, but **who tempted Satan** to sin against God Almighty? **The answer is absolutely no one at all!** Christ referred to this, when he said that **the devil was a murderer from the very beginning** in **John**

8:44 noted here. Jesus said, "*You are of your father the devil and the lusts of your father you will do he was <u>a murderer from the beginning</u> and abode not in the truth because there is <u>no truth</u> in him, when he speaks a lie he speaks of himself for <u>he is a liar and the father of it</u>.*"

If we review God's actions, sequentially as he decides the actual punishment for all of humankind we can see that God actually does so in the reverse. Let me clarify what I am referring to here. God did not curse Adam first, he cursed the serpent, then Eve, and afterward God cursed Adam then creation itself. Paul talks about this briefly within the book of Romans. Let us look at his reply here in the eighth chapter of the book of Romans. Paul begins to radically layout the plan of redemption for creation in the book of **Romans 8:18–23** whereby he cites *for I reckon that the sufferings of this present time are not worthy to be compared with the glory, which shall be revealed in us. For the earnest expectation of the creature waits for the manifestation of the sons of God. For the creature was made subject to vanity not willingly. But by the reason of him who subjected the same in hope. Because the creature itself <u>also</u> shall be delivered from the bondage of corruption into the glorious liberty of the children of God. For we know that the whole creation groans and travails in pain together and not only they but we ourselves also, which have the first fruits of the spirit even we ourselves groan within ourselves waiting for the adoption to wit the redemption of our bodies.* Now let me make this plain for some of us who may be following at a different pace below.

> *Romans 8:18–23 whereby he (Paul) cites: For I reckon (believe) that the sufferings of this present time (while we are alive here on earth), are not worthy (not on the same scale as) to be compared (incomparable) with the glory (to the highest level). Which shall be revealed in us (when we see Jesus during the Bema Judgment (only for those **who accept Christ as Lord,** and are given heavenly bodies and the rap-*

*ture if still alive at the time of Christ return). For the earnest expectation of the creature (expectancy of all animals, creeping things, fowls, etc., and creation itself) waits for the manifestation of the sons of God (the unveiling or the resurrection to life to live in unison via celestial bodies with Christ). For the creature (all animals, fowl, etc.) was made subject to vanity not willingly. (Subjected to punishment, the curse, corruption, decay and death via altered life style from God's original intent). But by the reason of him (Adam who disobeyed God)) who subjected (result of Adam's disobedience became a part of God's curse through no fault of their own);the same in hope. Because the creature itself, also shall be delivered (will no longer be subjected to the effects of the curse) from the bondage (harmful destructive impact of sorrow, death, disease, etc.) of corruption (decay) into the glorious liberty of the children of God. (Freedom to live harmoniously with God the Father, God the Son Christ, and God the Holy Spirit in his divine kingdom for all eternity with no possibility of crying, death or disease). For we know that the whole creation (all life on planet earth and the ground itself) groans (writhes with internal sighing or emotional grief) and travails (deep seated since of painful, sadness to potent to express externally) in pain together. (Self-explanatory) and not only they (all of the aforementioned) but we ourselves (believers in Christ as the Son of God) also, which have the first fruits (spiritual gifts and the earnest down pledge for rapture/redemption) of the Spirit even we ourselves groan within ourselves waiting for the adoption to wit the redemption of our bodies. (Transformation of our earthly bodies to heavenly bodies) P.S. **Note: the word of God says that flesh and blood cannot inherit the kingdom of God! Because Jesus said,***

God is a Spirit and those who worship him must worship him in spirit and in truth. (John 4:24)

Finally, man lives in the first heaven—i.e., the atmospheric heaven that consists of the troposphere, mesosphere and stratosphere. The everyday air, space we live, breath and play in that is accompanied by direct sunlight as well as gamma and beta rays nourishing plant life that sustains life here on earth for vegetative and food purposes. Humanity has inherited the delicate membrane of the protective shield of earth. Thus life on earth that is surrounded by the atmospheric membrane circle (Ozone layer) gives the planet protection from the extreme harmful Beta rays of the sun while simultaneously it nourishes, enriches as it balances the planet's food sources to sustain life on earth of all living species. **Genesis 2:4** reads as follows; ***these are the generations of the heavens (plural) and of the earth "man's residency" (first heaven) when they were created in the day that the Lord made the earth and the heavens***. It encompasses the area and expanse of our visible sky and just a little beyond where we launch spacecraft, the international space station, satellites and nuclear weapons, etc. Man lives on earth that God separated from the Seas, and sky—i.e., first heaven, when he formed it for all humanity, animals, fish, plant life so on and so forth. Review **Genesis 1:10** denoted here, "**And God called the dry land Earth and the gathering together of the waters he called Seas and God saw that it was good.**" The Ozone layer historically served as the protective membrane or shield against the sun's emission of x-rays, infrared heat, ultraviolet and gamma rays as well as radioactive neurons of the sun that man has degraded significantly with toxic carbons emitted into the atmosphere causing the "Greenhouse Effect." In addition, God (who is omniscient) was preparing a battlefield arena in advance for Lucifer and his fallen angels following their eviction or casting down from the third heaven. God has always resided in the third heaven and he was not going to yield his kingdom or eternal home to anyone. Therefore, God has restricted Satan to the second heaven where his domicile is now and ultimately will throw him directly on to the earth—i.e., the first heaven topography our residency. Review **Revelation 12:12**, which reads "**Rejoice you heavens (second and third) and you that dwell in them. Woe to the inhabiters of the earth (first heaven) and of the sea (there is no sea in the sky or second heaven or in third heaven) <u>for the devil is come down to you</u> having great wrath (anger) because he knows that he has but a 'short tim**e.'" The devil got beat at his own game. He thought that since he knew that God is an eternal being then so was he. Therefore, he would not die, per se, since the same God of Life who created Adam created and made him too. Therefore, he is also an eternal being with life everlasting. Consequently, neither was he worried about death initially. Eternal beings **never die** they *continue* to live on elsewhere in the spiritual dimension Satan reasoned among himself. God had to tell him yes you are an eternal being, thus, you will continue to live. However, **<u>I get to</u> decide where you shall live and where you will spend eternity and it is in hell**. Oops, Major gasp by Satan, for he had never heard of hell and there was no hell until <u>God created</u> it specifically for him and his angels. Hell is a jail for you and all fallen angels. **Christ said, hell, was not created for man but for the devil and his angels (Matthew 25:41)**. Satan realizes that once he is regulated down to the earth (the first heaven realm) that the Heavenly encrusted Mickey Mouse watch he has on his wrist actually "starts the clock" of the countdown to the imposition of his delayed sentence in hell. God knew what was going to happen before Satan caused Adam and Eve to rebel. Therefore, Jehovah was preparing the geography of Satan's downfall alongside his fallen angels even before the first blow. See **Isaiah 46:9–10** it reads, "**Remember the former things of old <u>for I am God</u> and <u>there is</u> <u>none like me</u> declaring '*the end from the beginning*' and from ancient times the things that <u>are not yet done</u> my counsel will stand and I will do <u>all my pleasure</u>.**" My Lord what a powerful self-declaration statement of God's divine power!

Conclusively, as promised, that sums up the matter relating to the T3 Heavens as it were.

Therefore, we can devote time to the next subject at hand—i.e., Luciferian supplemental interaction with man on an extremely amoral and personal level. Progressing forward to the narrative, I direct your attention to this sinister topic as we turn to the next chapter that deals with the Luciferian cohorts mating with humans, on earth with such diabolical debauchery against the Holy Creator of all life.

CHAPTER V

Nephilim: Fallen Angels

Angels who followed Lucifer into rebellion and outright warfare in the very "living room" of God exacerbated this unsuccessful coup de' tat by outrageous conduct on earth that followed their devious insurrection. This heinous act was so profane that its characterization is accounted treasonous intentional infliction of insult toward God. Even though God knew that this act would occur in advance (God is omniscient) he had to let it play out although it was despicable abomination in his sight. This is another tragedy of fallen angels overlooked generally in Christendom. This is probably because the subject matter is horrible to discuss and sometimes it may be challenging or complicated to explain fluidly because it may not resonate quickly among Sunday school parishioners who are more accustomed to digesting or consuming subject matters about the "milk" of God's word and not the "meat." Review **Hebrews 5:12–14**; cited here, "**For when the time you ought to be teachers, you have need that one teach you again that which be the first principles of the oracles of God, and are become such as have need of <u>milk and not of strong meat.</u> For everyone that uses milk is unskillful in the word of righteousness for he is a babe. But strong meat belongs to them that are of full age even those who by reason of use have their senses exercised to discern both good and evil.**" Additionally, some may be uncomfortable with the subject matter itself thus making it harder to get people to listen or be attentive long enough to understand its impact upon the world or us.

Nonetheless, although it is something usually omitted when discussing often overly repeated themes such as tithing, offering and giving of gifts to the ministry as **the main subject** when preaching on Sundays (Sabbath Day is Saturday) in most churches today. Essential truths like this are lost. They call it "prosperity" gospel. Nevertheless, we can't "cherry pick," which subjects of God's words we like to talk about because it brings money in the treasury or coffers of the various congregations while intentionally deleting or leaving out hard subjects. The Bible declares that *"all scripture" is given by inspiration of God and is profitable for doctrine, for reproof, for correction, for instruction in righteousness, that the man of God may be perfect (mature) thoroughly furnished for all good works* (**2 Timothy 3:16–17**). God commands us to speak sound doctrine. Read **Titus 2:1** that says **but as for you speak the things that are proper for sound doctrine.** The reasoning simply because the goal is to **present every man/woman (person) mature in Christ Jesus Our Lord and Savior.** Now back to the subject matter of ascertaining approximately when did this debauchery against God occur as we continue seeking answers to evil in heaven and earth? The word of God, tells us approximately *when* this incendiary conduct occurred by stating that "in the beginning" God created the heaven and the earth. This requires some clarification here. This is referring to the created heaven and earth where man resides. The Third Heaven where God always have dwelled obviously already (always) existed for that is where God has always lived. Additionally, this is where God has always existed. Therefore, it always coexisted with God and did not require *creation*. It already existed as the supreme domain or residency of God Almighty. Therefore, it is not referring to the heaven of heavens per se or the third heaven where Paul describes his ascension for a heavenly glimpse or vision (**2 Corinthians 12:2**).

Listed here, **I knew a man in Christ above fourteen years ago (whether in the body) I cannot tell or whether out of the body, I cannot tell God knows such a one caught up to heaven.** Hmmm so, which specific heaven is the author referring to here? Either it is directly referring to the second heaven where Satan dwells currently or the first heaven—i.e., our atmospheric cosmos where we reside. God created these two heavens by his spoken word. Look at **Genesis 1:1** denoted here, "***In the beginning, <u>God created</u> the heaven and the earth.***" We can logically conclude that the second heaven where Satan temporarily dwells or has access to was already there because that is the realm where he was exiled unto after leading his doomed followers. After they attempted or tried to complete a hostile merger and acquisition of heaven under his demonic, authoritarian, blasphemous conduct in the third heaven—i.e., God's Living Room. How can we logically presume this is accurate? We will query the biblical narrative to pinpoint support for this premise. After the Battle Royal, when the Archangel, Michael and his angels defeated Lucifer and his angels which resulted in Lucifer's eviction. The devil had to reside elsewhere but the question is where? However, more importantly *when* did this happen? This either occurred just prior to the creation of man on earth or just after God created man on earth. Satan's rebellion in heaven had already occurred and expulsion or eviction to another realm out of God Almighty's holy presence occurred immediately. Therefore, since Satan's expulsion to the earth was not completed at the time—i.e., the "first heaven" because this is a futuristic event that will take place with him entering/possessing the human body of the Antichrist. Since his expulsion from the Third Heaven where God dwells supreme that leaves only the second heaven where he is now temporarily as the only other location for him to be or on earth itself. Consequently, the second heaven must have already existed then for his forced exile there upon his usurpation. Furthermore, if we look at **Job 1:6–7** God inquires where Satan had been travelling to or from on his unassigned reconnaissance missions.

Although God already knows, he asked Satan because he wanted Satan to know that he knew what his evil intentions were for humanity. These scriptures are cited here in **Job 1:6–7**, "***Now there was a day when the sons of God came to present themselves before the Lord and Satan <u>came also among</u> them and the Lord said unto Satan whence cometh thou or modern translation where are you coming from? And Satan answered the Lord and said from*** *going to and fro in the earth and from walking up and down in it.*" These are some poignant scriptures. The reason is it tells us a couple of imperative things if we just ascertain its composition aptly. First, it tells us that the "*sons* of God" came to "present themselves" before the Lord. However, it is referring to the "sons of God" in the *celestial* (Heavenly) *realm,* not the terrestrial (earthly) domain where we live. Nevertheless, Satan came also among them. This imagery is masterful. Now watch this, for this is telling us that the sons of God—i.e., holy angels, in the celestial dominion are prostrating themselves and giving account of their activities unto the Lord and Satan came among them. Even the Devil submits himself before the awesome power of God Almighty and Jesus Christ as Lord! Lucifer brings his evil persona before God Almighty to give account of his actions or whereabouts. Satan's banishment or forced exile from the third heaven at this point of man's existence was not yet finalized but is a work in progress.

Therefore, we can reasonably conclude it has to be the second heaven just above where man lives that I described earlier prior to starting this topic. Additionally, in **Job 1:6** expresses to us that the <u>sons of God</u> came to "present themselves" before the Lord. Now before we go any further we must ***divide the word of truth rightly*** here as **2 Timothy2:15** directs us to do. What sons of God? God has not yet created man. Remember stay with me reader, I am referring to ***before*** the <u>creation of man</u> or the earthly heaven and earth where we reside. Therefore, this eliminates us. Animals logically were not created yet either. This eliminates them. More importantly, they do not fit this category anyway. Sorry animal rights lovers. They just do not measure up to this high standard which by divine decree is that "**man was cre-ated**" <u>in the image</u> of **God**. Look at **Genesis 1:26**. So much nonsense predicated upon the evolution of primates to humans—i.e., according to the author of "The Origin of the Species" by Charles Darwin, referred to as Darwinism. This is another satanic lie implanted to trick or deceive otherwise reasonably, intelligent persons seeking the origin of man. God created man period! Creationism period no ifs, no ands or buts about it at all. There was no evolutionary transition from animals to man. Nevertheless, continuing with the analysis, so that leaves angels as being the sons of God.

Since angels, are the only created beings on the scene during this epoch? Then by the process of elimination, it must be them. I am referring to Angels too as the "sons of God" allegorically. Since initially, all angels came to worship before the Lord *prior* to the creation of man including Satan who was originally identified as Lucifer. How do we know this? We know this simply by reviewing previous scriptural references including **Isaiah 6:3–4** and **Revelation 4:8–10**. Both scriptures cited below sequentially.

> ***Isaiah 6:2–4*** *Above it stood seraphim each one had six wings with two he covered his face, with two he covered his feet and with two he flew and one cried to the other Holy, Holy, holy is the Lord of hosts the whole earth is full of his glory. Now Revelation 4:8–11; and the four beasts had each of them six wings about him and they were full of eyes within and they rest not day and night saying Holy, holy, holy Lord God Almighty which was which is and which is to come. And when those beasts give honor and thanks to him that that sat on the throne, who lives forever and ever. The four and twenty elders fall down before him that sat on the throne and worship him that lives forever and ever and cast their crowns before the throne saying you are worthy O Lord to receive glory and honor and power for you have created all things and for thy pleasure they are and were created.*

Predicated from the documentation of the abovementioned scriptures we can logically reach the appropriate conclusion therein. This conclusion simply is that Angels in their original estate, *prior to the war in heaven*, worshipped God and bowed before his throne adoring the Godhead harmoniously in a spectacular display of heavenly worship. Again, it could not be man because we are discussing *prior* to the creation of man. Therefore, there was only God and the holy angels. In addition, look at (**Genesis 6:1–5**) herein is another place prominently where the phrase "the sons of God" expression is documented. Let us analyze this a little closer in detail conclusively to grasp the context that it is referring to angels. It begins by saying that when **men** began to multiply or increase via birth, **after** the creation of Adam and his descendants in accordance to God's commandment to them to go and multiply which they did via intimacy with their wives and lovers that *daughters* **were** *born* to them. Continuing it says in the second verse that "the sons of God" saw the "daughters of men" that they were beautiful or fair. It is obviously referring unto two different species, because there is no need to say the "sons of God" and the "daughters of men" if they are the same species. One only has to say, men and women or sons and daughters as opposed to declaring the "sons of God" and the "daughters of men." The author wants us definitively to understand clearly that this is an intermingling of angelic beings with natural mortals so the author purposefully tells us this precisely so that we do not miss the concept. Let us continue this probe.

Examine verse **Genesis 6:4**; here the WOG (words of God) says **that there were "giants" on the earth in those days, and the sons of God came in (mated sexually) with the daughters of men and they bore children to them**… **Those mighty men were of old, men of renown**. Whew, this is powerful! Interestingly, it appears that the "giants" on the earth were a byproduct (genetic mutation) to the sexual mating or **cross breeding of humans with angels**. We call these beings Nephilim. It is imperative to note that there was no prior mentioning of "giants" on the earth *until* we reach the scriptures regarding "sons of God" with the "daughters of men." A closer look reveals that prior to the creation of man, angels did not appear to mate or have (sexual contact) with each other yet alone with any human being. Therefore, this is why this specific illicit behavior taken by some fallen angels became so reprehensible to God, that he takes drastic action to wit, immediately imprisoning some of them to the realm of the abyss until the Day of Judgment.

Review **Jude 1:6**. Which is denoted here, "**And the angels who did not keep their <u>first estate</u> but left <u>their own habitation</u> he hath 'reserved in everlasting darkness' unto the judgment of the Great Day**." The reason this behavior is illicit or immoral is due to the fact that *God created* the woman for the man **_not_** for the angels. There is not a single scripture anywhere in the WOG referring to angelic sexual contact with each other *before* the fall of man! Do not take my word for it. Search for yourself...from Genesis to Malachi of the Old Testament, which comprises (39 books) and from Matthew to Revelation of the New Testament comprised of twenty-seven books...not a single scripture period in the King James Version of the Bible! However, during the war in heaven because of angelic rebellion/insurrection or a failed coup d'etat. Fighting violently spreads throughout God's Living Room for the very throne of heaven itself as angels go to battle. Holy angels and fallen angels fight violently in the presence of God Almighty. This has to be the epitome of disrespect, insult and outright evil on a grand scale. Some of these demons are so evil that God had to act impromptu causing their current detention occurrence (being held) temporarily under darkness (as we saw above) in chains until the judgment of the Great Day (**Jude 1:6**). Imagine for just a second, you have invited guests inside your home for a social gathering of your selection and a fight breaks out among them at your elaborate holiday planned festivities or social gathering. How would you feel as the host? What would you do? How would you or I, react to this disgraceful display of hostility in our humble abode insulting us as the hosts? My Lord what spawned such diabolical activity? Wow! Finally, some of these renegade angels or demons were so lustful upon man's creation they began sexual mating with the daughters of men (mortals) by the sons of God (fallen angels).

Look at **2 Corinthians 11:14** listed here, it reads, "**And no wonder! For Satan himself '_transforms_' himself into an angel of light**." Naturally, these angels transformed themselves into human forms when mating intimately with women or the daughters of men. Regardless, to what forms they took to complete the cross breeding or intermixing with the daughters of men. Logically, their appearance did not repel the women with whom they were mating. It is difficult to mate with someone who exhibits any image or trait deemed unattractive to you. Alternately, whose appearance is so grotesque, heinous and inhumane causing ones repulsion. Naturally, this would result in being so extraordinarily offensive that you would fear them or become offended by the mere sight unless, the attacker/individual became violent toward the victim thereby forcibly, physically assaulting the victim sexually against his or her will via raping.

Angels both good and miscreants can transform themselves into alternative life forms. One of the first times we see this is in **Genesis 18–19** chapters. Here is where the outcry to God Almighty regarding the sin of the twin cities of Sodom and Gomorrah has reached heaven's gate. We pick up the story outlined for us in **Genesis 18:20–22: and the Lord said because the outcry against Sodom and Gomorrah is great, because their sin is very grave, I will go down now and see whether they have done altogether according to the outcry against it that has come to me, and if not I will know. Then the men turned away and went toward Sodom but Abraham still stood before the Lord.** Here is a good place to just pause a second to grasp what just happened here. Look at the last sentence of the scripture again if you will, for it says *"the men turned away from there and went toward Sodom"* **but Abram remained still before The Lord.** What men? Abram (God later changed his name to Abraham father of many nations) was the only man present here with God Almighty, who came to inform Abram of his intentions and there were two angels and Abram or Abraham. Men do not accompany the Lord whenever he comes down from heaven. Even if they did, why would they be present there or even necessary? What actual purpose would they serve if they were present which they were not? What are they going to do? They have no celestial power, authority or jurisdiction. So again, what would be the purpose for having men to accompany the Lord? Historically, holy angels have always accompanied God as he moves through the T3 heavens and beyond. References regarding their presence with the Lord is rampant throughout scripture since their known or referred unto as the "heavenly host." Here are a couple of quick examples of such times angels of the Lord appearances happen one in past time and a couple of future occurrences with God or on God's behalf. One occurrence was when God confirmed Joshua as his messenger to replace Moses who has now died as the children of Israel were about to enter into the Promised Land.

See **Joshua 5:15** cited here as it reads, "**And he said, nay but as _captain_ of _the host of the Lord_ am I now come. And Joshua fell on his face to the earth, did worship, and said that unto him what saith my Lord unto his servant and the 'captain of the lords' host said loose thy sandal from thy foot for the place wherein stand is holy.**" Another time they will appear is when angels will accompany Christ when he returns to the earth to finalize God's decrees upon the earth and all inhabitants thereof. View **2 Thessalonians 1:6–8** which reads, "**And to you who are troubled rest with us when the Lord Jesus shall be revealed from heaven with his mighty angels in flaming fire taking vengeance on those that know not God and that obey not the gospel of our Lord Jesus Christ.**" Angels appeared to announce the holy birth of the Messiah in **Luke 2:11 and 14** noted here. "**And the angel said unto them fear not for behold I bring you good news of great joy which shall be to all people. For unto you is born this day in the city of David, a Savior that is Christ the Lord. Glory to God in the highest and on earth peace, good will toward men.**" Returning to our narrative, God decides to send two angels to record (for God already knows) what is actually happening there inside Sodom and Gomorrah and destroy those cities.

See also **Genesis 19:1 and 13** Cited here, "**Now the two angels came to Sodom in the evening and Lot (Abraham's nephew) was sitting in the gate of Sodom when Lot saw them he rose to meet them and 'bowed himself' with his face toward the ground.**" **Now Genesis 19:3, "But he (Lot) insisted strongly so they turned in to him and entered his house. Then he baked unleavened bread and they ate.**" This reminds me of instructions within Paul's letter to the Hebrews listed here in **Hebrews 13:2, "Be not forgetful to entertain strangers for thereby some have entertained angels unawares.**" Boy, I want to tell all of you about an encounter with a holy angel so badly. However, I will refrain because I stated earlier that I get annoyed when others tell accounts of seemingly braggadocios events. Therefore, this applies to me equally as well. Therefore, I continue with our narrative **_excluding_** this testimony. Simply put they did not know they were angels at all is Paul's translation! Furthermore, these scriptures details for us that the **_angels entered_** Lot's house, **_ate a feast_** and **prepared to sleep** before disturbances caused by homosexual neighbors outside who wanted to have intercourse with holy angels whom they *mistook* for men. Logically, these angels were not walking around with their wings exposed or in such a different format from the residents of Sodom and Gomorrah. Otherwise, the citizens would all have been alarmed at such a magnificent presence and recognized that they were in the presence of "heavenly" hosts or angels. You cannot just fold wings up and tuck them away under a trenchcoat or underneath a smock or robe. Another time we see angels transforming from their natural estate, was when Lucifer spoke through the body of the serpent inside of the Garden of Eden causing Eve to bait Adam.

Consequently, they both sinned against their God who planted them there. Satan did not appear in his natural form. Why not? He knew that he in his raw, natural, unholy angelic estate or appearance would have problems with Adam/Eve welcoming him or accepting him. *It is imperative for us to keep in mind that Adam and Eve were only aware of the appearances or presence of God and the animals they were not yet aware of angelic beings per se which Lucifer now Satan was.* Satan's appearance in his natural estate quickly would had identified him as an enemy of God to both of them or at least caused suspicion. Remember, Adam and Eve at that time, only interacted with or knew of God Almighty, all of the reptile's insects, fowls and the animals as well as their own offspring. So if Lucifer appeared in his fallen angelic form they would have asked him, who in the...(You know what I wanted to say) so I will substitute and say...who in the world are you? Whoa, narrowly escaped before using another word there! Nevertheless, Satan *alternates his form* to assume the serpent's body and beguiles Eve. Review **Genesis 3:1**. Noted here, **now the serpent was more cunning than any beat**

of the field, which the Lord God had made, and he said to the woman Has God indeed said you shall not eat of every tree of the garden? Not only did he *transform* completely he did so in the <u>form of a reptile</u>—i.e., snake's body! Another occurrence when demons or fallen angels enter into animals' bodies' illustration occurs in the Book of Matthew. Specifically **Matthew 8:28–34.** Here this time, it occurred when pig farmers were escorting their herd of bacon and ham; I mean pigs, around for sale when they encountered the Son of God, Jesus Christ. Another narrative explanation in further detail listed here, two men who were possessed of evil demons inside the coast of the Gergesenes came out of the cemetery or tombs as Christ was walking by. The Lord's word, describes them as being so violent that no man could walk by this area since these two demons inside of the bodies of men, powerfully instilled with rage, strength and evil. Naturally, that meant they would attack almost anyone… except the King of Kings—i.e., Christ Jesus the Lord! Both demons whom were in possession of human bodies—i.e., *a transformed* state of existence, instantly recognized Jesus Christ, as the Son of God. They inquired or asked Jesus not knowing why he was there, **did he come to torment them** *before the time appointed* by God for their punishment and rebellion in God's Living Room. Immediately, they asked Christ, since he was going to cast them out of the two men, which they knew he was going to do. They requested that Jesus upon his commandment (after disembodying from the two men) that they not be sent to Sheol/Hades/Hell or to the realm of darkness if they could embody the herd of swine. **<u>Christ had mercy</u>** even on **demons** and allowed them to go into the body of pigs who were just grazing grass for nutrition. The Bible tells us that after departing from the men bodies upon Jesus's orders, they embodied the herd of swine. Afterward, the herd of pigs ran violently down the hill into the sea where they drowned.

Naturally, now that the pigs were dead they needed new alive bodies to possess. Nevertheless, as we, all can see these demon/fallen angels *transformed* themselves within the bodies of the pigs via possession. Furthermore, another alternative time was when the angel, Gabriel, appeared to both Daniel in the Old Testament, **Daniel 8:16** and to the Virgin Mary in the New Testament in **Luke 1:26–31**. Close inspection of this verse reveals that Mary was "troubled" at what *he said* to her and **not** *his appearance* (**Luke 1:28–29**). Here is the story as told by the physician Luke. The holy angel Gabriel approaches the Virgin Mary with a greeting saying to her; **Hail you that are highly favored, the Lord is with you blessed are you among women!** And when <u>she saw him,</u> she was troubled at <u>his saying</u>. She was *not* troubled at his appearance, image, or what he looked like. **She was troubled at his saying and cast in her mind or reflected what manner of salutation or greeting this was.** Therefore, a reasonable deduction is that *he altered his form* to appear similar to a regular person and not a strong member of the heavenly host whose residency is usually near the throne of Almighty God! Summarily, this is not, a normal Sunday school sermon. Neither are the times that we are living in now "normal" times. Consequently, just to ensure that we are all on the same page as Morris Day, the singer/songwriter asked in his song, what time is it? The answer is these are the End Times! More definitively described as the time on earth preceding the imminent return (TBD date known only to God) of the Son of God, Jesus Christ, from heaven to return to the earth in his Second Advent! Stay tuned no commercial breaks, it will be awesome and in two specific stages. During the first stage, Christ will come to receive all believers unto himself to escort them to his heavenly Father. Whereby upon a short pause phase (unknown actual length of time) after introducing all saved souls to his Father. Afterward, in the second phase, Christ will return to the earth and set his feet upon the Mount of Olives according to **Zechariah 14:4,** which will split in half then returning to judge the quick and the dead on earth. Afterward, he will set up the **Divine Theocracy of God Almighty, that is, a government controlled, governed and ruled by God and his Son Christ, and the Holy Spirit only forever!** Gear up Saints of the Most High God, your redemption draws nigh. Hereafter, we transform or flow to the next chapter for discussion.

The next chapter for review is entitled the shot heard across heaven. This specific phrase of words historically or euphemistically revolves around the assassination of President, John Fitzgerald

Kennedy, whose murder in Dallas, Texas on November 22, 1963 sent Titanic, tsunami shockwaves around the world. I have taken the liberty to borrow it from that era while adding a minor modification to apply it to this literary expose because this shot is "even louder." The unimaginable killing of President Kennedy had both national and international consequences for the Nations of the world, not just America. Therefore, its reference as the shot heard around the world became a thunderous sound. The shot heard across heaven's plateau is much more troublesome to the ear due to its direct and indirect impact upon all of humanity and beings. It's louder because of the total, encompassing magnitude of its sphere—i.e., in heaven, earth, spiritual, natural, international, national and eternal consequences of its colossal reach involving all of life species...more imperatively mankind. Therefore, this shot without exception includes those currently alive and those yet to be born, those who have lived, those who died and those who are alive and will die!

CHAPTER VI

The Shot Heard Across Heaven

The nebulous of this war in heaven is obviously a mystery. We must then carefully examine all references to it, whether overtly or covertly. The Apostle Paul refers to this as the "mystery of iniquity" in **2 Thessalonians 2:7**. The reason that it is a mystery appears to be quite evident. How or why did a perfect angel, created to be a beautiful, shimmering light, become the enemy of his Creator? Satan's *creation occurred* in heaven, as all angels were. Each was fully mature to the best of our finite knowledge and with no scriptures to support any other assertions ever explaining or illustrating baby, juvenile or youthful angels. The youthful, juvenile or children angels or one's you see on cartoons or in the painting of the so-called European "master artists"—i.e., Renoir, Leonardo Divenchy, Michelangelo, etc., are the concepts of human artists imaginations, envisions or renditions only. The word of God **never tells** us anywhere in the holy scriptures about "baby angels." Synonymously, yet eerily similarly, Adam and Eve were *"created"* **on earth** as mature or grown adults.

For our purposes, we will describe or use the term *created* as meaning *unborn* but made by God Almighty **with life**—e.g., angels were *not born* but God *created* them with life. Oppositely we will use the term **born** as meaning all other beings born as experiencing natural birth, but with God as (ultimate *Creator* who utilized a surrogate process—i.e., birth) to create other life forms e.g. man. Therefore, being *born* by contrast in our context here will mean they went or underwent through the *natural birthing process* to come into existence with God still as their Creator but using an indirect methodology to provide life to the birthed being. Whereas created means they didn't go through the various stages of development—i.e., sperm fertilizes egg, causing conception inside of the womb, then causing descent of the fertilized egg down into the canal of the fallopian tube, thus becoming a zygote, continuing its travel after the first trimester to the uterus now as an embryo. Ultimately upon completion of the second trimester, transitioning into the third trimester to a fetus, just before birth thereby becoming an infant or newborn. Consequently, resulting in the full consummation after a normal cycle of human incubation/gestation inside the mother's body for a period of approximately nine months it is ready to begin it final descent to life outside the mother's body. Now, that the three trimesters of birth or born development (horribly detailed by me) completed resulting in a birthed human being. Consequently, allowing for the first time, that the born being is no longer very dependent upon the host (mother) for continued survival or incubation **inside** the womb. The "born" being whether man or animal, has life as a newborn upon birth; after the opening of the cervix via the vaginal cavity or via *caesarean section* into the new world sustaining life now independent of the mother as a separate, new born baby. Contrastingly, Satan, as all angels or demons are "created" "*celestial* (heavenly) creatures" and all men as Adam was are "*terrestrial*" (earthly) creatures. See **1 Corinthians 15:40**; noted here that says, "**There are also celestial bodies and terrestrial bodies but the glory of the celestial is one and the glory of the terrestrial is another.**" However, Adam and Eve are the **only two** *adults "created"* **human** beings exclusively! They were fully-grown and mature at the time of their creation. They were *__not born__* as all other humans were. ***Adam and Eve have this in common with angels of their existence into life***. Therefore, Adam and Eve had no mother or father in the *traditional* since as you and I had in our lifetime. Even Jesus Christ the Son of God was "born" via the power of the "Holy Spirit' in the womb of the Virgin Mary. This simply means that Christ's birth into this world was synonymous like all of us or other human births are into this realm with one **Major exception!** **Jesus Christ was not conceived** from, *of or by* the spermatozoa of a fallen, sin inherited man. Therefore, he was born by the fertilization of the egg in the Virgin Mary's uterus by **Holy Spirit of God** to maintain his holy nature at all times throughout his tenure (33 years) on this earth from birth to death, to resurrection, rapture to ascension period **NO EXCEPTION**! Continuing with the narrative regarding Adam and Eve's creation as adults simply means they could/should reason cerebrally, psychologically, emotionally, responsibly as well as maturely act or behave like adults. Then again maybe the two of them—i.e., Adam/Eve are the standard-bearers of *infantile thinking* as grownups or irrational logic when it came to obeying God. Nevertheless, we are no better. Actually, God holds the two of them to an adult standard of accountably and responsibility after their combined actions of disobedience in the Garden of Eden. They both received curses and both evicted from the Garden of Eden immediately after their disobedience. Adults are evicted from premises not youth or children. Children are "escorted" out with their parents, for they are not held responsible for dereliction of non-payment of rental or mortgage notes, as are the adult parents. Nevertheless, since they are with their parents during the eviction process they receive the same fate albeit escorted away from the premise as well. **Note carefully that Adam and Eve were both evicted from the Garden prior to the birth of any of their children**! Review **Genesis 3:23** detailed here that reads, "*Therefore, the Lord God sent him out* (evicted) *of the Garden of Eden to till the ground from which he was taken. Adam /Eve evicted in Genesis 3:23. Eve did not bare Cain the eldest son of her three sons (the others sons were Abel and Seth) child until Genesis 4:1 that reads Now Adam knew (mated sexually) with his wife Eve and she conceived and bore Cain and said I have acquired a man from the Lord.*" God did the **exact same thing** to Lucifer after he led an angelic revolt in heaven. God expelled him from his holy presence immediately. Alternatively, you and I, once upon a time, were children, who over time "developed" and are still trying to mature and grow up. The Apostle Paul in **1 Corinthians 13:11** says it aptly by saying, *when I was a child I* *spoke as a child I understood as a child, I thought as a child, but when I became a man, I put away childish things.* This comparative contrast analysis of created versus being born is an to attempt to clarify or make it easier for us to comprehend a complicated paradigm which simply is, "birth" requires a longer process of *psychological development* than does "creation." Furthermore, the process involving birth means that the species whether humans or animals once born requires a longer period of acclimation, nurturing, familiarization as well as exposure to ones surrounding. This will allow total immersion into the milieu thus safely developing as well as completely comprehending via lessons learned acceptable and unacceptable behavior. Specific instructions along with experiences passed on to one for educational, directional or behavioral insight so that one should comprehend what one should or should not do. Where one should or should not go, as well as what things that may pose risks, threats versus things or others that are innocuous to ones continued survival. The contrasting principle appertaining to angels versus man, means, that angels were "created" in heaven and man was *created (Adam/Eve) then successive generations are born* on earth. Each possessed diverse abilities or capabilities either enhanced or diminished predicated upon purpose, duty, responsibilities or designated assignments from God. They have unique capabilities—i.e., humans versus angels, because of their physical composition—i.e., created beings, versus born beings, as well as duties assigned to them by God. God made or intentionally designed man a little lower than the angels in terms of *abilities* **not in** *relationship* to himself! See **Hebrews 2:6–7** that reads *but one in a certain place (it was King David) testified saying what is man that you are mindful of him or the son of man that you take care of him. You have made him a <u>little lower than the angels</u> you have crowned him with glory and honor and set him over the work of your hands.* Man has a **closer** or more intimate relationship to God than angels do, because man is the **only** created/born being who mirrors **God's own image**. Additionally, man is the ***only created*** being that God's Son, Jesus Christ, **was sent to die** for or to atone for his willful acts of rebellion against God. See **John 20:21**; here is where Jesus said to them *peace be unto you as* _my **Father** sent_ **me so send _I_ you**. Furthermore, in **John 6:38** listed here, Jesus said, "_For I came down from heaven **not to do** 'mine own' will, but the will of **him who sent me**._" Summarily, the differences regarding being born versus created to this point vividly displays provisional insight into the unique or exclusive traits of both angels and men. Also, I have emphasized this prose to make the point that originally Satan (who was an angel) was not "governed" by time, matter or the laws of natural physics which we are bound by as human beings. However, unfortunately for him, he is now or will be soon shall I say receive direct effects of nature's governing laws! Although the direct impact or effects upon Satan overtime currently are negligible. Therefore, these dynamic events have no altering effects negatively speaking upon him currently. For instance time, physics and the laws of nature impact us e.g. aging, declining strength, getting wrinkles, lose hair, etc. Nevertheless, his time is running short, whereby God will limit his celestial abilities that he has historically enjoyed. See **Revelation 20:1–3** below, which reads:

> _And I saw an angel coming down from heaven, having the key of the bottomless pit and a great chain in his hand. And he laid hold on the dragon, that old serpent, which is the Devil and Satan and bound him for a thousand years. And cast him into the bottomless pit, and shut him up and set a seal upon him that he should deceive the nations no more till the thousand years should be fulfilled and after that, he must be loosed a little season._

Satan and his cohorts are the embodiment of pure, adulterated, spiritual evil! See **Ephesians 6:12**, that states, "**_For we do not wrestle against flesh and blood, but against principalities against powers against the rulers of the darkness of this age, against spiritual hosts of wickedness in heavenly places_**." Prior to Lucifer's fall, he previously had <u>direct access</u> unto the Lord without any encumbrances. So why did this all happen? This is the most imperative question in all of creation or galactic history. Why did the devil do it? How could any of God's created beings turn to be hateful toward the Lord of Hosts? The following paragraphs attempt to identify or answer this puzzling riddle.

The vitriol assassination of John F. Kennedy, while he was the thirty-fifth president of the United States of America in Dallas, Texas reportedly from the Dealy School Book Depository, is referred to as "*the shot heard across the world*" metaphorically. He was a beloved President in some circles despised in others. Yet, the motivation for killing him is not all that clear per se if you talk with the average ordinary citizen who was alive at that time of his assassination including me. Albeit I was a child at that time approximately four to five years old. The primary question everyone wants answers unto or know is why kill President Kennedy? Alternatively, put another way, what was the reasons for the assassination of President John F. Kennedy? There are infinite theories and conspiracy theses that only conjure up more questions than it does answers that may never ever be resolved this side of the eternal divide. Analogously, the same question posed slightly askance we ask about the Luciferian War in God's Living Room. Albeit, it has the some differing connotations, but some similarities too. However, to a much greater depth, extent or magnitude. Why did Lucifer instigate a War against God yet alone within in God's Living Room? Fret not fellow citizens of the third Heaven, a.k.a. the Paradise of God, nor any other enlightened reader, because the word of the Lord does give us enough information although not as much as we would like to make rational conclusions, deductions and observations as to when as well as why it all happened.

Genesis 1:1 tells us ***in the beginning God*** **created the heaven and the earth**. However, we can deduct from the scripture that the War in Heaven had already occurred—i.e., *prior* to earth's creation. How can we have such a leap in logic someone may ask to ascertain this conclusion? We can look at the Scriptural proof, listed in **Job 1:6** that reads **the "sons of God" came to present themselves before**

the Lord and _Satan_ came also. These are critical clues! The reason is, it tells us three important things that maybe overlooked by casual observation.

Primarily, the phrase "in the beginning" God created the heaven and the earth. First, it tells us _when_ by stating that "in the beginning" God created the heaven and the earth. Some clarification necessary here. This is referring to the _created heaven_ and _created earth_ where man resides. Neither one of these specific venues (earth and man's heaven or sky) **did not** exist prior to God directly and specifically bringing them into existence by his spoken word. Heaven where God always have dwelled obviously was already present for that is where God has always lived. Additionally, where God has historically resided God did not create. It already existed, as did God within his divine, supreme, sovereign domain or residency of God Almighty. The Godhead—i.e., God the Father, God the Son and God the Holy Spirit has no beginning of days and no ending of life, he has always been, he currently is and he shall and will always be as is with Christ and the Holy Spirit! Since God has always been, that means his residence throughout the cosmos and the galaxy has always existed as well. Therefore, it is not the heaven of heavens, per se, or the third heaven, where Paul describes his ascension for a heavenly glimpse or vision. See **2 Corinthians 12:2**. Abbreviated listing here… **Such a one caught up to the third heaven**. Consequently, it is either directly or indirectly referring to the second heaven where Satan dwells currently or the first heaven—i.e., our atmospheric cosmos where humankind dwells. Lucifer and Satanic angels were already created in heaven that is why they had the ability _"to go to and fro"_ in the earth for they **were already alive**. Study **Job 1:6–7**; herein noted for it says, **"Now there was a day when the sons of God came to present themselves before the Lord and Satan came also among them and the Lord said unto Satan From where did you come? So Satan answered and said "from going to and fro in the earth and from walking back and forth on it."** Satan's banishment or forced exile from heaven (God's Living Room or the Third Heaven) at this point of man's existence is complete. Additionally, we can establish this as a fact predicated upon Satan's reply to God when queried about his activity as well as his name change from Lucifer to Satan. More on the imperativeness of the distinction meaning of the name change shortly. However, for now let me assist the reader via navigation to the main point of this critical context or insight into establishing the fact that evil existed "prior" to the creation of the earth. Let us travel back through time imaginatively to the Garden of Eden if you will, when God just recently created man. The serpent (Satan) comes to tempt him shortly after his creation and assigned duties on earth. Now, for him to do that so soon after man's creation. Means that he <u>was already corrupt</u> or evil. Which he was and we have seen as identified as Satan came into God's paradise on earth—i.e., Eden. He did so to disrupt the harmony that God was trying to establish with Adam and Eve upon his newly created earth with his newly created species—i.e., Adam who was created in his own image. The temptation of Eve occurs quickly in only the *very third chapter* of Genesis first verse listed here; **Genesis 3:1, "Now the serpent was more subtil than any beast of the field which the Lord God had made and he said unto the woman, Yea hath God said you shall not eat of every tree of the Garden?"** Eve in her naiveté responds by telling **<u>lies and adds</u>** to God's words by *saying* that they couldn't even "touch" the tree by divine decree by God. God ***never*** said that! She did! Adam's creation happens in the second chapter of the same book. Review **Genesis 2:7**, denoted here, that says, **"The Lord God formed man from the dust of the ground and breathed into his nostrils the breath of life and man became a living being."** Yet his downfall occurs within the **next chapter**—i.e., **the third.** Furthermore, we know that evil existed *before* the Garden of Eden was completed because within the Garden of Eden there were ***two trees*** that had specific names, one was the **tree of life (tree one)** and the other was the **tree of the knowledge of good and evil (tree two)**. See **Genesis 2:17,** *<u>"But of the tree of the knowledge of good</u> <u>and evil,</u> you shall <u>not eat</u> for in the day that you eat of it you shall die."* There is a negative annotation associated with only one of the two trees God planted within the Garden of Eden. Logically, in order for this specific tree to exist or its implantation within the Garden of Eden, means that evil already existed. Otherwise, where did evil come? The Devil already knew when he entered into the serpent's body in the Garden of Eden, how to deceive, scheme, plot, mislead, lie and murder. Satan had already completed one phase of his deceptive nature or act of high treasonous rebellion in heaven with holy angels, whom he lied to who have now transitioned into fallen demons. Satan cohorts were masquerading themselves then and now as angels of light as does Satan. See **2 Corinthians 11:14– 15**, denoted here, that says, **"And no marvel for Satan himself is 'transformed into an angel of light' therefore, it is no great thing if his ministers also be transformed as the ministers of righteousness whose end shall be according to their works."** Therefore, who in the world were Eve and Adam comparatively speaking to angels regarding resisting Satan as it appertains to deception? They were woefully outmatched, outflanked, outtalked and outplayed by Lucifer as he disguised himself inside the serpent's body to beguile Eve. Therefore, this is why his eviction happened originally. Satan now kicked out of the third heaven has landed within the second heaven, his temporary residency. Since Satan's banishment is not exclusively to the earth realm just yet, he still has limited access to God from the second floor balcony of heaven. Also, Satan and his minions that have not been restricted to Hades (some of them have been due to gross wickedness) see **Jude 1:6** noted here again that says, *"And the angels that did not keep their proper domain but left their own abode he has <u>reserved in everlasting chains under darkness</u> for the judgment of the great day."* Nevertheless, not all of them have been restricted to the earth realm exclusively completely yet. Therefore, they can travel back and *forth as lighting* between earth and the second heaven. Review **Ezekiel 1:14** listed here: ***and the living creatures (angels) ran and returned as the appearance of <u>a flash of lightning</u>.*** Fallen angels presence forever excluded, unwelcomed and banned from God's Living Room in the **third heaven is complete**. Satan <u>**eternally banished**</u> from God's Living Room if you will, his throne, presence and seat of authority over all domains visible and invisible for all eternity. This sentence imposition is upon all of Satan's comrades of fallen angels too. No exceptions! All of them must use their collective memories of how spectacularly beautiful

God's Living Room looked to reminisce about the beauty of God's temple now and forever. I can certainly see why they are so angry now knowing what awaits them in the rapidly approaching future forever. Regretfully, seeing they once upon a time, long ago, were residents inside of God's Living Room.

Satan nor any of these fallen angels never will ever see the interior of the Great Hall of Heaven inside of God's Living Room again! This is a powerful statement because Satan's and their creation occurred in heaven. Once upon a time, it was their nest if you will. Satan previously walked in harmony with God, once upon a time. Satan has seen the face of God, once upon a time. Satan walked in the mountain of God, once upon a time. Satan reported directly to God about his daily activities…once upon a time. Now, Satan's privileges near the throne of God irrevocably and eternally stamped revoked. Satan nor any of his angels, forbidden anywhere near the throne of God…**for all time**. Nevertheless, fallen man redeemed by the blood of Jesus Christ, who has never seen the mountain of God…at any time, nor the face of God…at any time, neither the Living Room of God…at any time, who has consistently struggled in his walk most of the time. Failing daily because of sin of God's holy glory, as he walks unharmoniously, before God…some of the time. Will be provided an opportunity within God's time, all because of **Jesus Christ, the Son of God, at one time, obeyed the voice of his Father in due time to save mankind,** will get the sacred privilege of not only seeing all of the aforementioned invisible things regarding God, but to live eternally with Christ and God there forever. How prolific this is going to be to Satan's ego and existence. Satan's expulsion from heaven and man's welcoming or invitation to come live with God in heaven through Jesus Christ Our Lord! Hallelujah! Thank You Father God for sending Jesus Christ, Thank You, Lord Jesus Christ for doing the will of your Father to save our souls, Thank You, Holy Spirit of God for indwelling us along the way to preserve our eternal soul now and forever is all I can say!

Secondly, another interesting clue here is the identification of Lucifer for the very first time as "Satan' in the word of God. This is a very imperative clue attributable to the fact that Satan is not your everyday name. This name has a specific meaning (as do all names with God) directly connected to the character of the celestial/terrestrial being upon revelation of identity by God. The name Satan is a Greek word derived from the Aramaic language "Satanas" meaning adversary, nemesis, foe or enemy to describe him. What a coincidence! Not hardly though, Lucifer's name was changed by God so all the cosmos would understand what he represents—i.e., evil against God forever! Here is a coincidence for the record. The American jurisprudence system of our form of statutes (rules of law) in America said to be *adversarial* in nature, to protect the integrity of our Constitutional rights and liberties as stated by law…which when properly translated would be "Satanic." Nevertheless, we continue with our topic at hand. God wants us to know that Satan is his nemesis. His former name forfeited forever.

No longer referred to as Lucifer or bright and morning star from this point onward in the word of the Lord. Satan has lost all radiance in the heavens of his former shining star status as well as his close association with God or Christ Jesus. God views him as a rebel, an enemy, a dimming light of darkness. Satan's sentence meted out by the Lord God is reservation for the judgment of the Great Day. Satan along with his co-conspirators here noted in **2 Peter 2:4 and 9** says, **"For if, God spared not the angels that sinned, but cast them down to hell and delivered them into <u>chains of darkness to be reserved unto judgment,</u> verse 9. The Lord knows how to deliver the godly out of temptation and to <u>reserve the unjust</u> unto the Day of Judgment to be punished."**

Furthermore, but more importantly the amalgamation of these two scriptures—i.e., **Genesis 1:1 and Job 1:6** says that Satan came also. Back in the Garden of Eden, Satan clearly represented or identified as "the serpent" that beguiled Eve. God Almighty wants us to know exactly who the Instigator in Chief is, in sin, spanning the globe, time zones, the T3 heavens and heavenly atmospheres so God identifies him to us all as Satan. Because Satan is not your everyday name neither is Lucifer. Let us probe a little further to grasp this enemy of God's kingdom names and actions to comprehend the scope of his wickedness. However, these names have diametrically different meanings. Satan actually means "enemy" while Lucifer's origin means "morning star" or light of the morning star. Watch this here. Now when the name Lucifer is combined with his new name— i.e., Satan meaning is ominous. *It means, Enemy of the Morning Star's Light, which is Christ the Light of the world!*

Therefore, in essence we all should now see Satan as God sees him, an enemy of Christ and the light of the world without any hope in a failed cause. Something caused this demonic being to lust heavily after power, which in turn determined his downfall or sealed his doomed fate for all eternity. Let us analyze what Satan says to God as he presents himself along with the "sons" of God. I request that you make one key observation while doing so, which simply is this, underscore the fact that God **never asks** the other angels where they were coming from as he does Satan. See **Job 1:7** recited here; **and the Lord said to Satan, from where do you come? So Satan answered the Lord and said from going to and fro on the earth and from walking back and forth on it.** So why did the Lord not ask these other angels *where they* were coming from? Something to make you same hmmm… On the other hand, just wonder for a second or two, then ask yourself the same question which is *why did he ask only Satan that question* and *none* of the others angels? The answer is not as astonishing as much so as is the question. The answer is God knew why and where those angels were coming from as they presented themselves before him. **God sent** all of them on various assignments to the earth.

See **Zechariah 1:9–11** cited here, "**Then I said O my lord what are these? And the angel that talked with me said unto me, I will shew thee what these be and the man that stood among the myrtle trees answered and said. These are them whom the Lord hath sent to walk to and from through, the earth and they answered the angel of the Lord that stood among the myrtle trees and said we have walked to and fro through the earth and behold all the earth sitteth still and is at rest.**" Wow! There was no need for the Lord to inquire of their activity for God sent them. Satan on the other hand, self-dispatched to the realm of earth with no assignment, designation or God sanctioned purpose or instruction to go to the earth. Satan does as most of us do when we want to venture inquisitively. Satan somewhat just went *his own way* (Frank Sinatra said *I did it my way* in one of his songs) doing his own "thang so to speak" sic (slang intended for emphasis). Albeit, God never sent Satan near earth for any reason or purpose. Satan had his own plan for the people of the earth. Unfortunately, as we all see so vividly via misery, pain or sorrow now in our everyday lives. Additionally, as well on the constant, barrage of negative "breaking news" of tragedies unfolding almost hourly somewhere in the world. This includes but isn't limited to murders, kidnappings, international distribution of child pornography via compact disks, tapes, movies, wars, domestic and international terrorism, modern day enslavement, prostitution rings, drug cartels killing on wholesale level anyone who interferes in their business, etc. Furthermore, there is additional scriptural support that shows God does send holy angels to earth to report back with a status report see **Zechariah 6:1–8** listed here below;

And I turned and lifted up mine eyes and looked and behold there came four chariots out from between two mountains. And the mountains were mountains of brass, in the first chariot were red horses, and in the second chariot were black horses, and in the third chariot were white horses and in the fourth chariot were grisled and bay horses. Then I said unto the angel that talked with me what are these my lord, and the angel answered and said unto me these are the four spirits of the heavens which go forth from standing before the Lord of all the earth. The Black horses which are therein go forth into the north country and the white go after them. And the grisled go forth toward the south country. And the bay went forth and sought to go that they might walk to and fro through the earth. And he said Get you hence walk to and fro through the earth so they walked to and fro through the earth then cried he upon me and spoke unto me saying behold these that go toward the North Country have quieted my spirit in the North Country.

Unfortunately, for Satan he *was not* one of the angels sent by God on any mission to earth. Satan's reply is striking. He tells the Lord that he is coming *from the earth after going to and fro (back and forth) in the earth* and walking up and down in it. Reemphasis necessary here to declare or repeat that Lucifer, now called Satan (enemy) which means that his expulsion or eviction from the third heaven where God dwells into the second heaven happened already. However, during this period he still *has limited* access unto the Lord without permission specifically to go within the kingdom of God itself. Nevertheless, could someone curiously or logically ask how come or why does Satan still has permissible though restricted/allowed access to some contact with God? Well the answer to this question clearly discoverable in another scriptural reference to give us a clue. The scripture is **Revelation 12:10**. Satan according to this scripture *is "the accuser" of the brethren* (OT/NT worshippers of God). This is exactly what he was doing in Job's case. Satan intentionally was accusing Job of serving God for self-serving purposes other than out of genuine affection or devotion to the Lord. Satan cannot believe that a created being would just want to serve God without wanting "quid pro quo" something for something or be served like him. He genuinely believes that one must have an ulterior motive of some kind like himself! Satan's mentality is; what is in it for me only. Otherwise, I do not or I refuse to participate in the endeavor. So how can these people just want to serve the Lord without any quid pro quo?

God makes a permanent decision regarding Lucifer/Satan's fate. Which simply is that he has to be *eternally exiled* from God's Living Room in the third heaven! No ifs, ands or buts. However, Satan will not leave voluntarily without a fight. Satan acts like most humans do when evicted from a home, apartment or place of residency they previously occupied in good standing. Now that they have diminished or degraded this *good standing* due to either non-payment or chronic late payment of rent, fees, etc., or other violations of the lease agreement. Upon formal notification to them regarding eviction served upon one that, they **must vacate** the premises. Thus, be evicted. Suddenly, without any warning, they just act out violently requiring the involvement of the Sheriff, Constable or Police response out to scene to enforce the eviction notice: with the understanding that law enforcement can deploy any reasonable force that is necessary to effect such eviction including arrest or deadly force if required.

Thus, the shot heard across **heaven** sounds loudly. The specific scripture recited several times already during the writing of this book. Specifically, I am referencing, the scripture **Revelation 12:7–9**, which says, "*And there was war in heaven, Michael and his angels fought against the dragon, and the dragon fought and his angels, and prevailed not neither was their place found anymore in heaven. And the great dragon was cast out, that old serpent, called the Devil and Satan, which deceives the whole world. He was cast out (eviction) into the earth and his angels were cast out with him.*" These scriptures vividly tell us about the Monster of all battles catastrophic consequences involving humanity and demons. The Sheriff of Heaven, Michael, the Archangel and his angels, God called upon, forcibly to evict the usurpers from God's Living Room due to their rebellion in the very presence of God himself! Herein after, I want to visit the initial premise regarding God not allowing wars on earth that I began with during the opening query into this book's introduction or purpose just to connect the dots in your mind how wars became a part of the human tragedy of events here on earth.

Clearly, we can see from these scriptures **that war actually started in heaven** (God's Living Room) **way before** it started here on earth. The WOG tells us that, Michael, the Archangel and his angels (i.e., all classes of the holy angels aforementioned) fought against Satan, the dragon and his angels did fight back. (I recap Revelation 12:7–9.) *And war **broke out in heaven**, Michael and his angels* *fought with the dragon and the dragon and his angels fought. But they did not prevail <u>nor was a place found for them in heaven</u> any longer. So the great dragon <u>was cast out</u> <u>that serpent of old called the Devil and Satan</u> who deceives the whole world he was cast out to the earth and his angels were cast out with him.* This battle in the height of its ferocity as well as grandeur is unequaled to all of the battles (even if) combined simultaneously on earth that was fought by humans! The summary or analysis of this scripture follows here. The Bible tells us that Satan did not win verse 8. In addition, it tells us that neither *was their place* (original habitat) found anymore in heaven (Jude 1:6, Isaiah 14:12)—i.e., the third heaven where God dwells, verse 8 as well. Furthermore, the word of God tells us that the great dragon was cast out, that old serpent, called the Devil and Satan, which deceived the whole world he was cast out into the earth and his angels were cast out with him, verse 9. Lucifer's referral to as "old" because he has been around for quite some time. Remember he walked majestically in the mountain of God and in the Garden of God in Eden masquerading himself as a serpent. This is quite interesting because it sheds some light on this dark issue—i.e., why did Satan rebel against God?

The book of Isaiah delineates some of the reasons why Lucifer rebelled against God Almighty. First, I will provide you with the context in paragraph or sentence format. Afterward, I will itemize each specific instance of the five I wills of Lucifer **Isaiah 14:12–14** that says, **"How you are fallen from heaven Lucifer Son of the morning! How you are cut down to the ground, you who weakened the nations! For you have said in your heart *I will* ascend in to heaven, *I will* exalt my throne above the stars of God, *I will* also sit on the mount of the congregation on the farthest sides of the north, *I will* be like the Most High."** Now itemization follows below for quick view:

<u>Isaiah 14:12–14</u> lists what's known in Christendom or referred to as the five I wills of Satan:

1. *I will* ascend into heaven
2. *I will* ascend my throne above the stars of God,

3. *I will* also sit on the mount of the congregation on the farthest side of the North
4. *I will* ascend above the heights of the clouds
5. *I will* be like the Most High

Summarily, the devil wanted to be exalted "higher" than God himself and do a hostile takeover of heaven. Historical precedence established by Lucifer caused the entire predatory business practice of Hostile Mergers and Acquisitions here on earth. Evil originated from within, inside the mind of the most sinister being who ever lived that we see happening all over the earth. Satan's actions both in heaven and on the earth is responsible for causing chaos, family or historical brand businesses dissolution, pensions wiped out, college tuitions for offspring all but nonexistent. These actions have erased life-savings destroyed or depleted beyond restoration financial rainy day funds leaving misery in its wake. This all started in the *very presence* of God in the mind of a ***demonic angel***. However, the Lord tells Satan that Sheol or Hell will be his destination. Review **Isaiah 14:15**. Denoted here; **yet you shall be brought down to Sheol.** Clearly, we can see here that Satan wanted worship like God and that he wanted to show himself that he was "God"; he wanted to sit in the temple of God (**2 Thessalonians 2:4**). Oops Lucifer wrong floor. The complexity of Satan's rebellion is multifaceted or has many causes if we examine the word of the Lord carefully. Another factor in Satan's demise that we can review is located within the book of Genesis. This generally is a quite often overlooked or is a glanced over in fact if not examined in depth could easily lead to misunderstanding. **Genesis 2:7** tells us **that God formed man (Adam) from the dust of the earth**. Adam's name actually when translated into Hebrew means man. Here in the perfect paradise on earth, Satan makes his damaging move. Nevertheless, not only does Satan choose to rebel against God he enlists his followers including man. How is that so? Well, if Bible scholars are right, as well as the interpretation of scripture is balancing appropriately here regarding one third of the Cherubs followed Lucifer in his angelic rebellion. Review **Revelation 12:3–4** listed here. "**And there appeared another wonder in heaven and** behold a great red dragon having seven heads and ten horns and seven crowns upon his heads. And his tail drew '*the third part of the stars of heaven*' and did cast them to the earth and the dragon stood before the woman, which was ready to be delivered for to devour her child as soon as it was born." It is so profound that it causes all heaven to wonder. Whom or what did Satan desire so fiendishly is a rational question posed. The answer to this question simply is Satan coveted dominion and authority over God's crown creation... Man after he lost his position in heaven among the celestial sons of God who once upon a time adored him because of his beauty, wisdom and intellect.

We will do some biblically based research and creative deduction to grasp further insight into this devilish, murderous mind of Satan. Christ called *Satan a murderer from the beginning* **John 8:44**. From the beginning of when or what? The answer here is from the beginning of the creation of man on earth as well as angels in heaven. It is imperative that we keep in mind that **no angels** *prior to* **Lucifer** **lying** to them had *ever heard* a lie. There were no liars in heaven but the devil himself! This is one of the reasons that Jesus Christ called Satan a murderer and the "father of lies" and lying as aforementioned in John 8:44 verse starting this paragraph... Satan murdered them by *deceiving* them into rebellion against the Lord. Consequently, because of God's holiness, God had to impose upon all of them the required punishment of the sentence of death in hell to all of them. Furthermore, we must remember that there was **no hell initially** as well. God created all and it was good.

See **Genesis 1:31** cited here, "**Then God saw everything that he had made and indeed, it was <u>very good.</u> So the evening and the morning were the sixth day**!" Clearly, there is no mention of hell's creation or existence during the creation of the cosmos or the T3 heavens by the Living Holy God of Israel. It occurs after the rebellion of fallen angels in heaven. Furthermore, hell's creation derived out of a need to relocate these fallen angels after eviction from God's Living Room in heaven. Therefore, **God created hell exclusively <u>for</u> fallen angels** and not men. Here is scriptural support for this premise. Review Christ's words here in **Matthew 25:41, "Then he will**

also say to those on the left hand, Depart from me you cursed into everlasting fire (hell/Gehenna/hades) _prepared for the devil and his angels_**."**

God created hell because God had to have a place to punish or send fallen angels to after their heavenly insurrection to overthrow his holy kingdom. All of the angels who followed this diabolical scheme of war with Lucifer/Satan against God upon listening, following, fighting and adhering to these lies "died instantaneously" internally. Their entire effervescent heavenly glow became darker and dimmed by their treason. Consequently, since these fallen angels became aware of the eternal fate awaiting them in hell on the final Day of Judgment for man and angels. They continue their rebellion against Almighty God and fight on violently against humanity on earth attempting to cause as many who will follow them to be dammed beings too. Satan looked upon man as **inferior** to him, thus he should be worshipping him instead of God. There is the _theme of superiority/inferiority complex_ goes again. Does this evil premise or statement seem eerily similar to an often-repeated theme or sound familiar to you at this point? It does to me. I am referring to the evil theme of _white supremacy_. Satan's ideology was, if their creation—i.e., angels and humanity is not about them worshipping me, well then they should die. I am _superior_ to all of God's created beings and I deserve worship.

I am intellectually superior to them. I am more beautiful in appearance in comparison to any of them. I have been places within God's realm that they have not even seen. Therefore, I conclude, I am superior to all of them. Once Lucifer learned of his unalterable eternal fate that is not amendable, appealable or reducible in any way he lost his mind. All hell literally breaks loose in his mind. Therefore, he unilaterally decides as he reasons to himself something along the line as or like well; if or since I am going to suffer for all eternity, then I better make a plan for humanity to join me in my suffering. Misery loves company and where I am going to my understanding, it is a very miserable place. Since I have received eternal damnation to hellfire forever anyway, no matter what. I am not going alone! Another key point to bear in mind is that Lucifer received formal notice already regarding his mandatory time in hell for his actions almost immediately once he thought about his crimes.

Review **Isaiah 14:12–15,** listed here, **"How are you fallen from heaven O Lucifer son of the morning? How are you cut to the ground you who weakened the Nations for you have said in your heart; I will ascend into heaven. I will exalt my throne above the stars of God. I will also sit on the mount of the congregation on the farthest sides of the north. I will ascend above the heights of the clouds I will be like the Most High."** The key verse is **number 15.** Here Satan receives the actual formal sentencing of heavens most wanted criminal it says, **"Yet, you shall be brought down to Sheol (hell) to the lowest depths of the pit."** Satan knows what his eternal sentence is by God *before* its actual implementation. We refer this, to a specific terminology in the criminal justice system of American jurisprudence. The phrase or terminology we know it by is a "**delayed sentence.**" Whereby the convicted person(s) receive formal sentencing—i.e., to a term of imprisonment or incarceration inside a penal institution or mental facility for any specified period by a court of law handed down by a Judge or jury. However, before actual requirement to surrender in person to authorities to begin the formal term of detention, imprisonment or incarceration. The convicted person(s) is allowed time to take care of personal matters. This includes but is not limited unto taking care of financial matters, assisting with the living conditions or arrangements of an ill or impaired relative or loved one.

Furthermore, assisting the State with additional prosecution testimony or cooperating with ongoing investigations in other related cases to the accused/convicted case as a material witness. Generally, these events occur "prior" to ordering the convicted persons physical (in person) surrender for confinement—i.e., to report to a penal or mental institution to begin serving the prison term imposed. The most recent prolific or high profile public examples of this type of sentence is the one we all have witnessed involving disgraced lawyer, Michael Cohen and former National Security Advisor, Lieutenant General, Michael Flynn. Some readers will recall that both of them were associated with Donald Duck's...I am sorry, I mean Daffy

Duck's…pardon me again Daffy. I meant to say Donald Trump's personal lawyer/fixer for years. Among some of his duties were the handling of controversial matters discreetly for Trump. This includes, **_alleged_** "hush money" payments to porn stars, models or adult film stars in exchange for their silence. If this occurred, as alleged by Cohen, who made the payments, arranged the deals and coordinated the process at Trumps behest just before the election. These are explosive criminal allegations that if proven true, is a violation of the Hastings Act. This specific Act is a Federal crime that makes it illegal for anyone to receive or affect an election through bribery, gifts or extortion in exchange for their silence about knowledge of any information that may prove negative to a Presidential candidate if released just prior to the election. Cohen alleges, as does Stormy Daniels, whom received one the payments from Trump/Cohen.

It is vital to mention that allegations against Trump that have not been proven yet in any court of law. He is a "sitting president" (currently in office) who by current Department of Justice (DOJ) _guidelines memo_ to staff prosecutors (fictionalized interpretation) that a sitting President cannot be tried while in Office. A Federal Judge just ruled that is not true. This decision in his ruling located in regards to Don McGhan, former White House Lawyer, under Trump recently ordered to testify and is an **_untested theory_** that a sitting president cannot be tried for alleged crimes in a court of law. I would add if this is true this would make him above the law. If that is true then what in the world good, is the United States of America's Constitution? The answer would be it is about as important as a blank piece of parchment. Michael Cohen alleges that porn stars, mistresses, call girls, models, playboy bunnies or escorts who allegedly had adulterous sexual relationships with Donald Trump over a period under his watch according the narrative. In addition, Cohen was allegedly involved in a predatory practice known as "catch and kill" negative stories or press information regarding Trump before they could get out to the mainstream pressrooms or network news stations for publication or broadcast. Those stories or the rights to them effectively abandoned once money allegedly paid to the owner for their silence and waiver of rights to the story forever. This may be a good thing in disguise too because there they will live on in infamy during every news cycle in a frenzy of gossip, innuendo, insinuation and reports by "anonymous sources." Michael Cohen voluntarily pled guilty to some charges (tax evasion and lying to Congress) and his plea was accepted.

Therefore, it became a conviction and Michael Cohen received a three-year's sentence in Federal Prison for his crimes relating to his alleged romps for rump... I mean Trump "sarcasm" intended. I reiterate that if Trump were a private citizen, he would have received an indictment and formal prosecution charges too just like Michael Cohen did. However, as President he is receiving current immunity or Presidential treatment. Nevertheless, Michael Cohen's extension of time to remain out of prison for a short period so that he could testify before Congress, provide additional support to the Independent Special Prosecutor's Office and the Attorney General's Office in Manhattan about his direct knowledge of the Trump finances, dealings as well as other potential criminal related matters, etc., Summarily, he will begin serving his actual prison sentence sometime this summer. Finally, the Judge allowed him to remain "free" until he had an undisclosed (HIPAA Protection—i.e., Health Insurance Portability and Accountability Act) surgical procedure that would had been difficult for him to obtain while incarcerated. Alternatively, General Flynn on the other hand is still awaiting imposition of sentencing at the writing of this book—i.e., December 2019. Albeit he has already pled guilty to lying to the FBI during a criminal investigation. Good Lord will this ever end? Now, refocusing specifically back to the topical narrative, Lucifer had to figure out a plan, because he had a big problem. To wit the problem he had was figuring out how he was going to cause man's death. Especially, since God was in a perfect union with man and he is the God of Life. Lucifer concluded I know what I will do.

Ahh, I will deceive and outright lie to them just as I did with those angels who chose to follow me in rebellion. Furthermore, they will join me in the lake of fire, which is Satan's intent for all. Review (Revelation 19:20). Originally, demonic angels, who started out living in heaven with God and Christ, had **never heard** a lie **until Lucifer told** them lies when he enlisted their support in his hostile takeover scheme attempt of heaven. Thereby causing them to lose their life, habitat and original place with Almighty God. This is why Jesus said that Satan was a murderer and a liar and the father of lies recited here in **John 8:44**, "*You are of your father the devil and the lusts of your father **you will do**. He was **a murderer from the beginning** and abode not in the truth because **there is no truth in him** when he speaks a lie he speaks of his own for **he is a liar and the Father** of it!*" Satan murdered those angels allegorically (spiritual death) whom he lied unto so he could obtain their help in fighting in heaven. However, they did have a choice in the matter. They were fully-grown, mature and intelligent created angels synonymous to Satan. This made them more than capable of asking God for themselves, if they believed they were not included in any future plans that God had appertaining to them. What was prohibiting them from inquiring directly with God what God's plans were regarding their estate? They were in heaven already, they had independent relationships with God apart from Satan (we saw that when the "Sons of God" *presented themselves* before the Lord) in **Job 1:6.**

Therefore, each angel, in his own right, could have asked God in person, to ascertain what the situation was involving their status with God **before** they chose to become traitors to their Creator! They exercised their choice to join Satan in this grandiose act of evil without ever considering the consequences of eternal banishment from God and heaven itself as it related to them. Nevertheless, Satan as well as all fallen angels because of their rebellion or "War in God's Living Room" received eviction from heaven eternally. Consequently, failure to inquire, ascertain or ask cost them their eternal future as well as innumerable pain and sufferings. **Jesus said in Luke 13:28,** "There shall be weeping and wailing and gnashing of teeth when you shall see Abraham and Isaac and Jacob and all the prophets *in the kingdom of God* and **you yourselves** (unrepentant men and fallen angels) thrust **out on Judgment Day!**" This includes fallen angels who will be thrown into the lake of fire on this day as the final judgment for their actions causing the "War in God's living room" while following Satan to this doomed end on D-Day in heaven. Meanwhile, Satan could care less about any of them or anyone else for that matter. Satan focused then and now upon himself as usual, because he had all of the aforementioned attributes of God's grace bestowed upon him. He was attractive, dazzling, charming, smart, whom transformed himself into a murderer, liar, conniving, deceitful, outspoken as well as cunning Demon Prince. Satan must have thought to himself that God was going to assign him to the earth as head angel in charge.

Here he would reign supreme and would be worshipped just as God himself was being worshipped. (Romans 8:25) How can we know this with some degree of certainty? Review the book of Job again for imperative clues. Start with the very first clue. **Job 1:7** says that "**when asked where he coming from Satan's reply was from going to and from in the earth and from walking up and down in it.**" Satan gives the exact same answer on a separate occasion in the second chapter of Job the second verse to the same question from God. Key point of observation is, why was Satan going to and from the earth and walking up and down in it when God *__never sent__* him there as part of any assignment? There is **no record** anywhere in the Holy Scriptures where God *sends* Satan to the earth to check the State of the Earth for him with instructions to return with a status report. Therefore, one must logically conclude, that Satan *went on his own* for a purpose that God did not sanction, order, direct or approve. Satan self-dispatched to earth without any direct orders for his own purposes not any that were associated with God or Christ Jesus. Another way to consider this is to reason that he went outside of his jurisdictional boundaries or "off the reservation" to seek his own will…not the will of God. What Satan did not realize was that God already knew his sinister motives. **Hebrews 4:12** tells us that **the word of God is quick and powerful…and is a "discerner" of the "thoughts and intents" of the heart.** Furthermore, as we, all know God is omniscient—i.e., all knowing. Therefore, not only was God unworried he had already prepared for this evil tyranny in advance. We shall see how by continuing to read the words of this book.

Although Satan wanted to believe, that God choose him (self-appointed deception) because he was *in his mind* superior to all other angels, to rule over other beings (Adam/man) he was sadly mistaken. Satan got the single choice question incorrect. Wrong answer!

Delusion is a powerful mindset that entraps its victim into doing *outrageous things* e.g. like starting a War in God's Living Room. God never had any such intentions for Satan or any other created being for that matter! Jesus stated you **shall worship** the **Lord thy God** and **him only** shall **you serve** in **Matthew 4:10**. God had **only one** person in mind for eternal rule or worship besides himself… JESUS CHRIST his only begotten Son! No Exceptions! Scriptural support is discoverable at **Hebrews 1:8** that reads, **"But unto the Son (Jesus Christ) Thy throne O God, is forever and ever…"** If one will carefully review this scripture. You will notice that God the Father, refers to Jesus Christ here as, God the Son, as God. This reference is rarely noticeable in the word of God. Albeit this is one of the few times that this occurs in scripture. See also **Hebrews 1:13**, which says, **"But to *which of the angels* did he say at any time, sit on my right hand until I make your enemies thy footstool?"** (This includes Satan he is a fallen angel remember)

Actually, angelic worship remains unhallowed, unsanctioned neither allowed nor considered by God for men. Its practice unquestionably forever ruled **strictly forbidden** by God. Read **Colossians 3:18,** which says in part, **let no man beguile you of your reward in a voluntary humility and "worshipping" *of angels* intruding into those things that he has not seen vainly puffed up by his fleshly mind.** Read also, **Romans 1:25**, that states, **"Who changed the truth of God into a lie, and worshipped and served the creature more than the Creator, who is blessed forever. Amen."**

Satan goes off to ponder *another failed* attempt by him to gain any kingdom for himself. Therefore, he unilaterally decides that he will take another course of action. However, what could that possibly be? God had already sentenced him to eternal damnation with immutable consequences. No appeal, no plea-bargaining, no negotiation, no time off for good behavior. Therefore, he alternates his plan strategically. Satan makes another plan to strike at God. Satan decides to go after man directly, God's *peculiar creation* in all of the cosmos in the Garden of Eden. Read **1 Peter 2:9** verse listed here that says: **"For you are a chosen generation, a royal priesthood, an holy nation a peculiar people that you should show forth the praises**

of him who has called you out of darkness into his marvelous light." God called Adam out of darkness in the Garden of Eden, after, he fell victim to his own disobedience to God. Although he did so through deception, instigated by Satan, did not alter the result. God has been calling man ever since this horrible turn of events out of darkness. God is doing so even now via Our Lord and Savior, Jesus Christ, as we sojourn this life with its difficulties. Whimsically travelling, confusingly, stumbling along as we ride on "the carousel of life." Our God is doing so, at this very moment—i.e., eternity present that we may escape this present evil world. Bible support located or referred to in **Galatians 1:3–4** as it says, "**Grace be to you and peace from God the Father and our Lord Jesus Christ who gave Himself for our sins that he might deliver us from the present evil world according to the will of our God and Father.**"

Additionally, Christ declared in **Matthew 18:14, "Even so, it is not the will of your Father, who is in heaven that one of these little ones should perish."** Satan's intent is to murder man! Remember, Jesus said that Satan was a murderer from the very beginning. He will not take no for an answer. God's crown jewel of creation is man. How can we be certain of this or for sure with absolute certainty someone may ask? Well the answer is discoverable in the body of evidence in the Bible should be quite clear and convincing. Here are just a few examples. Man is **_the only_** creature created in **God's own image**! **See Genesis 1:27.** That reads **so God _created man_ in his own image** in the **image of God** created he him male and female created he them. God so **_loved man_** (the world) as described in **John 3:16** noted here; **For God so loved the world that He gave His only Begotten Son that whoever believes in him should not perish but have everlasting life!** God the Father **sent** his only Begotten Son, Jesus Christ to **die in man's place** for the punishment of **man's sin** against God.

Review **John 17:3** listed here; **and this is life eternal that they might know thee the only true God and Jesus Christ _whom you have sent_.** This is astounding! God demonstrates his love for man through action. Many people say they love this person or that person. However, what have they actually done to prove, show or

150

demonstrate it besides merely saying so? Years ago, Michael Jackson's youngest sister, Janet Jackson, recorded a song entitled "what have **you done** for me lately." This musical lyrical rendition asks in a direct form **what you have done** to prove or demonstrate the fact that you love me as you so easily say you do. God can show unequivocally what he has done to demonstrate and display to the entire galaxy in both heaven and earth that he loves man! The well-documented word of God in chapter after chapter, verse after verse and event after event, what he has done to display his love for humanity. **No other creature** in heaven or earth has received such **unconditional love from God** than has man! I challenge anybody, anywhere to show me any such grand display via the word of God, whom God has shewed affinity to, mercy for and love beyond anyone's wildest imagination comparable to that than man! I will make it easier; just show me one example, just one other created being that God has demonstrated love beyond words for than man! This challenge has no expiration date whatsoever just in case one may be wondering either! Now, back to our narrative. Satan has some tactical, strategic and logistical problems. He has to devise a way to cause a disruption in the harmonious relationship between God and Adam. How can he? The word of the Lord tells us **that God and Adam walked in the cool of the day together. (Genesis: 3:8)**. Therefore, the enemy must discover a way to destroy the harmony between God and Adam.

Satan misunderstood the depth of God's love for man a little more than he dared believe, which man sometimes himself does not quite comprehend then or even now for that matter. Therefore, Satan wanted to hurt the core of God's heart. King David mused to himself as he stated; **what is man, that you oh God are mindful of him or the son of man that you considers him** documented in **Psalm 8:4**? Satan although gifted, beautiful, perfect as well as intelligent originally was envious of man. The reason is attributable to man's image. Although Lucifer possessed astounding qualities and many aforementioned attributes, he **quickly realized** that, **he was not created in God's image** as man was. This poor little demon's awareness of this fact must have broken his little devilish heart beyond repair.

Let us examine how the story unfolds from a biblical perspective. Documented within the book of Genesis, the creation story told by God directly to Moses. However, one has to look no further than at **Genesis 2:1–2** vs. the Bible declares that **God rested from his works.** Obviously, God did not rest because he was physically tired. It simply means that *God completed all of the provisions to sustain life independently upon the earth for man to live.* Now review **Job 1:6.** Here **Satan presents himself to the Lord with the other sons of God (angels).** Nevertheless, remember, he tells the Lord that he is returning from the earth and walking to and from, as well as up and down in it. Unquestionably once banished from heaven—i.e., the third heaven where God lives Satan quickly visited the earth. He wanted to sabotage the plan for paradise that God had for the earth and the people on it (albeit there were only two initially) as he had already did in heaven. Satan wasted no time with Adam; he quickly set his lustful eyes upon Eve. However, Adam was his intended ultimate victim. **God created <u>Adam first,</u> in the image of God as well as for the glory of God.**

Afterward, God created Eve from Adam's rib or secondly. Furthermore, Eve's ***<u>creation occurred so she would be Adam's helper.</u>*** Consequently, Eve was *a copy* from *an original.* Additionally, God created Eve ***<u>for</u>*** Adam. See **Genesis 2:20** denoted here; **And Adam gave names to all cattle and to the fowl of the air and to every beast of the field but for Adam there was not found a *<u>help meet</u>* for him.** That means Eve possessed many of the attributes but lacked originality. Let me elaborate in detail here before someone quickly distorts the meaning of this point. Falsely alleging, accusing or saying that women are not original or this passage has nefarious undertones, subjugating the woman by innuendo regarding her unique status before God and man. Not only is this, misogynistic, it is sexist, demeaning, discriminatory and blatantly false as it strikes against God's intent for the significant essence of women's role in life. In addition, it is preposterously stupid as it belittles the innumerable, enriching contributions that women make to our world every day! The woman is the cradle of life, *not* man; the woman is the Mother of us all, *not* man. The woman is the giver of life to us all, *not* man.

The woman is the carrier of life, *not m*an. The woman is the nurturing guardian of life, *not* man! My point is something **completely opposite** of such foolishness and evil thinking.

More people in recorded history refer to their mothers in positive, uplifting, inspirational, devotional, conversations than they ever will or do their fathers... Hmmm, deservedly so. If one refuses to believe me just watch professional athletes regardless to the sport venue when quickly pictured on the sidelines after making some sensational play via broadcast on live TV screens after making some spectacular point. Quickly when they are aware that the camera lens points directly at them they send messages, blow kisses, make gestures or say loudly from the sidelines "I love you mom"! Rarely does any of them say I love you dad. **Even Our Lord and Savior Jesus Christ**, just before his spirit departed from his body on a wooden cross at Calvary for our sins, made provisions for "**his mother**" in the flesh—i.e., the Virgin Mary, when he instructed his disciple John "**to behold your mother and Mary, his mother, to behold John now as her son!**"

This instructional guidance is located in **John 19:26–27** versus. From that day forward until Mary's subsequent physical death, John took her into his home as he cared for her daily needs and wellbeing as Christ instructed him to do. Jesus Christ never made or said anything recorded about his "father" in the flesh "Joseph" in his dying declaration. Summarily, the point I am attempting to illustrate is relatable with a useful tool we all use at one time or another—i.e., "copy machines" in some form or capacity in our daily life at work or at home. Therefore, you know from personal experience that many times the copy is either too light or dark. On the other hand its not quite as clear as we would like it to be occasionally, or the print is to large or small, etc. Essentially this copy of the original has flaws or undesirable traits that does not quite measure up to the original that we must keep for documentation purposes.

Essentially the "original" print has some *key characteristics* in its *overall structure or composition* that our facsimile lacks. It was the same with Adam and Eve. God made Adam from "**the dust**" of the ground noted in **Genesis 2:7** here; **And the Lord God formed man** of *the dust of the ground* and breathed into his nostrils the breath of life and man became a living soul. However, Eve was made from "Adam's rib" (who is now flesh) Genesis 2:22 listed here; and the rib, which the Lord God had taken from the man, made him a woman and brought her to the man. Stay with me patient readers, now Eve is *composed of flesh* while Adam "structure" *is dust*. All this simply means is that Eve was a "copy" from an original. Obviously, anatomically, as well as gender wise God constructed each differently because of the diverse purposes for which each was created. It is extremely imperative to denote as well as focus upon specific scripture here. Look at 1 Corinthians 11:7–9 for it reads, "For a man indeed ought *not* to cover his head forasmuch as he is *'the image' and 'glory' of God*: but *the woman* is the 'glory of the man.' For the man is not of the woman but *woman from the man neither* was the man *created* for the woman but the woman for the man." Eve was made from Adam's flesh "symbolizing unity" with man *not inferior* or *superior* but to serve different roles in equal capacities in regards to their relationship (helping) parenting and serving each other as well as unto the Lord while Adam was created from dirt to the glory of God to serve God.

God saw that he needed a helper. Their coexistence was to be harmonious assisting each other in both practical as well as divine devotion. Adam (man) would not have to toil through life alone but with the companionship, support and encouragement of the woman as they collaborated in life till death did them part. This is the *only difference* narrated out to highlight or convey to the reader. Do not read into or imply anything else by this statement no more or any less. The difference I am highlighting is to emphasize *is in their being* or in their "molecular structure" their physical composition, versus their status, station or position before God or men. Allow me to explain this in another simplified way here if I may. Although each member within a band may play a different instrument, each with its own distinct sound or beat. Yet together they are all playing the same song, to the same beat with the same rhythm to have a harmonious song appreciated for the ensemble of complimentary or diverse instruments, harmoniously blended or enmeshed together as one chorus. As aforementioned, many times copies lack some of the exact characteristics of an original although it is similar to it in many aspects. There are some instances where a copy cannot be used e.g. in a court of law, certain documents must be the original only. Therefore, the war between the sexes did not start with the feminists groups mouthing off talking about their equal status with men. I just wonder who is really causing all of this confusion… Hmmmm… I think maybe its Lucifer.

This war started back in the Garden of Eden instigated by Satan (actually it started in heaven)—i.e., the subject of our quest, trapping Eve, in causing outright rebellion against God by Adam. Whoa that is another book…let me desist right here on that subject matter! Satan has a knack or affinity with a passion for starting wars whether it is in heaven above or earth below. He is a provocateur, a saboteur and a liar who wants anyone whom has a harmonious relationship to fight among or against each other. Satan creates division whenever or wherever he can. Beelzebub (Satan's alias) understands what Jesus stated listed here in **Mark 3:25, "And if a house be <u>divided</u> against itself, it cannot stand."** The point that I over emphasized here is that a copy although it does contain the essential elements of the original is useful and is a duplicate of the original. It has all of the functionality, importance, traits, characteristics, data and qualities and serves as the image of the original. However, occasionally it presents some vulnerabilities that poses risks or challenges as a valid substitution. Simply due to the fact that as it lacks some minor aspects of resiliency, authenticity, clarity as well as legibility or defensibility presented within the original. This relates to our story in the sense that the tempter took full advantage of Eve's naiveté as (a copy of Adam) while he deceived her into rebellion and disobedience against God. Remember our thesis here is to explain why Satan even wanted or caused a War within God's Living Room.

As usual, thieves always want something they either do not own or did not create, nor purchased, neither worked to obtain. Satan was no exception. Jesus referred to Satan as a thief (**John 10:10**) He wanted the kingdom of God. This Denzel Washington of angelic beings wanted something he did not own or deserve…primarily worship. Sorry Denzel, it is only referring to your popular appeal among the female population did I include your name. My apologies Mr. Washington. Satan said to himself that it could all be mine for the taking. This is where he completely miscalculated, with whom he was instigating an all-out war. Just like most of us from time to time forget the awesome power of Almighty God. The Lord God title of Almighty God exists for a reason. God alone is omnipotent—i.e., all-powerful! Essentially, because *all power* is God's *exclusively*. See **Romans 13:1** recited here it states, **"Let every soul be subject to the higher power for <u>there is no power</u> but the power of God and the powers that be are ordained of God."** Jesus said, <u>**all power**</u> **is "given" <u>unto me in heaven</u> and <u>in earth</u>** in **Matthew 28:18**. Unlike Satan who was trying to *"steal power."* Jesus Christ inherited divine power from his Heavenly Father. The WOG (word of God) tells us that there is **no power** but the power of God.

This is aforementioned in **Romans 13:1** above. Temporal secular government powers, governmental institutions or entities derive their *only limited* "authority" not power, **from God**. Powers per se that exist of either Nations, States, or Governments, etc., are ordained of God to maintain order only on earth. Therefore, when Satan and his little minions, supervisors, or appointees whom staff ranks above yours at work start huffing, puffing at you angrily, or menacingly as they do on occasions. Threatening or telling you, they have "power" over you (laugh) then reply to them either (mentally so you can keep your job) or verbally your choice. However, prepare for the secular consequences (potential firing) that they are lying and are all imposters, pretenders or phonies. Because there is **no power** but **<u>the power of God</u>**. Say it aloud to yourself until you believe it! For there is NO Power but the Power of God! Another way to peruse this is to look at this with our utility electric companies. All of us have electricity in our homes to turn on any electrical appliances of our choice whether it is the television, computers, irons, stoves, etc. Therefore, we walk around all day flipping light or power switches up and down telling our children lies that we pay the bills so we have the power. No, we do not; we tap into the electrical grid of what-ever electric utility provider of our choice that allows us authority temporarily do as we please. However if we ever fail to pay the bill or our service is interrupted for late payment or mix up of any kind. We see who really who has the power it is the electricity provider we can flip our little switches up and down all day to no avail. If the Power Company turns the power off—i.e., stops the flow of electrical energy to our residence for whatever reason we see who really has the power. They do and not us.

Conclusively, we see that Lucifer had a plan to attack the core of God's eye by attacking the only beings created in the "image of God" himself in heaven above or earth below. All other beings creation derives from an image God imagined them to be or decided how they should look or exist. However, this is extremely important to comprehend. When God decided to create man, God created an image of himself! My Lord the wonder of the Mighty One of Israel! Glory to God in the Highest! Next, we direct our attention to the Arrogance Satan displayed when contemplating his strategy for heaven and earth's dominion under his governance…therefore, he thought, lol.

CHAPTER VII

Satan's Arrogant Strategy

The secular jurisprudence or legal system in America requires there to be a motive to prove the elements of first-degree murder. What is a motive then? The definition of motive's summation relates to *a reason* for doing something, especially one that is hidden and not obvious. Therefore, a motive can simply be summed up by saying it is the "why" someone did something specifically regardless to the outcome. However, before proceeding further let me ask a couple of questions. What could Satan want so bad or desired so much that would have caused him to rebel against his Creator? Did his devious craving for this object, person, place, or thing have that much value that he would risk eternal separation from God Almighty to acquire or obtain it? Let us turn to our primary source—i.e., the word of God for some clues and possible answers to these questions. Recall we are seeking Satan's *motive* now in our ongoing journey to comprehend Lucifer's rebellion in causing this all-out War in God's Living Room!

The books of Isaiah and Ezekiel provide us with interesting insight to some reasons or motives why Lucifer chose to take this *unforgivable course* of action. **Isaiah 14:12–20** outlines specifically Satan's plan and strategy. The word of God tells us that on numerous occasions Lucifer describes vividly his wishes; Lucifer imagines in his heart; *I will ascend into heaven, I will exalt my throne <u>above</u> the stars of God, I will also sit on the mount of the congregation. I will ascend among the heights of the clouds...I will <u>be like</u> the Most High!* (**Isaiah**

14:13–14). Oh my Lord! The devil wanted not only to be like God, he wanted to be above him! Detailed in each instance, the devil says, I will do this I will do that. I, I, I is the primary selfish motive that drives the details of his sinister plot against Almighty God. This selfish, egotistical lust for power and worship distorts his mind to a hypnotic, blinding ambition in which he never considers the eternal consequences of his action… However, be careful not to judge so quickly. This is the same **_I will_** that actually motivates each of us in our idiosyncratic desires as well. However, God tells him in verse 15, no you are going to the _lower_ parts of Hell/Sheol. God judges Lucifer on the spot! God says to him you will not be _ascending_ you will be forever in a _descending_ state while burning. Nevertheless, as aforementioned the book of Ezekiel also provides a glimpse of Lucifer's mindset to accomplish his arrogant strategy, which is the usurpation of God's Kingdom. Let us explore Ezekiel's (God inspired) perspective of this aspect of the narrative here. God allows the prophet Ezekiel to use a symbolic king or a substitute here to explain Satan's plans to begin this expose. However, the prophet eventually moves away from this "stand in" or substitute as he identifies the actual culprit by name to ensure that all of us understand whom he really is proactively describing.

Here is scriptural proof. Begin reading **Ezekiel 28** for this narrative, Ezekiel begins speaking against the King of Tyre who through his wisdom, exceptional business acumen, savvy, wayfaring trading skills and military might, etc., amasses enormous material wealth and begins self-exaltation. Continue reading this chapter until you get to **Ezekiel 28:13**. Here is where I request the reader to concentrate or focus more attention because here is where the transition begins to identify Lucifer/Satan as the real culprit God is identifying as the Usurper in Chief.

Ah, but ponder briefly upon **Ezekiel 28:13** verse just for another second. Here is some specific verbiage that lets us know this is not, the King of Tyre. Subsequently per se—i.e., the substitute persona that Ezekiel has been using to this point in the narrative. If one, were to ask why is this not him? Okay, let me describe why not. **Ezekiel 28:13** says, I quote, **"You were in Eden the Garden** of God." Now, let us analyze this a little further. Genesis tells us that there were only a finite number of *persons or beings* in Eden, the Garden of God. These persons, reptiles, or animals were Adam, Eve, the serpent (Satan) who spoke via the serpent in the garden. We **definitely know** that the King of Tyre was not in the Garden of God in Eden during the temptation of Adam. Therefore, his elimination occurs almost instantaneously as the potential identifiable person or being. Further descriptive analysis tells us via **Ezekiel 28:14,** *you were the "anointed Cherub" (we previously identified in detail the categories or groups of angels) the ones that are fallen or who joined Lucifer in this angelic rebellion are called Cherubs or demons now. Satan came from this very group." The group Lucifer derived from is Cherub. Naturally, the King of Tyre was not an Anointed angel. Neither was he in the mountain of God (Garden of Eden) as the scripture continues to tell us along with these other aspects. You walked back and forth in the midst of fiery stones (this is speaking of Lucifer here) not the King of Tyre which Ezekiel starts out by telling us. Nevertheless, alas verse 15 gives us another key point that if overlooked would distort the identity of the culprit. Lucifer was "created" as a <u>perfect being</u> in terms of appearance, physique, character, stature, etc. Tragically, it concludes with his downfall which is captured in the phrase "until iniquity" was found in you.*

However, a careful analysis of the descriptive word **created** is needed here, simply because the author which is God himself, did not use **born**. Men are born through the natural process of fertilization, incubation, gestation then birth. Angelic beings do not go through this process at all, for God created them. Nevertheless, we can just use our common sense here to understand this critical difference. All terrestrial (earthly) beings have come into existence only by a mother (maternal host with unfertilized egg) and father (paternal donor of sperm to fertilize egg) with the (**only exception being Jesus Christ, who was <u>born</u> of the Holy Spirit of God**). <u>**Notable exceptions**</u>: Also, Adam and Eve who were <u>**the only created humans**</u> ever in the cosmos! Contrastingly, all celestial (heavenly) beings, specifically angels came, into existence as the "Spirit of God" <u>**created**</u> angels with life. **Absolutely none of them was born of a female via the normal pregnancy**, incubation gestation period from conceptual birth, as we know it. Nephilim are not **celestial** beings they are a hybrid of both **fallen angels** and **human female** species that came into existence because of angelic rebellion mating (sexual intercourse) with the daughters of men.

Birth or being born begins with the fertilization of egg—i.e., spermatozoa to fertilize egg which then becomes a zygote to embryo formation of the fertilized egg inside of womb of mother where all essential systems of life began to form, to fetus whereby complete process of development is finalized to birth of new born baby. Now, I have rudimentarily and quite possibly misinformed or confused the readers with an oversimplification of the natural birth of terrestrial life here on earth. I return to the topic at hand.

Essentially, Lucifer's arrogant strategy was to start a hostile takeover of the harmonious Kingdom of God. Look at **Revelation 12:7 it says, "And war broke out in heaven Michael, his angels fought with the dragon and the dragon, and his angels fought."** Satan wanted to rule heaven with his vision for eternity. Pass out heavenly assignments to others; receive praise, riches, glory, honor and worship. This is the equivalent of heavenly stolen valor. Satan wanted to live among the stars as a Honeymooner and say to himself. How sweet it is! This was reminiscent of the lingo used by Jackie Gleason in his heyday as "the star" of the original *Honeymooners* television show. If you are forty-five or younger this is a show, you probably would have no idea what I am talking about. So please pardon me here for inserting an antiquated flashback television show to illustrate a perspective. Nevertheless, I cordially invite that you continue reading on through to the final chapter of this book this antiquated flashback notwithstanding. Lucifer wanted to be a real honeymooner. Satan wanted his co-conspirators, now fallen angels, to join him in a wicked, masterful enterprise, unparalleled or unmatched in the canon of celestial history by switching seats in heaven. Simply put, Lucifer wanted to play a game of "musical chairs" in heaven on a carousel to remove God from his throne and place himself atop the newly formed apex of eternal power. This concluded with being nothing more than demonic *daydreaming or illusionary despondency* that was flawed, futile and fatal for all who conspired with him eternally!

Satan believed that he could win this celestial rebellion by fighting, intimidation, using violence, deception, amalgamated with widespread chaos, lying and stealing authority at all costs. Jesus said **the thief (Satan) comes to steal, kill, and destroy (John 10:10).** Satan envisioned a kingdom where he ruled instead of the Supreme rightful owner and Creator God the Father, Christ and the Holy Spirit of God. Satan's arrogant strategy was simple, direct and fatalistically flawed instigation of a War in God's Living Room. Not only did Satan receive condemnation or divine judgment but also the angels now demons were judged with him and God reserved a seat in darkness forever for all of them. See **Jude 1:6** that reads **and the angels that did not keep their proper domain but left their own abode. He has reserved in everlasting chains under darkness for the judgment of the great day.**

Well, Satan did not understand some simple aspects of Almighty God. Primarily, where God stated that he **would not share his glory with another** this includes Lucifer. Listed in **Isaiah 42.** Again, keep in mind the Godhead—i.e., no one *outside* of the Godhead (Father, Son and Holy Spirit) will God share his glory with ever! God will share "*his love*" with all who are *willing* to accept it but not **his honor or glory** period! Lucifer quickly discovered that was never any part of the divine plan of God for him or any other angel that God created. Read **Hebrews 1:5 and 13,** "That says **for unto which of the angels said he 'at any' time. Thou art my Son this day have I begotten you. Again, I will be to him a Father and he shall be to me a son? But to which of the angels said he at any time sit on my right hand until I make your enemies your footstool?**" Naturally, the answer to these questions is to *none of the angels* did God the Father ever say any such things ever! He did not whisper it; nor did he insinuate, suggest or imply it at all! Furthermore, he did not declare it and he certainly did not ever think of it in any way, shape, manner or form. The Devil just **lusted** for it because he envied God in his selfish quest for worship and praise because of the corrosive nature of his egotistical, grandiose, grotesque, exaggeration for self-praise of his beauty.

Contrastingly, here, in **Hebrews 1:14** we see another duty of the angelic hosts outlined in detail to wit, *it is to minster to man* as opposed to being worshipped like Satan coveted and craved so much. This is what God wanted Satan and the other fallen angels to do instead of receiving worship. They were to assist us as worshippers of God Almighty. This specific holy scripture reads; **Are they (angels) not all ministering spirits sent forth to minister for them who shall be heirs of salvation?** This is what happens when individuals, angels, man or otherwise who do not know the "plans of God" strike out on their own *contrary* to the plans of God seeking fate from whimsical, errant actions only to suffer dire consequences in the process. *We **are not** the "Masters of our Fate" or the "Captains of our Destinies"*... **God exclusively all alone is**! This is a calculated lie told by the enemies of God to people who are hurting, suffering, discriminated against, brutally beaten, economically distressed, impoverished, malnourished, educationally isolated, poor or downtrodden to "blame them" for their current station in life.

There is a part of this lie, which may be inspirational or has uplifting connotations if not considered in context of its overall implications or inferences. Therefore, it is misleading due to its partial appeal that is tantalizing, mesmerizing as it lures one into its web of deception. No one can alter their destiny via will power, effort, or desire alone **without** God...you cannot take destiny into your own hands. God alone is the Architect of all destinies. Let me provide an example if I may here. I implore you not to get politically correct or critical here dear readers for the perspective that I am conveying is for *the example only*. It is not designed to mock, belittle or demean anyone in anyway. *Shamefully now in today's society with the advent of "social media" we must resort to detailing or explaining every little nuance microscopically for out of concern that someone (namely boneheads) will take it out of context*, become "offended" and start publishing it online or going viral or some other idiotic nonsense protesting needlessly. Not everything stated by someone has ill will or malicious intent necessarily because it is a different perspective than one's own. Geesh. Nevertheless, here is the point I want to illustrate. Persons who suffer from or are affected by dwarfism or are midgets **(again this is not to mock, belittle, demean or slander them in anyway)** but *only* to demonstrate or illustrate the example. No matter how much *they will*, desire or try, they cannot dunk a basketball into the rim of a regulation height hoop without artificial assistance of some kind. They will or must require physical help from taller persons, trampolines or ladders, etc. No matter how much of the inertia or aforementioned principles of will power they may display. Some dreams do not come true. All of us need to stop lying to ourselves, our children and others talking utter rubbish about we control our destiny, **No we do not!** God alone does period! God as the Supreme Creator controls everything. **God is the only one with power!** Read **Romans 13:1** again slowly if necessary to comprehend the sincere meaning. It says, "**Let every soul be subject to the 'higher power' and there** is **no power but the power of God**."

We discussed this a little earlier but I added it again for emphasis. So if you do not have any power (which the word of God tells us we do not) how in the world can you control anything especially your destiny I dare ask? Another example that I would like to include here is the one involving Lucifer/Devil/Satan/Beelzebub whichever title you care to call him by regarding his destiny. Analogously, Satan can't no matter how much he may or would want to try or attempt to amend (**NOT THAT HE WOULD FOR HE IS THE APEX OF ALL EVIL**) *alter or change his destiny* or date within the lake of fire burning with brimstone where he will suffer day and night for all eternity. Jesus said that hell was not created for man but for the devil and his angels (Matthew 25:41). Yet, Satan's fate, forever immortalized from a line from Stevie Wonder's song entitled "*signed, sealed and (will be) delivered*" on the Great and Notable Day of the Lord.

Next, we transition to the terrain borders, boundaries or battle lines including the battlefield arena in which this galactically spectacular war's continuation from heaven will occur. This war's violence extends or transcends over expanding times zones, dimensions, supernatural and natural equators, visible and invisible empires, epochs and millennia of history both in heaven and on the earth as this heinous treachery unfolds. This war started in God's Living Room. However, this war does not and will not cease there in heaven. Its terminal phase descends for further warfare on planet earth's topographical landscape.

CHAPTER VIII

Battlefield Arena

The actual beginning of this heavenly battle described as stupendous fought on all levels of the T3 Heavens. Initially, it had to be a dazzling array of might, strength, power and strategy. For this was a battle to usurp the throne of God. This was not your casual walk in the park looking for someone to mug or rob or a nation to conquer. This battle makes all of the wars on earth seem like a simple mud wrestling contest in comparison. This fight is for the throne of GOD Almighty, winner takes all! If one were to think about it for just a moment, this fight was reminiscent of a previous predictable fights' outcome here on earth as it were. The fight I am referring to is the Battle of Little Big Horn, commonly referred to as Custer's Last Stand. Albeit, he fell and was defeated, Custer believed that it was his divine legacy to be the one holding the "line for liberty" for colonial Americans via his last known defense. Actually, this was nothing more than the repugnant invasion of the autochthonous American Indian homeland utilizing militarily force to subjugate and conquer the Nomadic populations of American Indian tribes who shed their blood and tears to repel, via antiquated, immensely overpowered weaponry and tactics via military invasion while claiming self-defense their heritage and lands. Now, for those of you who either are unaware of this fight and its aftermath or have forgotten some key points this quick review should update you.

General Custer was a renowned, well-respected military officer (even if imagined in his own mind) whose legacy even if self-embellished, rose among some circles while disputed by others to that of his grandeur. Supposedly, Custer's history romanticized in the Calvary of the US Army is debatable among supporters and detractors alike. George A. Custer was a Lieutenant Colonel in the ranks of Union Army of The United States of America. Albeit there exist some controversy between the two ranks held by Custer, I optioned for the higher rank for this prose. Essentially, in the regular US Army, Custer was a Lieutenant Colonel but he attained the rank of major general or two-star in the Volunteer Army of the United States, which was a precursor to the National Army of the American Union. This was a methodology for *citizen soldiers* to enlist and serve the country while quickly amassing or raising large forces of soldiers unlike militias governed by the United States Constitution. Additionally, they are governed or regulated by State Constitutions for enrollment, enlistment and are supported by State finances, regulations and infrastructure, chain of command, etc.

Therefore, I ask for the purist, historical readers pardon in advance while using the higher ranking. I will refer to his higher rank attained throughout this narrative as a matter of military courtesy. The reason is for just like General Custer, my father, my son, Jason, as well as myself all served our Nation's Military Armed Forces. Each of us having worn our Nations uniform under arms to protect and sworn in, to defend the Constitution of the United States against all enemies foreign and domestic. All three of us proudly served the Nation with distinction and received various military citations, ribbons, awards, and honors. Furthermore, we are three generations of Honorably Discharged Veterans of the Armed Military Forces of the United States of America who served our country faithfully to our God given ability. Therefore, synonymously I accord the Honorable General George A. Custer the highest regard for he gave the ultimate sacrifice in service to his country. Jesus said in **John 15:13, "Greater love hath no man than this that a man lay down his life for his friends."**

My Branch of service is the United States Marine Corp—i.e., USMC or Marines for short Oorah! My father served in the same branch as General Custer—i.e., the United States Army and my son is a US Navy Veteran. Practically, these military forces guard our country and our way of life in America. Having served with distinction, I will esteem Major General Custer the honor and respect due his name because of his military service rendered to a grateful nation on behalf of his service to his country. General Custer's Eurocentric definition or valuation of his boyish good looks, golden hair, signature mustache, unkempt military attire and quick charges a.k.a. "Custer's Dash" into the American Confederate Army defensive formations during the American Civil War as well as the American Indian Wars battle positions or lines of defense, brought Custer fame as well as contempt. Custer never saw a fight that he did not like or neither that he should run from. However, in every life, there is a moment for *reflection*, which is designed to cause one to ponder the road travelled thus far to ascertain or evaluate it in relation to the intended destination (destiny), whether near or far. Nonetheless, or at any rate, General Custer did not *recognize his moment of reflection* as he decided to attack the American Indian tribes pushed further into the countryside militarily to make room for the ever-increasing encroachments of the arriving whites from Europe and those being born on American soil. However, although the Indians voluntarily gave up vast lands or sacred territories as well as space for peace, it never seemed to be enough. Therefore, they united after notification of some heinous acts against their brethren as well as the demand for more land to keep the peace between the Indians and the ever rapidly swelling numbers of white Europeans arriving to the Americas.

Alas, the stage now set for Major General, George Armstrong Custer to have his shining moment in the sun. Here was the Golden Boy's grandest opportunity of them all. For if General Custer could singlehandedly defeat the likes of a powerful Indian hegemony, comprised of Crazy Horse, Red Horse, Black Moon, Chief Gall, Crow King, Sitting Bull et al, he would undoubtedly go down in history as the greatest of all military commanders produced by West Point bar none. The annals of history literature books published in America would be inundated with grand myths, lies, falsehoods, untruths, gallantry, intrigue, heroic tales galactically superior or greater than any lies told to date on the level of Greek and Roman mythological "gods of war" namely Custer would had become an American Mars or Achilles respectively. Well then again may be not… Remember once upon a time, we heard the story, that Christopher Columbus "discovered America." America was already **inhabited** when Columbus arrived to the shores of this country by Native American Indians, Mayans and now the "new migrants" whom Trump calls *illegal aliens* who **were here first**—i.e., the Mexicans, **way before** the arrival of the *Mayflower* at Plymouth Rock in or around 1607.

I repeat here Jesus said the devil is a liar! Nevertheless, there was something terribly flawed in his plans. Primarily, Custer *overestimated* the strength of his exhausted Calvary. Secondly, he grotesquely *underestimated* the combination of Indian tribes assembling against him. Thirdly, he failed to consider the disadvantages of a lightning fast Calvary assault that meant they had little to no artillery support that contributed to its speed of attack. Finally, he failed to assess the unified intellect of veteran Indian Chiefs. All who were individually more experienced, qualified veterans of warfare and prepared to fight than was he. History tells the rest of this story which ends in the tragic defeat of the U. S. Seventh Calvary at the Battle of Little Big Horn. General Custers's decimation was engulfing to the point of obliteration! General Custer because of wounds sustained died in this battle along with his brother, Tom Custer, a two time Medal of Honor recipient and his nephew. The point for including this exhaustive historical battle's dissertation that I want to convey to all readers is to compare or contrast this with the actions of Satan regarding his attack within God's Living Room in heaven. This is exactly what Satan did in his attack upon the throne of Almighty God. Satan **overestimated** his strength while he simultaneously **underestimated God's power.** Unfortunately, the Indians would later pay for winning this battle with their lives on the trail of tears death march, which by the way was only revenge for Custer's defeat. Ironically, the American Indians are in the same situation that Satan finds himself in… Sort of speaking—i.e., more on this perspective following here.

American Indians forced remandment upon reservations is godlessness epitomized. Thus, they are a sovereign people within their sovereign country contained within borders. Therefore, the US

Government doesn't have to (neither do) they provide any social services to them at all unless it's trying to collect revenue from a casino under the guise of taxes. If they do, it is minimally to the point to make it nonexistent. God has temporarily remanded Satan to the realm of the Second Heaven's reservation. Therefore, Lucifer resides in this heavenly atmospheric reservation for the fallen demon he is now. Satan failed to consider God's omnipotence. He microscopically examined his own resources without taking into consideration that he was fighting against Almighty God. This Golden Boy of angels committed a heavenly disaster equaled only by General Custer's blunder here on earth. Satan will make one Last Stand before his ultimate defeat on the "Little Big Horn" of earth. Satan fell in love with a romanticized version of himself, as did General Custer as opposed to the realistic finite version of his true capabilities. Thus, judgment in eternity will be much kinder to General Custer than it will be to Lucifer. Ah the idiosyncrasies of life! God watched the battle not worried about its outcome or his nemesis. God knows that his power is absolute, unequalled anywhere in the cosmos! (**Romans13:1**).

The sad thing about this is how many of us underestimate the awesome power of the Holy One of Israel. Satan has been on a downward spiral ever since he started a war inside the very Kingdom of God. After banishment from God's Living Room he was *casted down* to the second heaven where he temporarily resides, from there he will be *cast down* to the earth (first heaven where we reside) which is coincidentally our next topic. Finally, he will be *cast down* to hell and the lake of fire forever in a constantly descending movement away from God Almighty and Jesus Christ Our Lord! Review **Revelation 20:10 cited here, "The devil, which deceived them, was cast into the lake of fire and brimstone where the beast and the false prophet are. And they <u>will be tormented day and night forever</u> and ever."** My God, My God. How horrible is the thought of burning eternally day and night with no chance of reprieve ever. Que Sera Sera. Alas, we arrive to the discussion of our realm or the First Heaven of the T3 heavens—i.e., level one ground floor of the three heavens.

Those who are familiar with warfare, wars, battles, military conflict, incursion campaigns, etc., understand that the key to being victorious is always determined by knowing the battlefield peculiarities or particular specifics. Simply put, not only do you need to understand the enemy tactics, capabilities, weaknesses, strengths, strategy or chokepoints you are fighting against, but also you must intuitively understand the terrain where the battle will be fought. Naturally, Lucifer in his many voyages going to and *fro in the earth and from walking up and down in it* since the dawn of creation knows the earth's topography, landscape and geography due to his many reconnaissance missions here to planet earth from many moons ago. Therefore, whenever his final banishment to the earth occurs. Satan will attempt to make his Last Stand. He and his coconspirators will be more than ready to fight. The earth is an excellent battlefield to fight upon as Lucifer sees it. Some of the reasons why that is, can be attributed to the fact that the earth is totally governed by unholy beings (some without Christ)—i.e., humanity unlike heaven. Heaven's rules are by divinity different from man's immorality or mores. Heaven's rules are holy, sacred and divine all of the time eternally. Heaven is where God governs all dominions. This is the sphere or locale of the Holy Lord God Almighty, who dwells supreme governing in his holy estate forever albeit briefly physically separate from man.

In addition, Holy angels **do not occupy any** of earth's terrain **_unless_ or _until_ specifically sent by God on a mission** to minister to the heirs of salvation (believers) in Jesus Christ. Lucifer has assistants on the earth he has no helpers in Heaven. Lucifer likes earth because he knows he has many advantages over man on earth's landscape that he did not have in heaven against his peers—i.e., other angels who threw him out of heaven along with his unholy angels. For example, Satan and his unholy angels are stronger, physically different and able to do way more things than mortal men can as they by original divine design are vastly superior in intellect, composition, knowledge as well as strength than is humanity. Remember, unholy angels have seen the face of God, the kingdom of God and once worshipped Almighty God in person face to face as former occupants of the very Living Room of God's inner sanctuary where all believers in Christ (which we have not seen) to date, yet want to go forever to live with the Lord. Therefore, there exists an imbalance of ability or power between the two beings one being celestial and the other, man being terrestrial. Earth is idea for Lucifer to wage final warfare upon because he has an audience that is easily influenced by him (humankind) because we have an ***inherited predisposition*** to sin since we naturally **inherited** the fallen DNA of Adam/Eve.

This is another reason why Jesus said that flesh and blood could not inherit the kingdom of God. Man's flesh is sinful, fallen and flawed along with sin infested in every part of man's existence—i.e., his thoughts, desires, actions and mannerisms. Satan loves earth topography for he can wreak havoc throughout the cosmos unchecked or free willing style. For Satan, earth is familiar contestable ground where he has an advantage unlike in heaven where he did not after the fall of man in the Garden of Eden. Satan earned some property rights that granted him some privileges that he will exploit in his Last Stand for a kingdom of his own. God must allow Satan some freedom within earth's realm or the first heaven because of Adam and Eve's willful disobedience. The reason is God is just and Satan *did not force* Adam or Eve to do anything against their own will… The two of them did acts as independent, mature adults as they voluntarily disobeyed God's commandment willfully as we all voluntarily choose to sin in our personal lives as well. Even though we know better or the truth of God's word and commandments forbidding us to act so sinfully occasionally.

Furthermore, another reason why earth is an attractive battlefield for Satan is relatable to the fact that on earth there are more victims other than just the fallen angels. Originally, in the Living Room of God, Satan only had his angels as the victims or casualties of instigating a rebellion against the Lord. Now on earth he has humankind as potential victims in the ongoing battle or fight with God in play too now. This is a very critical point. Because God loves man and has demonstrated his love in so many ways culminating with the sacrificial death of his only begotten Son, Jesus Christ, as our substitutionary offering his holy shed blood to placate God The Father's holy justice for the atonement of our willful sin. Review **Hebrews 9:22** listed here, requiring shed blood for atonement of sin; **and according to the law, almost all things are purified with blood and without the shedding of blood there is no remission.**

Now, that preparation for the battlefield itself is completed. The next requirement is for the warriors who will fight within this battlefield arena on this contested landscape of the earth's soil need review of its warriors. Therefore, we focus some attention to look at the combatants. The warriors themselves must gain access to the battlefield to fulfill their roles here. Even if that role is to die on its facade. Well one opposing set of warriors are already here—i.e., humankind. They are just awaiting the arrival of Lucifer along with his horde of demons to usher in the greatest battle among humans and fallen angels this side of the eternal divide. Ready or not…herrrrrrrrre's Satan. Jesus said, "**Behold I saw Satan as a 'bolt of lightning' _fall_ from heaven**" (**Luke 10:18**). Also, see, **Isaiah 14:12** that reads, "**_How are you fallen from heaven O Lucifer son of the morning how are you cut down to the ground!_**" This descent, Satan's second fall, emanating this time from the second heaven will serve as Satan's eviction notice from the second heaven to the earth when it occurs. Currently, he can go to and from the earth, back to the second heaven's promenade deck level and back to the earth at will. After this push to the earth from God, he will not be able to go back and forth ever again. With an exception that will be explained at the appropriate time. Therefore, let us examine his activity on earth during his brief stay here after this God imposed descent.

CHAPTER IX

Lucifer's Descent to Earth: First Heaven

One note to keep in mind every time God evicts Satan he falls or descends from one level of the T3 Heavens down to another lower level; forever prohibited from ever attaining that previous level again. For example, after his expulsion out of the third heaven he could never go back to the third heaven. Well, when the time comes for his expulsion from the second heaven (soon coming event) he can never go back to the second floor balcony to accuse the brethren anymore. Jesus's return to the earth euphemistically referred to as the Second Advent of Christ is a much-anticipated prophetic event worldwide. Well, contrastingly, Satan's fall or arrival to planet earth is not looked upon favorably at all not even by him. Satan once effortlessly moved about the mountain and Garden of God with ease. However, once confined to the earth he is going to be angry. I will take the liberty to refer to the fall of Satan to the earth as *Lucifer's Second Descent.* Satan accuses all believers when we sin, directly to God Almighty and the Lord Jesus Christ. Satan does so day and night from the second floor balcony of heaven looking up to God and screaming as loud as he can about all of the things that we are doing sinfully against God. See **Revelation 12:10** that says, "***And I heard a loud voice saying in heaven, Now is come salvation, and strength and the kingdom of our God and the power of his Christ for <u>the accuser of our brethren is cast down which accused</u> them before our God day and night.***" Jesus's reply to Satan's accusations against us was, is and forever shall be until we receive *glorified heavenly bodies* is **Father forgive them for they know not what they do (Luke 23:24).**

Jesus reply does not mean that we do not understand our actions of sinful disobedience or the temporal satisfaction of the sin itself. See **Hebrew 11:25**, it *says,* ***"The pleasures of sin are only for a season."*** Christ reply is twofold; first, he is interceding with his heavenly Father on behalf of redeemed believers of humanity citing that humans were born into sin after Adam's choice to sin. Furthermore, Jesus tells his Heavenly Father that he has **paid the price in full** for the penalty associated with sin. Review Romans 6:23 here that says, **"For the wages of sin is death but the gift of God is eternal life through Jesus our Lord."** Christ by shedding his holy blood as the atoning sacrificial lamb satisfied God the Father's threshold. Sin has a very high price. God requires that innocent blood pay for the guilty party actions. This demonstrates God's disdain for any evil. I hope that it will make us think twice too before we sin once we comprehend the enormity of price that must be paid for committing sin against the Lord God. One little brief anecdotal story to implant here to enhance this point is the first child by David and Bathsheba died to atone for the adultery committed by the two guilty adults. The innocent child's blood was required. Although both of them were forgiven, but the child who did no wrong died.

See **2 Samuel 12:12–15** here that says, **"For you did it secretly but I will do this thing before all of Israel before the sun. So David said to Nathan I have sinned against the Lord and Nathan said to David the Lord has also put away your sin you shall not die. However, because by this deed you have given great occasion to the enemies of the Lord to blaspheme *the child who is born to you shall surely die*."** My God the wages of our sin. Nevertheless, Hallelujah! Thank You Lord Jesus Christ! Christ as our High Priest intercedes on our behalf asking for mercy as well and compassion since he sympathizes with our weakness after we confess our sins because Jesus was tempted in all points as we are yet without sin! *{I recite reference scriptures,* **Hebrews 4:14–15**, *that reads,* **"Seeing that we have a great High Priest, who *passed through the heavens*, Jesus the Son of God, let us hold fast our confession. verse 15, for we do** *not have a High Priest who cannot sympathize with our weakness. But was in all points tempted like as we were yet <u>without</u> sin."}*

Secondly, Jesus is saying that man does not "understand" how horrible sin itself offends God who is the epitome of Holiness and causes God unimaginable grief emotionally if you will. All sin has a powerful, direct, negative impact upon God personally causing God to grieve in his heart. **See Genesis 6:6** verse, which *reads, "And the Lord was sorry that he made man on the earth and he <u>was grieved in his heart</u> for the thought of his (man's) heart were evil continually."* God <u>was grieved</u> because his crown jewel of all created beings and the only one he exclusively created *in his own image* intents and thoughts of his heart was evil continually. Jesus said be Holy for the Lord your God is Holy. See **1 Peter 1:16, "Because it is written, be holy for I am holy."** This is attributable to God's Divine nature of Holiness is why sin is so offensive to the Lord God of Israel.

Continuing with our current theme, however, there is one exception; whereby Lucifer's return is allowable to a previously evicted level upon his eviction from a previous higher level of occupancy. This involves the realm of the first heaven of man's domicile. Satan will be allowed back briefly to earth (first heaven realm) to start the End Time war. **See Revelation 20:1–3,** which reads, "*Then I saw an angel coming down from heaven, having the key to the bottomless pit and a great chain in his hand. He laid hold on the dragon that serpent of old, who is the Devil and Satan and bound him for a thousand years and cast him into the bottomless pit and shut him up and set a seal on him so that he should deceive the nations <u>no more, till the thousand years were finished.</u> But after these things 'he must be released' for a little while.*" Satan fought with Michael the Archangel in a vain attempt to remain in heaven—i.e., the third heaven within the very presence of God. Since he lost this fight, he fully understands that his days are numbered. How does he know this? Satan realized this when God cast him out of Paradise into the second Heaven with the ultimate banishment being to man's time zone on earth—i.e., the First Heaven. Mortal men on earth are governable by time here. Read **Ecclesiastes 3:1 says to everything there is <u>a season and a time</u> to every purpose under**

heaven. For example, **a time to be born and a time to die**. There is no end time in eternity future! This is difficult to understand since all things that we do end at a certain period here on earth. Another way of putting it is, we don't have anything to compare eternity without ending unto, since we are measuring time in seconds, minutes, hours, days, months, etc. Therefore, theoretically, this usurpation against God by Satan could have been a thousand years or one day. Remember (**2 Peter 3:8**) cited here says, **but beloved do not forget this one thing that with the Lord _one day is as a thousand years and a thousand years is as one day_**. Objectively, eternity present for man once started (it began when God created Adam on the earth) never ends. Eternity is divisible into three parts. Eternity past, what has already happened, eternity present the current here and now or what is actually happening and eternity future what will happen as time passes on.

The Bible says **woe unto the inhabiters (humankind) of the earth and of the sea** (all fish or animal life) for *the devil is come down unto you* having **great wrath (anger) because he knows that he has but a _short time_. (Revelation 12:12)**. Satan is furious because he recognizes that he must operate within time zones now. Alternatively speaking, Satan must conduct his unholy affairs within a specified period. Although Satan does not know God's plan he knows how God thinks. Therefore, he attempts to devise strategy both tactically and strategically based upon his former exposure to God. Satan knows that a millennium is a thousand years, so he deduces that God made the world in six days and rested on the seventh. Thus, Satan strategizes that regarding time, we are living in the period of 2002. (Jewish calendar would make this approximately year, 5,766 years) of recorded time on earth (Initial period when I started writing this book.)

Therefore, we are living two thousand years after the crucifixion of Jesus Christ approximately somewhere circa AD 30 or AD 33. Thus, logically the time from Adam and Eve unto Christ covered four thousand years and the death of Christ until now is two thousand for combined total of six thousand years. (Georgian calendar). Then rationally we must be living in the sixth millennium, next is the seventh millennium. Which is when God rested on the seventh day. Another way to view this is the seventh day. This is attributable to a day equaling unto a thousand years and a thousand years equaled to a day in the eyes of JEHOVAH (**2 Peter 3:8**). This is amazing! Jehovah God views all the time on earth as passed as just six days! Although to us, it seems like a long time. God Almighty says it is merely a short time. Remember, in eternity where God is, our time is only six days because HST records the clock that is used, Heavenly Standard Time. Next, we briefly turn our attention to some other reasons why Satan is angry besides the obvious one I just narrated. Then I will return to the main topic of Lucifer's descent to earth.

Additional Reasons for Lucifer's Wrath (Anger)

Satan knows that during the rapture—i.e., the snatching away of believers alive at the time of Christ first stage return to earth will start the clock of his final or Last Stand against God and Christ. Satan's temporary detention or detainment in the bottomless pit for a thousand years or one day stated above. See **Revelation 20:1–3** (HST), which reads, "***Then I saw angel coming down from heaven, having the key to the bottomless pit and a great chain in his hand. He laid hold on the dragon that serpent of old, who is the Devil and Satan and bound him for a thousand years and cast him into the bottomless pit and shut him up and set a seal on him so that he should deceive the nations <u>no more, till the thousand years were finished.</u> But after these things 'he must be released' for a little while.*"** Therefore, since Satan nor anyone else (*except* God the Father) knows when (the rapture) is going to occur (**Acts 1:7,** whereby Jesus said, "**It is not for you (us) to know <u>times or seasons</u> which the Father has put in his own authority**") Satan is intensifying his activity on the earth. Because the word of God tells us that during this period of rest, which will last one thousand years with Christ the rest of the dead lived not again until this time expired. Cited here in **Revelation 20:5** ***but the rest of the dead lived not again until the thousand years were finished. This is the first resurrection.***

Now it is vital not to confuse what the scriptures are telling us here. This is not the Second Coming of Jesus to the earth. However, it is the first stage of his return to resurrect those who have faith in him. Nevertheless, if someone insists on referring to this as the Second Advent of Christ we can state that it is in two parts. The initial part to retrieve his worshippers (*resurrection of the dead and the rapture amalgamated*) **and Jesus will descend from heaven with a shout with the voice of the Archangel and with the trump of God and the dead in Christ shall rise first according to 1 Thessalonians 4:16.** The word of God calls this the first resurrection repeated again from above **Revelation 20:5.** *But the rest of the dead lived not again until the thousand years were finished. This is the first resurrection.* The second part is when he will put down all earthly authority and install God's Kingdom over humanity forever. TBD—i.e., Too Be Determined by the Lord only. I nor anyone else in heaven above or earth below knows. This period coincides exactly with God's creation of the earth in six days resting on the seventh day. The LORD is duplicating it again. Therefore, the rapture could occur any moment now, as the Apostle Paul said within a "**twinkling of an eye**" (**1 Corinthians 15:52**).

Another reason for Satan's anger besides having to operate in man's time zones is Satan's knowledge that he has a short time left according to GOD'S time clock that is on HST. Satan is attempting to prevent as many people as he possibly can from partaking or involvement in the process of "Operation Rapture"—i.e., in the first resurrection or heavenly snatching away discussed earlier. Ultimately, he wants to stop anyone from going to heaven period. Why? Here is his arrogant strategy. If he can keep them here he thinks that he can intimidate them and all others left behind through his campaign of terror as he did with murders causing fear, desperation, death and despair in the Roman coliseum enacted upon first century believers for their faith in Christ. How can he succeed with this? Honestly, he cannot without our cooperation.

See Hebrews 2:3, which states, "**How shall we escape if we neglect so great salvation which at the first began to be spoken by the Lord and was confirmed to us by those who heard him?**"

However, he feels as if they will not submit and choose death that he can cause others to fear for their own lives and accept the mark of the beast. Satan believes this because he knows the dark *power of fear* combined with the fact that he has the *power of death*. Read **Hebrews 2:14–16** denoted here, "**Inasmuch then as the children have partaken of flesh and blood. He (Jesus) himself likewise shared in the same that through death he might destroy him *who had the power of death that is the devil* and release those who through fear of death were all their lifetime subject to bondage for indeed he does not give aid to angels but he does give aid to the seed of Abraham.**" The holy scriptures tell us **that God *has not* given us the spirit of fear *but of power* and of love and of a sound mind! (2 Timothy 1:7).** Although the mark of the beast figures prominently in this sinister scheme that will be implemented by Satan of psychological and emotional terror to intimidate people on earth to avoid death by those who fear death or dying. I will avoid further narration on this subject until the designated chapter devoted to its inclusion in this battle to refocus upon our mission here to expound on additional causes for Satan's anger and his descent to the earth. Remember, initially Satan started this fight in the very presence of God in the highest heaven and was expulsed from heaven **(Revelation 12:7–8).**

Cited here, **And war broke out in heaven Michael and his angels fought with dragon and his angels fought but they did not prevail nor was a place found for them in heaven any longer.** However, the outcome or aftermath of this battle *will be determined* on the earth *regarding humanity*. Here is scriptural proof, **Revelation 12:12** states, "***Therefore rejoice O heavens and you who dwell/live in them. Woe unto the inhabitants of the earth (you and I) and the sea, for the devil has come down to you having great wrath/anger because he knows that he has a short time!***"

The final battlefield arena is now planet earth between God and the devil if you will. Satan's "dishonorable discharge" from heaven shifted the battlefield or arena from heaven to earth for governorship. However, he will continue to fight against the holiness of God on the earth against the people of God (especially against those of us who believe that Christ is Lord) but also against mankind in general per se. Man was created in the image of God, no other creature or being in the cosmos has this unique identity. The earth has the things that God created to sustain our life upon it—i.e., animals, grain, food, fruits, vegetables, seas, oceans, lakes, rivers, streams, brooks, air, mountains, hills, valleys, etc. Therefore, Lucifer in his numerous travels since the creation of earth has had plenty of time to study the battlefield. Keep in mind (He was going back and forth up and down in it for quite some time Job 1:7) as he plots against his enemies, mankind per se and believers in the Lord Jesus Christ specifically. See **Psalm 37:12** as it states, "**The wicked plots against the just and gnashes upon him with his teeth.**"

The geography and the atmosphere of the earth alone itself means nothing to Lucifer. Satan is after the people on it so he weighs his attacks in coordination with the battlefield itself. He has a role in the devastating death toll in tornadoes, hurricanes and other natural phenomenon. Here is biblical support for such a premise. **Ephesians 2:2** reads, "**In which you once walked according to the course of this world, according to *the prince of the power of the air...*"** Paul tells us here in Ephesians that Satan **is the "Prince of the Power of the air."** Therefore, one can readily understand that periodically, Satan unleashes the "power of the air" that spawns tornadoes, hurricanes and other violent wind related power when directed against humans causing death and destruction in its path. Are you still unconvinced? Let us review the book of Job for more clues into the satanic power associated with the air that Satan periodically unleashes to kill his enemies—i.e., humankind and those who worship God. This is a short recap of the life of the man of God, Job, who avoided evil and worshipped God. God informed Satan of Job's desire to serve God and remain holy **Job 1–5**.

Denoted here, "**There was a man in the land of Uz whose name was Job and that man was perfect and upright and one that feared God and eschewed evil. And there were born unto him seven sons and three daughters. His substance was also seven thousand sheep, and three thousand camels, and five hundred yoke of oxen and five hundred she asses and a very great house-**

hold. So that this man was the greatest man of all of the men of east. And his sons went and feasted in their houses everyone his day, sent, and called for their three sisters to eat and to drink with them. And it was so when the days of their feasting were gone about, that Job sent and sanctified them, and rose up early in the morning, and offered burnt offerings according to the number of them all; for Job said, It may be that my sons have sinned and cursed God in their hearts. Thus, Job did continually."

Satan replies to God that Job had a selfish purpose in doing so which he told God that Job only did so because you bless his work, provide him with safety, wealth, etc., so that was no big deal. Satan actually challenges God that if God will let him attack Job, God will see how fast Job will reject God and curse him to his face. God accepts the devil's challenge and offer and allows Satan to attack Job but not take his life. Review **Job 1:11** here for clues. Here is where Satan used his awesome power as the prince of the power of the air for it reads: **"*a great wind* (tornado) came across the wilderness and struck the four corners of the house and fell on them and they are dead" to kill Job sons and daughters who were drinking wine in the eldest brother's home (Job 1:19).** Believers in Christ are not to be disheartened because Lucifer is the "prince of the power of the air." The reason being he is just that *__a prince__*. Christ is **"King"** over all elements! We all know Kings outrank princes in authority, stature, power, governance, etc. Here I will show one prime example where the King of Kings, Jesus Christ displayed his divine authority over the elements on earth while living as a man. Are you familiar with the story? If so outstanding, if not here is a recap here for biblical support; see **Matthew 8:23–27.** Christ enters a boat along with his disciples and falls asleep as they were travelling from one location to the next. During the journey *a violent wind tempest* (hmmm I wonder who caused that Satan maybe) threatened to kill all of them. Yet look at **Matthew 8:26** for the key verse in this narration for it says *__Christ rebuked the winds and the sea and there was a great calm.__* My LORD what a mighty King we have in Jesus! However, there is more credence following below in the story of Job. We will begin by looking at the dialogue between God and Satan regarding

Job. Job was a man who revered God and tried in earnest to live a humble, godly lifestyle in the sight of the Lord.

God inquires in **Job 1:8 as to whether or not during Satan's travelling back and forth to the earth did Satan consider Job's voluntary willingness to serve God honestly while avoiding evil**. Naturally God was embarrassing Satan here by contrast and comparison in the sense that the Lord was showing him that here is a man unlike yourself a fallen angel who wants to sincerely serve me and live an honest lifestyle in my sight. Satan rhetorically replies in **Job 1:11, "That there is a hidden motive, why Job serves God as he does."** Job only does so because God protects him, blesses him with substance, property, resources, etc. Furthermore, Satan challenges the Lord regarding Job as he tells the Lord: **but now stretch out your hand and touch all that he has and he will surely _curse you_ to your face!** God accepts Lucifer's challenge and allows Satan to move against Job's family, livestock, workers and property. However, God forbids Satan to attack Job's body or take away his life. The next phase of the story begins in earnest as the events unfold rapidly with dire consequences for Job.

God agreed in principle in **Job 1:12** to allow the devil broad discretion and latitude with "restricted permission" to attack Job property initially. **Review Job 1:12** here as the Lord allows Satan permission to touch the resources within Job's orbit: **And the Lord said to Satan behold "all that he has" is in your power only _do not_ lay a hand on his person. So Satan went out from the presence of the Lord.** Specifically, God's only restriction was that the devil **_would not_** be allowed to harm, injure maim, afflict or kill Job. However, the devil had another plan in mind. Although Satan was prohibited by God to kill Job, Satan decided to utilize the same tactic he did back in the Garden of Eden. Adam was Lucifer's target in Eden, as was Job now, but the devil got Eve first, who got Adam to sin against God for him. Satan concluded if it worked then this scheme would work now. Satan calls this "attack by proxy." Satan's strategy was to _kill Job's family first,_ in addition to other tragic events to get Job voluntarily cursing of God to his face. Although, God directed Satan specifically not to kill Job. However, there were **no restrictions** on his family.

Therefore, Satan _killed Job's children_ as we observed above by using a tornado. See **Job 1:19.** Tornados a.k.a. **"airpower" from Satan as the prince of the power of the air.** However, prior to this, there was a series of unfortunate news for Job as described vividly in **Job 1:13–19.**

These specific scriptures delineates for us the events. Essentially these are as follows; **the Sabeans, who killed his servants, as they took them away verses 14–15, confiscated Job's oxen and donkeys. Afterward, mistakenly called the "fire of God" (which was actually caused by Lucifer) fell down from heaven as it burned up Job's sheep and servants who were watching the sheep verse 16. However, there is additional unfortunate news as it arrives at Job's doorstep while this sole survivor was telling Job the misfortune that had befallen him without any warning.** Finally, this updated bulletin is heart piercing, gut wrenching, mind numbing traumatic event as it is without any question the most ominous that any parent can ever experience. The breaking news by the individual survivor tells him in **Job 1:18, "Your sons and daughters were drinking wine in your elders son's home when suddenly _a great wind (tornado)_ came across and stuck the four corners of the house and it fell on the young people and they are dead."** This is additional proof that Satan is the **_"prince of the power of the air"_** as noted earlier in **Ephesians 2:2.** This was done in addition to the other attacks upon his cattle, servants, etc. All of these events began immediately after Satan left from the presence of the Lord who told him all that Job had was **in the power of the devil's control** _except his life_ **Job 1:12.** Unbelievably, none of these things worked according to the devil's diabolical scheme—i.e., killing his children, kidnapping his servants, stealing his livestock, which nearly caused him to go bankrupt. Despite his enormous personal grief, Job still refused to sin or curse God.

Look at **Job 1:22** cited here that says, **in all this Job sinned not nor charged God foolishly.** The devil switched tactics. He requested permission from God that would allow him directly to attack Job's body. **He was granted the ability to do so still he _was not allowed_ to take his life (Job 2:6). Satan immediately attacked Job with**

severe boils from the crown of his head unto the soles of his feet. See Job 2:7. Consequently, we see in these events orchestrated by Lucifer that the battlefield is now on earth against the people of God specifically. The devil will use anything including the natural elements such as wind to attack persons who have placed their trust in the Invisible God of Israel. Summarily, this will conclude our narration on additional reasons for Lucifer's anger. Next, we review some other heinous individuals who will assist the devil in his violent rule of dictatorship upon the earth prior to Christ's Second coming. However, before doing so we will preview some of the current events shaping our world preparing its landscape for the arrival of the Wicked One.

Current Events

However, this is not an isolated attack on earth upon an Old Testament believer only. It is coming to a theater near all of us on the earth soon too! This is the transition of the war in heaven—i.e., fighting in God's Living Room to becoming the war on earth… Fighting in *our* living rooms. This follows Satan's expulsion from heaven permanently. See **Revelation 12:9, "So _the great dragon_ was cast out that serpent of old, called the Devil and Satan who deceives the whole world, he was *cast to the earth* and his angels were cast out with him."** Let us explore some additional evidentiary proof from God's word to see how. Begin looking at **Revelation 13:2–18.** These particular scriptures describes ominous details for all humankind that are alive on earth during that epoch. Essentially, *it describes the ascension of the Anti-Christ reign of terror on earth.* I will summarize the text here. However, I highly recommend that you read it in its entirety at your leisure and pleasure when and if you choose to do so.

Summary of this passage indicates that the Anti-Christ, the False Prophet and the Beast will work collectively together to deceive the entire world—i.e., unsaved /unrepentant (humanity to worship the Antichrist and receive the mark of the beast 666) and if anyone chooses not to do so, he/she initially will not be allowed to buy or sell anything. Subsequently, The Antichrist will receive a mortal wound that is usually fatal and *recover* from this wound (via counterfeit resurrection which is simply the devil enters his body as his own spirit departs) which will cause all those who dwell on the earth to conclude ***who is able to war or fight against him? Read Revelation 13:4 listed here, "So they worshipped the dragon who gave authority to the beast and they worshipped the beast saying who is like the beast and who is able to war against him?"*** Apparently errantly concluding that the Antichrist is "divine," they attain this deceitful conclusion because of this demonic miracle (false resurrection) via physical recovery from a head wound as the scripture states. **One of his heads** (secular political leader) was *wounded unto death this act will cause worldwide manipulation of the masses of deceived people to accept, worship and praise the Devil. Since the devil always coveted worship, he will get what he wants albeit temporarily through the false narrative of embodying the Antichrist's human corpse body. All who worship him will thereby doom for all eternity their immortal souls to unspeakable horror, pain and suffering of eternal damnation via the second death in hell separated from the love of God forever.*

The Antichrist transferred or granted power by the devil himself to blaspheme God, his holy name and those who dwell in heaven this includes holy angels, raptured believers, Christ the Lord and OT/NT and Tribulation saints who have risen with Christ in the first resurrection during phase 1 of Christ's Second Advent. Christ will come directly to the earth in Phase 2 of his Second Advent. Look at the ironic difference between the two ways of worship—i.e., proffered between God and the Devil. Look at **Revelation 22:17**, denoted here, **"And the spirit and the bride say come, and let him who hears come, and "whosoever will" let him come drink the water of life freely."** God allows the individual to choose his or herself, which I annotated in the purpose for this book within the paragraph on the external book cover. However, Satan contrastingly, will kill and force anyone who rejects worshipping him as we just read in Revelation 13:5. However, later Satan turns up the ante by executing all tribulation saints who refuse to worship his godless beast by beheading anyone who rejects his name or number to accept or receive tattoos upon their bodies (**Revelation 13:15, Revelation**

20:4). Herein the entire scripture referenced for your perusal if you opt to read it now below.

And the beast, which I saw, was like unto a leopard and his feet were as the feet of a bear. And his mouth was as the mouth of a lion. And the dragon gave him his power and his seat and great authority. And I saw one of his heads as it were wounded to death and his deadly wound was healed and all the world wondered after the beast and they worshipped the dragon which gave power unto the beast and they worshipped the beast saying who is like unto the beast? Who is able to make war against him? And there was given unto him a mouth speaking great things and blasphemy and power was given unto him to continue forty two months. And he opened his mouth in blasphemy against God to blaspheme his name and his tabernacle and them that dwell in heaven. And it was given unto him to make war with the saints and to overcome them and power was given him over all kindred's and tongues and nations and all that dwell upon the earth shall worship him whose names are not written in the book of life of the lamb slain from the foundation of the world. If any man have, an ear let him hear he that leads into captivity shall go into captivity he that kills with the sword must be killed with the sword. Here is the patience and faith of the saints, and I beheld another beast coming up out of the earth. And he had two horns like a lamb, and he spoke as a dragon. And he exercises all the power of the first beat before him and causes the earth and them that dwell therein to worship the first beast. Whose deadly wound was healed and he does great wonders. So that he makes fire come down from heaven in the sight of men and deceives them that dwell on the earth by the means of those miracles which he had power to do in the e sight of the beast. Saying to them that dwell on the earth that they should make an image to the beast. Which had the wound by a sword and did live. And he had power to give life to the image of the beast that the image of the beast should both speak and cause that as many as would not worship the image of the beast should be killed. And he caused all both small and great rich and poor free and bond to receive a mark in their right hand or in their foreheads. And that no man might buy or sell save he that had the mark or the name of the beast or the number of his name here is wisdom let him that has understanding count the number for it is the number of the beast for it is the number of a man (666) or six hundred threescore and six. (Revelation 13:2–18)

This entire passage of the Holy Bible denotes specifically what I am referring to regarding the war on earth that started in heaven transitioning the battlefield to the earth. Satan will make war with the saints and all those who hold Christ to be divine (**Revelation 13:7**). **It was granted to him to make war with the saints and to overcome them. And great authority was given him over every tribe, tongue and nation.** Initially, he will prevail against believers in Christ and overcome them. In verse **Revelation 13:7**. However, because of the sovereign power of the holiness of Jesus Christ, he will be defeated. Here we shift our focus to ***approximately*** when these events will culminate in the utter destruction of the evil one that Old Serpent, the Red Dragon eternally identified as the satanic cherub and his minions whose evil ways have devastated all of humanity and some of the heavenly angels for the last time. This is the most difficult chapter to attempt to have a valid scriptural detailed essay about. The reason is exactly attributed to what Jesus said in **Acts 1:7**: "**It is** not for you (all of us) to know *the times or the seasons (when these events occur)* that the Father has reserved into his own hands or authority according to the word of God."

Consequently, this leaves us at a distinct disadvantage. Especially since so many false prophets, preachers and self-proclaimed "Bible scholars" are running around telling people that they know when (eternity future) yet to happen, significant events to come—i.e., the rapture, date of the Second Advent or return of Christ back to the earth. Alternately, that they know the Antichrist's identity, etc., and when prophetic events under God's sovereign eternal control are going to occur. These events individually as well as collectively herald the Second Coming of Our Lord Jesus Christ back to the earth. Truth told it is *not possible* for a man to know these things **unless the Spirit of God** reveals it to him directly and it must be 100 per cent accurate to meet the biblical standard! Close enough does not count when you attempt to tell someone God said something or provide clear insight into holy prophecy. Again we all need to stop lying to one another or ourselves… **For the time will come when they will not endure sound doctrine but according to their own desires having itching ears**…as stated in **2 Timothy 4:3.**

Either conversely listed in **Colossians 2:18** that says **let no one cheat you out of your reward taking delight in false humility and worship of angels intruding into those things, which he has not seen,** *vainly puffed up by his fleshly mind*—i.e., *our own imaginations.* There is no room for 99 percent right if God said it as one would allege then it is 100 percent right every time. **God is not a man that he should lie nor the son of man that he should repent as stated in Number 23:19.** The Old Testament required death for the prophet if it was not exactly, as one alleged God said it would be mandatory 100 percent every time period was the standard! Scriptural proof can be located in **Deuteronomy 18:22** and **Deuteronomy 13:5** both listed here that says, **"When a prophet speaks in the *name of the Lord*, if the thing does not happen or come to pass that is the thing, which the Lord has not spoken. The prophet, has spoken it presumptuously, you *shall not* be afraid of him,** verse **13:5.** But that prophet or dreamer of dreams

shall be put to death because he has spoken in order to <u>turn you away</u> from the Lord our God, who brought you out of the land of Egypt and redeemed you from the house of bondage, to entice you away which the Lord your God commanded you to walk. So, you shall put away the evil from your midst." However, this does not mean that we cannot review the biblical record, rightly divide the word of God as commanded us in **2 Timothy 2:15.** That **cites study to show yourself approved of God a workman that need not to be ashamed *"righty dividing"* the word of truth.** Also, we can use Godly wisdom, as outlined in **James 1:5,** that states, *"If any of you "lack wisdom" let him ask of God who gives to all liberally and it will be given him, "* employ common sense and avoid reckless, self-serving, distortions as well as plain old sound logical reasoning or sense to understand the overall goal of God. Which is for all of us in due time…to be where, the Apostle Paul reported God wants us to be forever. Listed in **Ephesians 1:10**—i.e., where God and Christ are, **that in the dispensation of the fullness of times (end of this age) he "might gather together" in one *all things* in Christ both *which are in heaven* and *which are in earth* even in him.**

Essentially God wants to unite all who worship Christ his Son as Lord. This includes the host of heaven's holy angels, Old and New Testament saints, resurrected and raptured believers in Christ, tribulation saints and worshippers of God that are currently located in different places (nations of the world) under **one tabernacle** of the Lord God of Israel. See also **Revelation 21:3**; which reads: **And I heard a loud voice in heaven saying, Behold the <u>tabernacle of God is with men</u> and <u>he will dwell with them</u> and they shall be his people. God himself will be with them and be their GOD! My, My, My Lord what outstanding news!** All of us saved by faith through the blood of Christ will be with God and Christ and dwell with them forevermore.

Therefore, we need to be pragmatic, cautious, disciplined, realistic as well as honest so we can humbly accept or conclude a certain common sense understanding that has eluded us because of incessant lying to ourselves and allowing others to deceive us. There is a limitation to what we know or can honestly say about God Almighty.

We need to quit lying, pretending or self-pontificating as though we **know everything** we need to know or can know about Our Lord Jesus Christ. I pose this question to all of us (myself included): how can the finite know, understand or explain the infinite wisdom, persona, and glory of The Heavenly Father without his divine help or inspiration of his Holy Spirit with certainty. Deceit is rampant in our everyday life because of the influence of the devil, the world and our flesh that it is now spilling-over into discussing concepts about or relating to Christ the Lord or Our Heavenly Father and it needs to stop immediately. Therefore, beginning with myself, I pledge that I will only tell you the truth of God's word without trying to impress you with lies, untrue revelations or prophetic statements that the Lord Our God has not revealed or shown unto me because of evil pride, self-aggrandizement and crowned with puffy imaginations made up within or by my own fleshly mind. Accountability and truth telling is paramount when speaking God's word or writing points of view about God's intentions for humanity. Rather this is on paper or made in speeches because many people reject or turn away from God by the hypocritical or intentional deceitful words of professed believers.

The very best that we can simply desire is an *"approximation of the period"* of times that these things may take place without lying on God saying he told me that it would be so and so blah, blah, blah. Especially if it contradicts the documented words of the Lord God of Hosts of Israel and his Christ entrusted into our stewardship temporarily for our age to read, live by and correct our sinful conduct daily. Thereby attempting to impress upon others namely those of the household of God that one's (theirs) relationship with Christ is closer opposed to others that is utter non-sense. **For God is not a respecter of persons (Romans 2:11).** Furthermore, for the record neither am I! Now that I have exhaustively narrated this perspective, I return the focus of our journey.

A current review of the hostility, threats, rumors of wars made by competing world powers, such as the USA, Russia, Iran, the United Nations, the European Union, NATO—i.e., North Atlantic Treaty Organization, the revived Rise of the Roman Catholic Church, North

Korea nuclear capabilities, constantly making threats to neighbors and distant countries alike with regularity. Additionally the ascendancy of the Arab Kingdoms military, resurgence of Russia and its cold war diabolical challenging antics against the West as well as the total modernization of its nuclear military forces and conventional weapon's platforms. The KGB Master murderer, Vladimir Putin of Russia has been bragging about hypersonic nuclear weapons. What Godless insane person would talk like that understanding the devastating power nuclear weapons capability—i.e., burning of human flesh with fire would say such evil! All of these things are occurring so that the battle of Armageddon can happen here on earth.

Jesus said there shall be wars and *rumors of wars* see that you are not troubled for all these things must come to pass but the end is not yet! (Matthew 24:6). Furthermore, the rapid ascendancy of the Chinese to an excellent military, economic, political powerhouse especially because of their incessant espionage and stealing industrial, classified, military, technological secrets from the West specifically the United States of America! Currently, they are now nudging the United States for world hegemony in terms of world influence enlarging their military footprint in Africa the Far East in Pakistan, the South China Sea and elsewhere. Someone please tell Trump the (The Great Wall of Chinas') construction around their wall was designed or built to keep the population **inside** the boundaries of China (Our Land) ***not* immigrants** out. Japan has increased expenditures into its military capability along the Pacific Basin. North Korea acting out with impunity at the world's condemnation whenever it launches a "rocket" from various platforms while simultaneously threatening to destroy the United States in an all-out war. All because a spoiled, wild boar masquerading despot little fat man, Kim Jung Un, who has insecurities especially the "Napoleonic Complex" while he seeks International recognition or attention by any means necessary including ruthlessly murdering anyone he wants too inside (and some outside including his own half-brother) North Korea including relatives of his own family with impunity.

The continued guerilla hit and run style of terrorist attacks throughout the world more recently in Brussels, Belgium, Paris,

France, across the Horn of Africa, etc., are accelerating with alarming intensity as well as frequency. We see the increasing continued mission creep in Syria slowly luring American military forces there, while the ongoing battle wages on endlessly via perennial wars that continue in Iraq and Afghanistan. Actually, all of the aforementioned events are partial derivatives of the transferred "war in heaven" to the "war on earth." The events read like the book of Revelation and other books of the word of God in contemporary terms when attempting to understand the approximation of the time the battle on earth between the forces of light and eternal darkness converge into all-out war on the earth.

However, these are not the only ones; the expansion now includes India and Pakistan into nuclear weapon owners as well as regions of Africa specifically the South African government. The Israelis who are my favorite people and God's too. Also, possess the "Goliath Option"—i.e., the nuclear bomb, in a vain attempt to keep it from terrorist or war from attacks by God's nemesis—i.e., all Muslim-Arabic pseudo caliphate nations that hate Israel. Iran is trying to enrich plutonium and uranium, to build centrifuges and other key ingredients to acquire this monstrosity Weapon of Mass Destruction. Iranians claims they want it for peaceful power of electricity when the entire world knows it has acquired the technology and now or will soon have nuke capabilities for militaristic conquering ambitions for the Middle East. Therefore, the question is... Approximately, when will the Anti-Christ revelation to the world happen, thereby culminating in the complete transfer of the *war from heaven* to *the war on earth* and the world's mass deception is complete via misleading counterfeit miracles, signs and wonders into debauchery unheard of or unseen since the dawn of humankind on earth?

Although no one—i.e. (human on earth) can say for sure without God's direct revelation, we can look at the current events to get a clue to "approximate" the period. Currently, the world and everyone in it knows that something has to give. All we need to do is look at the state or climate of hostility within our world. Given the current exponential explosion in the occurrence of dynamics worldwide—i.e., violence, hate, wars, regional conflicts, nationalism, populism, racism, cynicism, terrorism, racial superiority attacks, famines, murder, abortions, drought, crime, kidnapping, modern slavery, same sex marriages, decline in faith in the true God—i.e., global apostasy, wholesale genocide of people, drug and human trafficking, child pedophilia, pornography, etc. Now just think for one moment or for a second if you will about this situation. Jesus Christ referred to those of us who believe that he is the Son of God, as the salt of the earth. Scriptural support for this perspective is denoted here in **Matthew 5:13 that reads, "You are *the salt of the earth* but if the salt loses, its flavor how shall it be seasoned? It is then good for nothing but to be thrown out and trampled underfoot by men."** Now this entire point simply translated means that salt by its very nature is a "preservative" that keeps things from spoiling fast or rotting out before it is consumed especially when it comes to food products. The American Indians did not have refrigerators back in the days when they rode on the open range terrain in the vast landscape prior to colonial conquest of America their country.

The American Indians had no way to store, keep or preserve their uneaten kills and sometimes they couldn't travel far with small children due to enemy tribes and invading whites nearby with all of the buffalo, deer, elk, moose or other wild game they killed on the open ranges of this gigantic continent. Therefore, they would pour large volumes of salt into the carcass to "preserve" it until they had an opportunity to finish consuming whatever parts they had not eaten just yet. Analogously, Christ's reference to believers as the "salt of the earth" simply means while we are alive here we are "keeping" or preventing thus *preserving this world* albeit briefly from being hell on earth for ourselves and all others too. Even though we daily exhibit undesirable traits via our failures, sins, faults, problems, idiosyncrasies and imperfect lives habitually coming short of the glory of God Almighty. Yet imagine what this world would look like when all of the believers in Christ have been raptured out of the world. The existence on the earth of *all believers* as *salt is preserving the world* as we know it today even though it is deteriorating rapidly to greater levels of a decaying state. Otherwise, even though believers are imperfect we are the only thing that is *holding/preserving* this fragile world together from utter debauchery and madness and I guess one could argue that is not saying much. If you think it is bad now, baby you have not seen nothing yet!

One day my friend, it certainly will be worse and more horrible than you can ever imagine after the rapture. There will be **no believers** left behind. Tribulation saints will not be the salt of the earth because they are born again (i.e., accept Christ as Lord) during the reign of terror of the Antichrist. Simply put the judgment of God has already started and there existence is coincidental as it runs parallel to the advent of the revelation of Satan's son on earth. Therefore, it will be just a little while before they pop up on the radar screen of life during the End-Time showdown. Nonetheless, even when they do, Satan kills them for their testimony of Christ later during the actual tribulation period. **See Revelation 15:2 and Revelation 6:10–11** combined scriptures below that cites:

And I saw as it were a sea of glass as it were mingled with fire and them that had gotten the victory over the beast and over his image and over his mark and over the number of his name stand on the sea of glass having the harps of God. Revelation 6:9–10 denotes when he opened the fifth seal. I saw under the altar the souls of those who had been slain for the word of God and for the testimony which they held. And they cried with a loud voice saying how long O Lord holy and true until you judge and avenge our blood on those who dwell on the earth? Then a white robe was given to each of them and it was said to them that they should rest a little while longer until both the number of their fellow servants and their brethren who would be killed as they were was completed.

Note, these tribulation saints attain the victory over the evil one by sacrificing their lives as martyrs to Christ choosing rather to die than accept the eternal soul damming mark of the beast or the name of his number on their bodies. All of these events are setting the stage for the arrival and disclosure of the Man of the Hour, Lucifer in the flesh! A.k.a. The Antichrist. The devil's expulsion for the final time thrown out of the heavens completely to the earth where he will display his second act. This is the reason why the battlefield shifts to the earth. Satan started a war in heaven, expelled to the second heaven, continued fighting, accusing and attacking believers in Christ even to this day. He will be thrown out of the heavens for good as aforementioned and continue fighting on the earth. Satan's antichrist revelation will occur accompanied by a hypnotic, demonic inspired following by the entire world as they marvel after him. For he shall do mighty signs and wonders which will cause all to worship and adore him who have not been saved by the blood of the Lamb of God, Jesus Christ.

See **Revelation 13:8 that says and all that dwell on the earth shall worship him whose names <u>are not</u> written in the book of life of the Lamb slain from the foundation of the world**. Let us discover together the biblical evidence to support such strong assertions. The books of Timothy, Thessalonians and Revelation provide some clues that apply here. We will begin with the book of Timothy first. Simply because it contains a phrase that is critical to understanding biblical concepts and phrases that are initially opaquely vague. Let me show you what I mean by this statement. Turn your Bible to **1 Timothy 4:1** it reads here verbatim **"Now the Spirit expressly says that in _latter times_ some _will depart_ from the faith, giving heed to deceiving spirits and doctrines of demons, speaking lies in hypocrisy, having their own conscience seared with a hot iron."** This requires division or analysis to understand specifically the author's intention. So starting with the initial sentence whereby it says now the Spirit expressly says that. Now the Spirit refers to the "Spirit of God" or the "Holy Spirit" makes a specific declaration as he tells the author/minister, Timothy that in the "latter times." Latter times phrase directly refers to the time just prior to the revelation and

Second Advent or Return of Jesus Christ to the earth in two distinct phases one to rapture believers in him to himself and the second is to come to the earth and place his feet on the Mount of Olives to Judge the world. Here is additional inquiry or analysis demonstrating the perspective.

Eternal Time is divisible into three periods. These are past, present and future. Timothy was not referring to *his time—i.e., when he was alive.* The reason is that if he were there would be no need to say "latter times" because at the time of his writing, via inspiration of God's Holy Spirit, he would have said our time or present time then. In addition, he was not referring to *past time* for he would not need to state something that has already occurred. Common knowledge and historical awareness would simply be understandable. Furthermore, logical rationale would be self-explanatory unto the facts attributable to historical records of such an event alluded to by him through either storytelling or recitations referring to it or via documentable or factual observations. Finally, there is no need of prophesying about something that already occurred. For it is a matter of historical record if the event has already happened relating to its significance or its fulfillment. Prophesy relates to "future events" that are "<u>yet to happen</u>" not already occurred or past events or current ones for that matter. Simply put that is recitation.

Now, we can explore what the book of Thessalonians reveals about our current topic—i.e., the time *approximately* just before or around the return of Christ and an all-out war on earth between good and evil that started in God's Living Room. Look at **1 Thessalonians 5:1–3** the authors tell the Thessalonians and us that actually **there is no need that he writes to any of them regarding the times and seasons regarding the return of Christ to the earth. Simply because they already know that, the day of the Lord will come as a thief in the night.** *This means suddenly, surprisingly and unexpectedly.* **Paul, Silvanus and Timothy state that when "they" in the world who have rejected Christ as there Savior desire and proclaim "Peace and Safety" then sudden destruction will come upon them verse 3.** This will either be by declaring an armistice with the Antichrist or a global craving for Peace and safety because of the constant wars, death, worldwide terrorism and misery that will be heaped upon the world at a pace unseen or unparalleled in human history. All of this relates or connects to or arises due to the Antichrist's existence and revelation on earth—i.e., the devil incarnate. Remember, "the Anti-Christ" is the devil in human form! Here is biblical support located in **Revelation 13:2,** "*The dragon gave him his power, his throne and great authority.*" He has **no mercy for any human whatso-ever** especially those of the household of Jesus Christ. Furthermore, review **2 Thessalonians 2:1–2** whereby the ministers of God directs the believers in Christ in Thessalonica not to be confused, nor upset about the return or coming of the Lord Jesus Christ **as though it has already past** because he provides the biblical formula for Christ's return in the third and fourth verses of this book.—i.e., **2 Thessalonians 2:1–4** and **9**, which reads:

> *Now brethren concerning the coming of our Lord Jesus Christ and our gathering to together unto him. We ask you, not to be soon shaken in mind or troubled either by spirit or by word or by letter as if from us as though the day of Christ has come. Let no one deceive you by any means. For that Day will not come unless the falling away comes first and the man of sin be revealed 'the son of perdition.' Who opposes and exalts himself above all that is called God or that is worshipped, so that he sits as God, in the temple of God showing himself that he is God. Verse 9: the coming of the lawless one is according to the working of Satan with all power signs and lying wonders.*

Further analysis of the above-mentioned scriptural reference provides us with definitive information. It says in the first sentence that the authors'—i.e., Paul, Timothy and Silvanus, did not want us to be without information or ignorant regarding the coming of the Lord Jesus Christ and our gathering together to him. However, just as importantly they demand that the believers do not panic or become despondent regarding the news that Christ has already come. The authors warns the believers in Christ not to be deceived by any means neither by anyone because the day of Christ has to meet ***two specific criteria*** prior to his arrival here on earth. Specifically, the first condition that is to be met is that there must be a "falling away" or disbelief in his return and in the holy tenements of the word of God. This is an apostate attitude or I don't believe in the promises of God's word or of God's deliverance mentality anymore will be pervasive throughout the world but more **specifically among the professed believers** in Christ. The word of God says they will say things like where is the promise of his return since all things remain as they were for years yet there is no sign of his coming. Read **2 Peter 3:4, that says, "Knowing this _first_ that there shall come in the last days _scoffers_ walking after their own lusts and saying, where is the promise of his coming? For since, the fathers fell asleep all things continue as they were from the beginning of the creation."** This level of doubt, mocking, scoffing and ridicule as it grows and permeates throughout the body of Christ will cause many to be deceived as they agree with this evil attitude toward God and Our Savior the Lord Jesus Christ. Simply because they do not understand that God is intentionally *delaying or suspending,* the imminent return of Christ because he does not want any to be lost.

Review John 6:39, "Jesus said this is the will of the Father who sent me that all he has given me I _should lose nothing_ but raise it up at the last day!" Also, review **2 Peter 3:9, that says, "The Lord is not slack concerning his promise as some men count slackness, but is longsuffering to us-ward _not willing_ that _any should perish_ but that all should come to repentance."** The second condition **that must** be met before Christ Second Advent or return to the earth is that "**the Antichrist**" **mandatory revelation** to the whole world must occur, as he is *unmasked* with his true diabolical identity and purposes. Although there will be many antichrists there is only one true ANTICHRIST who is the epitome of the personification of Satan. See **1 John 2:18** that reads **it is the last time and as you have heard that antichrist shall come. Even now, there are many antichrists. Whereby we know that it is the last time. The revelation of the Antichrist is crucial to the Second Coming of Jesus Christ**. Here is some of the reasons why. Jesus Christ revelation as the Son of God unto the world with a ministry that lasted only three years. Christ crucifixion occurred for the sins of the world on the thirty-third anniversary of his divine birth in the womb of the Virgin Mary by the overshadowing power of the Holy Ghost upon her. Analogously, Christ revelation to the world was a *pivotal event* in the ongoing battle of good versus evil on the earth.

Therefore, the devil not willing to be outdone or overshadowed wants to replicate his own version of **revelation** in his counterfeit copying of God's activity. Satan desires or wants to replicate his own *godlike persona* through his demonic offspring, **the Son of Perdition**—i.e., **The Antichrist**. Obviously, the son of Satan is alive and well on planet earth awaiting his unholy revelation to the world. He will do sinister exploits, false miracles, e.g. causing fire descending from heaven, all kinds of witchcraft, wizardry, sorceries and demons entering into dead bodies providing false or *fake resurrections* or *zombies* on earth. Satan's son creates black magic with ease and unimaginable horror unseen by humans ever since the creation of the world. The Devil in the flesh is his true honor. He is the Evil King and High Priest of Darkness. Bar none. Remember the devil is a celestial being while we are terrestrial ones. Therefore, he has access to a cadre of mind-blowing capabilities and skills that he will display by a mere snapping of his fingers. Christ did miracles upon the earth. Therefore, Satan says to all demonic forces of darkness lets highlight our unique talents too. We are not going to be outdone on earth by God or his Son, Jesus Christ. Christ Jesus has a dual nature. Christ is both a _celestial_ (heavenly/spiritual) very divine Godhead member deity entity. Furthermore, Jesus through his physical holy birth via the womb of the Virgin Mary is also _terrestrial_ (earthly) being born in the flesh. Jesus said in **John 4:24**, "**God is a Spirit and those who worship him must do so in spirit and in truth**." Recall this is the final battle or Satan's Last Stand as he opposes God from a descended war that he initiated in God's Living Room in the third heaven that is now in its terminal phase.

However, there is additional scriptural support as aforementioned, that connects or is a nexus regarding our quest in the book of Revelation. This concerns our current topic occurring *approximately just* before or around the return of Christ and an all-out war on earth between God and Satan. John the Revelator, who God granted "limited exposure" to see the vision from Christ, describes the Great Supper of God for all the carnivorous birds or fowls of the sky. They have an invitation from God himself to eat the carcasses of those whom God assembled as combatants and warriors to the Battle against Christ. Therefore, I cite **Revelation 19:17–19** to support this assertion here, which says, **"Then I saw an angel standing in the sun. And he cried with a loud voice saying to all the birds that fly in the midst of heaven. Come and gather together for the supper of the great God that you may eat the flesh of Kings, the flesh of captains, the flesh of mighty men. The flesh of horses and of those who sit on them and the flesh of all people free and slave both small and great. And I saw the beast, the kings of the earth and their armies gathered together to <u>make war against him</u> who sat on the horse <u>and against his army</u>."** However, before proceeding further into our spiritual journey to understand how, why, when and who started all wars in heaven above and earth below. I want all readers to see another *significant point* just illustrated in the last sentence. Which simply is the devil has **deceived** <u>the whole world</u> to fight against Christ and his holy legion of angels and believers in "Satan's Last Stand" on earth before eternal judgment's sentence imposition upon him! The war that Lucifer started in God's Living Room in the third heaven has now transferred via descent to the earth of the first heaven as it has all the armies of the world assembling to fight against **Jesus Christ the Lord! Oh my God!**

The devil has actually convinced, deceived, cajoled and brainwashed them into thinking albeit it foolishly that they can win against Christ. It is not only fool hearty or asinine to fight against Michael the Archangel. It is also futile all to no avail. However, glory be to God in the highest heaven; it is utterly suicidal or another thing altogether that reflects a monumental depravity of reasoning, extreme oxygen deprivation to the cranium and utter cataclysmic dissolution of the frontal lobe of the cerebral cortex to try to fight against Jesus Christ the Son of God. This desperate act results in a colossal degeneration of blood flow to both left and right brain hemispheres of all organic matter of the Dura Mater material of the brain matter interrelated to the mind. Baby, it is a whole another ball game trying to **fight against the Son of Almighty God, Christ Jesus Our Lord!** Years ago, as a matter of fact, in 1927, African-American Civil Rights activist, James Weldon Johnson, wrote a book of sermons entitled "Gods Trombones," in one of his sermons he said "Your arms are too short to box with God! I think that these specific words of Mr. JWJ sermon is applicable to these nimrods trying to fight against Christ! No wonder they will be on the bird's menu for dinner. Either way the outcome is disastrous without any doubt. This is astonishing and tragic news for all of them because the outcome is already determined. See the conclusions at **Revelation 19:20–21** that reads, **"Then the beast was captured and with him the false prophet who worked signs in his presence by which he deceived those who received the mark of the beast. And those who worshipped his image these two were <u>cast alive</u> into the <u>lake of fire burning</u> with brimstone and the <u>rest were killed with the sword which proceeded from the mouth of him </u>who sat on the horse and _<u>all the birds were filled with their flesh</u>_."**

Consequently, predicated upon these inclusive illustrations you can now see that the "war in heaven" (God's Living Room) has been completely transferrable to the War on Earth. Its evolution from the diabolical mind of Lucifer. All the way down to the misguided incantations of the likes of Adolf Hitler, Attila the Hun, Julius Caesar, Nero, Charlemagne, Cleopatra, Alexander the Great, Shaka Zulu, Idi Amin Dada, Genghis Khan, Pol Pot the infamous death baton drum major of the heinous Khmer Rouge murderers in the killing fields bordering Cambodia, Laos and Thailand. Saddam Hussein and others, Just to name a few murderous villains of antiquity and the present day.

Interestingly, where does this leave humankind in general and specifically believers who accept the mercy of God via Jesus Christ atoning death for their sins both during these horrendous events to come on earth and eternally specifically? Let us review the scriptures for details outlying the events for both groups of persons with more details to explain the situation regarding their eternal destiny according to the word of God.

First, we will look at the good news then the bad news as it were. I will start this chapter by displaying God's reaction to the wickedness of man originally in the Garden of Eden then forward toward the climax of prophetic events. God expelled or kicked Adam and Eve out of the Paradise of God for their rebellion. God did so because of three primary factors from my perspective. Primarily, because his holy nature and his righteousness requires that *no sin* be near him period. Secondly, he wanted man to understand that there is a consequence for willful disobedience to his holy authority. Finally, there existed precedence already for God's action. God had already expelled Lucifer and his evil angel cohorts or mental minions from heaven for their sin. Therefore, God simply continued with this theme of expulsion from his presence when addressing consequences for sin/rebellion against him even though this time it was Adam and Eve. God sovereignly concluded that the two of them—i.e., Adam and Eve were no different in that sense. Although God loves man, he could not ignore his outright rebellion because he loved him and just say oh it is no big deal, Adam and Eve just had a bad day so I will wink at their sin and disobedience to me. God's holy persona demands that all who approach him be and remain holy at all times. No exceptions! Furthermore, we see a major shift in God's reaction to worldwide rebellion during the Noahic Flood whereby man's evil became so outrageous that God made a decision to eliminate _all life forms_ that he created in the Old Testament because of the wickedness of man.

See **Genesis 6:7** listed here, **"So the Lord said _I will destroy man_ whom I have created from the face of the earth, both man and beasts creeping thing and birds of the air for I am sorry that I made them."** However, God because of his love for man makes a way for man's salvation or atonement through the substitutionary deliverance through Christ Our Lord despite our collective wickedness. For me personally, the worst scriptures I have ever read is located in **Genesis 6:6–7** verses **whereby God declares that he is "<u>sorry</u>" that he made man because the thoughts of his heart is evil continually**. After this, I think the next sad scripture with an eternal positive consequence is the crucifixion of Christ for our sins. It is horrendous to read the accounts in the gospels how Christ suffered at Calvary for all of us. However, I Thank God for Jesus Christ! For without Christ willing to suffer and lay down his life for our sins we would have no chance at all to see God's holy face. Yet alone receiving salvation from The Lord God of Hosts divine judgment against all sin by both man and angels. Bible proof exhibited in Jesus words in **Matthew 26:38–39.** I have listed here. **"Then he said to them my soul is exceeding sorrowful even to death. Stay here and watch with me. He went a little farther, fell on his face, and prayed. Saying my Father. <u>If it is possible</u>, let this cup pass from me, nevertheless not as I will but as you will."**

Apparently, we all now know that God's answer was it is not possible for there was and there is no other way for fallen humanity's redemption, or salvation, from eternal destruction and not suffer the same eternal fate as Lucifer and his fallen angels if you will not die for them. This is the paramount reason there is no other way for salvation through any other than Jesus Christ Our Lord and Savior. Next, we focus on what happens to believers during this time referred to as "Jacobs's Trouble" this is good news for all those who believe that Jesus Christ is Lord. Afterward, as promised, I will deliver the bad news as it was.

CHAPTER X

Rapture

God has a plan (good news) to redeem his people from the earth *prior* to the all-out war between Satan, the devil in the flesh (The Antichrist), his False Prophet and the Beast along with his unholy angels and with mankind armies aligning themselves with Satan against Christ and his armies in heaven here on earth. If readers (who are believers in Christ) will recall God has done the same feat before in history—i.e., saving those who have put their faith, hope and trust in his divine deliverance. For those who may not be believers yet in Christ let me provide some biblically based examples for you to digest as you consider making the eternal choice regarding the salvation of your soul. Here are just a couple of well-known examples that most of us already know (new converts or those sitting on the fence can review) that can shed some illustration of God's handiwork to rescue believers in him. God flooded the entire world by water for forty days and forty nights because man's sin was so rampant. Yet, **_he saved_** Noah and his entire family including daughters in laws. Don't tell me it's not important whom you marry because here is an example involving these three women for marrying into the right family per se. Obviously they were unrelated to each other until they married into Noah's family uniting in holy matrimony to Noah's three sons which resulted in saving their lives.

See **Genesis 6:7–8 and v11** that says, "**So the Lord said I will destroy man whom I have created from the face of the earth both** man and beast, creeping things and birds of the air for I am sorry that I made them. However, Noah found grace in the eyes of the Lord v 11, the earth was also corrupt before God and the earth was filled with violence." Naturally, we all know that globally all died *except the people and animals inside of Noah's Ark*. Another glowing event in the OT occurred as the Egyptian Army pursued the children of Israel as they fled Egypt after four hundred years of slavery. They had to cross the mighty Red Sea Basin over to safety. However, this sea blocked their path to freedom. For it was too deep for the carriages, mules, and people, including those with women and children who were fleeing for their very lives, running away from Pharaoh and his formidable army who were determined to kill all of them. The vast and mighty sea was in front of them and the enslavers armed with weapons were behind them. They were sandwiched within a dire strait, not knowing which evil would be worse of the two, that is dying by the stampeding horses, chariots, or being impaled by lances, spears, daggers and swords of the Egyptians.

Comparatively, versus drowning having their lungs overfilled to capacity as they choked beneath the waves of the mighty, swift moving currents in the depths of the Red Sea. Naturally, as they feared what was about to happen unto them. **God delivered them from a certain obliteration** by having Moses stretch out his arms over the depths and the waters of the Red Sea. See **Exodus 14:21–22** that reads; **Then Moses stretched out his hand over the sea and the Lord caused the sea to go back by a strong east wind all that night and made the sea into dry land and the waters were divided. So the children of Israel went into the midst of the sea on dry ground and the waters were a wall to them on their right hand and on their left.** Afterward, God had Moses stretch out his hand back over the sea to begin causing the sea to be as it was before. Subsequently, when the Egyptian army tried following them upon the dry ground, God killed them by allowing the water to return to its original posture. Now, there are some skeptics, or maybe even a believer, or two. Whom may say something similar, or along the lines (musing internally) that saving eight souls in an Ark is one thing and killing Pharaoh's army are peanuts compared to the mighty task set before the Lord, which is to save millions of believers worldwide simultaneously during this period. Really, you think. God asks Abraham the Father of all Nations in **Genesis 18:4**, **"Is there anything too hard for me?"** God told Jeremiah, the weeping prophet, the formula how to get impossible tasks for man but not God completed or resolutions to difficult dilemmas in **Jeremiah 33:3**.

Whereby God tells Jeremiah, **"Call unto me and I will answer you and show <u>you great and</u> <u>mighty things</u>, which you do not know."** Jeremiah concludes in **Jeremiah 32:17** the following as he says to the Lord in prayer; **Ah Lord God you have made the heaven and the earth by your great power and stretched out arm and <u>there is nothing too hard for you</u>**! Jesus Christ in **Matthew 19:26** positively states **"that with man this is impossible but <u>with God all things are possible</u>."** Therefore, now that we know that *nothing is impossible* with God since **everything is possible with God**, the question juxtaposed in a different format. Essentially, something along the lines of how will God accomplish this monumental feat for millions of believers in Christ worldwide simultaneously some of whom have actually already passed (died) in Christ and those whom are alive at the time of his Second Coming? I am glad that this may be an hypothetical question posed by anyone who has doubts, concerns or may not be quite sure if there is even a plan of deliverance like we saw in the earlier two examples. Therefore, I will answer this hypothetical, highly probable or more likely than not question directly from the word of God. God's escape plan for his people is ordered in **Revelation 18:4,** which says, **"Come out of her my people,"** **unless you share in her sins and her plaques**." God is commanding his people to come out of the world so that his retribution upon all evil can commence in earnest. The Almighty God's methodology to do this is by what's known in Christendom as the rapture. However, the first question one may have prior to examining this situation is; what does the term Rapture mean in terms of applicability and has it ever occurred before in the word of God? The English word rapture isn't necessarily spelled out in God's word per se. The word rapture actually comes from the Latin verb word rapio which means, "To catch up" or be "taken away." However, its occurrence has actually happened on more than one occasion within the context of God's word in both the OT and NT.

Additionally, **1 Thessalonians 5:9** provides another perspective it says **"For God has not appointed us (believers in Christ) to wrath, but to obtain salvation (deliverance) by our Lord Jesus Christ."** Clearly God will not sit idly by while this horrendous, evil angel inspired war is going on neither will he allow his people to suffer through this violent upheaval or war on earth. God will be proactive by removing his people away from this war supernaturally, via rapturing—i.e., snatching away! Some other reasons for this snatching away suddenly of believers both deceased and alive are located in the word of the Lord that tells us more about this in various books of the Bible. Here, I direct our attention or search to see this interesting phenomenon in detail. First, let us recall what the term rapture actual meaning is afterward, we will review the scriptures for any previous occurrences as an example of God's power or ability to remove his people from disaster. Although there are several variations to this terminology biblically when pastors, ministers or believers in Christ refer to this term. They are referring to the actual, sudden, whisking away of believers physically from earth to heaven or into Christ's immediate presence. My, my, my! Just think about it for a second within a twinkling of an eye, it does not matter what the person is doing. One second they are on the earth and the next second they are in the eternal presence of the Son of God forever!

Jesus mentioned it when he said, "There shall be two in the field, one shall be taken and the other shall be left" (Matthew 24:40). However, one may rationally ask, did this ever occur in the Old Testament era? The answer unto this question is yes it certainly did! Let me set up the background story for you to review at your own leisure. Enoch was the son of Cain who actually murdered his brother Abel. However, Enoch pleased God immensely. Wow, that is a contradiction, that a man who would murder his own brother had a son who so pleased God Almighty that God acted immediately upon his behalf. Enoch did please God so well, that *God snatched him* away after allowing Enoch to live 365 years prior to this event. Actually, he so pleased God in his daily living that God raptured (took) him right out of the earth into heaven! Enoch's rapture is recorded in **Genesis 5:24: And Enoch walked with God and he was not for "God took" him**. Our Georgian calendar has 365 days to mark a year. I surmise that God honored Enoch again by the universal use of this calendar in modern times—i.e., for each year of Enoch's life; **Genesis 5:23** tells us how old Enoch lived on earth before he was snatched away by the Lord. It **says all the days of Enoch <u>were three hundred and sixty-five years.</u>**

It is my humble opinion that God allows one day in each year for a total of 365 days to celebrate if you will or to honor the righteous servant of his by marking it on the calendar of each year. Western civilization specifically uses the Georgian calendar whose total for the year is 365 days. This to me is more than a mere coincidence it is the divine hand of God at work. However, every person is free or can decide for his or her self what this actually means. I respect your opinion if you so disagree. Paul, the Apostle, tells us that (the rapture) is a mystery and that it **<u>will occur</u>** *within a **<u>twinkling of an eye at the last trumpet</u>**! Here is the specific biblical reference located in **1 Corinthians 15:51–52** vs whereby **Paul says, "Behold I show you a mystery we shall not all sleep (die) but we shall all be changed, in a moment in "a twinkling of an eye" at the last trump, for the trumpet shall sound. For the trumpet will sound and the dead will be raised incorruptible and we shall be changed."**

Nevertheless, there is another example of this occurring in the Old Testament as well. There was a prophet named Elijah who had an understudy named Elisha. Elisha was a precocious person as most youth are and he wanted to understand how God performed miracles via Elijah on earth. Actually, Elisha wanted a "double portion" of the blessing of God to be granted unto him when asked by Elijah what did he want from him. Since God had told Elijah that he was taking Elijah to heaven as recorded in **2 Kings 2:9.** The entire narrative surrounding *Elijah's snatching away or rapture* is located in **2 Kings 2:1–11**. God took Elijah into heaven as Elisha helplessly watched in earnest. The actual scriptural reference is **2 Kings 2:11** as it says: **and it came to pass as they went on and talked that behold there appeared a chariot of fire and horses of fire and parted them both** asunder and <u>Elijah went up by a whirlwind into heaven</u>. My Lord, the power of the Mighty God of Jacob! The point in all of this is to display that God is able to supernaturally, take persons directly from earth to heaven. The rapture is God Almighty's *elevator* if you will from the first floor of earth's heaven directly unto the third floor of God's heavenly kingdom! Logically, he can reverse the direction if he so desired but that is a story for another day. Nevertheless, here is a quick example of God doing so. God literally does this in the reverse (not quite so with rapture) in his expulsion of Lucifer from God's Living Room. Lucifer goes from third floor of heaven down to the first floor of the earth via the *elevator express* to hell. I am referring unto the direction only. Naturally, Satan's expulsion from heaven occurred by force by the Archangel Michael and his angels.

The point is clear here. God says goodbye Satan. Go to earth, then to hell imprisonment itself for all eternity since you are so unhappy here in heaven. Lucifer's descent to the earth after his eviction and banishment from God's Living Room forever is actually unbelievable mystique wise. What in the world was Satan thinking. However, it is analogous to Adam and Eve who like Satan were inside of paradise rebelled then expelled for their evil conduct. Summarily, to this point, I have provided the readers with examples of this occurrence in the Old Testament. However, a logical question by a skeptic could simply be; are there any examples in the New Testament? Well not surprisingly, of course there is a prophetic (yet to occur) event denoted here. Look inside the book of Revelation specifically for one account. Specifically the eleventh chapter of the book of Revelation deals with God's two witnesses spreading the gospel to the world during the Great Tribulation Period. I (along with some other believers) theorize that these "*two witnesses*" will be Enoch and Elijah for they are the only two people who **never died** from OT times. I will discuss this subject in more detail following this narrative along with my support for the theory that they are the two witnesses. Naturally, only God knows for certainty whom they are. Worldwide people receive persecution, arrests, trials and unspeakable horror by the evil tyranny of the Antichrist (Lucifer in the Flesh) and his cohorts—i.e., The False Prophet and The Beast. Death is by beheading which is the only option for anyone who refuses to accept the mark of the beast or the name of his number—i.e., 666.

Subsequently, these final two witnesses sent from God from heaven are spreading the gospel unto the entire world and have the power to kill any who would hurt, harm or injure them by fire coming out of their mouth and burning their attackers to death into little cinders. God's Mandatory death methodology in this manner is prescribed or to be carried out specifically this way. See **Revelation 11:5** for it reads as follows; **and if anyone wants to harm them "fire proceeds from their mouth" and <u>devours their enemies</u> and if anyone wants to harm them, <u>he must be killed</u> in this manner. God's orders!** Eventually, these two witnesses from God are killed by the demonic, angelic, King of the bottomless pit Abaddon/Apollyon. See **Revelation 9:11** as it reads, **"And they had a king over them. The angel of the bottomless pit whose name in Hebrew is Abaddon but in Greek he has the name Apollyon" and Revelation 11:7** that says **"When they finish their testimony** (God's two witnesses) **the beast that ascends out of the bottomless pit (Abaddon/Apollyon) will make war against them, overcome them and kill them."** This evil angel, called Abaddon in Hebrew or Apollyon in Greek, is only the fourth angelic creature ever identified by name in the King James Version of the Bible. This is the Bible used by Protestant believers (the others are Michael, Gabriel and Lucifer/Satan as previously noted) whose description as arising out of the bottomless pit, with his other demonic angels whom are vividly and frighteningly described.

This description as follows **having crowns of gold on their heads, locusts like horses prepared for battle, the faces of men with the hair of women, with breastplates of iron, locusts with scorpion like stingers to torment men for five months** according to **Revelation 9:7–11**. Afterward, these grotesque, locust like creatures will attack the two witnesses of God after they finish their mission of worldwide evangelism warning about the judgment of God, the kingdom of Christ, etc. The entire **ninth chapter of Revelation** describes these dreadful creatures from Hades. Furthermore, the citizens of the earth celebrate the death of God's two witnesses, refuse to bury them in a grave and allow their bodies to sit openly on the ground for all to see because of the constant torment of their ministry. Additionally, to show their gratitude for the death of these two Godly witnesses they give gifts to each other celebrating the death of these two men. Yet, **three and a half days later, the Spirit of Life from God enters into their bodies as they stood upon their feet. And great fear fell on those who saw them.** See **Revelation 11:11** Now watch what happens next in **verse 12**: "*It reads and they heard a great voice from heaven, saying to them 'come up here' and they ascended up to heaven in a cloud and their enemies watched them*" *(italics mine).*

This is clearly an example of **the rapture or snatching away** of their physical bodies from the earth directly into heaven. Afterward, the plagues of God began to occur upon all those whom are here on the earth during what's known as the Great Tribulation Period with unbelievable magnitude of devastation, misery and human suffering. The word of God informs us all that the power of punishment from God will be so overwhelming that men will seek death and it will flee from them. Review **Revelation 8:6** that says, **"In those days' men will seek death and will not find it, they will desire to die and death will flee from them."**

The most prominent time this occurred not only in the NT but in the entire word of God Almighty is when Jesus Christ the Son of God was raptured out of the earth! Most believers and ministers today omit this fact or are simply unaware that Christ was raptured out of the earth. Jesus did both he <u>resurrected first</u> from the dead {Matthew 28:6, Mark 16:6,14–19, Luke 24:1–5, John 20:3–17} then he <u>was raptured</u> Acts 1:9–11 out of the earth via <u>his ascension</u> directly into heaven where he is seated at the right hand of God. This is the most powerful example in the entire word of God regarding or relating to this mysteri-

ous phenomenon. Jesus Christ, Enoch, Elijah and the two witnesses of God along with all believers in Christ at the (time of his return) will share this exact same experience—i.e., they will be raptured or snatched away directly into heaven. Elevator going up anyone? I am old enough that I remember the time as a little boy you had to tell the elevator operator which floor you wanted to arrive at or be let off on upon entrance onto the elevator on the mezzanine floor... Well I will request the third floor of heaven. However, this time Christ is the Elevator Operator and only he will decide which floor anyone exits! Problem my friends there are only two floors heaven or hell.

Another major reason the rapture will occur simultaneously for all believers is directly relatable to the Holy Spirit of Jesus Christ, a.k.a. the Holy Ghost, the Spirit of Life, the Spirit of God, etc., is because he currently indwells, lives within or embodies all persons who like myself believe that Jesus Christ is the Son of God. A quick overview of how the Godhead operated in various times in various ways will provide us with a more detailed analysis of the ministry of the Holy Spirit. Remember the Godhead is composed of three eternally existent different deities uniquely, forever related via Divine holiness unto the Lord Our God. These are; God the Father, Jehovah-Yahweh, God the Son, Jesus Christ and God the Holy Spirit. All three work divinely together with each member of the Holy Trinity. However, occasionally each member of the Divine Godhead primarily at various times ministers as the prominent Holy Personage working as mentioned independently, yet united. Carrying out divine acts to save man during various times in the evolutionary pilgrimage of man here on earth. God (Father, Son, and Holy Ghost) herein after referred to as **FSH** my new phrase or moniker for Our God does this during humanity's quest to find God.

Rather more aptly stated, by "keeping it real"—i.e., to tell the truth, to say God trying to find, save, rescue and to help lost humankind. Let me tell you what I mean by this. During the Old Testament Times, we see the ministry as well as actions by God the Father in the OT period. He walked with Adam in the Garden of Eden. **Genesis 3:8** God the Father, was the invisible helmsman, that steered Noah's Ark as Noah and his family were navigating upon the rapidly rising floodwaters that continually deluged the earth for forty days and forty nights with rain that killed **_every living_** creature other than those inside of the Ark. **Genesis 7:17–23.** The Father displayed himself in the burning bush to Moses on Mount Sinai. **Exodus 3:2–6.** God the Father displayed his mighty acts in Egypt to force Pharaoh to let his people go. **Exodus 10, 11, and 12.** He drowned Pharaoh's entire army, chariot riders, equestrians and horses as they pursued the children of Israel into the Red Sea (symbolism) for blood of Christ. **Exodus 14:24–30.** God the Father gave Moses the 10 commandments on tables of stone atop Mount Sinai (**Exodus 34:4).** God the Father fed the children of Israel 40 years in the desert as they wandered around on an approximately 500-mile trip until that unbelieving generation died out. **Deuteronomy 29:5 and Judges 2:10.** God the Father delivered King David when he, as a youth fought against an adult man who just so happened to be a giant named Goliath (**1 Samuel 17:49–51).** God the Father fed Elijah via ravens as he fled from Jezebel (**1 Kings 17:6).**

These are just a few of the miraculous acts of the Holy Father of Heaven on prominent display in the OT era. Now, I shift the trajectory to the Ministry of the God the Son or Son of God, Jesus Christ actions in the NT epoch. Some of the miracles of Christ where he turned water into wine at the marriage feast (**John 2:1–10).** Jesus Christ walked on water displaying his power over the elements, nature, gravity, etc. (**Matthew 14:22–33).** Jesus calmed the stormy seas after his disciples awakened him for fear they would drown (**Mark 4:35–41).** Jesus healed the ten lepers, the lunatic and the blind (**Luke 17:11–19, Matthew 12:25–28, John 9:1–12).** Jesus Christ resurrected Lazarus from the dead (**John 11:38–44).** Jesus caused the lame man who sat by the pool of Siloam for years to take up his bed and walk (**Luke 5:17–26**). Jesus Christ released the legion of demons inside of the man who cried out in the cemetery for years (**Luke 8:30–33**). Jesus returned Jairus, the Centurion's daughter from death back to life with only himself, Peter, John, James and the Centurion within the room with him when this miracle occurred (**Mark 5:22–43**).

Finally, the Son of God, Christ Jesus voluntarily hung on a wooden cross for the sins of the whole world! (**Matthew 27:32–56**). This fact or feat denoted in all four gospels; **Luke, Mark and John** are the other three places where this is discoverable. Remember Christ said **in John 10:18, no one takes my life from me I lay it down to do the will of my Father who sent me to save that which was lost**. Currently, during the present day era (our lifetime) which is the post New Testament era or the after-testament period of time that we are living in now. Unequivocally, we see the divine ministry of the Holy Spirit of God especially to all of us who believe that Christ is Lord. The Holy Spirit raised Jesus from the dead after he laid in the tomb of Joseph of Arimathea for three days (**Mark 16:9**). However, before I continue outlining some of the work attributed to Holy Spirit of God's ministry in the world, I would like to take this opportunity to mention a very imperative aspect for all of us to consider or keep in mind as we interact with the Spirit of God.

Specifically, we must remember as a precautionary warning, for all of us to understand. That he (The Holy Spirit) is the most _sensitive member_ of the Divine Holy Trinity of FSH—i.e., Father, Son and Holy Ghost. We through our sins can quench or grieve him directly by our actions, words and imaginations. Remember or be informed that Jesus stated whosoever blasphemes or continually resists the convicting power of the Holy Spirit or speaks evil of anything against him is in danger of committing the **unpardonable sin**. Which leads to eternal hellfire. Jesus said **all sin spoken against me and or my Father is forgivable**, but he who **does insult** to the Spirit of Grace **is unforgiven** in _this world_ or in the _world_ **to come**! Christ exact words cited in this specific scripture in **Matthew 12:31, "Therefore, I say unto you, every sin and blasphemy will be forgiven men, but the blasphemy against the Spirit will not be forgiven men.**

Anyone who speaks a word against the Son of Man it will be forgiven him but whoever speaks against the Holy Spirit, <u>it will not be forgiven</u> him either <u>in this age or in the age to come</u>." This means not only during one's lifetime but also for all eternity. Now, continuing with identifying the ministry of the Holy Spirit acting as the primary member of the Holy Trinity in our realm of life—i.e., the natural world during this contemporary epoch. The Holy Spirit overshadowed the womb of The Virgin Mary to "fertilize" the egg inside her womb to ensure the total or complete encapsulation of the holy integrity of Christ's birth (**Luke 1:35**). This cemented his holy nature forever without the donation of any man's contribution **validating** that Christ **remained Holy from birth till death** (which is ***the holy nature he always had*** with his Father in heaven) before agreeing to come to the earth in the form of a man (flesh) to save fallen man. See **Hebrews 2:14 that reads, "Forasmuch then as the children** (believers in Christ) **are partakers of flesh and blood (human) he himself (Jesus) likewise took part of the same that through death he might destroy him that had the power of death that is the devil."**

This is extremely significant! **<u>Christ was not conceived by a man</u>** as is the normal process of the childbirth between men and women or male and female of any species. Therefore, Christ **did not** have, possess or could not exhibit **any traces** of the fallen sinful DNA nature and the lusts thereof of humankind. **Jesus was, is and will forever be Holy as he reigns with his Father in Heaven!** The Holy Spirit is he who teaches us all things of Christ so that we can understand them to apply them practically in our daily lives. See **1 John 2:27** that says, **"But the anointing which you have received from him which abides in you and you do not need that anyone teach you but as the same anointing teaches you concerning all things and is true and is not a lie and just as it has taught you will abide in him."** Logically, we should know, that all three—i.e., **FSH** are working together in *divine synchronization* to affect the will of God the Father on earth as it is done in heaven. The Holy Spirit intercedes via prayer on our behalf through words that cannot be spoken. See **Romans 8:25** that states, **"Likewise the Spirit also** helps our infirmities for we know not what we should pray for as we ought but the Spirit itself makes intercession for us with groaning <u>which cannot be uttered</u>. The Holy Spirit of God raised Jesus from the dead!" (Acts 1:1–2 and 9). The Holy Spirit of Christ sent angels to release Peter from prison after the death of Christ so that he could strengthen those followers and others to whom Peter was sent to preach the gospel (**Acts 12:7**).

The Holy Spirit of Christ warns us to guard our garments (keep our faith genuinely) so that the world will not see our nakedness or shame via hypocrisy or a sinful lifestyle (living in sin openly) while proclaiming faith in God (**Colossians 1:10**). The Holy Spirit gives us courage to speak the truth of God openly in the face of death threats, peril and dangers. **Matthew 10:19** and **Acts 4:13**. The Holy Spirit comforts us in times of danger, anxiety or restlessness. Jesus said, "**If I don't leave, the (Comforter) Holy Spirit will not come**" (**John 16:7–13**). The Holy Spirit after the death of Christ began the apostles' ministry by appearing as cloven tongues on the mouths of those who believed at Pentecost in the upper room (**Acts 2:1–12** and **Acts 11:15**). The Holy Spirit guided Paul to his ministry after his conversion to Christianity throughout the realms of Thessaly, Corinth, Asia Minor, Galatia and Ephesus (**Acts 9:1–31**).

The Holy Spirit provided us with all of the authors of the books of Acts forward culminating with the Book of Revelation. The Holy Spirit is the Guardian of the Holy scriptures for the word of God says that **all scripture is given by *inspiration of God* and is profitable for doctrine, for reproof, for correction for instruction in righteousness that the man of God may be complete thoroughly equipped for every good work (2 Timothy 3:16–17)**. The Holy Spirit descended in the bodily shape of a dove to fly directly from heaven to land upon the shoulder of Jesus Christ to signify or proclaim that Jesus is the Son of God to the world (**Luke 3:22**). **The Holy Spirit restrains the revelation of the Antichrist until he is taken out of the way! (2 Thessalonians 2:7)**. Thus, we have seen how the divine trinity of Almighty God works independently yet united. Christ said **my Father and I are one**. Now let me revert to the rapture just to emphasize some vital points. Remember Paul tells us something very interesting regarding the resurrection of believers who have already died, thereby mentioning the rapture of all believers in Christ even those who will be alive when Christ returns and The Antichrist set loose on the earth to wreak havoc unparalleled in human history. We will look at this now together. I will start with **1 Thessalonians 4:13–17** Paul says,

> *But I do not want you to be ignorant, brethren, concerning those who have fallen asleep, lest you sorrow as others who have no hope. For if, we believe that Jesus died and rose again, even so, God will bring with him those who sleep in Jesus. For this, we say to you by the word of the Lord, that we, who are alive and remain until the coming of the Lord, will by no means precede those who are asleep. For the Lord himself shall descend from heaven with a shout. With the voice of an archangel and with the trumpet of God and the dead in Christ shall rise first. Then we who are alive and remain shall be **caught up together** with them in the clouds to meet the **Lord in the air** and thus we shall always be with the Lord!*

Finally, this is how the rapture will be possible for all believers around the world. OH My Lord this is extremely powerful and inspiring! Paul tells us that we will be caught up (raptured) to meet the Lord in the air. What a welcome! If you are down this should pick you right up without fail instantly! No pun intended. Conclusively, we can see how God Almighty will accomplish saving or removing all believers in Christ simultaneously from the earth prior to the onslaught of evil that will distress the entire globe. Now, let us see what Paul says regarding The Antichrist, is where the rubber will meet the road to cement the premise of rapturing or snatching away or caught up whichever terminology, you want to apply here. We will not have to venture far way through our Bible to find it. Let us look at **2 Thessalonians 2:1–12** Paul declares,

---

Now brethren concerning the coming of our Lord Jesus Christ and our gathering together to him. We ask you not to be soon shaken in mind or troubled either by spirit or by word or by letter as if from us as though the day of Christ has come. Let no one deceive you by any means, for that day will not come <u>unless the falling away comes first and the man of sin is revealed</u>, the son of perdition, who opposes and exalts himself above all that is called God or that is worshipped. So that he sits in the temple of God showing himself that he is God do, you remember that I told you these things. And now you <u>know what is restraining that he may be revealed in his own time</u>. For the mystery of lawlessness is already at work <u>only he who now restrains will do so until he is taken out of the way and then the lawless one will be revealed who the Lord</u> will consume with the breath of his mouth and destroy with the brightness of his coming. The coming of the lawless one is according to the working of Satan with all power, signs and lying wonders and with all unrighteousness. Deception among those who perish because they did not receive the love of the truth that they might be saved and for this reason, God will send them strong delusion that they should believe a lie that they all may be condemned who did not believe the truth but had pleasure in unrighteousness.

Clearly, Paul is telling us that the only thing that is holding back or restraining the revelation to the world whom the Antichrist is or his actual identity is **because the Holy Spirit of God presence is still on earth embodied inside each believer in Christ Jesus as Lord**. The Holy Spirits' continued presence on earth is delaying or preventing the Antichrists' identity or revelation to the world. Paul explains the actual reason why this is occurring in this scriptural passage as well. The Apostle Paul tells us that the "mystery of lawlessness" is already at work. Furthermore, that God will send non-believers *a strong delusion* so that they *will believe the lie* and be condemned together with the evil one because they <u>did not love the truth</u> that could have saved them. Nevertheless, there is more to be discovered in another book of the word of God. It can be found in the book of **Romans 8:11** verse *that states, "But if 'the spirit of him who raised Jesus from the dead 'dwells in you' he who raised Christ from the dead will also give life to your mortal bodies through 'his Spirit who dwells in you!"* However, there is even more saints of the Most High God and all others who may be reading this book. Review **2 Corinthians 1:21–22** which reads **now he who <u>establishes us</u> with you in Christ and has "anointed us" is God who has <u>sealed us</u> and given us "the Spirit" in our hearts <u>as a guarantee</u>!** This is the crux of the matter! Now that all believers have been "sealed" with the *"Holy Spirit in our hearts"* as a guarantee. When the Holy Spirit is removed and taken out of the way (returns back to heaven) as did Christ on his ascension/rapture to the Godhead in heaven. Everywhere the Holy Spirit is indwelling, residing, occupying simultaneously (embodied inside of believers in Christ) which we read earlier elsewhere, will be removed or snatched away to heaven also. Believers in Christ have this hope, of our collective whisking or snatching away, since he *<u>is in our hearts as a guarantee via our sealing and</u>* anointing by God of his divine presence.

Therefore, all of us will be snatched away within an instant within a **twinkling of an eye** according to Paul in **1 Corinthians 15:51–52** listed here, **"Behold I tell you a mystery we shall not all sleep, but we shall all be changed in a moment, in the twinkling of an eye, at the last trumpet. For the trumpet will sound and the** dead will be raised incorruptible and we shall be changed." Also, See **Ephesians 1:12–14** denoted here, "**That we should be to the praise of his glory who first trusted in Christ in whom you also trusted after that you heard the word of truth the gospel of your salvation in whom also after that you believed you were _sealed with that Holy Spirit of promise._**" Summarily, these scriptural passages simply declares that we have been sealed with a pledge as we have seen and when the redemption of the purchase comes due—i.e., the redemption of our bodies purchased possession since the down payment is secured via the Spirit of God.

Our complete redemption and purchasing and whisked away is the actual translation here is solidified or guaranteed! Conclusively, that said, these are just some of the examples of displayed moments when one or the other members of the divine trinity was acting as the dominant holy being on the stage of life. It goes without saying that these are just a few examples of individual yet joint administrations of the Godhead into the affairs of human and angelic history in heaven above and earth below but there are many more.

Additional reasons or purposes for the Rapture of believers in Christ is mentioned by the Apostle Paul who tells us that our mortal bodies which are corruptible (subject to decay, death, disease) must put on or be renewed by immortal spiritual bodies (like Jesus upon his resurrection) that is incorruptible in order to live in Paradise with Christ. **See 1 Corinthians 15:53–54 vs.** Listed here; **for this, corruptible must put on incorruption and this mortal must put on immortality. So when this corruptible has put on incorruption and this mortal shall have put on immortality then shall be brought to pass that saying that is written O Death is swallowed up in victory.** In addition, Paul informs us that flesh and blood cannot inherit the kingdom of God. **1 Corinthians 15:50 noted here, "Now I say brethren that flesh and blood cannot inherit the kingdom of God nor does corruption inherit incorruption."** Furthermore, Paul tells us how, whom, as well as when the snatching away or rapture will occur in **1 Thessalonians 4:14–17.** Repeated here **for if we believe that Jesus died and rose again even so God will bring with him those who sleep in Jesus. For this we say to** you by the word of the Lord that we who are alive and remain until the coming of the Lord will by no means precede those who are asleep. For the Lord himself, will descend from heaven with a shout, with the voice of the Archangel and with the trumpet of God and the dead in Christ will rise first. Then we who are alive and remain shall be caught up together with them in the clouds to meet the Lord in the air and thus we shall always be with the Lord. This is why it is so imperative to be born again.

Jesus said in **John 3:3**, "**That unless a man is *born again* he cannot see the kingdom of God**." Unfortunately, the devil via **the Antichrist** and other enemies of God, including the False Prophet and the Beast, will deceive many people trying to explain the sudden, mysterious disappearance of millions of people around the world all seemingly with no rational explanation. They will use phrases such as "God" has judged these evil people—i.e. (true believers in Jesus Christ) "unworthy" to remain on earth when in fact it is just the opposite. God does not want his people to suffer with the world during this tumultuous time on earth. Essentially, the devil, fallen angels as well as all people who do not love Christ will keep lying until the Day of Judgment. **There is nothing new under the sun** says the Lord in **Ecclesiastes 1:9**. Here we transition or focus our attention to the Great Tribulation Period, and what that means for the war on earth that actually spawned in heaven. For those of you who are unfamiliar with this period in Christendom let me narrate a little about what this period means to all of humanity. Look up cheer up and get up saints of the Most High God of Israel! God has promised that his people will not suffer during the Great Tribulation as we saw above.

CHAPTER XI

Great Tribulation Period

Just to ensure that all of us are on the same page—i.e., both neophytes, new comers, those whom are veterans of faith and those who will become believers in Christ. What is the meaning or definition of The Great Tribulation period? The Great Tribulation period comprises a seven-year period just prior to the Second Return of Jesus Christ to the earth. This will culminate when Christ will put down all human authority, dispel the devil, the Anti-Christ, the False Prophet and The Beast and all evil for good and set up the Theocracy of God on the new earth forever! Theocracy meaning God centered and ruled kingdom. This period is divisible by two, forty-two and a half months intervals—i.e., three ½-year periods, which when added together give you seven years total. After this horrible period has expired and Christ has vanquished his enemies eternally, he leads the redeemed of the earth inside of his Father's peaceful Kingdom. Christ establishes a true theocracy or government completely ruled by God. No more ministers, preachers, pontiffs, clerics, bishops, pundits or anyone else assert to be running the show or speaking on God's behalf. God himself is in complete control to live in harmony and govern redeemed man in person face to face.

See **Revelation 22:4** cited here, "**And there shall be no more curse but the throne of God and of the Lamb shall be in it and his servants shall serve him and _they shall see his face_ and his name shall be in their foreheads.**" Sadly the Tribulation Period of time on earth is where all hell breaks out literally including worldwide deaths, catastrophes, wars, famines, pestilences and utter chaos whereby misery comes in many forms, suffering and despair will exceed all known records of adversity for man on the earth to date. Christ said that if it had not been for the mercy of God shortening those days, no flesh would be saved alive during this period (**Matthew 24:21–22**). Wow! Question, does this sound familiar? It should… Remember the Noahic flood wherein *only eight souls* survived the deluge of water for forty days and forty nights sent from God *that killed everything* and *every being* man, fowl, fish, insect, plant or animal. Synonymously, this period characterized by unbelievable natural disasters, plagues, murders, wars, lawlessness, conflict and judgment of God, etc., causing death all over the world at an alarming rate.

However, this period is divisive in that it has two separate, equal epochs. Albeit both periods on earth ruled by the authoritarian Antichrist (devil incarnate in human flesh) diabolical dictatorship, what happens during each period is slightly different. We will ascertain how it breaks down here via the analysis of Christ words to his disciples during one of his sermons in the WOG. Herein is the scenario or scene. Jesus is atop of the Mount of Olives describing in vivid detail for his disciples what the end of the ages will look like here on earth during the first period explained by Christ in **Matthew 24**. The battle on earth is affecting every aspect of life and persons on it during this sinister period.

Located within **chapter 24 of Matthew**, Christ talks vividly about the **Great Tribulation** below in these bulleted highlights:

- Jesus warns his disciples in **Matthew 24:4–5** *not to be deceived by false Christs* claiming to be him.
- Jesus tells his disciples that there were be *wars and rumors of wars* (Matthew 24:6–7) **with pestilences and earthquakes.**
- Christ says **this** *is only the beginning of sorrows* (Matthew **24:8).**
- Christ tells his followers **they** *will be arrested, murdered, and hated* (Matthew 24:9–10) **many of them will be offended.**

- Jesus warns **false *prophets will rise up and deceive many* (Matthew 24:11).**
- Lawlessness abounds; ***the love of many will wax cold* (Matthew 24:12).**
- Christ says that one **must endure until the end to be saved (Matthew 24:13).**
- Gospel of the kingdom of God **must be *preached worldwide* as a witness, *then the end comes* (Matthew 24:14).**
- Son of God tells them that the *"**abomination of desolation**"* **will occur spoken of by Daniel the Prophet (Matthew 24:15).**

Albeit many critical or key points are mentioned by The Son of God here as he foretells the end of time. The most significant point made by Jesus here appertains to the abomination of desolation. The utmost significance of the abomination of desolation requires a detailed analysis as opposed to highlighted bullet points like those above. Therefore, let me divide the word of God here more succinctly. This is a deviation from Christ's earlier points because here the Messiah actually connects them with the OT prophet Daniel, who warned of this event. This subject matter requires a little detailed analysis from the <u>OT law of God Almighty</u> spelled out concerning the temple. God strictly forbade just anyone doing service in the temple and anyone just walking up to the temple to do as he or she pleases per se. Solomon was careful as he explained to King Hiram of his intent to build a temple unto the Lord his God. Solomon says in **2 Chronicles 2:4, "Behold I am <u>building a temple</u> for the name of the Lord my God to dedicate it to him to burn before it sweet incense for the continual showbread for the burnt offerings mornings and evenings on the Sabbaths on the New Moons and on the set feasts of the Lord our God."** This is an *<u>ordinance forever</u>* to Israel. Furthermore, God warned Moses to ensure that he told Aaron his brother **not to come at all times** to **the holy place** to be mindful when he walked into the holy place—i.e., Holy (behind the Veil) because God would be there in a cloud upon the mercy seat. *The exact words are documented for us in **Leviticus 16:2, "And*** *the Lord said unto Moses speak unto your brother Aaron that he come not at all times into the holy place within the Veil before the mercy seat which is upon the ark that he die not for I will appear in the cloud upon the mercy seat!"*

Here God Almighty outlines some of the **restrictions that God placed** upon service *within the temple.* So that we can gain a better understanding of what is the "abomination of desolation" Daniel the prophet prophesied about and referred to by the Son of God in **Matthew 24:15.** The Tabernacle of the Lord originally established in a tent not an actual building whereby the Ark of God rested (**2 Samuel 7:2**). **"Then the King said unto Nathan the prophet, see now I dwell in a house and the ark of God dwells within curtains."** The very first actual temple or building structure to worship God Almighty was not constructed until Solomon the son of King David built it. **1 Kings 6:14 so Solomon built the house and finished it**. Although King David wanted to build the Temple of the Lord, God denied him the right to do so because God told David that he had shed men's blood in battle. **1 Chronicle 28:2–3, "Then David the king stood up upon his feet and said hear me my brethren and my people as for me, I had in my heart to build an house of rest for the ark of the covenant of the Lord and for the footstool of our God and had made ready for the building. But God said unto me thou shall not build a house for my name because you have been a man of war and hast shed blood."** This fact alone demonstrates that God is holy, that he would not allow hands that shed blood to build him a place where sacrifice or worship to him would occur. Furthermore, God tells Moses that Aaron and his sons are to consecrate themselves before going into the tabernacle of the Lord. **Leviticus 22:2 God forbids and doesn't allow anyone with the following physical issues to be priests these are; lepers, blind persons, maimed, broken feet, hunchbacks, dwarfs, eye defects, eczema, scabs or eunuchs. Leviticus 21:17–22.** Now Look at **Numbers 1:51. God tells Moses that whenever the tabernacle (tent as it were then) of the Lord is taken down to be moved any "outsider" who comes near it is to be put to death**. This term *outsider* here is used to designate or identify anyone who was a foreigner or stranger—i.e., Gentile who traveled with the fledging Hebrew State as they were seeking to acquire the promised land of Canaan. People of the same ethnic group have no need to identify himself or herself or any member thereof as an outsider. Therefore, it is explicitly referring to people who are non-Hebrew. Allow me to provide a very powerful example of someone who was not a Hebrew, but was an actual "outsider" but accepted the Hebrew God, Jehovah as her God.

The person I am referring to is none other than the great grandmother of King David, Ruth who was initially a Moabite. Ruth's mother in law Naomi (Hebrew) lost her husband (Elimilech) and both of her sons (Mahlon and Chilon) they all died. Mahlon was Ruth's first husband. The family was merely traveling when all three men died. Naomi bids both of her daughters in law Orpah and of Ruth to turn back to their own country (Moab) and people. Because there was nothing she could do for either of them because of this unfortunate turn of events since she has lost all males in her immediate family. She kissed both of them and Orpah returned to her land of nativity. However, Ruth would not depart from her mother in law. Ruth pleaded with her not to ask her to leave ever again as recorded in **Ruth 1:16, "*For where you go, I will go, and where you lodge, I will lodge, your people shall be my people, and your God shall be my God!*"** Subsequently, God blesses her for her steadfastness, loyalty and faith with a new husband (Boaz) and a special, direct, genealogical line to King David and the lineage on earth relating to The King of Kings, Jesus Christ the Son of God. Now that I have provided readers with an example of what constitutes an outsider, I redirect our focus to the narrative of why God forbade outsiders from service and entering into the temple which when it occurs creates the "abomination of desolation."

God specifically tells Moses to inform his brother Aaron, who is now by divine decree, from God, the **First High Priest** of the temple of God. This is equivalent to George Washington's election as the First President of the United States of America. However, it has a superior calling. Because God designated Aaron to lead worshippers and carry out the ordinances of the temple dedicated to the name of

God. George Washington, as a slaveholder and owner merely governed other slaveholders and owners. While they themselves enjoyed all the privileges and benefits of freedom. What hypocrisy! They were willing to fight and did die to deny others the rights or freedoms they enjoyed while simultaneously holding other people as their chattel. Jesus said do unto others, as you would have them do unto you. Actually, Christ goes much more in depth. Review **Matthew 7:12** here, Jesus said, "**Therefore whatsoever you 'want men to _do unto_ you' _do also to them_ for this is the Law and the Prophets.**

I am sure that George Washington and other Constitutional authors, signers and slaveholders' didn't want the African slaves they held against their will under constant threat of lynching, whipping with bull whips, cruel servitude and other atrocities wanted them to hold them as slaves or deny them their freedom. So why did they **_do this unto them_** as slaves? Satan is truly the Arch-Cherub of all lying and evil wonders in heaven above and earth below as he deceived them into believing the lie that they are superior. Nevertheless, The Lord tells Moses to inform Aaron about the specific duties involving regulations regarding worship and access to the holy of holies. This is the designated place where God would appear above the mercy seat behind the partition or veil inside the tabernacle/temple (tent at this time) to meet with the future descendants of Aaron who may serve as High Priest or priests in successive future generations or descendants of Aaron role within the Levitical Priesthood. See **Leviticus 21:17–23.** "**Speak unto Aaron saying whosoever he be of thy seed in their generations that hath any blemishes, let him not approach to offer the bread of his God. For whatsoever man he be that hath a blemish he shall not approach, a blind man, or a lame or hath a flat nose, or anything superfluous. Or a man that is broken footed or broken handed or a crookback, or a dwarf or he that hath a blemish in his eye or be scurvy or scabbed or that his stones broken. No man that hath a blemish of the seed of Aaron the priest shall come nigh to offer the offerings of the Lord made by fire, he hath a blemish. He _shall not_ come near to offer the bread of his God. He shall _eat the bread_ of his God both of the most holy and of the holy. Only he _shall not go in_ unto the**

vail <u>nor come near unto the altar</u> because he hath a blemish that he _profane not_ my sanctuaries for I the Lord do sanctify them."

Carefully examine verse 23. Closer inspection of this scripture provides direct commandment from The Lord God; it says only **_he shall not_ go <u>_near_ the _veil_</u> or _approach the altar_**, lest he **profane my sanctuaries**, for **<u>I the Lord sanctify</u>** them! Furthermore, not just anyone can be a priest because one chooses this as a profession. God tells Moses whom he will allow only to have this distinctive, special duty—i.e., the Levites. Read **Numbers 1:49–50** and **Numbers 3:6. Only you shall not number the tribe of Levi, neither take the sum of them among the children of Israel. But you shall appoint the Levites over the tabernacle of testimony and over all of the vessels thereof, and over all things that belong to it, they shall bear the tabernacle and all the vessels thereof and _they shall minister_ unto it and _shall encamp round_ about the tabernacle.** Additionally, God informs Moses and Aaron that Aaron and his sons shall attend to their priesthood, but any **"outsider"** who comes near **shall be put to death.**

Review **Numbers 3:9–10 here, "And you shall give the Levites to Aaron and his sons; they are given entirely unto him from among the children of Israel. So you shall appoint Aaron and his sons and they shall attend to their priesthood <u>but the 'outsider' who comes near shall be put to death</u>."** God decides to take the tribe of Levi and make them his priests since the firstborn of all are his. God selects this specific tribe of the twelve tribes of Israel for elevation for ministerial duties inside the tabernacle. Afterward, their role in the temple ordained an everlasting priesthood role on this side of the eternal divide in lieu of every firstborn male. See **Numbers 3:12–13, "Now behold I myself have taken the Levites from among the children of Israel instead of every firstborn who opens the womb among the children of Israel. Therefore, the Levites shall be mine. Because all the firstborn are mine, on the day that I struck all the firstborn in the land of Egypt, I sanctified to myself all the firstborn in Israel, both man and beast."**

Conclusively, we can see by this specific listing of characteristics below, the person serving as priest or High Priest must meet in order to have access to God behind the veil inside the tabernacle of the Lord *with access* to his altar. **The most significant requirement is they cannot be an outsider**. They are listed here below as a quick recap:

- Only Levites from the tribe of Levi (**Numbers 1:49–50**)
- Male (**Numbers 2:43 and Numbers 4:2**)
- Thirty to fifty years old in age (**Numbers 4:3**)
- Veil and altar are both sanctified (made holy) by God himself (**Leviticus 21:23**)
- *No outsiders* this includes anyone who *is not a Levite* or a *foreigner* living among Israelites (**Number 3:9–10**)

Next, we focus on how the abomination of desolation occurs by the person who violates all of the perquisite traits above and dooms himself for all eternity. The sacred temple of worship to God Almighty during the End Time events construction on earth in Israel is required one final time prior to the Second Advent of Christ. The Temple's construction is required for two essential reasons. Herein this is how and is where the Antichrist will commit the *abomination of desolation* that causes ruin by standing where he should not be standing. Additionally, the Orthodox Jews will begin to worship the Lord God of Israel in compliance with the historical provisions mandated by the Torah—i.e., first five books of the Bible. The Western Wall aka the Kotel, in eastern Jerusalem, Israel is the only portion of what once upon a time was part of the expanse to contain the temple of Solomon. I will briefly recap the original history of this sacred place singled out for the God of Israel's devotion. King Solomon built the first temple circa 10 century BCE (Before Common Era) as foretold by God. However, Nebuchadnezzar razed this temple to the ground for Israel's rebellion against Yahweh. This Babylonian King took the Israelites as captives including the prophet Daniel after burning and destroying Jerusalem. Later after the restoration and return of the exiles during the conquest of Babylon by the Persians and Medes, eventually the temple reconstruction albeit on a much smaller scale occurred or proceeded by several different groups over a twenty-year period.

Some of the more prominent groups and or individuals were Zerubbabel, the Hasmoneans and King Herod the Great. Subsequently, the Romans destroyed the *second temple* when Titus of Rome butchered many of the Jewish citizens and residents all for the glory of Rome in the year 70 AD (Anno Domini). Contemporaneously, the world awaits the "final temple" reconstruction prior to the return of Jesus Christ. Someone may ask why in the world we are awaiting the rebuilding of the temple. The reason is very simple. Orthodox (Hebrews) Judaism will faithfully continue to serve their God in the way, customs, rituals or practices of their ancestors have since Israel became a nation. This requires animal sacrifice specifically within the temple dedicated to Jehovah. Currently the Muslim Dome of the Rock or Mosque of Omar is the onsite resident of the location where the temple is to be rebuilt. Somehow, naturally or supernaturally this temple mosque will be removed so the Orthodox Israelites can rebuild the final temple of worship to the Lord their God. Remember a key point here; rebuilding or reconstructing the traditional temple in Israel is paramount to the People of Israel. However more importantly the temple mandatory rebuilding will design or rebuilt so that the Holy Scripture regarding the abomination of desolation act fulfilment as prophesized by Daniel and Christ. For this heinous specific act will occur within these hallowed walls as I will demonstrate. The rebuilt temple will have servants, attendants and others no doubt.

However, only **Levitical Priest** whose ordination by God in the traditional manner can do the actual work in terms of ministerial duties pertaining to the temple. This lineage of Levitical Priest will be determined by DNA testing for authenticity or verification for service. See the section above references relating to the specificity or requirements of this ministerial service. Although, the only way to serve God Almighty now is to accept by faith—i.e., to believe in his Son, Jesus Christ as Lord, as do all Christians including the "Messianic Jews" believe this to be true. Which by the way it is the only way. See **John 11:25** Jesus stated, "**I am the resurrection and the life he who believes in me though he may die he shall live**. Furthermore, the Bible says **there is no other name given under heaven whereby we**

must be saved" according to **Acts 4:2. "Nor is there salvation in any other for <u>there is no other name under heaven given among men</u> by which we <u>must be saved!</u>**" The Orthodox and the Hasidic Jews accept Jesus as a Holy Prophet, but desire to serve their God, as did their ancestors through the shed blood of animal sacrifices, which they plan to do once the third and final temple reconstruction to the Lord occurs in Israel. Here is where the problems begins.

CHAPTER XII

Outsider inside God's Temple

Since, the Antichrist will have authority over all people on earth at this time via commercial services, law, police, military forces, business, trade, commerce, shopping, legislation, industry, etc. No one can buy or sell anything without the mark of the beast. See **Revelation 13:15–18,** listed here: **he was granted power to give breath to the image of the beast that the image of the beast should both speak and cause as many as would not worship the image of the beast to be killed (tribulation saints). He causes all rich and poor, free and slave to receive a mark on their right hand or on their foreheads. That _no one may buy or sell_ except one who has the mark or the name of the beast or the number of his name, which is 666.** Quadriplegics, those with birth defects, etc., whom are non-developed, or unborn with or dismembered in war, accidents, etc., of hands or arms will be included as well.

For the mark is on the forehead if they have no hands or extremities**.** In addition, read **Revelation 13:7–8** listed here that says, **"And it was given him to make war with the saints (tribulation) and to overcome them and power was given him over <u>all kindred</u> and tongues. And nations and <u>all that dwell upon the earth</u> '_shall worship him_' whose names are not written in the book of life of the Lamb slain from the foundation of the world."** This includes but is not limited to food, water or any commodities. If anyone refuses to worship this beast, he/she execution ordered via the antichrist. The mannerism in which these persons death occurs is also significant too. Specifically, the word of God says each of them receives beheading. However, what about the Jews? Satan knows they will never just follow his false Christ so he makes a treaty or covenant with them.

See **Daniel 11:20–24** noted here, "**There shall arise in his place one who imposes taxes on the 'glorious kingdom' but within a few days, he shall be destroyed. But not in anger, nor in battle and in his place shall arise a vile person to who they will not give the honor of royalty. But he shall come in peaceably and seize the kingdom by intrigue with the force of a flood. They shall be swept away from before him and they shall be broken. And also the prince of the covenant and _after the league (treaty) is made with him_ he shall act deceitfully for he shall come up and become strong with a small number of people. He shall enter peaceably even into the richest places of the province and he shall do what his fathers have not done nor his forefathers he shall disperse among them the plunder spoil and riches and he shall devise his plans and he shall devise his plans against the strongholds but only for a time.**" The Devil in the flesh will lie to them and tell them they can worship and sacrifice to their God freely as they so choose.

Yet a series or turn of events will go against him and he will be angered and enraged to break this covenant. **Daniel 11:30–32 says, "For ships from Cyprus shall come against him. Therefore, he shall be grieved and return in rage against the holy covenant (peace treaty for Israelis to 'freely worship' their God) and do damage. So he shall return and show regard for those who forsake (break, abandon, void) the holy covenant and forces shall be mustered by him and _they shall defile the sanctuary_ fortress. Then they shall take away (stop/forbid) the 'daily sacrifices' (sanctioned animals worthy of sacrifice upon the altar of God and place there the abomination of desolation (substitute a unclean animal of sacrifice) upon the altar of God Almighty." This he will do in lieu of the Hebrew custom of Kosher, animals God allowed in Old Testament times for animal sacrifice unto himself—i.e., shedding of blood of innocent animals for man's guilty actions of sin.** The Antichrist will demand that the Hebrews no longer worship or sacrifice to the God of Heaven and earth but **that they _must worship him_ because he is taking away the daily sacrifice (Daniel 11:31)**.

The Antichrist commits two specific violations of God ordinances against himself and to the Hebrew people inside of the temple of the Lord. One he himself should not be in there (desecration) for he does not meet the criteria of those God allowed inside the temple. He is profaning God's sanctuary that he himself sanctified by being inside the temple of the Lord of Hosts. However, just as deviously he takes a non-kosher (unclean/unapproved of by God) animal and sacrifices it upon the altar of God to show his disdain and contempt for God Almighty. (Abominable Desolation) This happened in antiquity when Antiochus Epiphanes slaughtered a pig on the altar of God inside of the Hebrew Israeli temple in Israel. Stay tuned God has something in store for him in a flaming hot hell front row seat reservations in his honor! Furthermore, let me include here a very imperative point so as not to confound the readers. I will include a mandatory notification here for the record that God **no longer requires** animal sacrifice—i.e., shedding of innocent animals' blood for the forgiveness of guilty man's sins.

For we have the **eternal sacrifice of Christ** atoning death and shed blood at Calvary for the remission of our sins. Let us review some imperative scriptures to support this truism. Review **Hebrews 9:11–15** denoted here that says, **"But Christ came as High Priest of the good things to come with the greater and more perfect tabernacle not made with hands, that is not of this creation. Not with the blood of goats and calves but with his own blood. He entered the Most Holy place once for all having obtained eternal redemption. For if the blood of bulls and goats and the ashes of a heifer, sprinkling the unclean, sanctifies for the purifying of the flesh. How much more shall the blood of Christ who through the eternal spirit offered himself without spot to God cleanse your conscience from dead works to serve the living God? And for this reason he is the mediator of the new covenant by means of death for the redemption of the transgressions under the first covenant that those who are called may receive the promise of the eternal inheritance."**

Now we transition to **Hebrews 9:19–26** here: **"For when Moses had spoken every precept to all the people according to the law, he took the blood of calves and goats with water, scarlet wool, and hyssop and sprinkled both the book itself and all the people. Saying this is the blood of the covenant which God has commanded you. Then likewise, he sprinkled with blood both the tabernacle and all the vessels of the ministry. And according to the law almost all things are purified with blood and without shedding of blood there is no remission. Therefore, it was necessary that the copies of the things in heaven should be purified with these but the heavenly things themselves with better sacrifices than these. For Christ has not entered the holy places made with hands which are copies of the true, but into heaven itself now to appear in the presence of God for us. Not that he should offer himself often as the High Priest enters the Most Holy Place every year with the blood of another he then would have had to suffer often since the foundation of the world but now once at the end of the ages he has appeared to put away sin by the sacrifice of himself."**

Now **Hebrews 10:12–17**, **"But this man after he had offered one sacrifice for sins forever, sat down at the right hand of God. From that time waiting till his enemies are made his footstool for by one offering he has perfected forever those who are being sanctified. But the Holy Spirit also witnesses to us for after he had said before, This is the covenant that I will make with them in those days says the Lord I will put my laws into their hearts and in their minds I will write them. Then he adds their sins and their lawless deeds I will remember no more."**

Finally, **Hebrews 12:1–3**, **"Therefore we also since we are surrounded by so great cloud of witnesses, let us lay aside every weight and the sin, which so easily ensnares us, and let us run with patience the race that is set before us. Looking unto Jesus the author and finisher of our faith who for the joy that was set before him endured the cross, despising the shame, and has sat down at the right hand of the throne of God for consider him who endured such hostility from sinners against himself, lest you become weary and discouraged in your souls."**

Nevertheless, the Orthodox Judaists (Hebrew followers of Levitical Laws) believers will still construct and restart all of the animal sacrifices, daily devotions and prayers to the God of Israel as did their ancestors in the middle of the desert in Israel. The Devil in the personage of the Antichrist himself is going to walk right into the newly rebuilt temple in Jerusalem and *say I am god* now you must worship me or die! See **2 Thessalonians 2:3–4, which reads in part, "Except that man of sin be revealed (exposed) the son of perdition who _opposes_ and _exalts himself_ above all that is called God, or that is worshipped: so that he as God sits in _the temple_ of God, showing himself that he is God."** Therefore, these acts when applied contextually constitute the "abomination of desolation" prophesied by Daniel and reemphasized by Jesus Christ the Son of God. Here is why. Simply put this cannot be the temple in heaven because the devil has already been banished from the third heaven where God dwells forever so it must be the temple on earth.

This we noted in earlier narrative expose specifically **Revelation 12:7–12**. This demon is preparing others to provide him with ministerial services, to himself via self-proclamation that he is God. He should not even be _in the temple_ because of his **Gentile heritage** yet alone sitting at or near the altar of God! The evidenced rationale for such premise listed as follows via the recap of those thought worthy by God to approach his altar to do service inside of the temple of the Lord.

Priestly Traits Recap

Furthermore, if you will recall from our earlier listing of Levitical priesthood traits or characteristics he violates most of them. I have recited them again for your quick review. He **meets one** of these requirements. He is a male. Other than that zero match. Since his identity is unknown, presently we can also assume he does not meet the age specification too;

- Only Levites from the tribe of Levi (**Numbers 1:49–50**)
- Male, Numbers 2:43 and **Numbers 4:2**
- Thirty to fifty years old in age (**Numbers 4:3**)

- Veil and altar **are both sanctified** (made holy) by God himself **(Leviticus 21:23)**
- **No outsiders** this **includes anyone** who **is not a Levite** including **foreigners** living among Israelites **(Number 3:9–10)**

The most imperative of all these violations is that **he profanes and pollutes the altar of God** with **his presence** as a (foreigner and outsider) **in the temple of God** simply by approaching it. Summarily, this is **the abomination of desolation** as explained by Christ in **Matthew 24:15–21** that reads *Therefore, when you see the abomination of desolation, spoken of by Daniel the prophet <u>standing in the holy place</u>* **(where it ought not stand in the temple of God) for the aforementioned reasons. Verse 21 reads,** *for then there will be "great tribulation" such as has not been since the beginning of the world until this time no, nor ever shall be.* Essentially, Christ words translated here means when you see a *<u>foreign or outsider</u>* non Hebraic person (Levite) inside of the temple "standing" where he ought not be standing—i.e., behind the veil, in the holy of holy, place reserved **only** for the High Priest during the Old Testament epoch location. This is the **"abomination of desolation"** that makes ruin or "profanes and pollutes" the temple of God here on earth inside the Israeli Holy Temple Mount. Now we move our discussion to the topic of the second period of the Great Tribulation.

The second period of this tribulation event is also the exact same period of time forty-two months or three and a half years for a total of seven years when amalgamated together. Furthermore, this is when all of the lies, deception, false promises told by satanic forces are exposed and the judgment of God begins to take place exposing the Antichrist for *who he actually is*—i.e., **the devil in human flesh.** Essentially, the Antichrist will solve global crises during the first half of the seven-year period with astounding answers and keen accuracy or insight that creates resolutions or solutions to complicated problems, climate emissions of greenhouse gases via international treaties. However, while simultaneously, encouraging or allowing petrochemical companies to search for alternative methods to fossil fuels while polluting the atmosphere everyone breaths. The Antichrist will assist with astounding accuracy (devil inspired) gimmicks to resolve some of the problems highlighted as follows. Destabilizing wildlife preserves, that prevent the overhunting and killing of animals to the brink of extinction. Fostering scientific exploration with emerging technologies to enhance and increase survival rates of all on earth. Brokering of armistice treaties to mitigate wars among hostile nations, famine food control disbursement to underdeveloped or exploited people and countries. Medicinal innovations to care for the sick and elderly, as well as eradicate some debilitating diseases afflicting humanity. He will increase energy distribution of power in a seemingly equitable way that appeases opposite forces or kingdoms. The Antichrist answers to seemingly unsolvable issues makes it appear that his level of wisdom, insight, knowledge and judgment are "divine." However, none is divine at all. They are demonic answers because of previous access to the Living Room of God insider "celestial knowledge" that he had. Remember he is the devil in the flesh. The devil has seen things in God's kingdom that we desire to see and will in due time God willing.

The word of God calls these *performing signs or miracles* of demons. Look at **Revelation 16:14**, listed here: "***For they are spirits of demons performing signs*** **which go out to the kings of the earth and of the whole world to gather them to the battle of the Great Day of God Almighty**." Consequently, as peace begins to rapidly deteriorate among nations, countries, neighbors, races, tribes and people the truth starts to emerge. Because wars and problems began rapidly, deteriorating armistice agreements globally resulting in open warfare. Hostilities began to reoccur in preparation to move all nations toward the Battle of Armageddon as the Great Day of God Almighty approaches. **Review Joel 2:1** here, "**Blow the trumpet in Zion and sound an alarm in my holy mountain let all the inhabitants of the land tremble. <u>For the day of the Lord is coming</u>.**" The Antichrist will revert to authoritarian brutality to maintain a façade of order and peace worldwide. This will be a very diabolical authoritarian rule over the people of the earth who do not believe that Jesus Christ is Lord. The rejection of Christ's holy authority ushers in the unholy authority of the most dreadful persona ever created... Satan himself! Ready or not... The Devil is on his way!

Satan as aforementioned always wanted to occupy reptile or human flesh. Biblical support for such a premise is located in the narrative back in the Garden of Eden. He already used the serpent's bodily form within the Garden of Eden to deceive Eve. See **Genesis 3:1.** That reads, **now the _serpent_ was more _subtil_ than any other beast of the field, which the Lord God had made. And he said unto the woman yea has God said you shall not eat of every tree of the garden**? However, a logical question asked; as to why would the devil want to inhabit a human body? It is clear or easy to understand why. If the devil gets inside of a body or transform himself unto a human form (body), he can easily deceive those who are human a lot quicker than he could if he maintained his celestial form. The process called assimilation is what he is after. In addition, he wants a human body so that _humans worship_ him. He wants to have this experience while he is assimilating or mimicking the voluntary worshipping of God the Father and God the Son, Jesus Christ, as they are worthy of worship. **Naturally no other creature in heaven or earth is worthy of worship besides the Lord God!** Additionally, a similar example, of when Satan desired a body occurs upon or after the death of Moses. The devil in Round two waged a fight with the Archangel Michael for the body of Moses. Recall if you will they already fought in heaven during Satan's eviction.

See **Jude 1:9**, cited here that says, **"Yet, Michael the Archangel, in contending with the devil _for the body of Moses_ dared not bring against him a railing accusation but said the Lord rebuke you."** Satan knew, if he could get Moses's body or get inside of that body and appear to have survived via a (false resurrection by identity theft posing as Moses) or claiming by lying that God changed his mind about Moses death due to his service to the Lord. Because he was a faithful messenger delivering the children of Israel from Egypt as God commanded, he would have been easily able to deceive the tiny struggling nation of Israel as they were entering into the Promised Land. However, he missed the point. Moses was not always obedient to God as most of us are not "**always**" obedient to our God.

We struggle daily with our faith, mixing with our works, the world, our fleshly, lustful desires, the devil and actions to serve our God as well. Here is a brief digression from our topic thereby allowing discussion, mentioning or reviewing a couple of examples of Moses disobedience to God. Ultimately, when amalgamated these acts of rebellion led up to God's *decision not* to let him or his brother Aaron enter the Promised Land. God allowed Moses to "see" the Promised Land albeit he was not allowed to enter it along with the people he led out of Egypt under God's divine power. First, Moses killed a man an Egyptian (**Exodus 1:14).** Secondly, Moses told God to have his brother Aaron or someone else go be the Prophet in lieu of himself (who tells God what to do?) (**Exodus 4:10–17).** Moses informed God that Aaron, his brother, was more *articulate* than was he (**Zipporah his black wife** saved his life) then by cutting the foreskin of her son's genitals and throwing it in front of him. This satisfied God's requirement, it encompassed *the shedding of blood* for the remission of sin. Keep in mind Zipporah knew to do this for she was the daughter of Jethro the Priest of Median.

See **Exodus 3:1** here, **"Now Moses was tending the flock of Jethro his father in law, *the priest of Midian* he led the flock to the back of the desert and came to Horeb the mountain of God."** Thirdly, he violently struck the rock twice by the waters of Mereibah or "water of strife" when God commanded him to simply *speak to the stone* so that water could flow to the thirsty tribes as they travelled upon the desert floor enroute to Israel from Egypt to attain deliverance. Review **Numbers 20:8 and 12** here, **"Take the rod you and your brother Aaron gather the congregation together then the Lord spoke to Moses and Aaron. Because you did not believe me to hallow me in the eyes of the children of Israel. Therefore, you shall not bring this assembly into the land that I have given them."** Furthermore, Moses who was angry at Israel when he broke the original Ten Commandments *tablets by throwing them to the ground* as he walked down the mountain when he discovers Israel's sins against God in the wilderness of Zin. Review **Exodus 34:1, "And the Lord said to Moses cut two tablets of stone like the first ones and I will write on these tablets the words that were on the**

first tablets, which you broke." Fortunately, for him though, No problem, God made another copy from his heavenly Xerox Copier Eternity Brand Model. Consequently, because of all of these things God finally decided he could not go into the Promised Land. Now back to our narrative.

Nevertheless, it is imperative to remember as the Master Counterfeiter; Satan wants to perform every feat that Jesus Christ did to prove to himself and his fallen angels that he is a god. Jesus Christ came in human form in the body shape, form and likeness of a man to save fallen man from eternal destruction. Additionally, it is equally important to keep in mind that demons at this current hour of eternity present are actively being totally deceived by Satan. Satan is cunning, conniving, convincing, charismatic and clever as the fight from God's Living Room in heaven is relentlessly spreading like a malignant cancer upon the human landscape here on earth. Satan's deception and lies to the fallen angels did not end with just one lie he told them while they were with God in heaven then that is it. It was not a one-time deception and now they are forever deceived, Satan is still ***proactively deceiving*** these fallen angels by lying and saying things like or something to the effect. I have figured out a way we can get back into the third heaven, even now at this very moment even though we are sliding and spiraling downward. I *theorize* that Lucifer is telling them lies something along the line specifically like; we are just on a heavenly roller coaster ride. Demons, I want you all to keep in mind, Lucifer, I believe tells them; the roller coaster ride *goes down* before it "comes back up."

Therefore, as the Phoenix we will arise from the ashes of our dilemma and reenter the third heaven to take our rightful place on "my" throne now occupied by God Almighty and his Holy, Only Begotten Son Jesus Christ who is seated at his right hand! Additionally, he always seeks to transform himself as an *angel of light* within the environment that best suits his deceptive activity according to **2 Corinthians 11:14** denoted here that reads, "**And no wonder For Satan himself *transforms* himself into an angel of light.**" He does not want to appear in his natural estate form for many reasons. Among some of these are he is bound by the authority of God from doing so generally. Yet Satan witnessed the power, combined with the significance of being in human form as he saw Jesus Christ the Son of God assumed human form to be a blessing to all people who put their eternal hope in him for salvation. Review **John 3:16 that tells us, "For God so loved the world that he gave his only begotten Son that whosoever believes in him shall not perish but have everlasting life."** Furthermore, he would not be as effective, because Satan would be readily detected and obvious in his celestial body and many would know whom he is. So little to no chance fooling anybody there. Therefore, the dragon disguises himself like a chameleon blending into the fabric of the milieu to carry out his well-orchestrated, diabolical schemes of murder, theft, death and destruction. Jesus said **the thief (Satan) comes to steal, kill and destroy (John 10:10).**

The sheer horror, despair, death, disease, destruction, dismay that happens to all of the inhabitants on the earth during this period is unimaginable. This can be attributable unto the ultimate magnitude of the devastating widespread chaos, pain and suffering that will happen during this span of time on earth. The enormity of carnage that sweeps the globe is unfathomable in human history! Unbelievably, all life isn't extinguished but is very near total annihilation had it not been for the mercy of God who shortens the days of their horror. Jesus said that _no flesh would survive_ if not for the "mercy of God" listed here in **Matthew 24:22, "If those days had not been cut short, <u>no one would survive</u> but for the sake of the elect, those days will be shortened."** My Lord! Furthermore God promised that he would never kill all life on the earth again as he did during the flood saving only Noah and his family. Review **Genesis 8:20–21** cited here, **"Then Noah built an altar to the lord, and took of every clean animal, and of every clean bird and offered burnt offerings on the altar and the lord smelled a soothing aroma. Then the Lord said in his heart I will never again curse the ground for man's sake, although the imagination of man's heart is evil from his youth <u>nor will I again destroy every living thing as I have done.</u>"**

The word of God says that ***men will seek death in those days and will not find it they will desire to die and death will flee from them in Revelation 9:6.*** Herein is another strange quirk as to why some bad people seem to live forever while decent good people seem to die earlier in life during one's life span in general. The reason is that God is ***intentionally*** keeping these wicked people alive to punish them slowly for their rebellion against his Son Jesus. We have all heard various and different people periodically at some point throughout our lifetime say something to the effect that "good people" always die young and the bad ones "stay alive" and seem to live longer lives. This is true to an extent. However, it is not for the reason they assume it to be. Primarily, God is allowing some sinister people to live longer in hopes that they *will repent.* God's motives and sense of justice is brewing something very different on the horizon for all who reject Christ Jesus. Review **2 Peter 2:9** cited here that says, "**The Lord knows how to deliver the godly out of temptations and to reserve the unjust unto the Day of Judgment to be punished.**" God's intention is benevolence initially. James the brother of Christ on earth said that God considers by comparison to a farmer who awaits the latter rain prior to harvesting his crops and not just the first or former rain.

See **James 5:7 that reads, "Therefore be patient brethren until the coming of the Lord, see how the farmer waits for the precious fruit of the earth waiting patiently for it until it receives the *early and latter* rain.** Analogously God is waiting until all those who will repent in the latter times acceptance (later on) of salvation by faith just as the ones who were saved in the earlier or former time prior to the onset of the tribulation era. Remember Peter said **it is not the will of the Father that any should be lost.** Read **2 Peter 3:9,** listed here that says, "**The Lord is not slack concerning his promise as some men count slackness but is longsuffering to us-ward not willing that any should be lost but *that all* should come to the repentance.**" Secondly, if they go on unrepentant and continue to reject Christ as Savior then God will justifiably allow their eternal punishment for they are without excuse seeing that they had plenty of time to repent and serve Christ as Lord but rejected him. Review **Romans 1:20** cited here: "**For since the creation of the world his invisible attributes are clearly seen being understood by the things that are made, even his eternal power and Godhead, so that they are *without excuse*.**" Therefore, they are worthy of God's punishment. This enables the full torrent of God's wrath releasement upon those of us who *do not obey* or *believe* God.

Look here at **Romans 1:18, "For the wrath of God is revealed from heaven against all ungodliness and unrighteousness of men who suppress the truth in unrighteousness.**" God has ordained seven angels with the last seven plagues of his judgment to pour out their bowls with his indignation upon the earth and all inhabitants thereof. See **Revelation 15:1** that says, "**Then I saw another sign in heaven great and marvelous *seven angels having the last seven plagues* for in them the wrath of God is complete.**" Paul the Apostle said **God has not appointed us to wrath but to obtain salvation through Christ in 1 Thessalonians 5:9.** However, the exception involves *"tribulation saints" whom will go through some of this anguish.* Tribulation saints are all persons who will not accept Christ as their Savior **until the exact time** of the dispensation of these plagues began striking the earth during their ministry (while the Great Tribulation Period is occurring on the earth) of the two last messengers or olive trees who stand by the Lord of the whole earth—i.e., our God.

See **Revelation 11:3–4** listed here that says, "**And I will give power to my two witnesses and they will prophesy (preach) one thousand two hundred and sixty days in sackcloth, these are the two lampstands standing before the God of the earth.**" Their ministry will last approximately half of the entire Tribulation period, which is seven years—i.e., is 3.5 years before they meet their demise. One can presume from this that this is just like in the days of Noah who kept saying that God was going to cause it to flood which is his judgment and that it was going to rain while he preached on sunny days. Jesus alludes to this himself by providing two poignant or glaring examples of not paying attention or considering the gravity of God's warning until it is too late.

Review **Luke 17–31** denoted here, **"And as it was in the days of Noah so it will also be in the days of the Son of Man they ate, they drank, they married wives they were given in marriage until the day that Noah entered the ark and the flood came and destroyed them all. Likewise as it was also in the days of Lot they ate they drank and they bought they sold they planted they built but on the day that Lot went out of Sodom it rained fire and brimstone from heaven and destroyed them all. Even so will it be when the Son of Man is revealed in that day he who is on the housetop and his goods are in the house let him not come down to take them away and likewise the one who is in the field let him not turn back remember Lot's wife."**

This is why I can state unequivocally, those who accept Christ as their Savior **_prior_** to the Great Tribulation will not be involved in this event. Remember early on way back in the beginning when discussing what it meant to be "saved" this is what I was defining. Simply put to "be saved" means to be _spared_ of God's righteous indignation upon a rebellious creation that actually hates the Lord from the judgment of God that is coming upon all those angels/demons and mankind that don't want to obey God! Consequently, this means that we must all make a choice, with a decision that has either great reward or horrifying implications for all eternity upon our souls… i.e., choosing a side. Therefore, we arrive at our next venture, which each person must actually choose a side.

CHAPTER XIII

Choose a Side

The movie regarding Forrest Gump was a brilliant adaptation of a man who was somewhat dimwitted, naïve, maladaptive yet a likeable character. His ability to run from those who bullied, taunted, teased and harassed him because of his quirky behavior eventually led him to meet the President of the United States. Analogously, believers in Christ are somewhat like Forrest Gump. The reason I say this, is because we are running from the enemy of Christ daily in our personal lives, who is bullying, taunting, teasing, tempting or beating us up as we are struggling against the world, the flesh and the devil. However, more importantly we are just as naïve, dimwitted and backward souls, as was Forrest Gump. No wonder Christ referred to believers as "sheep." Similarly, just like Forrest Gump's dimwittedness and running ability got him to meet the President of the United States our "dimwittedness or simplicity through faith' in Jesus Christ his Son will get us to meet the God of the cosmos! Paul calls this the simplicity that is in Christ, which is our faith. Read **2 Corinthians 11:3** listed here that says, **"But I fear lest somehow as the serpent deceived Eve by his craftiness so your minds may be corrupted from _the simplicity_ that is in Christ."** One day all of us those who believe and non-believers that Christ is Lord will meet the God of Israel and his heir apparent, Jesus Christ the Lord in person! We will get a personal, up close interview with him in all of his sacred glory. This is why it is paramount that each of us make a monumental decision in our life. Yes, we must actually choose a side. Jesus when told by his disciples that they encountered others who were preaching in Christ name, whom they did not know, attempted to stop them from proselyting. Consequently, because they did not know them, the Disciples of Christ attempted to stop them from preaching about Jesus. Jesus replied, "Leave them alone…" Jesus told them for he that *is not* with me *is against* me (**Luke 9:49–50**).

Wow! There is no such thing as far as God is concerned about "neutrality" you are either with (Christ) or against him! Christ says in **Matthew 12:30, "He who is not with me is against me and he who does not gather with me scatters abroad."** This is a good place to transition or pivot to define or *delineate our role in this quest* within this fight between opposing forces of eternity. It is the fundamental aspect of all of events or contests that members of diverse teams be "chosen or selected" to compete in the field of endeavor they are engaged. Furthermore, this means that the member themselves must agree in principle to participate on behalf of the team they are representing. Subsequently, this means they must *choose to be on one side* or the other of **opposing sides** in the respective event or in any type or kind of contest. Professional teams select, draft or choose promising college players or free trade veterans from other teams they believe will help them win sporting crowns, titles or championships. Children in adolescent years go to playgrounds and other areas of youthful assembly to either choose a team to play on or against to represent their team pride. This simply means they must choose to be on a team. High Schools and collegiate athletes all compete against each other while representing their school's side in athletic and academic contests. Well my friend, it is the same here with our eternal souls held in the balance.

We must make a decision to either accept Christ as Lord or face rejection by him on the day of our judgment. Simply put, we must choose a side to be on in this eternal contest of God versus Satan. Let us explore some biblical examples of other saints who choose a side to fight on or for to outline the imperativeness of this perspective and why it is such a critical issue for us.

The man Joshua was a devoted follower of God and was the first assistant of Moses the prophet of God. Joshua faithfully executed his duties and took commands from the prophet, led the army of Israel along the way via Moses direction and was a faithful supporter of Moses and a believer in God Almighty. Subsequently, upon Moses's death, prior to the children of Israel going into the Promised Land, God directs Joshua to lead the embryonic Nation of Israel in its fragile estate into the Promised Land after God denied Moses this privilege or honor for his insolence. God tells Joshua to be courageous, obedient to his leadership and observe the commandments of the Lord in order to receive God's blessing and divine protection. God directs Joshua to seek his divine intervention, guidance and steadfastness as he goes about the service of the Lord now as its Captain. I have outlined the specific scriptures for you here below, see **Joshua 1:2–7** that says,

> *Moses my servant is dead now therefore arise go over Jordan you and all this people <u>unto the land that I give to them</u> even to the children of Israel every place that the sole of your foot shall tread upon that have I given unto you as I said unto Moses. From the wilderness and this Lebanon, even unto the Great River the river Euphrates <u>all the land of the Hittites</u> and unto the great sea toward the going down of the sun shall be your coast. There shall not any man be able to stand before you all the days of your life as I was with Moses, so I will be with you. I will not fail you nor forsake you. Be strong and of good courage for unto this people shall you divide for an inheritance the land which I swore unto their fathers to give them. Only be strong and very courageous that you may observe to do all the law which Moses my servant commanded you turn not from it to the right hand or to the left that you may prosper whithersoever you may go.*

Joshua obeys God's commandments to him thereby leading Israel into their triumphant route over their enemies as they begin to occupy the territory (land that was not originally theirs) that God promised to them in their inheritances. Remember the Hebrews came out of slavery from Egypt into the Promised Land. Joshua's time on earth as an emissary for the Lord was coming to a close after living for 110 years. Joshua in his farewell address to the new nation of Israel provides them with a detailed history of the emerging nation, the story of its conception, the activities of those who came before him until the present day at that time. Joshua cautions the nation to ***make a choice***. Look at **Joshua 24:15** cited here, "**And if it seems evil to you to serve the lord, <u>choose for yourselves</u> this day whom you will serve. Whether the gods, which your fathers served, that were on the other side of the river, or the god of the Amorites <u>in whose land</u> you dwell, but as for my house and me, we will serve the Lord.**" Clearly the prophet of God in his own way says to the emerging nation they can make whatever *choice* they deemed appropriate in terms of a belief in what many humanitarians refer to as a "higher power." Joshua tells them directly **that for my house and me we will serve the Lord**! Joshua made that choice as you and I must make ours. There is no way around it.

Further display of this is explainable again with the prophet Elijah playing a prominent role in trying to convince young men to "make a choice" when it comes to God Almighty. Let us pick up the story background to lay the foundation of its occurrence as it unfolds in the **eighteenth chapter of 1 Kings**. Elijah challenges them all to stop deliberating or debating back and forth between their two diverse opinions. He demands that they <u>choose a side</u> one way or the other as fact then move on. Elijah says to them sternly either way make a choice! (**1 Kings 18:21**). Elijah spoke these words to a large group of people—i.e., prophets of Baal and King Ahab on Mount Carmel. They had departed from God. Nevertheless, to quiet their consciences they had begun to worship false gods. Yet their consciences still bothered them. They wondered if they were right. Thus, they were undecided. They "halted" between two opinions. The Hebrew word halted actually means, "danced." They were dancing between false religion and the worship of the True, One and Only God of heaven and earth Jehovah. Therefore, the prophet drew a sharp contrast between false religion and true faith in God Almighty. He said, in **1 Kings 18:21, "How long will you waver? How long will you dance back and forth? If the Lord be God, follow Him! If your false religion is true, follow it." You have to stop dancing and wavering between two opinions. "And the people answered him not a word."** How could they? What he said was obvious. It is suicidal to waver back and forth on such an important subject! The salvation of our eternal soul is at stake. Heaven and Hell are at stake! Wake up and come over to one side or the other. After all, it is your choice either way. My recommendation is echoed in the word of the Lord that is prescribed on the cover of this book from **Deuteronomy 30:19 that says, "I call heaven and earth as witnesses today against you, that I have *set before you life and death, blessing and cursing; therefore choose life*, that both you and your descendants may live."**

Just like these OT-Old Testament believers, some current believers in God have gone astray and begun to worship false gods. Succumbing to false doctrines and doctrines of demons e.g. same sex marriages and other beliefs and worshipping of angels, which God strictly forbids. See **Colossians 2:18** denoted here, **that says, "Let no one cheat you of your reward taking delight in false humility and <u>worship of angels</u> intruding into those things he has not seen vainly puffed up by his fleshly mind."** Along with deities or false gods of their <u>*own choosing*</u>. However, their consciousness will began bothering them to the point that it will occur to those who are going astray currently, that they need to awake out of their slumber and make a choice for Christ. They will start having a sense of despair because there is an unhinged connection to the true God of Israel that is lingering among their thoughts. This may explain why some people who have wealth and worldly possessions still feel "empty" inside. The hole in their spiritual DNA/RNA is only fillable by the blood and with the love of Jesus Christ. I propose we all make the choice for Christ whom humanity refers to or is aka, the Great Physician.

Essentially all of us must make a choice and choose a side or make a decision as to whom we will serve. We are no different from them in that sense. Everyday across the world in sports venues, teams, relationships, friendships or social circles people choose whom to love, befriend, associate with or unite. Life demands a decision in daily life. Therefore, since the consequences here are so enormous one must also understand that this choice is an eternal one that is unalterable once one faces Christ Judgment or the Bema seat (where believers are judged)when he/she decides where all will spend eternity—i.e., either with Jesus or with Satan in hellfire. The Great White Throne Judgment seat reservations occurs for all nonbelievers. Review here **Revelation 20:11–15, "Then I saw a great white throne and him who sat on it from whose face the earth and the heaven fled away. And there was found no place for them. And I saw the dead, small and great standing before God and the books were opened. And another book was opened which is the Book of Life. And the dead were judged according to their works by the things which were written in the books. The sea gave up the dead who were in it, and Death and Hades delivered up the dead who were in them. And they were judged each one according to his works Then Death and Hades were cast into the Lake of Fire. This is the second death. And anyone not found written in the Book of Life was cast into the lake of fire."** However, there is an unexpected pleasant twist in this dilemma. Although we are making a choice in a sense, the choice in many ways has been made for us. Allow me to provide more clarification in the following narrative. God says, via Christ you **have not** "chosen me" but I have **chosen you**!

Read **John 15:16–19, "You did not choose me, but I chose you and appointed you that you should go and bear fruit and that your fruit should remain that whatsoever you ask the Father in my name he may give you. These things I command you that you love one another if the world hates you, you know that it hated me before it hated you."** Wait a minute! I just spent some time elaborating or describing how we all must make a choice for Christ, yet here the WOG (words of God) clearly states that we were "chosen" by *Christ* to be his disciples (believers). How can this be reconciled via the scriptures with the contrasting perspectives? Ah, now we will review to explore a little further to ascertain the balance between God Almighty choosing humanity to have faith in his Holy Son Jesus Christ versus us choosing God to live through or by faith in his Son Jesus Christ.

Let me began here with **1 Peter 2:9** here it says, **"But you** (believers in Christ) **are 'a <u>chosen</u> generation,' a royal priesthood, an holy nation, a peculiar people that you should show forth the praises of him who has called you out of darkness** (fallen state of man) **into his marvelous light (holy estate) of Christ."** The eternal Heavenly Father Jehovah knows all. God is Omniscient. Therefore, because he does he works all things **according** to the counsel of his own will. See **Ephesians 1:11 that reads, "In him we have obtained inheritance <u>being predestinated</u> according to the purpose of him who *<u>works all things according to the counsel of his own will.</u>"** I am not sure how many of you are familiar with the story of the child prophet Jeremiah. If you are outstanding, if not let me provide a few key points regarding his life to illustrate this matter. Jeremiah was a child when the Lord called him to the ministry and he tells the Lord at the time of his calling that he is only a child when God directs him to go the people of Israel to preach his word. See **Jeremiah 1:5–10** listed here, **"<u>Before</u> I formed you in the womb, I knew you. <u>Before</u> you were born, I sanctified you. I ordained you a prophet to the nations. Then I said ah Lord God behold I cannot speak for I am a child/youth. But the lord said to me do not say that I am a child/youth. For you shall go to all, to whom I shall send you and whatever I command you shall speak. Do not be afraid of their faces. For I am with you to deliver you says the Lord. Then the Lord put forth his hand and touched my mouth and the Lord said to me. Behold I have put my words in your mouth see this day I have set you over the nations and over the kingdoms to root out and pull down to destroy and to throw down to build and to plant."** I will analyze these scriptures in more detail following below.

Jeremiah (just like Moses did) attempts to avoid preaching to his countrymen by responding to the Lord that he is *only a child* thus he is not equipped or mature enough to have any dialogue with adults yet alone to preach to them regarding their lives or about their conduct that is askance of God's will. **Jeremiah 1:5–8.** God's response to Jeremiah is quick and direct. God tells the child prophet that *before* he formed Jeremiah in the womb *he **knew** him...before* you were born **I sanctified** you, I **ordained you** to be prophet to the nations. Several key points are observable here in the dissertation that if not reviewed more specifically may casually go unobserved. First, God tells Jeremiah that ***before* he** formed Jeremiah in the womb that **he knew** him. We need to consider the totality of the concepts here God wants this child prophet and all of us to understand. Among them is that Jeremiah's birth happened by "the will and hand" of God as all births are. One's mind may not be able readily to grasp the enormity of this because of the finite understanding of the human brain on earth. God is telling this child prophet (as well as us) that your existence (birth) did not happen as an accident, a mistake or because your human parents desired it to be so. **Your existence on earth is by divine decree only!** God is telling Jeremiah that you were in ***my mind*** "before" you were in your mother's womb! *Remember early on during the introduction to this book, I alluded to this very fact that we (all) beings man or animals **originated "in the mind" of God** in heaven **before** life ever began for us anywhere in his sovereign universe.* My God, this is awesome! In addition, by the way this applies to each of us collectively and to each of us independently not just Jeremiah.

I believe God is telling all of us something here. Grant me some latitude to expand upon this subject shortly as I deviate from our primary subject matter momentarily before getting back on track. Never let anyone say to you again that abortions are correcting mistakes made by people who want to have the **right** to choose when to give birth or they have **an absolute right** to decide when to abort an unborn child. **NO RIGHTS ARE ABSOLUTE ANYWHERE IN THE COSMOS!** People especially Americans are always talking about their "rights." I have a right to this; I have a right to that et cetera. Slow down just a bit. The artificial implementation or invocation of your *citizenship* "labeled rights" **do not exceed** the authority of God Almighty's commandments to all of us. Mathematics is a specific science that uses exact numbers, integers, algebraic equations e.g. associative or distributive theories, formulas (E=MC2) theorems (Pythagorean Theorem A2+ B2= C2), equations, including fractions and denominators whereby all things are reduced to the **Lowest Common Denominator or LCD**. Therefore, God has reduced all of us to the LCD period. Essentially, this says that all of us regardless to temporal titles or labels used to identify our roles here as stewards whether that be presidents, governors, bishops, kings, ruler, police officer, firefighter, etc. God holds humanity to the exact same standard no exceptions period. Because all of us are reduced or identified to God Almighty by the Lowest Common Denominator as **human beings.** This applies to all, American or not, rich or pauper, free or slave! This celestial deception via Lucifer's interference, attributable or due to the lie, man utilizes from Satan as the causation of **abortion** by man to terminate life as he/she sees fit. Man tries to alter God's sovereignty and plan of life thus by invoking demonic lies declaring _artificial rights on demand_ according to birth family, heritage, ethnicity or citizenship. God must or has to be laughing hysterically when anyone asserts his or her self-declaration of rights. Anyone's self-declaratory rights means absolutely nothing to the Lord God of Hosts! God will simply say to any such challenger to God's divine authority as he did to Job, **where were you when I laid the earth's foundation? Tell me if you understand,** listed in **Job 38:4.** Please recall or remember the difference between "created" and "born" from earlier discussion.

This is a critical point. Simply because it illustrates those children whom are aborted, **_God knew each and every one of them before_ they were created** via birth process then aborted (murdered) within the womb of their mother. We know this because God tells the child prophet Jeremiah that he knew him before he planted him in the womb of his mother and knew his name prior to the advent of his birth! Abortion's interference within the birth cycle thus not allowing birth or terminates the process of coming into life via "born" or alive outside the mother's womb independently of her is murder. God will have a discussion with each person on his or her personal interview with him on Judgment Day to explain his holy intent for the aborted fetus he knew before they were born then abruptly killed. Regardless, to their role in the murdering of *unborn* aborted *children* in the womb of their mother where they were supposed to be in the safest cocoon imaginable until their actual birth. Unfortunately, her womb became their tomb. Returning to our topic, God is simply stating that we (all humanity) predestination or **chosen by God** to exist on earth, **before** we were ever **born** on earth.

See **Ephesians 1:4–5** which reads in part, "***Just as he chose us in him (Christ) before the foundation of the world… V5 having predestined us to adoption as sons by Jesus Christ to himself according to the good pleasure of his will.***" Praise God! This tells us several things. Among them is that God knows our name, race, gender, ancestors, tribe, death, suffering, tribulations, etc., in advance. Furthermore, this tells us that God knew everything about him/us *before* he/we ever took his/our first breath on earth. Nevertheless, Jehovah God goes on to inform Jeremiah that **he sanctified** (separated/made holy) Jeremiah **before** he was born. Conclusively, God Almighty tells Jeremiah that you were **predestined,** ordained, sanctified, known and **chosen** by **me before** you ever came into existence on earth. We will look at additional Holy Scriptures to solidify our narrative a bit more. Jesus stated in **John 15:16**. "*You **did not choose me** but **I chose you** and **appointed you** that you should go out and bear fruit and that your fruit should remain that whatever you ask the Father in My Name he may give you.*"

Clearly the Lord was talking with his disciples and informing them of their ministry to go out unto the world and labor to evangelize about the gospel or good news that he (Christ) came to save the world (believing mankind) from eternal separation and judgment from God. Christ **chose** his disciples thereby granting them a reprieve of having to choose him. Summarily, this balances with the WOG in this sense that God does the ***choosing initially*** and we reply or respond **by accepting** that invitation by ***our choice*** if you will by serving him voluntarily. Furthermore, just as we can *accept the invitation* from Almighty God we can also *choose to reject* or decline this open invitation to eternal life. Thereby receiving the unalterable diametrical opposite—i.e., eternal death which some have chosen to do all to the dismay of their own soul. **Jesus** said in **John 6:44, "No man can come to me _except_ the Father who sent me <u>draw him</u> and I will raise him up at the last day."** I now direct our focus to the next topic regarding this transitional war on earth from heaven to The Antichrist or the devil in human form on earth.

CHAPTER XIV

The Antichrist

I will begin this topic with the words from the **1 John 2:16**, which reads, *"Little children it is the last hour and as you have heard <u>the Antichrist</u> is coming, even now many anti-Christs have come by which we know that it is the last hour."* What is specifically so significantly mystifyingly evil about this person that strikes terror in the heart of man? Many people want know who is he. Where is the Antichrist at right now? Is he alive on earth now? Is it possible to stop him before assuming his role as God's nemesis on earth? Before, I try to answer some of these questions directly with answers within the words of God. Let us search what the word of God has to say about this cursed individual. Jesus said in **Matthew 26:24, "The Son of Man will go just as it is written about him but woe to the man who betrays the Son of Man it would have been better for him if he had never been born than to betray the Son of Man."** We know that when Jesus initially spoke those words that he was referring to Judas Iscariot, **but not just** only to or about him. The key to understanding this verse is expanding its meaning applicability to others than just Judas Iscariot. Many people pray for the return of Our Lord and Savior, Jesus Christ to return, as we should as commanded by God and Christ for us to do. However, we must understand **before** Jesus comes back, the **Antichrist must** come **first** and *<u>be revealed</u>* to the whole world just as Christ was revealed to the whole world as the Son of God. The world has seen some truly evil people living on its landscape since its creation by God Almighty. Nevertheless, there are **only two people** *ever* referred to as **the Son of Perdition** in the word of God.

They are **Judas Iscariot and The Antichrist period!** I will briefly discuss the former then the latter in more detail after a brief analysis of the phrase "Son of Perdition." The Son of Perdition is a unique phrase or title. Therefore, I will do some inquiry into its meaning before moving on to the application to the two people that I have already mentioned above. This title's origin has very dire consequences for its owners. Jesus referred to this title when he said I have lost none **except** the "son of perdition." See **John 17:12** that I have listed here as Jesus was praying unto his Heavenly Father said, "**While I was with them in the world, I kept them in your name. Those whom you gave me I have kept and none of them is 'lost' *except* the 'son of perdition' that the scripture might be fulfilled.**" Simply put Jesus told his Father and Our God that only one person is lost (doomed) of those disciples you gave me. However, Christ emphasizes that he is lost, so that the word of God's fulfillment occurs as God has decreed. The original Greek meaning of this word "perdition" means destruction or doomed to a specific fate because of the persistence of evil or the ultimate embodiment of evil. Consistently throughout scripture Greek (Aramaic) is referred to as the original language because of the conquest of the Greeks during Alexander The Great's reign of terror on the Middle Eastern culture topography including Jerusalem, Israel as prophesied by Daniel the prophet, was the dominant linguistic tongue. This usually happens as conquerors dominate a region or people via violence they replace native or indigenous laws, speech, language, customs, mores, principles or way of life and edicts, etc., with their own to further subjugate the vanquished people whom are under their own ruling authority. Naturally, this nullifies or negates historical practices of self-identify in all of its forms and in some instances, eradicating the host identity completely for total immersion or assimilation into their own value system or lifestyle practices of what is the preferred way of life contemporaneously. For examples, the ancestral African slaves and their descendants (African-American or Blacks today) were conquered, kidnapped and shipped to the Americas lost not only their own historical values, mores, or way of life they lost the ability to identify themselves.

All of them denied, deprived and prohibited from the use of native African names, tribes or unique self-identification labels. Afterward, when auctioned off at the slave trade on the auctioneer's block, then given European names thus erasing forever all vestiges of self-awareness or name identity that connected them to their African Continent or heritage. The purposeful, intentional result of these amalgamated heinous actions forever destroyed the umbilical cord of blacks to their ancestral heritage and connection to their motherland of Africa with no trace of whom *they were*, whom *they are* or whom *they could become* forever! Now, reverting to the "Son of Perdition" meaning per se, regarding this evil definition of the persons who have been cursed thereby forever by God that cannot be eradicated. This evil is inheritable, transferable or transplantable to someone or even unto an animal for that matter. The Antichrist, the Bible says obtains his power from Lucifer himself. Therefore, it is transferable in that sense or application. **Review Revelation 13:2 that says, "Now the beast, which I saw, was like a leopard his feet were like the feet of a bear and his mouth was like the mouth of a lion. The *dragon (Satan)* gave *him* his power, his throne and great authority."** This is one example of the transfer of evil authority from one diabolical being unto another. Another type or way it is accomplished is by demonic possession inside a body of or by an evil deity. Review **Luke 22:3–5**, it says, **"Then entered Satan into Judas surnamed Iscariot being of the number of the twelve and he went his way, communed with the chief priests, and captains how he might betray him (Jesus) unto them and they were glad and covenanted to give him money."** This is an instance of perdition being transplantable. The final example I would like to use is humanity to illustrate the inheritability of perdition. All of us inherited evil from Adam and Eve. Eve is the mother, of All-Evil on earth... Adam is "humanity's" stepfather of evil (apart from Lucifer who is the **undisputed father-King of All-Evil** in heaven and earth) here on our planet by proxy as he listened to the lie of Lucifer after he deceived Eve.

Judas Iscariot is a unique person in many regards. He was a disciple of Christ, treasurer, professed believer, spy, snitch, thief and a traitor. Judas was always concerned about money (as we see from the illustration just above) for we see him always lurking about when the topic involved cash. Another glaring illustration occurred when the alabaster box of expensive perfume was broken on the head of Christ to anoint him prior to his crucifixion that Judas Iscariot spoke out against it. Judas's response was that the perfume box (alms potential) for more money if sold instead of poured on Christ head and feet would have helped the poor. Superficially, this seemed like a good reason on the surface of motives without inquiring any further. However, Judas Iscariot was unconcerned about the poor or why this box potential financial yield could had a separate benevolent use for another good purpose to help those in need of financial ruin. Judas was concerned about how he was going to get his fuzzy little hands on it. However, this liar and thief had no intentions to do any such good for anybody other than himself. He carefully hid his ulterior motive underneath the sheet of deception. Judas Iscariot was not concerned about the poor as he professed he was by declaring such a pejorative. His only motive was when no one was looking as the treasurer he planned to steal the money. How do we know this for sure someone may ask?

We know this because Jesus rebuked him in **John 12:7–8** verses by saying **you have the poor with you always**—i.e., and there will be many more opportunities for you to help them **but me you don't have always leave her alone for she has done this for the day of my burial.** Christ said this because he knew Judas would betray him and that he was a thief who consistently stole from the moneybox that he kept. See **John 12:5–6** that outlines for us this thief's genuine sinister motive for it says, "**Why was this fragrant oil not sold for three hundred denarii and given to the poor? This he said not that he cared for the poor but because he was a thief and had the moneybox and he used to take (steal) what was put in it.**" My Lord, liars usually are thieves and thieves are usually liars to conceal their thefts. Clearly, Judas Iscariot was no exception to this premise.

Judas Iscariot, just like Bernie Madoff, the hedge fund profiteer, swindler, crook, thief and liar who stole millions of dollars from family and friends. Bernie Madoff cared for no one other than himself. Bernie had no remorse or consciousness about whom he hurt with his theft. Over time Bernie Madoff, via propped up Pyramid schemes, embezzlement and fraud of exorbitant deceptive trade practices in modern history, exceeding that of Michael Milken, another convicted liar and thief. Whose predatory (theft) business practices in the mid-nineteen eighties, caused financial havoc and ruin across the American landscape. Michael Milken's crimes were responsible for destroying lives, fortunes, profits, companies, careers, dreams, aspirations and well known bedrock solvent financial institutions during his phony paper money heyday schemes. Milken created an empire of vast wealth via stolen money along with valueless, worthless annuities or junk bonds wrecked the economy of the United States with devastating consequences for those directly and indirectly affected by its orbital sphere. Michael Milken's illegal activities or rippling waves of financial tsunami drowned out billions of dollars overnight via cascading domino effects upon vast corporate and family owned small business holdings alike.

Bernie Madoff, Michael Milken, and Judas Iscariot all had full-time jobs as professional thieves, conmen and liars. Judas betrayed Jesus in the garden of Gethsemane (**Luke 22:47**) with a kiss for thirty pieces of shekel. See **Matthew 26:14–16** that cites then **"One of the twelve-called <u>Judas Iscariot</u> went to the chief priests and said what are you willing to give me if I deliver him unto you? And they counted out to him thirty pieces of silver. So from that time he sought opportunity to betray him."** Review another example of his treachery in **Luke 22:47–48** that states **and while he** (Jesus Christ) **was still speaking, behold a multitude and he who was called Judas, one of the twelve, went before them and <u>*drew near to Jesus to kiss him*</u>, But Jesus said to him Judas are you <u>*betraying the Son of Man with a kiss*</u>?** Judas had worldly sorrow afterward once he knew that they intended actually to kill Jesus via crucifixion. Therefore, Judas later regrets this act of ultimate betrayal of Christ the Son of God Almighty, then commits suicide by hanging himself in the field of blood. Judas's ministry for Christ rarely mentioned as some of the others like Philip, Peter or John. I always wondered why that was the case. However, I guess I knew somehow deep inside that, the answer was that he was concentrating on the next theft from the box. Judas accompanied the arrestors sent from the Sanhedrin Council to seize/arrest Christ person for blasphemy against God. Judas gave the "signal," *which was **the one that I kiss** is he who proclaims to be the Son of God* as they appeared angrily in the garden with torches lit, drawn swords and clubs to effect the arrest of Christ by force if need be. See **Mark 14:44–46,** here **"Now his betrayer had given them a signal, saying <u>whomever I kiss</u> he is the one seize him and lead him away safely, as soon as he had come immediately he went up to him, Rabbi, Rabbi and kissed him then they laid their hands on him and took him away."** We know this because Christ asked Judas do you betray the son of Man with a kiss as he approached Christ in the garden of Gethsemane. Read **Luke 22:47–48 cited above.**

This kiss or act in contemporaneous times is referred to as the "Kiss of Death." This moniker has followed the Sicilian mafia as well as other extremely violent murderous gang members or groups of international criminal cartels around the world. The reason being the perception of its appearance as an insidious betrayal both personally as well as professionally. Clarification regarding this issue here by the following simple explanation generically speaking. Kiss or kisses generally convey or demonstrate an act or display of endearment intending to convey affection for the one kissed. People kiss all the time those who they endear, love or appreciate. Kisses are the quickest publicly accepted form of greeting and romance allowed in societies around the world. Whenever families members reunite or arrive safely from flights, cruises or destinations and venues to greet or meet loved ones whom they temporally were absent from during their respective hiatus or travels they will publicly kiss each other. Enemies generally do not kiss each other for any reasons. Historically, it is considered an act of aggression, insult or gesture of belittling to humiliate by *kissing someone* you are at war, despise, hate, have ill will or feelings about or toward.

Subsequently, the act of arrest or seizures of one's person against one's will involuntarily including enemies on any level is viewed as a hostile, aggressive movement designed to humiliate the arrestee, kidnapped or seized person pseudo-sinuously amounting to a feeling of dread or death like grasp almost figuratively speaking. Therefore, the amalgamation of the two opposite dynamisms simultaneously—i.e., apposite actions, one designed to convey the message that one cares and the other viewed as one that seeks forcefully to impose upon one ill will, humiliation/subjugation creates the "kiss of death" component for the victim. Consequently, **Jesus identifies Judas as the Son of Perdition** when praying to his Father; he said I have lost none except the **son of perdition** who later as he attempted to kiss Christ pretending that he cared for him while simultaneously betraying him "using the kisses" as the identifying act symbolically on Christ person as he was to be arrested. This is aforementioned in **Luke 22:47–48 above**. It appears to me that the kiss disguised as "the signal" because the hour of the day was dark that is why they brought torches and lanterns with them due to low visibility and they needed something to vividly identify or point out Christ to the arresting authorities among them. Importantly we should recall or remember that during this period of civilization there were obviously no lights, public light poles, or any illuminating equipment that would allow visibility to be sharp, precise or where one could so clearly see or identify with certainty faces among people who bore striking resemblances even at short distances was challenging. Summarily, Judas's personal rejection of Christ, via betrayal appointed Judas Iscariot, to this dire fate by *choosing* not to repent. Albeit he was in Christ's presence or inner circle as a disciple.

Furthermore, Judas Iscariot was the *son of perdition* and destruction walking along the path of his life's course toward his doomed fate which is exemplified by his betrayal of Christ. Judas's incessant theft due to his love of money. The word of God says in **1** Timothy 6:10 the **"love of money is the root of all kinds of evil from which some have strayed from the faith in their greediness, and pierced themselves though with many sorrows."** Judas's frequently was pilfering from the moneybox, his suicidal death, his direct rejection of the offer of God's love accorded to him via the opportunity/chance as one of the original twelve Disciples of Christ here on earth. I repeat for emphasis Judas Iscariot was among the *first twelve* Disciples of Christ. This is mind blowing. Judas had an honorable, coveted, granted recognition or invocation by God my fellow believers, newcomers and non-believers in Christ. It is second only to the **one woman** "<u>chosen</u>" by God to be the "mother" of Jesus Christ, here on earth exclusively, the Virgin Mary. I briefly digress from discussion of Judas Iscariot, as I propose that we all pay homage and devote some attention to the monumental; honor/salutation given unto the Virgin Mary by the angel Gabriel dispatched by God to herald to her the good news recorded in **Luke 1:26–34** below:

Now in the sixth month the angel Gabriel was sent by God to a city of Galilee named Nazareth to a virgin betrothed to a man whose name was Joseph of the house of David. The virgin's name was Mary and having come in the angel said to her **Rejoice, <u>highly favored one</u> the Lord is with you blessed are <u>you among women</u>** *but when she saw him she was troubled at this saying and considered what manner of greeting this was. Then the angel said to her, do not be afraid Mary, for you have* **<u>found favor with God</u>** *and you will conceive in your womb and bring forth a Son and shall call his name Jesus. He will be great and will be called the Son of the highest, and the Lord God will give him the throne of his father David and he will reign over the house of Jacob forever and of his kingdom, there will be no end. Then Mary said to the angel how can this be since I do not know a man? and the angel answered and said to her, The Holy Spirit will come upon you and the power of the Highest will overshadow you therefore also that Holy One who is to be born will be called the Son of God.*

Many women were virgins at the same time The Virgin Mary was alive whose lineage connected or related to the DNA kinship of Abraham. Yet, Gabriel told the Virgin Mary, she was highly favored, chosen and selected, by God Almighty to be the vessel of distinction to give birth unto God's Child on earth! Analogously, many other men could had been among the first twelve disciples of Christ. However, Judas Iscariot, who ultimately betrayed him was hand selected by Christ to serve among him. I continuously use Judas's surname of Iscariot for distinction simply because Christ had two Judas's among his original twelve disciples. The other Judas identified or whose first name was Judas was the son of James. Review **Luke 6:13** that **reads, "And when it was day he called his disciples to himself and from them he chose twelve whom he named apostles. Simon whom he named Peter and Andrew his brother James and John, Philip and Bartholomew, Matthew and Thomas, James the son of Alpheus and Simon called the zealot, 'Judas the son of James' and Judas Iscariot who also became a traitor."** Further momentary digression here, I believe personally, that when Jesus disciples asked him whom was it that would betray him at the Last Supper. Christ does not identify the person by name. Actually, Jesus identifies the betrayer by act or action.

Look at **Mark 14:18–22**, denoted here that says, **"Now as they sat and ate Jesus said assuredly I say to you one of you who eats with me will betray me and they began to be sorrowful and say to him one by one Is it I? Another said is it I? He answered and said to them it is, one of the twelve, who _dips with me_ in the dish."** There was still some minor confusion because they were all dipping in the dish with Jesus. However, Jesus spoke specifically about it being **_he who dips_** his hand **in** the bowl **_at the_ exact same time** that I do. I theorize that if Jesus would have said it is Judas, because there were _two Judases_ who were disciples, later named as apostles that would have caused enormous confusion had Christ said it is Judas. All of them would have been disoriented, in disbelief, flabbergasted or shocked as well as suspicious of the *other* or innocent Judas—i.e., Judas the son of James. Then the apostles would have asked Jesus Christ which Judas? Now back to the main narration of the story. However, Judas

Iscariot forfeited this honorable selection by siding with the enemies of God and among spiritual wickedness in high places—i.e., evil angels of whom Lucifer is king. It was a highly coveted or esteemed positon for all eternity then, now and forever! Actually, the word of God says the wall of the City of the New Jerusalem foundation of heaven will have the names of the *first or original twelve apostles* of Christ emblazoned on it.

See **Revelation 21:14 cited here that reads, "Now the wall of the City had twelve foundations and on them were the names of the twelve apostles/disciples of the Lamb**." Matthias's name *will replace* that of **Judas Iscariot** on one of the foundations of **heavens twelve floors** just in case any of you were wondering about Judas Iscariot name in this scenario. Matthias replaced Judas Iscariot as the twelfth apostle of Christ after Judas Iscariot's betrayal. See **Acts 1:23–26** here, **"And they proposed two, Joseph called Barsabas who was surnamed Justus, and Matthias. And they prayed and said O Lord, who know the hearts of all, show which of these two, you have chosen to take part in this *ministry and apostleship* from which Judas by transgression fell, that he might go to his own place. And they cast their lots and the lot fell on "Matthias" and he was numbered with the eleven apostles."** Furthermore, we know that *Judas Iscariot name will not be there* simply because it **does not** say **ex-disciples** it says disciples/apostles. Finally, we know that the betrayer and thief name will not be there because of God's holiness allowing us to use common sense. God has never honored any evildoer eternally whatsoever! Without question, this is an eternal honor no doubt. Therefore, certainly this will not be an exception to God's divine holiness regarding the name of his Son's betrayer/apostle as one of heaven's foundations.

This is heavens "Hall of Fame" or "Ring of Honor" if you will. This is where those who via distinguished service unto the Lord God Almighty and his Only, Begotten Son, Jesus Christ are eternally recognized. Certainly, God in his holy, omniscient wisdom and glory wouldn't dishonor his beloved Only begotten, Son, Jesus Christ by etching in heaven's Hall of Fame the *one* who betrayed Jesus Christ unto death in the flesh. My God what an Honor they have and Judas would have had had he remained faithful to his Christ. Contrastingly, Judas Iscariot instead of an eternal honor will receive an eternal shame. Furthermore, history forever identifies Judas Iscariot as Christ's traitor. Thereby sealing his eternal damnation to his soul forever by utilizing his own limited freewill *choosing* rather to number among those who crucified Jesus. Thus nullifying his selection as a bishop of the Lord. Christ said that it ***would have been better*** for him if he **never had been born** (inherited this doomed fate) than to betray Jesus. See **Mark 14:21 here, "The Son of Man indeed goes just as it is written of him but woe to that man by whom the Son of Man is betrayed! It would have been good for that man if he had never been born."** Furthermore, Christ foretells of Judas Iscariot's betrayal of himself. Review it here whereby Jesus tells us in **John 13:18, "I do not speak concerning all of you. I know whom I have chosen but that the scripture may be fulfilled he who eats bread with me has lifted up his heel against me."**

Subsequently, Judas Iscariot now awaits shivering and trembling in horror in the abyss of total darkness of the bottomless pit for a temporal resurrection to kneel before the same Son of God. Whom he betrayed, willingly, voluntarily, greedily, only to look into his holy, fiery eyes of Christ the Lord, the King of all Kings, for the final imposition of sentence by Jesus Christ on Judgment Day. Judas Iscariot will receive no mercy for his dammed soul as one of the two "Sons of Perdition" suffering banishment to the flaming embers of an unquenchable hell fire prepared for Satan and his fallen angels. How do we know that Judas Iscariot will receive no mercy from the merciful God of Heaven and Earth? Someone could reasonably inquire or ask. We know so because of the words of the Son of God Jesus Christ himself confirms this to all of us. See Jesus words here in **Matthew 5:7. "Blessed are the merciful for they *shall obtain mercy*."** Simply put another way Christ said he who has shown no mercy shall receive no mercy! The brother of Christ here on earth James echoes his brother words in **James 2:13** here, **for judgment is without mercy to the one who has shown no mercy. Mercy triumphs over judgment.** Next, I elaborate about the second "Son of Perdition" a.k.a. the Antichrist.

The Antichrist also is the second Son of Perdition or destruction for he has a lot more damnable issues than does Judas Iscariot! Let us look at this sinister being and the unbearable pain he must endure for time immemorial because of his outright opposition to God Almighty! Whereas, Judas actually **betrays** Jesus Christ to the religious leaders of his day (the Sanhedrin Council) who ultimately delivers Christ to the Romans who actually crucified the Son of God on a cross for our sins and the sins of the whole world. The Antichrist actually "**portrays**" to be Jesus while simultaneously opposing him. One Son of Perdition, actually *__betrays__* Jesus—i.e., Judas Iscariot and the other Son of Perdition, the Antichrist *__portrays__* to be Jesus while opposing him! Wow, the cabal of hideousness never stops trying to spread its malignant cancerous tentacles of evil everywhere possible. When discussing the Antichrist—i.e., the world's most demonic, sinister, heinous and diabolical individual in the flesh (human form) this side of the eternal divide between spiritual and terrestrial beings. There are some completely logical questions regarding his evil leadership that requires further inquiry. For example, someone may ask, where, from whom, and how does he receive his global authority or dominion of all the people of the earth? Does anyone currently have that power that is transferrable to him? Who is that individual? Et cetera., etc.

Well, the word of God actually has these answers readily available so to speak. I will begin with the book of **Revelation 13:1–2**. The WOG—i.e., words of God—says here, "**Then I stood on the sand of the sea and I saw a beast rising up out of the sea having seven heads and ten horns and on his horns, ten crowns and on his head a blasphemous name. Verse 2: now the beast that I saw was like a leopard his feet were like the feet of a bear and his mouth like the mouth of a lion. *The dragon gave him his power, his throne and great authority.*"** Next, I will decipher these amalgamated scriptures a little more in detail using these same words from the original translation below.

Then I (John the Revelator) stood on the sand of the sea (seaside on the shore) while the vision (futur-

istic event to occur) that Jesus Christ was allowed by
his heavenly Father to show him. Revelation 1:1 and
I saw a beast (symbolism for man, Nations or entity),
rising up (coming into being meteorically) out of
the sea. Having seven heads (seven mountains) and
ten horns (10 leaders or kings/emperors) and on his
horns (symbol of authority) he had ten crowns (des-
ignates monarchs, kings, leaders or presidents repre-
senting countries). And on his head a blasphemous
(vile or against God/Christ) name. Satan in Greek
actually means 'enemy.' Now Revelation 13:2; now,
the beast (male satanic ruler) which I saw. Was like
a leopard (quick/fast) and his feet were like a bear
(strong foundation). And his mouth as the mouth
of a lion (devouring, loud, and commanding) and
the dragon (Satan/Lucifer) __*gave him*__ *(transferred*
to him) his power (principalities and powers, ruler
of darkness). All demonic angelic wisdom (powers of
divination, insight, witchcraft, sorcery and evil on a
grand scale) and his seat, realm and great authority
(spiritual wickedness in this world in demoted heav-
enly places). Also, See Ephesians 6:12 that cites for
we (believers in Christ/humanity in general) wres-
tle not (fight against) flesh and blood. (Terrestrial/
humans) But against principalities (demonic spirits,
celestial treachery, against powers against the rulers
of the darkness (unhinged evil) of this world. (All
satanic Lucifer inspired, orchestrated along with his
fallen angels spheres or corridors of power) against
spiritual wickedness (devilish evil) in high places
(invisible empires by spiritual beings—i.e., demons,
in ranking privileged) orders of world powers.

Further analysis of this scripture tells us other ominous things
of the coming ruler of darkness of spiritual wickedness in high

places that will be at a theater near us soon. **Revelation 13:1** tells us that **"This beast rises out of the sea having 'seven heads' and ten horns."** This is simply symbolic language that says he arises to life or comes to political power with great authority. Therefore, an analysis needed to comprehend this symbolism is as follows. Numerous sites around the world purportedly built upon "seven hills" for example Israel. Jerusalem's seven hills are reportedly; Mount Scopus, Mount Olivet, Mount of Corruption, Mount Ophel, Mount Zion both old and new Mount Zions and Antonia fortress. However, there are countless others but none are more prominent that Rome. This is important because although during the writing at the time of John the Revelator, as well as others, including the prophet Daniel, it was a mystery. Simply because not all of the other countries that have seven mountains were yet known (undiscovered) or held prominent hegemony militarily or economically in global affairs. During the revelation of Jesus Christ to the Apostle John, the Roman Empire was the dominant force on earth politically, economically and more importantly militarily. Furthermore, its revision again under the ten-nation confederacy or ten toes seen by Daniel in his double prophetic End Time message to this world seen by Nebuchadnezzar. Almighty God determined that there would only be seven empires appertaining to man's rule over the earth in humanity's pilgrimage in the world and they are as following according to the depiction of the image of man statue in Nebuchadnezzar's King of Babylon dream.

They are including his rule: Assyrian, Egyptian, Babylonian, Medes-Persians, Grecian, Roman, and the Revised Roman Empire or Ten Nation Confederacy of European Union 12 members currently (Britain/Brexit is already withdrawing from current twelve-nation confederacy Spain may be next). This is why nations that attempted world rule afterward have miserably failed e.g. Japan, Germany, Italy, Russia just to name a few who instigated world wars for world supremacy. All of them failed and will fail including our current world powers. Because they do not understand, neither do they believe, nor do they know the Lord God's decree regarding the Lord God' of Hosts imposed limitation on world dominance relating to man's governance on the earth's plateau. Jesus said in **Mark 12:24,**

"**Are you not therefore mistaken <u>because you neither know the</u> <u>scriptures or the power of God</u>?**" God's limitation upon man's rule on the earth mandates only seven *kingdoms of men* (coincidentally this balances with seven days of the week as well as the seven year tribulation period) until he sets up the eternal Kingdom of Jesus Christ his Son that will have no end. God promised King David, that his family lineage would forever rule upon the throne of Israel in perpetuity. Read **1 Kings 2:1–4** here, "**Now the days of David drew near that he should die, and he charged Solomon his son saying, I go the way of all the earth, be strong therefore and prove yourself a man and keep charge of the Lord your God, to walk in his ways to keep his statutes and his commandments. His judgments and his testimonies as it is written in the Law of Moses that you may prosper in all that you do and wherever you turn. That the Lord may _fulfill his word_ which he spoke concerning me, saying if your sons take heed to their way, to walk before me in truth with their heart and with their soul. He said you _shall not lack a man on the throne of Israel._**" **Jesus Christ** fulfills this _role permanently eternally_ being of the <u>family lineage</u> of **King David** in the flesh. Read the genealogical line of Christ in abbreviated form that establishes the word of God in this perspective.

See **Matthew 1:1 and 17** here that reads, "**The book of genealogy of Jesus Christ, <u>the Son of David,</u> the Son of Abraham.**" **Now verse Matthew 1:17, "So all the generations from <u>Abraham</u> <u>to David</u> are fourteen generations, from <u>David until the captivity</u> <u>in Babylon</u> are fourteen generations and from the <u>captivity in</u> <u>Babylon unto the Christ</u> are fourteen generations.**" Wow, my God this is awesome! This gives me goosebumps saints of the Most High God of Israel as well as any other reads of this book. Consequently the despot or rulers on earth do not comprehend God Almighty has sovereignly and divinely designated only so many kingdoms of man to rule period. Jesus told them you know neither the scripture nor the power of God. <u>I repeated this passage for emphasis sake only.</u> Read **Matthew 22:29, "Here Jesus answered and said to them, You are mistaken, not knowing the scriptures nor the power of God.**"

Furthermore, review **Daniel 2:1 and 39–43** listed here, "**Now in the second year of Nebuchadnezzar reign, Nebuchadnezzar had dreams and his spirit was so troubled that his sleep left him. But after you shall arise another kingdom inferior to yours then another, a third kingdom of bronze. Which shall <u>rule over all the earth.</u> And the fourth kingdom shall be as strong as iron inasmuch iron breaks in pieces and <u>crush all others</u> whereas you saw <u>the feet and toes</u> partly of potters clay and partly of iron the kingdom shall be divided yet the strength of the iron shall be in it just as you saw the iron mixed with ceramic clay. And as the toes of the feet were partly of iron and partly of clay, <u>so the kingdom shall be partly strong and partly fragile.</u> As you saw the iron mixed with the clay, they will mingle with the seed of men but they will not adhere to one another. Just as iron does not mix with clay. <u>And in the days of these kings the God of heaven</u> will set up <u>a kingdom</u> which shall <u>never be destroyed</u> and the kingdom shall not be *left to other people* it shall break in pieces and consume all these <u>kingdoms and it shall stand forever!</u> Glory be to God!**"

However, in our time—i.e., the last days (time era just before the second return of Jesus Christ to earth) it is to be revealed. See **Daniel 12:9**, whereby he was told by the angel of the Lord to "**seal up the book**" **until** the **end of days** arrive. This final king of the earth that will rule over man emanates from the confederacy that is emerging from the ashes of the Revised Roman Empire—i.e., the European Union. As foretold by Daniel in the scriptures just cited of the 10 toes narration. Now I continue our narrative regarding the identity in principle of this vile devil in the flesh.

This evil monster is none other than Sheol's seed, "the man of the hour," Lucifer's Golden Boy in the flesh...the Anti-Christ! The world is seeking his identity for many reasons some for curiosity others for clarity, some just want to know whom he is, others foolishly want to kill him as Herod, and others wanted to kill Jesus Christ when he was just a baby. Look at **Matthew 2:13** denoted here, "**And when they were departed behold the angel of the Lord appeared to Joseph in a dream saying arise and take the young child and** his mother and flee into Egypt and remain there until I bring you word for Herod will seek the young child to <u>destroy</u> him."

Nevertheless, this man, The Antichrist, has a diabolical origin in the bowels of hell and once they discover who he is, they are going to wish that they never would have known him. Seemingly, his identity is a mystery for now. Why that is, someone may ask? Well the reason is simple. Jesus Christ, the Son of God, lived for thirty three years on this earth and for thirty years of his life, Christ lived relatively in a shadow like estate, or obscurity so to speak or normalcy as it were without much fanfare or notoriety. Therefore, this made him almost anonymous or unknown to public scrutiny. Yet, once his revelation to the world through his public ministry became prominent. The entire world knew whom he was and is even to this very day so do we. Contemporaneously, it is approximately two thousand years after, the death of the Son of God, at Golgotha—i.e., the camp of the skull's hillside. Yet we are still talking about God's Son, Jesus Christ. Make absolutely no mistake about it so does the ceremonial entry into this world's stage will the arrival of Satan's Son or Imp be to our decaying world. The Antichrist secret concealment or hidden identity comprised for general reasons as well. Some of these reasons are specific and some are generic reasons simply put. Jesus preached publicly for three years. The Antichrist will do so for three and a half (forty-two months) years. See **Revelation 13:5.** Listed here, **"And he was given a mouth speaking great things and blasphemies and he was given authority to continue forty-two months"**—i.e., 3.5 years. Actually, he will rule the world for 7 years a combination of the two, forty-two months periods combined of the Great Tribulation of his worldwide reign of terror.

Some people on this earth are foolish enough or naïve regarding his authority and they actually attempt, desire, or want to kill him or at least try to harm him. Remember he receives a mortal would that was "miraculously" healed which causes the whole world to follow him declaring **who can make war with the beast?** God's word documents this in **Revelation 13:4**, which says in its entirety, **"So they worshipped the dragon who gave authority to the beast, and they worshipped the beast saying _who is like the beast? Who is_** *able to make war with him?*" Look at **Revelation 13:3, which** says, "**And I saw one of this heads as it were _wounded to death_ and his _deadly wound was healed_ and the entire world wondered after the beast.**" This is the first attempt but it may not be the last. Therefore, it is apparently clear for security purposes one of the general reasons for his obscurity is to mitigate many unsuccessful attacks to kill him. Subsequently, it may be argued that all of this (attempts to assassinate him) in a vain effort to "save the world" from this demonically controlled and possessed man who will terrorize them. Those who would attempt to kill him "think" that they could spare the world from this false Messiah that is to come via his meteoric ascendancy to world authority as a result of his sinister plans if they could just rid the world of his presence. Well, it is virtually impossible neither is it quite that easy for a couple of reasons one is **that God is not a man that he should lie** cited in **Numbers 23:19**.

Therefore, God has said that this man would appear on the earth and transform the world into a living hell via his campaign of terror and worldwide deception. God's word does not return unto him empty or void without accomplishing the thing whereunto God sent it. Review **Isaiah 55:11** that reads, "**So shall my words be that goes forth out of my mouth. It _shall not return_ unto void but _it shall accomplish_ that which I please and it shall prosper in the thing whereto I sent it.**" Thus, attempts on earth to kill The Antichrist, though well intended or embedded with nefarious undertones implemented depending upon the motives of the conspirators will be futile. The reason is quite simple; he **must** remain until he **fulfill his role** on earth as **God Almighty** has proclaimed he will do without exception! We all should know by now when God says something it *happens just* as God has declared it to be! It is **completely impossible** for it to fail. **Luke 1:37** states unequivocally to all of us, "**For with God nothing shall be impossible!**" In addition, the Antichrist will enter upon the world's stage apparently peaceful. He will not arrive thrashing the world into war initially or killing indiscriminately for no apparent reason, for then he would readily be identifiable as the Son of Perdition.

The Antichrist has to convince the world of two key points to ascertain or attain global hegemony. First, he must *destroy all hope* in Jesus Christ and Jehovah God Almighty as well as any worshippers of the true God of Abraham, Isaac and Jacob period on planet earth. No exceptions! This is the Anti or against Christ mode. Secondly, he must *mislead* the world via deception that he is the "Messiah" the "Christos or Christ" ___*anointed one of God*___ appointed to save the world from its destructive current course. He has to persuade and cause others to believe that he can lead peacefully as well as alter the destructive direction it seems to be hypersonically moving. This is the "Christ" mode. This is why he has the title of the "Anti-Christ." No one can hope to have converts follow them or do that just by walking in blazing saddles, guns rapid fire style killing indiscriminately initially like Yosemite Sam. The Antichrist cannot act like an out of control buffoon or demagogue violently starting chaos without rhyme or reason (current President Trump excluded) if he wants the world to follow after him which he does want the world to do. This would be a dead giveaway as to who he is if that was his modis operandi (method of operation) or entrance upon the world stage of leadership. Right now, no one on earth (outside of his immediate cabal) actually knows who he is or exactly where he is located.

Note: I said no one <u>on the earth knows outside</u> of his sphere of guardians. God always knows everything for God is omniscient—i.e., all knowing but God is not on the earth. The Bible tells us that God is in heaven. Rosemary's baby, the Antichrist protection currently shrouded by a cocoon of evil emissaries who will kill their own mother to protect him and his identity. The legions of corrupt fallen angels, along with disillusioned, demonically possessed, evilly inspired, satanically controlled humans who voluntarily, obediently, willingly with resolute passion and extreme dedication worship or serve him as the Ambassador of Hell. The Devil and the Antichrist both have a diabolical, tyrannical evil agenda for the entire world. However, we have enough scriptures that describe him or there exists specific criteria that this person must meet in order to claim the demonic bishopric. Consequently, this might point to whom actually he may be. The Antichrist is the angel of death. He is living, lurking, hiding in plain sight, peeking out behind his curtain of shadows until this world's stage emcee summons him by name. Once the global chaotic scene is set and his grand entrance on a cosmopolitan scale marshals the world into oblivion... Act 1. Stay tuned.

The devil is on his way! Years ago the twenty-six-time Grammy Award winning and counting and two time Oscar winner, song-writer, musician, author and musical genius, Stevie Wonder, wrote a song entitled "Superstition." The third stanza lyrical verses say the following words I quote: "'Very superstitious nothin more to say,' very superstitious **the devil is on his way**!" My Lord, this talented musical guru was actually aware of the entrance of the most sinister being this side of heaven and earth in one of his melodic hit tunes. Another thing that makes this even more inspiring to me is the fact, that Mr. Stevie Wonder is legally blind. This means to me he is more spiritually in touch with God Almighty than most of us who have our sight (vision) so to speak but we may or appear to be heavenly or legally spiritually blind! Therefore, unequivocally the person who is to be Satan's ruler on earth **must meet *every*** conceivable precursor trait of the Antichrist without exception, just as Jesus Christ met *every* precondition that he is the true Messiah sent from God with-out exception. I really have a problem mentioning the Antichrist with the Son of God in the same sentence. Pardon me, moving on. Some of the more dominant themes this Son of Perdition must meet are that **he must**:

1. Have a name when calculated adds up to or equates to **666** using a numerical system in Judaism by both worshippers and non-worshippers alike outlined in **Revelation 13:18**, which **states, "Here is wisdom let him who has under-standing callout the number of the beast for it is the number of a man, His number is 666.:**

2. He in some manner has a nexus or connects with the sym-bolism of the dreadful beast outlined in **Daniel chapter 7 and Revelation 12:1–5** and **Revelation 13:11–14**, high-lighted below:

Daniel 7:1–8, in the first year of Belshazzar, King of Babylon, Daniel had a dream and visions of his head upon his bed then he wrote the dream and told the sum of the matter. Daniel spoke and said, "I saw in my visions' by night and behold the four winds of heaven strove upon the great sea and four great beasts came up from the sea." Diverse from one another, the first was like a lion and had eagle's wings. I beheld until the wings were plucked and it was lifted up from the earth and made to stand upon the feet as a man and a man's heart was given it. And behold another beast a second like unto a bear and it raised up itself on one side and it had three ribs in the mouth of it between the teeth of it and they said thus unto it arise devour much flesh. After this, I beheld and lo, another beast as if unto a leopard, which had upon the back of it, four wings of a fowl the beast also had four heads and dominion was given unto it. After this I saw in the night visions and behold a fourth beast dreadful and terrible and strong exceedingly and it has great iron teeth it devoured and brake in pieces and stamped the residue with the feet of it and it was diverse from all the beasts that were before it <u>and it had ten horns</u>. **I considered the horns then there came up among them another little horn before whom there were three of the first horns plucked up by the roots and behold in this horn were eyes like the eyes of a man and a mouth speaking great things.** *Revelation chapter 12, now a great sign appeared in heaven, a woman clothed with the sun with the moon under her feet and on her head a garland of twelve stars. Then being with child, she cried out in labor and in pain to give birth and another sign appeared in heaven a great fiery red dragon, having seven heads, ten horns, and seven* *diadems on his heads. His tail drew a third of the stars of heaven and threw them down to the earth. And the dragon stood before the woman who was ready to give birth to devour her child as soon as it were born. She bore a male child who was to rule all nations with a rod of iron and her Child was caught up to God and his throne. Revelation 13:11–14, "Then I saw another beast coming up out of the earth, and he had two horns like lamb. And spoke like a dragon and he exercises' all of the authority of the first beast in his presence and causes the earth and those who dwell in it to worship the first beast. Whose deadly wound was healed he performs great signs so that he even makes fire come down from heaven in the sight of men. And he deceives those who dwell on the earth by those signs which he was granted to do in the sight of the beast telling those who dwell on the earth to make an image to the beast who was wounded by the sword and lived."*

3. Be a charismatic geopolitical leader, ready and willing to influence all aspects of human life including worship, religion, education, politics, legislation, law enforcement and humanities. This individual must have Roman ancestry or descent (bloodline) genealogy traceable according to **Daniel 9:26–27.** This will indirectly grant him authority or "legitimacy" to world hegemony within the ecclesiastical community proclamation or destiny over all Nations including the Jews with whom he will make a covenant or peace treaty that he will violate later causing them to realize he is the Devil via demanding that they worship him not the God of their forefathers. His religious background portrayal must appeal to the Roman Catholics (False Christianity), Israeli Judaists (Judaism) and Islam. The three major world faiths as it were.

4. Be a king, politician, president or secular ruler the world is willing to acquiesce its leadership unto who has geopolitical influence regardless to his lack of moral character and is willing to follow. Regardless to the blatantly obvious shortcomings of his individual moral character while willingly solving global issues as he gives the approval nod or eye wink to hateful rhetoric, merciless policies and immoral criminal conduct worldwide.

CHAPTER XIV

Continued: The Antichrist

Now for clarification we do not want to get this confused with other scriptures that are interrelated which may lead to distortion regarding the Antichrist's actual identity. For example, some biblical commentators cite the scripture regarding the King of the North prophecy refer to the Antichrist. Actually, that is inapplicable because the "King of the North" refers to the kingdom of modern day Iraq that derived its Kingdom from the Babylonian dynasty of Nebuchadnezzar. Whom down through the years derived it from Seleucid who was one of Alexander the Great generals who divided his kingdom among themselves according to the prophetic word of God. Whereby it stated they would do before Alexander ever lived after his unexpected death during the zenith of his power! This is the specific prophecy eventually fulfilled because of divine order regarding the heavenly decree appertaining to Alexander's four generals upon Alexander's prophesied death during the apex of his power. Review **Daniel 8:8** that reads; **therefore, the male goat grew very great but when he became strong the <u>large horn was broken</u> and in place of it, <u>four notable ones</u> came up toward the four winds of heaven**. A brief interpretation from the passage implemented here to make it plain for non-Bible readers, new converts as well as those who may be unfamiliar with God's prophetic words is necessary here. Repeat citation of **Daniel 8:8** says, "**Therefore, the male goat (King of the West) grew very great**"—i.e., **he became very** strong. (Alexander's title included the Phrase "great" Alexander the <u>Great</u>) but when he became strong (His ascent to power rose quickly) and Alexander was a world renown military leader conquering vast foreign lands in short spans of time while being known for his blitzkrieg attacks and keen military daring campaigns. The large horn was broken (the leader Alexander died some speculate that he was poisoned). Factually, he died at 33 years old just as did Jesus Christ the Son of God. Others not of his family lineage (posterity, sons or brothers) assume his vacated kingdom since he is now deceased. Then came four *notable* ones (four notable generals leaders assumed his place by dividing his vast conquered kingdoms came up toward the four winds north, south, east and west) provinces he unilaterally once held unitedly or singularly were divided among his four generals under heaven.

Alexander's generals did this after Alexander's untimely or unexpected death. The other three generals of Alexander were Hephastion, Cassander, and Ptolemy. See Daniel's prophecy regarding Alexander's ascendancy and premature death at thirty-three years old at the zenith of his young commandership of the army from Macedon, Greece. See **Daniel 8:8**. Furthermore, The King of the North ultimately during the Antichrist reign, attacks the King of the South and the Antichrist who will defeat both kings (discussed later). This means that the Antichrist would actually then be attacking himself, which is illogical, impossible and very improbable if we were to accept this interpretation. In addition, another issue that requires dispelling is the existence of the narrative that the Antichrist will not regard the desire of women, implying that he is a homosexual. This is another distortion cited in the book of Daniel that has an entirely diverse meaning when appropriately applied to dividing the word of God rightly as God's word directs us to do in **2 Timothy 2:15**. Which says, **study to show yourself approved unto God a workman that need not be ashamed <u>rightly dividing</u> the word of truth.** Historically, many scholars or theologians say this alludes to the Antichrist's homosexuality. Alternately, what they now call pansexual, multi-sexual or non-specific gender identification sexual. Translation this means one can sexually have who or what you want whenever you want it since you are nonspecific gender preference. All of this evil is an abomination to God Almighty. **God alone** designated us into our sexual identities as either male or female created he them.

Review **Genesis 1:27** here, **"So God created man in his own image in the image of God he created him *male and female* he created them."** God never created anyone pansexual, homosexual, asexual, lesbian, same-sex freelance sexual or any of the other sexual labels that satanic evil celestial demonic angels are whispering into the minds and thoughts of sexually lustful humans that is transforming our societies into a smorgasbord or cadre of devilish perversity. Although God instituted mating (sexual intimacy) between a man and woman, he did so with specific guidelines and restrictions—i.e., that they be married to each other *not* someone else. Furthermore, that there are limitations or boundaries that should not be crossed of sexual experiences that are balanced with some enjoyment between the husband and wife while in the process of procreation of their children. Not just, have a good ole time to see how many different experiences you can have on the open range Wild, Wild Western exploration style with as many diverse people or ways as one so chooses to experience. What in the world is going on in our minds, thoughts, and mannerisms today? These are *doctrines of demons* spreading lies in hypocrisy with *lying wonders* so the balanced natural desire within us for intimacy of the opposite gender prescribed by God (married couple) twists or contorts itself negatively. Thereby transforming itself into lust within us burns hotter than the embers of hell. Misleading, deceiving and misguiding humanity headlong into a head splitting, denial of the holiness of the living God of Israel and his Holy Son, Jesus Christ into sexual freedom revolution or an exponential diaspora of out of control sexual panorama jamboree free for all!

Review **1 Timothy 4:1–2** here: **Now the Spirit expressly says that in the latter times some will depart from the faith giving heed to <u>doctrines of demons</u> <u>speaking lies in hypocrisy</u> having their own conscience seared with a hot iron.** Furthermore, read **2 Peter 2:1–3, "But there were also false prophets among the people even as there will be false teachers among you who will secretly bring in destructive heresies, even denying the Lord who bought** them and bring on themselves swift destruction. And many will follow their pernicious ways because of whom the way of the truth will be blasphemed." The musical artist John Legend featuring rap artist, Rick Ross has a song that asks a specific question I think is appropriate here. John's song is entitled "Who Do We Think We Are? That is okay remember **_eternal residency_** is established by **_choice or choosing_** as we reviewed in the previous chapter. I know all whom disagree say we are big and bad, free and we can do whatever we want with whomever we want whenever we want to with our bodies. I certainly hear you and respectively disagree. However, just remember that one day you will die. I caution any who dare challenge God Almighty with such arrogance.

Death will touch everyone on the shoulder one day (unless raptured alive) and say it is time to go meet your God. I advise one to be more humble before then. Just wait until you die and come face to face with the Creator, the Holy God of heaven and earth on bended knee to ascertain his thoughts about a mere mortal challenging his holy divine eternal designation. Tell God then what you are bragging or boasting about now that you can do whatever you want, when you want with whomever you want to do it with. I just wonder what the Almighty's reply will be. Hmmmm. I think I have an idea that emanates from the word of the Lord. I will provide all such persons who are just so brave, brazen or stubborn with a preview here in **Hebrews 10:31** declares **it is a fearful thing to fall into the hands of the Living God.** Review also **Revelation 20:11–12** here **then I saw a great white throne and him who sat on it from whose face the earth and the heaven fled away. And there was found no place for them. And I saw the dead small and great standing before God and books were opened and another book was opened which is the Book of Life and _the dead were judged according to their works_ by the things which _were written in the books_.**

Tell me how that turns out for you then okay. I hope you have your bravo on that day too like you have now. Anything outside of God's divine designation or assignment is an abomination to the Lord God Almighty of Israel that succumbs to doctrines of devils or demons because of the love of pleasure. Read **1 Timothy 4:1–2** here, "**Now the Spirit expressly says that in the latter times some will depart from the faith *giving heed to deceiving spirits and doctrines of demons speaking lies in hypocrisy* having their own conscience seared with a hot iron.**" Continuing with our journey, another scriptural phrase that may cause misunderstanding whereby, it says, "*he will not regard the desire of women*" specifically. This particular passage may imply or become errantly interpreted that the Antichrist is gay or a homosexual if one does not properly balance the scripture with either contextual application or considerate review or insight as well as the actual connotation of what God is conveying to us. Nevertheless, this is a complete misnomer if this is one's interpretation of these scriptures. Because the actual reason refers to the fact that he will reject Jesus Christ the true Messiah. Whom the historical, orthodox Israelis and secular pagan countries, during the Old Testament epoch regarded as "the desire of women" to be the true Messiah and *the desire of all nations. Clearly this is* denoted in **Haggai 2:7** here that reads, "**And I will shake all nations and the *desire of all nations* shall come and I will fill this house with glory says the Lord of Hosts.**"

The desire of all nations was to be the arrival or coming of the one to bring deliverance or salvation from their present state of oppression at that time. Review the Disciples of Christ question here before his final ascension into heaven after his resurrection from the dead in **Acts 1:6,** therefore when they had come to him **saying, "Lord will you at this time restore the kingdom to Israel?** Jesus replied, **it is not for you to know the times or seasons which the Father has put in his own authority.**" Subsequently as we can see from the dialogue and documented scriptures this had nothing to do with his personal sexual preferences as much as it had to do with the restoration for the desire to restore or deliver the kingdom of Israel from Roman or Italian authority or governance. Thereby resulting or bringing about God's divine liberator Messiah, Deliverer like Moses whom all women wanted to give birth—i.e., the "*desire of all women.*" Consequently, the anti or false Christ *will reject* the true Christ *who is the desire of all nations and women.* This does not mean that he will reject the sexual attractions emanated to or for him from women nor does this mean that he is a homosexual. When the scriptural reference is divided aptly it has an entire diverse meaning than the superficial one proffered by well-meaning students of biblical canon or doctrine in some instances. Alternately, nor does it by the intentional misdirectional intent supplanting by nefarious characters who are, hell bent either upon deceit or deception via misleading rabbit trails in an attempt to thwart those who put their trust in Christ as Lord.

The Antichrist thus has specific goals he wants to accomplish in preparation for world dominance according to the prophetic scriptures. Among them is a one world, ecumenical false religion with him atop the helm see **Revelation 13:15**. Which in part reads, "***And cause as many would not worship the image of the beast to be killed.***" However, he is not just content with people worshipping him he wants to also "turn away" others who have remained (on earth) for whatever reason(s) they have been left behind or newly converted to Christianity called "tribulation saints" to deny Christ or fall away by apostasy. See **2 Timothy 4:3–4**. these amalgamated versuses state: "**For the time will come when they will not endure sound doctrine but after their *own lusts* shall they heap to themselves *teachers* having itching ears and *they shall turn away* their ears *from* the truth**". We can see that occurring now. Whereby some homosexuals who *want to live* "their way" (after their own lusts) have founded, discovered and attend "churches" that allow them to openly cohabitate. They can marry or live with their same sex "partners," which is called an abomination by Almighty God unto him, his words not mine.

Read **Leviticus 18:22: "You shall not lie with a male as with a woman. It is an abomination.**" These "churches or pastors" turn a blind eye or look the other way provided they *donate consistently* to the coffers of the congregation faithfully. An apostasy—i.e., falling away from the true faith in God **1 Timothy 4:1–4 and 2 Thessalonians 2:3, "Now the Spirit expressly say that in the *latter times* 'some will depart from the faith' giving heed to seducing spirits and doctrines of demons speaking lies in hypocrisy having their own conscience seared with a hot iron. Forbidding to marry and commanding to abstain from foods which God created to be received** with thanksgiving by those who believe and know the truth. For every creature of God is good and nothing to be refused if it is received with thanksgiving."

Now **2 Thessalonians 2:3**, "Let no man <u>deceive you</u> by any means for <u>that day</u> (day of the Lord's return) **shall not come** 'except' there '*comes a falling away first*' and that 'man of sin' <u>be revealed</u> the **Son of Perdition**." Thus an apostasy *differs* dramatically from false worship in that; false worship involves worshipping deities, statues, images, false gods including anyone or anything "other than" the Lord God Jehovah of heaven and earth who created all things. However, by contrast apostasy means the abandonment and renunciation of a political or religious belief period. Therefore, the scriptures are on point here as it describes in Timothy what will happen to some whom the Antichrist, the False Prophet and the Beast—i.e., the unholy cabal triumvirate have deceived.

Although there is a lot more to say about the Antichrist, I will cease at this point to narrate any additional data about him simply because the central theme of this book is not about him. Albeit he is a central character in fighting the transcendent war from God's Living Room in heaven to the first floor, if you will to the earth, to impact the outcome of events that are to come. Therefore, I move onto the next subject in our joint odyssey or travel, which is the False Prophet to continue our quest regarding the original fight in heaven that has cascaded down to the earth.

CHAPTER XV

The False Prophet

Our discussion involving this demonic "Attila the Hun" is over-powering in many aspects. The reason I state this is because, this evil prophet "misleads" or deceives many people into believing, worshipping and praising Satan's Son **intentionally against** the will of Almighty God. The False Prophet's main purpose is to destroy humanity's worship in the Only True, Holy God of Israel and his Only Begotten, Son, Jesus Christ as the Lord God. God commanded the Hebrews and all humanity in the original Ten Commandments given to Moses documented here in **Exodus 20:3, "You shall have no other gods before me."** Furthermore, the False Prophet, will **_kill anyone_** who resists his commandment to worship the image of the beast who advocates any other God other than his false god Lucifer. This sinister fellow, who will help the devil attain his celestial, demonic covetousness for worldwide, self-indulging, egomaniac, distorted craving for praise. Furthermore, the False Prophet, will cultivate and encourage the devil as he nourishes Satan's insatiable appetite relishing or self-regarded in high esteem upon a self-appointed pedestal to absorbing melodic self-adoration tunes, praise and egomania worship as an Imposter. Thereby self-enshrined while pretending to himself, fallen angels and all deceived persons who reject Jesus Christ as Lord, that his evil leader to whom he swore allegiance is a "god."

Actually, he is a god. ***He is…a god…a demigod of perversion***! The False Prophet, self declares or proclaims that the Antichrist is worthy of praise and worship as Our Lord God and his Son Jesus Christ are forever! This person is more than a False Prophet. He is also a deceiver, a worshipper of evil, the devil's right hand man. The False Prophet is the Devil's Advocate unparalleled by any other. He like Lucifer is a liar. The False Prophet is a uniquely masked man. For he will seem to be "holy" devout, benevolent, just, kind, humble, pious and just about any other essential *positive trait* that one would desire in a "consecrated" man. Yet he is the most dedicated deputy assistant of evil, or tyranny ever to live besides Satan. He serves as the Chief Architect as well as enabler of Lucifer's acquisition, sustenance and key pretender to attain and maintain worship for a while on the earth. He is the Messiah of Deception. He is the conductor of deceit within earth's cosmopolitan orchestra in a symphonic harmony of lies, deception, and false worship as well as the deification of Satan's beast. Leading all renegades both of demons and of unrepentant man who will descend into an eternal destruction with him in the lake of hell fire burning with brimstone where he is going ultimately to the unquenchable abyss of destruction.

See **Revelation 19:20** listed here, "**Then the beast was captured and with him the <u>false prophet</u> who worked signs in his presence by <u>which he deceived</u> those who received the mark of the beast and those who <u>worshipped</u> his image. These two were <u>cast alive</u> into the lake of fire burning with brimstone.**"

The words of God in **2 Peter 2:1–3** states, "**But there were *false prophets* among the people. Even as there shall *be false teachers* among you" who privily (secretly) shall bring in damnable heresies (false teaching or doctrine),** e.g., same sex marriage. **Even denying the Lord that bought them (by his shed blood and atoning death) via his crucifixion at Calvary for the sins of the whole world. And <u>many shall follow</u> their <u>pernicious ways</u> by whom <u>the way of the truth</u> shall be evil spoken of, and through covetousness shall they with feigned words make merchandise of you whose judgment now of a long time lingers not and their damnation slumbers not.**" This is another example where an individual who has cohorts or many who are like him (if the readers will recall earlier narration on the archangel) stands alone. For example, although there are many antichrists yet, there will be a primary **Antichrist** just like there has and will be many "false prophets" there will be only one primary Chief, False Prophet. We will unmask this worshipper of Satan as he enchants, mesmerizes and charms fragile lost souls by the drumbeat of evil with the purpose of deception with his exotic signs, miracles and wonders.

It is a little easier to spot a phony, fake, impostor, counterfeit or false entity once you have the authentic next to the pretender side by side for comparison or a thorough examination. Therefore, I will proffer such a list here to illustrate the perspective with this individual (False Prophet) by showing some of God's actual prophets who have always played a role in the transformation and direction into the spiritual lives of the people of God here on earth. Moses was the prophet that God called to go set his people free from slavery under Pharaoh as God appeared to Moses in the burning bush. Denoted here in **Exodus 3:10** whereby God commands Moses: "**Come now therefore and <u>I will send you</u> to Pharaoh that you may bring my people the children of Israel out of Egypt.**" Joshua was the messenger of the Lord who escorted the people of God (Israelis) into the Promised Land after Moses death who was forbidden by God to enter into the Promised Land. Cited here in **Joshua 1:1–2: "Now after the death of Moses, the servant of the Lord, it came to pass that the *Lord spoke to Joshua,* the son of Nun, Moses minister. Saying Moses my servant is dead. Now therefore arise, go over this Jordan you and all the people unto the land, which I do give them even to the children of Israel.**"

Jeremiah the child prophet was called the "weeping prophet" because he was used by God as a young prophet to turn the Jewish people back to him after their fall away from God while expressing great remorse for himself and Israel via his lamentations. Initially, the child prophet Jeremiah resists God and vainly attempts to persuade God that he is only a youth who certainly would have no influence over adults. Yet, alone his peers to convince any of them of the error of their ways. However, God rebukes him as documented here as follows in the book of **Jeremiah 1:5–8**. "**Before I formed you in the womb I knew you. Before you were born I sanctified you. I ordained you a prophet to the nations.** Then said I ah Lord God I **cannot speak for I am a child but the Lord said unto me Say not I am a child for you shalt go to all that I shall send you and what-soever I command you shall speak. Be not afraid of their faces for I am with you to deliver you says the Lord. Then the Lord put forth his hand and touched my mouth and the Lord said unto me Behold I have put my words into your mouth.**"

John the Baptist was the prophet who prepared the way of the Lord Jesus Christ's ministry here on earth. Review **Matthew 3:1–3** and **11** listed verbatim here from the holy scriptures: "**In those days came John the Baptist preaching in the wilderness of Judea and saying repent for the kingdom of God is at hand. For this is he that was spoken by the prophet Esaias saying the voice of one crying in the wilderness, Prepare you the way of the lord make his paths straight. I indeed baptize you with water unto repentance but he that comes after me is mightier than I whose shoes I am not worthy to bear he shall baptize you with the Holy Ghost and fire.**" Jesus Christ is not only the Son of God; he was a prophet, with the "Rod of Iron" and a sword—i.e., the word of God.

See **Revelation 19:15:** "**Now out of his mouth goes a sharp two edged sword that with it he shall strike the nations. And he himself shall rule them with a Rod of Iron. He himself treads the winepress of the fierceness and wrath of Almighty God.** Also, Review **Hebrews 4:12**: as cited **the word of God is quick, and powerful and sharper than any two-edged sword piercing even to the dividing asunder soul and spirit and of the joints and marrow and is a discerner of the thoughts and intents of the heart.**"

Christ came to convert the people to God Almighty! (**Isaiah 42:1–8**). "**Behold my servant whom I uphold mine elect in whom my soul delight. I have put my spirit upon him he shall bring forth judgment to the Gentiles. He shall not cry nor lift up nor cause his voice to be heard in the street a bruised reed shall he not break and the smoking flax shall he not quench he shall bring forth judgment to truth. He shall not fail nor be discouraged till** he have set forth judgment in the earth and the isles shall wait for his law. This says God the Lord he that created the heavens and stretched them out he that spread forth the earth and that which comes out of it he that gives breath to the people upon it and spirit to them that walk therein. I the Lord have called you in righteousness and will hold your hand and will keep you and give you for a covenant to the people for a light of the Gentiles to open the blind eyes to bring out the prisoners from the prison and them that sit in darkness out of the prison house. *I am the Lord that is my name, my glory I will not give unto another neither my praise to graven images.*" This is just a small fraction of the ministerial goal of Christ for specificity but essentially the whole word of God (Holy Bible) talks about the prophetic ministry of Jesus Christ!

Now that I have provided some examples of God's prophets. Let us look at the evil, False Prophet who is to come. It is essential to understanding this fellow as we do all prophets in the sense that he is a minister, a devout believer in the so-called god or "god" he serves. This maniacal demon is no different. He totally believes in Satan. Prophets unlike regular ministers, pastors or priests receive divinations, dreams, specific instructions, prophecies or visions directly from their God or "god" to further their respective deities' perspective to humans here on earth. He is sinister in every way imaginable. This is the High Priest of Hell incarnated in the flesh! This False Prophet will receive specific instructions directly from his "god"— i.e., Satan with all damnable lies, coaching, evil mandates, false and pretentious edicts, counterfeit, untrue blasphemies, misleading and perverse teaching, doctrines of demons, directing the world toward total unrestrained evil in every way conceivable.

If you think, it is bad now you have not seen anything yet by comparison! This demented demon cataclysmically full of evil whom *totally believes* that Satan's **lies are genuine truth will also lie**. Lucifer's Second Act has not even yet begun on this earth. This will not start until all of his cohorts are in human form wielding their carousel of satanic tricks that only the demons from the bottomless pit are capable of doing. (Satan deceived angels he knows for sure that he can deceive us.) However, the entire world is undergoing preparatory steps that will allow expedient implementation for Satan's Second Act strategically to deceive millions e.g. legalization of drug use including marijuana, hemp and other so-called recreational drugs. Also, the relaxation of policies, laws or rules for progressive inclusion of same sex marriages as normal. The legal adoption of children by openly homosexual and lesbian couples. Public "churches" that promote homosexuality, lesbianism and alternative life style choices as the new normalcy. Thereby distancing themselves from the traditional biblical mandate instituted by God himself regarding marriage between a man and a woman. This will result in wholesale deception unparalleled in human history, as many human beings will succumb to their diabolical schemes. While these evil emissaries are telling lies, displaying illusions, showing spectacular heavenly wonders of distortion and spiritual blindness due to their pernicious ways creating a dangerous world and place for families and people to live. It does not matter, for everyone is already high anyway. The word of God says, **"This know also that in the latter times or last days perilous times shall come" (2 Timothy 3:1).**

The False Prophet unlike the other prophets we have already noted **was not** sent from God! He is a demonically inspired being, sent from Satan, with a damnable pedigree and ministry with an evil agenda. He will be promoting and teaching lies with acrimony unprecedented in human history to a dying, suffering world. His ministry is perverse because it is deceptive for it has its genesis from the bowels of the abyss of dark secrets from the King of Darkness Lucifer himself. In addition, because he is "*ministering*" to the masses he will intentionally "mislead" many into destruction. Contrasted as we just saw from the leadership guidance and divinity from above via prophets of God who should speak the word of God in truth to a struggling humanity toward the salvation that is **only** via Jesus Christ! Bible proof is located in **Acts 4:12,** which says, "*__Neither is there salvation in any other for there is none other name under heaven given among men whereby we must be saved.__*" These actions collectively initiated by Satan, The Antichrist, The False Prophet, The Beast and their cabal of coconspirators including fallen angels and unrepentant man for worldwide delusion and deception are no small matter given the diversity of ethnic groups, countries, relgions and languages on earth.

Furthermore, this wholesale delusion that descends upon man leaves humanity in a quandary so to speak. Simply because they gestate numerous questions that humanity must try to resolve or answer before it is too late. Some of these questions are as follows; where does this False Prophet come from and how does he ascend to such a prominent role in the End Times? What is the significance of the False Prophet's ministry upon earth? When will the False Prophet enact his diabolical schemes for false ministry and satanic worship upon the landscape of humanity as the dawn arises drawing, back the curtain for the Final Act of evil within the world? Can humanity escape the clutches and talons of deception that is gripping humanity at a blistering pace? Consequently ushering in the will of Satan, which he always coveted in heaven—i.e., so that he receive worship, praise, honor, glory and riches for himself to satiate his selfish evil egomania because he is superior (self-deception in his mind) to all of God's other being in creation including man. Although the answers to these sinister questions are difficult to zero in on with pinpoint accuracy.

We still must seek God's will from his word to help us understand. In all thy getting, get understanding **(Proverbs 4:7)**. Summarily, I will attempt to answer some of these imperative lingering questions as we proceed onward in our quest to ascertain insight to understand debauchery tentacles outreaching schemes thereby better able to resist the devil so that we are not victims of his evil trickery. The word of God provides all of us with a sound formula as we struggle in our daily lives and upon our joint travel in this endeavor outlined in this mini-book. It says in **James 4:7, "Therefore submit to God. Resist the devil and he will flee from you."**

Naturally, we will refer to the word of God—i.e., the Holy Scriptures for the answers to these questions. **Revelation 13:11–18** provides us with our answers. First, I will write the entire passage in unity then attempt to divide it in smaller units for the readers to easily comprehend.

Revelation 13:11–18

Then I saw another beast coming up out of the earth and he had two horns like a lamb and spoke like a dragon. And he exercises all the authority of the first beast in his presence and caused all the earth and those who dwell in it <u>to worship the first beast</u> whose deadly wound was healed. He <u>performs great signs</u> so that <u>he makes fire come down from heaven on the earth</u> in the sight of men. And he <u>deceives those</u> who dwell on the earth <u>by those signs</u>, which he was granted to do in the sight of men. And he deceives those who dwell on the earth. By those signs, which he was granted, to do in the sight of the beast. Telling those who dwell on the earth to make an image to the beast who was wounded by the sword and lived. He was granted power to give breath to the image of the beast that the image of the beast should both speak and <u>cause, as many would not worship the image of the beast to be killed.</u> He cause all both small and great rich and poor to receive a mark on their right hand or on their foreheads. And that no one may buy or sell except one who has the mark of the name of the beast or the number of his name. Here is wisdom, let him who has understanding calculate the number of the beast for it is the number of a man. His number is 666.

Now smaller divisible units for easier comprehension. Further analysis of this reading says in verse 11, **I** (John the Revelator) **beheld another (second) beast coming up out of the earth, he had two horns like a lamb, and he spoke as a dragon**. This is our first imperative clue. He had two horns (symbols of ecclesiastical authority) that were like a lamb (meek, gentle or mild) Even Jesus Christ himself, the Son of God has this title as the "Lamb" of God. Review John 1:29 here that says, **"The next day John saw Jesus coming toward him, and said Behold the Lamb of God that takes away the sin of the world!"** Currently, the Roman Catholic Pope has two horns atop his MITRE that he wears…hmmmm, yet he spoke like a dragon (OT and NT symbolic identity for Satan). This factually is a contradiction in and of itself. This is attributable to essentially understanding the False Prophet's identity, role, false ministry and buttressing of the Antichrist's imagery worldwide. Simply because he will win people over via his meekness, gentleness or mildness so to speak. Utilizing his *lamb horns* of piety, compassion and meekness. Yet, he will blasphemously demand that all worship the devil. We will continue our analysis of this passage. **Revelation Verse 13:12** provides even more keen preciseness to this Master Minister of Deceit. This passage reads; **and he (False Prophet) exercises (displays or uses) all the power (authority) of the first beast (The Antichrist) before him (revealed in sequential order).**

Our examination now takes us unto **Revelation 13:13** this is a critical scripture. Let's see why for it reads: **for he (The False Prophet) does great wonders (signs and miracles) so that he makes fire come down from heaven (out of the sky) on the earth in the sight (witnessed by humans on earth) of men.** Now what an ominous coincidence or a dubious paradox this is for him. The reason I say this is that he along with the Beast and the Antichrist will face destruction by the same miracle element (fire) that he is displaying on earth to deceive humans into thinking that the beast is God from Jehovah God. Review **Revelation 19:20: "The beast was captured and with him the _false prophet_ who worked signs in his presence by which he deceived those who received the mark of the beast and those who worshipped his image. These two were cast alive into the fire burning with brimstone."**

Continuing with this theme/topic, fire coming out of the sky is not an easy feat, for the atmosphere around us is saturated with moisture formed from the clouds as well as dew. Also, the evaporation process that occurs daily via reverse osmosis from trees to the air absorbing carbon dioxide by the trees emitted by humans. Afterward, giving off life sustaining oxygen from the trees for humans and all other life forms. For situational awareness if you will, recall this feat—i.e., of fire coming down from heaven in the sky was accomplished by Elijah as he killed 102 soldiers (in sets of 2 x 51—i.e., each group of 50 soldiers had a captain that made it 51 each) of King Ahaziah. Who was the son of the wicked King Ahab and his spouse, the evil Queen Jezebel, whose godless son Ahaziah summoned Elijah to court for interrogation without God's permission (**2 Kings 1:9**).

The next scripture is **Revelation 13:14**. For it reads, "**And deceives them that dwell on the earth by the means of those miracles which he (False Prophet) had power (ability, capability and authority) in the sight of the beast (Antichrist). Saying to them that dwell on the earth, that they (people on earth) should make an image (statute or digital portrait) to the beast, which had a wound by a sword (some kind of violence) and did live**." This is conclusive that this is referring to the Antichrist, for he is the political leader whom receives a mortal wound but lives. It is imperative for me to ensure that there is no confusion here so I will clarify a point that may be easily misconstrued. The Beast and the Antichrist are the same person. The terminology here is interchangeable at various times throughout the dissertation. The Antichrist is called a beast by God Almighty became that is exactly what he is a **"lion" (a beast) seeking whom he may devour as denoted in 1 Peter 5:8**. Jehovah God considers these characters to be beasts. Among the reasons is their merciless, violent, wholesale genocide and homicidal activities upon the people on the earth at this time. Predatory beasts act purely upon natural instinct to hunt, kill and devour for food for their own survival without regard to morality or a consciousness of mercy. God considers the activity of these individuals during their binary, forty-two months (7 years total—i.e., The Great Tribulation Period) tenure no differently. All of their amalgamated actions causing death, despair, misery, horror, terror and unspeakable brutality while killing people is why God Almighty considers them beasts.

Continuing with our narrative. **Revelation 13:15** reads, "**And he (False Prophet) had power to 'give life'** *(cause to come alive or speak)* **to the image (statue or digital image/portrait) of the beast/antichrist, that the image (likeness) of the beast/antichrist should both speak, and cause as many as would not worship (bow down to) the image of the <u>beast be killed</u>.**" The word of God says **that there is nothing new under the sun in Ecclesiastes 1:9.** Well this is certainly true in this incidence as it is in all events appertaining to Gods words. This happened at least twice in antiquity or in what's referred to as the Old Testament period. The first time it happened was when Aaron who ultimately became the first High Priest in Israel, made the molten calf and misled the children of Israel into worshipping a false god since Moses remained atop Mount Sinai for what to them seemed like an eternity. See **Exodus 32:15–23** as it reads: "**And Moses turned and went down from the mountain and the two tables of the Testimony were in his hand. The tablets were written on both sides on the one side and on the other side, they were written. Now the tablets were the work of God and the writing was the writing of God engraved on the tablets. And Joshua heard the noise of the people as they shouted; he said to Moses, There is a noise of war in the camp. But he said it is not the noise of the shout of victory nor the noise of the cry of defeat. But the sound of** *singing* **I hear. So it was** *as soon as* **he came near the camp that <u>he saw the calf and the dancing</u>. So Moses anger became hot and he cast the tablets out of his hand and broke them at the foot of the mountain. Then he took the calf, which they had made burned it in the fire and ground it to powder and he scattered it on the water and made the children of Israel drink it. And Moses said to Aaron what did this people do to you that you have brought so great a sin upon them? So Aaron said do not let the anger of my Lord become hot you know the people that they are set on evil. For they said make us gods that shall go before us as for this Moses the man who brought us out of the land of Egypt we do not know what has become of him.**"

Clearly, we can see via this narrative that Aaron was acting "like" a **<u>False Prophet</u>** by making, fashioning, leading and allowing the children of Israel to **worship** the _Calf's Molten image_ in defiance of the true and Only God of Israel. Aaron should had known better for he was Moses's brother and the Prophet of Moses when God told Moses that he allowed Moses to be as God unto Pharaoh and Aaron his prophet. Review **Exodus 7:1** listed here that reads; **so the Lord said to Moses see I have made you as God to Pharaoh and Aaron your brother shall be your prophet.** Thus, Aaron should had understood at least that The Lord God was using these forty days and forty nights to explain to Moses the origin of life, creation of the world and all things relating to life up to Moses day. Remember there was no complete accurate recorded history anywhere in the world to explain events originating in the Garden of Eden, the Noahic Flood, and the Tower of Babel, etc., "prior" to Moses life.

Therefore, God used this time to tell him how, when, why and the purposes for God's creation of all life began as the Divine Creator of all heaven and earth. Naturally, Moses as a man tired became hungry and thirsty and was provided ample time to sleep, eat. I suppose that he may have actually fasted being in the very presence of God and may had to periodically relieve his body of excrements as needed away from God' sight per se and began the next day to document God's true account of sin, life, death and mankind's unique relationship to him. However, I do not know with certainty either way. Recall I informed readers that when I did not know something I would tell you honestly. Furthermore, God Almighty commanded his will to Moses by his own finger by inscribing his orders, divine commandments and his expectations or instructions to man on how to live upon his earth via the 10 commandments as well as all other ordinances. Therefore, the children of Israel who were at the foot, floor or bottom of the slope of Mount Sinai, upon the plateau plain inside the valley near Mount Sinai simply did not fully understand or know specifically what happened to Moses in his prolonged absence. Simply because they did not have access to any social media accounts—i.e., twitter, Snapchat, Facebook or news bulletins or CNN updates to inform them what Moses and God were doing or could possibly be talking about for forty days and forty nights.

See **Exodus 24:18** that tells us how long the two of them talked together cited here: "**So Moses went into the midst of the cloud and went up into the mountain and Moses was on the mountain forty days and forty nights.**" Furthermore, one should bear in mind the children of Israel's collective "state of mind" under the duress circumstances they had recently encountered after becoming free from slavery for 400 years. They had been held as slaves in bondage for decades (some accounts have it four hundred years other accounts have it two hundred years) I opt to believe God and say it was four hundred years of bondage. All readers are free to accept their own belief either way. By any account, it was for a very long time by the Egyptians and newly released by the hand of God via Moses leadership to freedom in its embryonic stage. They did not know how to "live free" for eons since they were slaves against their will and forced to do all sorts of menial tasks as others prescribed, demanded or desired times or ways other than their own. Therefore, to the newly released slaves freedom represented any or all forms of self-expression or sensual desires to bring happiness anyway, they so choose to display it. They errantly believed that anytime they waited beyond any reasonable period determined by themselves. Alternatively, several seconds without a quick answer to them was a reminder of their forced rigor or hardships in Egypt or that God had abandoned them since he could not care for them in the vast, barren land where they waited for Moses to come back from the mountaintop.

Now the children of Israel demanded *microwave answers*—i.e., *a quick resolution or reply* to any hard questions or situations for they had in their perspectives "waited long enough" as slaves in Egypt and were unwilling at this point in their lives about to sit patiently or idly by to see what would happen next. They wanted to *act independently* now that they *were independent* or choose for themselves, their God, their faith, their religious beliefs, etc., etc. In addition, they may have thought that Moses was dead or killed by a wild beast somewhere in the rugged mountainside while somehow leaving them as orphans as they were trying to move on without him or God. The children of Israel quickly forgot God (as we all do) right after he performed a miraculous deliverance from Pharaoh's bondage in Egypt, including drowning Pharaoh and his entire army of horsemen and chariots who were in "hot pursuit" of them as they fled for their emaciated lives. Next, I will discuss the second time this type of false worship event led by a false prophet occurred in the Holy Scriptures.

Another time it happened was when Nebuchadnezzar made his image and required all persons to face and worship his image or statue upon the penalty of death if one refused whenever they heard the clarion call to do so. Review **Daniel 3:1–6** denoted here: **"Nebuchadnezzar the king made an image of gold whose height was threescore cubits and the breadth thereof was six cubits he set it up in the plain of Dura, in the province of Babylon. Then Nebuchadnezzar the king sent to gather together the princes, the governors and the captains, the judges, the treasurers, the counsellors, the sheriffs and all the rulers' of the provinces to come to the dedication of the image which Nebuchadnezzar the king has set up. Then the princes the governors and captains, the judges, the counsellors, the sheriffs and all of the rulers of the provinces were gathered together to the dedication of the image that Nebuchadnezzar had set up. Then an herald cried aloud, To you <u>it is commanded</u>, O people, nations and languages that at what time you hear the sound of the cornet, flute, harp, sackbut, psaltery, dulcimer and all kinds of musick you <u>fall down and worship the golden image</u> that Nebuchadnezzar the king has set up. And whoso falls not down and worship shalt the same hour be cast into the midst of a burning fiery furnace."**

Consequently, this story is how we all have become familiar with Meshach, Shadrach and Abednego. The three Hebrew men who refused to worship or bow their knees to anyone other than the Lord their God, Creator of Heaven and earth! Even though they knew by refusing, they faced immediate death in the fiery furnace. However, I can include another time, which was when Haman tried to kill the entire Israeli people in the realm of the Persian King Ahasuerus after some of them refused to kneel to the image (statue) of the King.

Nevertheless, the Hebrew people were saved when Mordecai insisted that his niece, Queen Esther, reveal her identity as a Hebrew woman. Initially Esther resisted doing so until persuaded by her uncle Mordecai. Mordechai insisted that Esther tell the King about Haman's plan who wanted to kill all Hebrews in the Persian King Ahasuerus provinces without knowing that God had planted within the Persian King's harem, a beautiful girl whose name in Hebrew is "Hadassah," Her Persian (Iranian) name was Esther in his courtyard of women. God did this in advance because we know how she came to this prominent attention when the beautiful Queen Vashti refused to come into the King's Court when summoned by him. Subsequently, Esther became Queen when his first wife, Vashti, refused to come before him upon issuance of his royal edict as summoned to his royal feast. This would read in today's Modern day techno social media "terminology" parlance as #IamnotgoingtocomeOKing. God was already at work planting the foundation for Esther/Hadassah meteoric ascendancy to prominence to save the Hebrews before the order ever came about to kill them by Haman's sinister plot. Logically, as one can see these are just a couple of examples of "false prophets" doing their evil ministry to mislead otherwise God revering people astray. Now, I transition back to our primary subject matter on our journey that is the ministry of the False Prophet during the Great Tribulation Period of our time to come.

The False Prophet continues his deception in **Revelation 13:16**, by mandating that all persons no matter free or slave, rich or poor, must receive a mark on their forehead or their right hand. Look at **Revelation 13:16** here that says, "**He causes all both small and great, rich and poor, free and slave to receive a mark on their right hand or on their foreheads.**" This significant event highlighted more in detail in the next chapter of this book—i.e., the mark of the beast. However, I will highlight some of the problems with persons receiving such a mark here. By accepting the mark of the beast, one is actually choosing a declaration of loyalty. This proclaims ownership as well as whose side one is pledging allegiance as his/her Lord. It declares publicly that the Antichrist is your "god." It vows alliance or allegiance to him, rejecting the true God and Our Heavenly Father Jehovah of Israel. It signifies one's worship or devotion to the evil one on earth. It is a voluntary acceptance of Satan's counterfeit to God's authentic marking of his people. See **Revelation 7:1–3** listed here:

"After, these things I saw four angels standing at the four corners of the earth holding the four winds of the earth that the winds of the earth should not blow on the earth, on the sea, or on any tree. Then I saw another angel ascending from the east having the "seal of the living God" and he cried with a loud voice to the four angels to whom it was granted to harm the earth and the sea. Saying do not harm the earth, the sea, or the trees <u>till we have sealed</u> the servants of <u>our God on their foreheads.</u>"

The False Prophet has a couple of sinister ways to enforce this practice. First, he ensures that you cannot buy anything without the mark. This includes everything that you now use for daily living. It does not matter what the commodity or item is. If the item can be sold or purchased, you will not be able to buy or sell it because you do not have the access number to do so. Secondly, he will cause anyone without it immediate death by execution. Therefore, if one was thinking about being a true survivor off the land, via hunting or fishing and simply foregoing the numerical marking of the emblazoned, tattooed number of the beast/antichrist or the micro chipping of the same. This includes those who are amputees upon whose body the base of the hand extremity is nonexistent due to birth defect, accident or medical necessity amputation such as diabetes. The mark or number in lieu of placement upon their hand has a substitute location prominently placed on their forehead. Therefore, no one should entertain the idea that I have an excuse not to accept the mark or number due to impairment, handicap or disability.

The False Prophet will not allow refusal to accept the mark of the beast. He nixes that idea with just killing the people outright for him the problem's resolved as far as he is concerned. He does not care about you going to heaven at this point. He is just satisfied that you are no longer *here to witness* for Jehovah or Jesus Christ by your refusal to accept his name or his number. The outright defiance and or refusal to accept the mark of the beast or the name of his number which is 666 is treasonous that amounts to a capital offense warranting death's imposition immediately.

Finally, in **Revelation 13:18**, it says, **"Here is wisdom let him who understands calculate the number of *"the beast"* for it is a** "*number of a man*" *God* wants it completely understood exactly to whom he is referring. This confirms what I stated earlier about the beast and the Antichrist is the same person. It is a man with symbolic beast connotations to understand or comprehend his savagery upon humanity during his eighty-four months or seven-year tenure on earth. The Beast/Antichrist rule is divisible into two, forty-two month intervals of prosperity and then total debauchery under his murderous tutelage or governance. Summarily, we have reviewed some interesting actions that will be undertaken by the False Prophet who forces all who are living on the earth during his "evil ministry" to support the worship of the Antichrist. Nevertheless, let us look at some possible traits regarding his background before evolving to the next chapter. This individual does or should already know something about worship. You just do not walk outside and start a ministry especially if you have absolutely no idea the tenements of ministerial or ecclesiastical jargon or precepts of canon laws about the divinity of any deity.

Yet since he is *the False Prophet* that means that, the current faith or god that he is worshipping right now is a false god that is preparing him for his celestial rise to worldwide "false" evangelism to worship Lucifer as god. There are a couple of world religions right now on this earth that meet this criteria but one more so than any other—i.e., the Roman Catholic Church. The Roman Catholic Church forbids the clergy from marrying. This is diametrically opposed to the word of God. Review **1 Timothy 4:1–3** that has been cited numerous times already due to its applicability to events occurring in the world today. **"Now the Spirit expressly says that in the latter times some will depart from the faith. Giving heed to deceiving spirits and doctrines of demons. Speaking lies in hypocrisy having their own conscience seared with a hot iron. *Forbidding to marry* and commanding to abstain from foods which God created to be received with thanksgiving by those who believe and know the truth."**

However, we all know the history of child molestation of the numerous convicted and pending Archbishops, Cardinals, Priests and leaders of its flock that have gone on for decades within this tentacles of the octopus of the Roman Catholic Church. The tentacles of this pagan institution reach everywhere throughout the world. It is a mysterious hybrid combination, amalgamation or blend of religious and pagan deities, religious symbolism, artifacts, deceitful embellished history, including the Spanish Inquisition homicide/murder blood stained cloths on its hands, catholic canons, Pantheon of rituals, etc., with the "periodic" mentioning of the holy foundation of Jesus Christ when necessary. However, it simultaneously promotes, endorses, encourages and demands via prayer while promoting the Virgin Marian worship as the foundational aspects of it beliefs. The word of God expressly forbids worshipping **anyone other than God exclusively**! God declares that he is a (Jealous God) in **Exodus 34:14** that reads, "**For you shalt have _no other_ god, for the Lord whose name is Jealous, is a jealous God.**"

Furthermore, the word of God tells us in another scripture that **salvation** can **only** come via **Jesus Christ** _exclusively for all humanity._ **Acts 4:12** cited here; **nor is there salvation in any other for there is no other name given under heaven among men by which we must be saved.** Furthermore, Catholicism promotes and endorses worshipping of the dead "saints" that have departed this life for the next. This institution distinguishes itself from all other religious institutions in the world via some auxiliary practices for example, the Roman Catholic Church has its own bank, the vast holding of its current net value are estimated to be around 30 billion dollars in cash reserves. However, given the enormity, scope, breadth and vastness of its art collections, buildings, libraries, artifacts, lands and other holdings, the Holy See as it is referred to, true net worth is incalculable. The Roman Catholic Church has ambassadors from sovereign secular Nations that confer with the Pope on various matters of State.

Currently, during the time of the penmanship of this book, the American Ambassador representing the United States of America's interest with the Roman Catholic Church is Callista Gingrich. Not surprisingly, she is the (second) wife of Newt Gingrich, the former US House of Representatives powerful Speaker of the House. Good ole Newt a conservative Bible thumping' "Christian" Thunderbolt allegedly sent divorce notice paperwork to his first wife while she was fighting for her life on a cancer deathbed. God will forgive Newt just as if he forgives each of us. However, but I am just saying for the record we need to be aware that at times while we are throwing our Bibles and proclaimed Christian faith in the face of others. We need to humble ourselves before our God that we may remember some important truths. Such as Michael Jackson stated in one of his songs…If you want to make the world a better place, "*take a look at yourself*" and *make the change.* By starting with "the man in the mirror." Good ole Newt's whose former position in the American Constitution is so powerful as Speaker of The House, it is second in line after the vice-president in the Order of Succession to become President of The United States of America in the event of any unforeseen National or State tragedy to the sitting President. The Roman Catholic Church is its own sovereign entity or vassal if you will. Let me clarify what this actually means. If someone shoots and kills another person anywhere in Italy and runs to seek shelter (asylum) within or inside of the Vatican Church basilica, its walls or any of its structures. The Vatican police cannot just follow such an individual to affect an arrest of this person **without** the express, written consent and agreement by the Pope.

Now let us switch countries anywhere else in the world you commit that type of felonious, criminal offense and run inside any other local church, synagogue, temple or mosque and the police will cordially follow you inside the house of worship. They will handcuff you, arrest you, and then escort you to their vehicle for processing at police headquarters or a local precinct. The Catholic Church has its own "Praetorian Guard" if you will, the Swiss Guard a small but deadly, dedicated group of professionally trained solders. These soldiers are typically well-trained, veteran members of the Swiss corps of Gendarmes, who will drop threats to the Pope like a bag of potatoes. Originally founded in 1506 by Pope Julius II. That is approximately over five hundred years of existence. Someone may ask if these security personnel are that good then why didn't they stop Mehmet Ai Agca, an alleged Muslim terrorist when he unsuccessfully shot and attempted to assassinate Pope John Paul II. Well that answer is simple, the Pope skirted some of his security protocols recommendations to meet more people in an open air setting when hundreds and thousands of well-wishing people greeting, tugging, lunging, crying and reaching out to touch the "hem of his garment" toward him *which compromised* his security detail significantly. However, let us be very pragmatic or practical here as well. No one can prevent *all threats* directed against the security protocol for dignitaries, emissaries and elected officials. Especially when the overall designation is to thwart, mitigate, defend, or attempt protection from as many different threats as possible. There is no such thing as ultimate protection unless you have God doing the protection!

However, if you will recall, another infamous shooting attempt here in the heartland of America could be compared or is analogous to asking why didn't the United States Secret Service, stop John Hinckley Jr. from shooting and almost killing President Ronald Reagan as he left the Hotel enroute to his motorcade in Washington D.C. In fact, both of these men were shot in the exact same year 1981 along with President Anwar Sadat of Egypt who was killed because of his gunshot wounds. No one would dare question the professional marksmanship, willingness to die or the courage required to act as human shields (skilled training) during assassination attempts of these dedicated professionals. Neither would anyone question their espirit décor, devotion to duty, honor or prestige (which has taken major hits lately) prostitutes (spies) infiltration or penetration into their cocoon of secrecy to steal vital secrets of their tradecraft to protect American elected officials in Columbia who stole vital secrets while protecting President Obama.

Furthermore, the agents who risk their lives daily for their protectees and dignitaries without flinching in perilous times of threats visible and invisible to their assigned duties seem to go about these challenging tasks without minimal care for their own personal safety. Not even the famed Israeli Shin-Bet security detail professional's record is flawless. The reason is attributable to the fact that Yityak Rabin was shot and killed by a disgruntled Israeli law student and died because of his wounds on their watch. Therefore, as we see, no one is flawless. Now back to the main topic. The Roman Catholic Church has its own bank. Wait a minute say what about a religious institution regarding **_self-governing_** its own financial bank? A religious institution that is supposedly dedicated to "worshipping God" and converting souls has **its own** financial institution with vast holdings. The actual name of the Roman Catholic Church's bank is the Institute for Works of Religion (IOR). This bank founded in 1942 as the Vatican reorganized from the ashes of financial investment ruin as it almost went bankrupt in 1929. This bank is located, where else…within Vatican City. Because it is the official bank of an independent city—i.e., Vatican City it has its own special charter. Now let us briefly talk about an awkward situation involving this institution albeit it is a financial institution devoted supposedly to the official bank of an incorporated entity—i.e., Vatican City. It is a *privately* held bank.

There are undoubtedly secret activities that we will never know about that have occurred over the years shrouded in secrecy, dubious transactions, under the table deals or blind actions that have been happening on behalf of this institution to protect the enormous wealth of the vast Vatican empire for eons. However, some well-known scandals in public preview shed some light upon some previous allegations. For example, that the Vatican Bank made money from the deaths of Ashkenazi (European) Jews during the holocaust. Allegedly, it did so via insurance policies of the life of Jewish Italians. Here is how the scheme allegedly went down; the Vatican acted as a third party insurer for Jewish families during the World War 2. Since it was a *third party insurer and not a direct insurer* of lives of the misfortunate it did not have to pay these losses according to a court ruling. However, upon the deaths of many Jews who were killed by the Nazis during this period they refused not to pay on the claims but also they declined to release the assets of these victims to the families or survivors as a ruse invoked by particular executive level decision makers within this cabal of Bankers or "Judas Iscariots" collectively. Supposedly this was related to or shall I say it was attributed to the fact that many records were destroyed during the actual murdering, incarceration, forced slave labor, mass public executions, gassing as well as cremations or live medical experimentations causing excruciating deaths, upon the bodies of feeble, starving, defenseless people by the Nazis.

Therefore, the Vatican Bank simply denied access to their vaults ignoring claims; neither did they release any of the assets held by them in trusts to the rightful heirs, relatives or the estates of the property to the decedents families. The Vatican Bank a.k.a. IOR coffers swelled as a result of this sinister, devilish, financial, ecclesiastical embezzlement of wholesale transfers of illegal wealth from "bankers" of "God" from forced impoverished victims. Therefore, families victimization multiplied exponentially as they went away empty handed along with the agony compounded with the interest of the death of their loved ones. Also, the Vatican Bank *concealed* many records as well as hid Nazi war criminals as the allies searched all over Europe to find these mass murderers of innocent people many whom were women and children. Everybody walking around in robes and religious garb with MITRE up upon their skulls while holding books of praise with religious artifacts including crucifixes or with crosses around their necks were not holy. Although they appeared to be devout men reciting in Latin pseudo sacred phrases of worship as they were "pretending" to be archbishops, bishops, cardinals, or priests were wolves dressed in sheep clothing. All of the persons walking piously within the walls of the Vatican Bank, its Basilicas, cathedrals, rectories or facilities of worship were not all lambs. Some of them were ravening wolves who had or once upon a time—i.e., just prior to the arrival of the Americans and allied forces held German Luger 9mm para-bellum handguns or fully loaded automatic machine guns in their hands as they shot to death at point blank range into the heads of a vanquished people. Thank God, he knows every one of them and his judgment of vengeance will be upon their evil, murderous souls.

See **Romans 12:19,** listed here, "**Beloved do not avenge yourselves, Vengeance is mine says the <u>Lord I will</u> repay**." Unquestionably they are deserving of divine retribution because they are responsible for blindly, voluntarily, in orchestration conspired with the network of evil emissaries at the executive military level of the Third Reich. Making genocidal policies while marching in goose-stepping cadences, as they idolized, a maniacal, bloodthirsty devil identified as none other than the Fuhrer Adolf Hitler. They willingly did this while methodically, rhythmically, attired in black

Jackboots. Goose-stepping to drumbeats of hatred while carrying out genocide to the demonic inspired lie of (all white supremacists) ideology espoused by Hitler and his henchman as they went about killing innocent people. Supposedly, because of a misguided racial hatred, bigotry as well as self-underachievement of supposed lionized heroic bloodlines of superior accomplishments; while blaming others for their own failures instigated by Lucifer himself! Evil has no boundaries! Ironically, they were nothing more than hoodlums, or miscreants who failed within their own country and within a society that gave them every conceivable advantage over others (via institutional and outright racism) who excelled. Yet they still failed miserably. Allegedly, the Vatican Bank and its board of co-conspirators in direct complicity with the Nazis via trickery, deceit and treacherous acquisition of booty or loot held by the Nazis pilfered, plundered as well as ravished the Ashkenazi (European) Jews during this long "Krystal Night."

Jewish citizens confiscated, stolen wealth lay deposited as untold enormous amounts of stolen wealth in the vaults of the Holy See. Secondly, another allegation that has been alluded to supposedly occurred within the corridors or confines of the milieu within the Vatican Bank was the allegations of used deposited money to attempt to purchase fake securities from a Mafia linked counterfeit ring. Continuing, thirdly another levied allegation against the Vatican Bank is that it used millions of dollars to cover up the squandering of donated money estimated somewhere to be around 15 to 20 million dollars range for projects by catholic priests or *monks* who were residing in America. Specifically in Philadelphia at the supposed time of its occurrence. Some of them accused as thieves acting like pious souls who raised money for religious projects only to take the money via embezzlement schemes for irreligious escapades on themselves to live lives of luxury. Supposedly, the Vatican paid the debts off that these *friars* made to keep the news on the "down low" as not to arise any suspicion or alarms and possible criminal indictments so that all of the bad news about the high style living of presumed holy men was doing in the name of God wouldn't be exposed. Finally, another sad allegation levied against this behemoth institution is that it smuggled stolen gold in Poland to topple the communist reigning regime in the Warsaw Pact at that time. The scheme must have really worked well because today there is no longer any "Warsaw Pact" that Poland was a nation-member of which was the antithesis of NATO—i.e., the North Atlantic Treaty Organization which coincidentally still exists.

The purpose of this military alliance (NATO) is to assist America and its European allies to help each other to defend against the menacing Russian (Kharzars) Bear to the east. Surprisingly this seems like a real-world possibility of occurring sooner rather than later with the current strongman and KGB (America's CIA Counterpart) Colonel, Vladimir Putin as the Russian Federation's President. Putin is threatening everybody in the world to bring back the glory days of the USSR—i.e., Union of the Soviet Socialist Republic that groomed him for his role on the international stage today as it once encompassed all of Northern and almost all of Eastern Europa near its borders on the Baltic Sea! However, this move by him has awakened another *sleeping giant* the "Kings of The East" according to biblical prophecy, the Chinese, who are hungry for world domination or power as they steal, spy, scheme, lie, deceive and reverse engineer American industrial military and business secrets. Furthermore, China along with its spies are outmaneuvering the compromised, corrupt leadership in Washington D.C. under President Daffy Duck, of the United States of America who appears by all accounts to be cerebrally paralyzed mental midget of America. My apologies, sorry, I meant to say President, Donald "Daffy Duck" Trump who is mired in head-splitting, insurmountable criminal investigations after investigations his inaugural campaign is under investigation, his administration has numerous convictions already, his personal lawyer was convicted and is now in prison while other cases are awaiting trial. Donald Trump himself has just been impeached—i.e., a criminal trial held in the Halls of The United States Senate Chambers for a sitting president. **Oh my God.**

This has only happened **three times** in the history of The Republic. His acquittal all but guaranteed along partisan party lines. However, his impeachment will live on in infamy forever! Quick side notation, fake or false preachers are saying that God is supporting Donald Trump. This is not true. **God is Holy and has nothing to do with any evil.** Read **Romans 9:17, "For the scripture says to Pharaoh, For this very purpose I have 'raised you up' that I may show my power in you and that my name maybe declared in all the earth."** Just as God Almighty raised Pharaoh up to political authority to demonstrate, he is the only one with power. There is absolutely no question that the God of Israel is doing the same thing with Donald Trump. The Mighty Pharaoh of the Egyptian Empire while holding the Hebrew people of God as slaves was a mighty military and economic juggernaut that ruled everywhere over other kingdoms in its heyday. However, the God of Abraham brought it all to nothing. Look at Egypt today just to see it is nowhere near the grandeur and respect of its authoritarian governance over the world contemporaneously now. America under Trump's tenure is a colossal military and economic juggernaut that God is about to bring to nothing today unless we repent as did the people of Nineveh after God sent Jonah to them to warn of God's impending doom that his name is declared in all the earth. Furthermore, all of his businesses are under Federal scrutiny and investigations and his endowment Foundation just reached a settlement with the government to cease or dissolve and cease any charitable donations because of alleged kickbacks to his company or holdings.

Donald Duck Trump already has so many members of his administration under indictment, subpoena, either pending trial or imprisonment more than any other administration in American History. These cases involving Trump's inner cabal circle who acts more like a mafia criminal enterprise than the duly elected, sworn in, one part of the three branches of the American Republic. We as American citizens have forgotten that our blessings of prosperity, peace, and sustenance, National and individual defense come only from the Rock of Ages—i.e., the Holy One, the God of Israel. Not any political party, administration, president or ruler. Therefore, here is a warning to all of us as Americans. The word of God says in **Psalms 9:17, "The wicked shall be turned into hell and 'all' of the Nations _that forget_ God."** We need a national day of remembrance declaring that we have not forgotten The Lord Our God of

Jerusalem! ASAP. Trump's Administration has men and women performing mediocre feats of achievement at the level of mental dwarfs and criminals who may have possible Russian criminal connections or collusion.

There are so many legal inquiries into Trump's possible criminal conduct and his administration's disregard for Constitutional safeguards protecting citizens from tyranny of demagoguery. Collectively speaking that these acts could fill the Library of Congress catalog for decades to come. The word of God says in **Proverbs 14:34** that **righteousness exalts a nation but sin is a reproach to any people** this *includes* America **not excludes**! The Chinese are on the move globally so much in fact, that China just went out to the South China Sea, dropped anchor then unilaterally claimed International Ocean shipping lanes to construct a manufactured island while daring anyone to challenge their recent theft of vast sea-lanes containing food and untapped energy sources and supplies. Furthermore, this ocean's geography holds potential vast energy supplies of underwater wealth of untapped oil reservoirs that lies underneath its blue waters. The Chinese have moved resources to Africa to build infrastructure as well as place spies inside countries there that they are assisting via financial loans, grants, hiring indigenous workers, building railways, roads, bridges, etc., within their borders. The Chinese have sent "student spies" to America and around the world who assists their unrelenting espionage against American corporations institutions, banking, manufacturing, technologies, and military industries and know how. In addition, they have compromised, while successfully recruiting numerous Chinese-American nationals and other greedy citizens in their ongoing campaign of theft and covert transfer of knowledge of American highly classified technologies to mainland China—i.e., the People's Republic of China military apparatus.

They have conspired with the Russians, Iranians and North Koreans to hack into all aspects of American businesses to utilize malware to uncover troves or tons of corporate, military, utilities and banking secrets, modis operandi. They daily steal business or tradecraft applications, patented trademark secrets, compromising of industrial, military or privileged, confidential proprietary information while all the while bowing their heads, smiling and lying pretending to be humble. My apologies in advance to all readers here briefly. However, this segment connects with our overall exploratory quest regarding the War in God's Living Room. That has transcended to our Living Rooms. I will outline some grievances with our Redneck, Archie Bunker President that jeopardizes our collective security here before getting back to our main topic. Nevertheless, ignorantly, fool heartedly as well as without any exercise of cerebral matter involvement at all. Trump has passively assisted America's premier enemies including Russia, China, Iran and North Korea as he has played the game of musical chairs with so many cabinet members in his firing and expulsions in his version of ***The Apprentice-Washington D.C. style*** of critical high-level sensitive policymaking positions designed to protect the nation. Trump's egotistical carelessness and sloppy governing is providing less than thorough leadership as he blatantly refutes advice after careful, critical, informed, in-depth analysis of our enemies true or actual intentions by our intelligence agencies. Contrasted by their smiling benevolent often-propped up photo op sessions as opposed to their public acrimony and false statements. Alternatively, intelligence agencies via sophisticated intelligence gathering techniques by both human and non-human sources, directly proffer to the Office of The President of The United States of America through its PDB, Presidential Daily Briefing careful insight into our enemies intent. Sophisticated encrypted messages carefully complied by veteran intelligence collectors are totally disregarded, dismissed, and belittled publicly as he praised Putin while dismissing **sixteen National Intelligence agencies simultaneously of America's National Defense Directorate!**

Simply because this dodo cannot read or understand complicated schemes of elaborate words above the second grade level by this baboon buffoon as President. No wonder he lost a Billion Dollars in Casino investments! Who paid for these failures was it the Russian Mafia? Hmmmmm... Trump only needs an Etcho sketch toy to relate complicated intelligence matters. Allegedly, he constantly ignores or refuses to read or listen to others read to him (except Fox-News Channel Caravan of Clowns) for his own individual greed as well as skin or hide's sake. Donald "Daffy Duck" Trump could care less about the approximately 330 million American citizens except that little overly, privileged, cabal of misfits he calls family Ivanka, Melania, Eric, Don "Nutso" Jr., and Brandon but why does he forget about Tiffany his other child by Marla Maples from one of his three failed marriages. Donald Trump, blatantly, brazenly, ignorantly with stupefying consistency **ignores, publicly attacks or belittles** Americas Intelligence community, law enforcement personnel including the FBI (*his favorite whipping post because they are investigating his possible criminal conduct on myriad levels*) experienced senior military leadership professionals, skilled advisors and others while stating "**his gut and Putin**" (he is really fat) tell him otherwise.

What is actually happening on the world landscape? What a buffoon! America's security is savagely compromised or weakened as a direct result of such immature, infantile, ignorant stupidity as he takes the word of our sworn enemies over the word of our dedicated, career professionals who have kept America free for over 200 years and counting some giving their lives in the process. Furthermore, he lusts in his heart after his own daughter. What decent self-respecting father imagines an incestuous rendezvous intimately with his offspring by saying that if Ivanka were not his daughter he would probably be "dating" her when referring to Ivanka in a hypothetical conversation with radio talk show host Howard Stern? What Making America Great Again dad and President he really looks like to the world and non-leader he has turned out to be! The surreal fact that Trump said it actually means that he has at the very least "thought about"—i.e., a romantic interlude with his own daughter Ivanka, in his heart. She probably should never be alone with him and take Jared with her inside any private meeting. How evil and lustful wickedness. *Jesus Christ said, "For out of the abundance of the heart the mouth speaks. A good man out of the good treasure of his heart brings forth good things and an evil man out of the evil treasure of his heart brings forth evil things"* (Matthew 12:34–35).

"Furthermore, the word of God says by righteousness a Nation is exalted but sin is a reproach to any Nation. See Proverbs 14:34. In addition, the wicked shall be turned into hell and <u>all</u>

the Nations that forget God!" See Psalms 9:17, Matthew 15:19. Folks, this includes not excludes America. Donald Trump has not made America Great again; he has succeeded in making America "hate" again. Donald Trump is the Drum Major of demonic racism and White Power rallies throughout the country. While evoking and stoking the fires of "white supremacy" at his self-styled, ego promoting rallies as he disenfranchises, marginalizes and discredits all other non-white ethnic groups while making white Americans exude with fiendish pride as they publicly chant "send her back," "lock her up," and "build the wall" mantras echoing Nazi Germany behavioral themes of Pleasantville for white America! Pleasantville for Trump and his dim-witted, band of Trumpteers utopia is Pleasantville—i.e., a fictionalized domain where all other ethic or races of **Almighty God's created humanity** have been "eliminated" and only white people live in harmony with each other in America. Recall Adolf Hitler, *did the exact same thing* by holding "rallies" promoting bigotry, inciting violence and maniacally blabbing about "The Master Race." Before plunging the world into war causing untold millions of people murders and genocide in the name of "lebensraum"—i.e., self-perceived *needed* living space for "Anglo-Saxons" to live exclusively harmoniously as the self-proclaimed or so-called "Master Race." However, the delusional followers of Trump are not alone. The entire United States Senate both Republican and Democrats alike are all cowards.

They swore allegiance to the Constitution, yet they daily display loyalty to the "Godfather" Donald Trump and they are not executing faithfully the duties thereof. Because if they were they would draft the articles of impeachment to remove him immediately under the auspices of the twenty-fifth amendment of America's Constitution for mental incapacitation. Furthermore, they would expel him from office for his constant disdain, trampling on the rule of law outlined by constitutional provisions (all laws) including high crimes and misdemeanors before and while in office to remove him from office and the vote should be unanimous except Mike Pence as he presides as the President of the Senate. Unfortunately, even children can see that Trump is mentally unfit for Office. He tweets policy rather than provide news conferences or clear headed executive level direction via policies, enforcement of current laws or proposal/draft legislation forwarded to Congress other than "the wall." He displays top-secret classified data or information like a child throwing candy in the air in a store. He is incoherent, rambling, babbling and stumbling around. Trump errantly keeps talking about Alabama, draws a line on a government map with a sharpie pen to include Alabama when it **never** was in the path of the hurricane Dorian while ignoring areas actually impacted and where people right now are without essential power or resources necessary for survival. Hurricane Dorian hit Florida, North and South Carolina, while it was still active along the eastern seaboard. He goes to play golf during crises as the violent deadly hurricane is destroying lives and property. He did not know that Puerto Rico is part of America!

Yet they do nothing but hold the party line. All of the members of Congress that are not actively seeking removal from Office of this President should be indicted and imprisoned immediately for treason against The Constitution of the United States of America. James Comey, the former FBI Director, whom Trump unceremoniously fired, even though he had years left to serve under his ten-year congressionally enacted law tenure. Which was designed to keep an incoming President from firing (good luck with that law) an FBI Director, just because he does not like him (as Trump did) in his book entitled "A Higher Loyalty" initially sidetracked me by its title. I thought that Comey was going to argue his merits against all of the Trump enablers by showing that they each as elected officials owed a "higher loyalty" unto the Constitution of the United States as opposed to his actual premise of desired leadership traits. Yet, these folks are not alone in their stupor. In addition, others are equally misguided, deceived, privileged, greedy, so-called preachers, ministers and pastors who are blowing the same nonsense as they tell their congregations to vote for Trump. God never told any of them that. These are false apostles and false teachers. God never told any of them that.

The devil, or his demonic spirits as well as their own hypocritical hypothesis of what "God wants" told them. See God's words in **1 Timothy 4:1–2, Now the Spirit speaks expressly that in the latter** times *some shall depart* from the faith, giving heed to seducing spirits and doctrines of devils <u>speaking lies</u> in hypocrisy having their conscience seared with a hot iron." Now let me be very direct here. **God does not support evil or lying at all under any conditions regardless to who is doing it. Neither does God support liars ever!** Trump is a deranged, habitual liar! Trump vilifies women and children at the border as they live in inhumane conditions in detention centers. God told us to **pray** for leaders and those in governmental positions of trust, **not to VOTE** for them. Review the apostle Paul words here in **1 Timothy 2:1–3**, "**I exhort therefore, that first of all <u>supplications, prayers, intercessions</u> and <u>giving of thanks</u> be made for all men. <u>For Kings</u> and <u>all that are in authority</u> *that we may lead a quiet and peaceable life in all godliness and honesty.* For this is *good and acceptable in the sight of God* our Savior.**" Not a single word in these sentences mentioned anything **about voting, selecting** or **choosing leaders.** God does not care about your vote or who "you want" to be in political office per se. **It is God's choice exclusively. God alone** places into office **whom he will** period and he needs **no assistance** from any of us not even our "vote." Look at Daniel's words cited here regarding God's divine hand in man's kingdoms, national government offices, etc. **Daniel 4:17** says, "**This matter is by decree of the watchers and the demand by the word of the holy ones to <u>the intent that the living may know that the Most High rules in the kingdom of men</u> and *gives it* to 'whosesoever he will' and <u>sets up over it</u> the <u>basest</u> of men.**"

God will place whom he wants to in political offices of governmental leadership regardless to your vote. He wants *us to pray* that we may have peace in our hearts with freedom to worship Christ even though these leaders may be corrupt. Did all of the Egyptians vote for the Pharaohs? Logically of course, no they did not or the answer here is a resounding… No! God placed him there so that he could demonstrate his power from heaven against Pharaoh. See **Exodus 9:18** cited here, "**But indeed <u>for this purpose</u> I have 'raised you up' that <u>I may show my power</u> in you and that my Name may declared in all the earth.**" Could God be doing the same thing again raising Trump up to demonstrate his power that America is just a nation like any other and he alone reigns Supreme in heaven and earth! Watch out for these false teachers and preachers. Even Texas "good ole boy" Rick Perry, Secretary of Energy under Trump said that God ordained Trump to be president...but for what purpose not necessarily to display his talents because, Trump has none at all! Trump humiliated Perry by placing him in charge of the very agency he wanted to dismantle as Candidate Perry against Trump. Lol.

However, this is actually a good move because it gave Perry a much-needed education. Rick Perry did not know (prior to being sent humiliated by Trump) that the Department of Energy was also responsible for the maintenance, disposal, placement, concealment, safeguard and acquisition of Americas Nuclear Weapons. Apparently, America and the world has not learned anything from the two previous World Wars. Do not worry, with America's unmitigated embracing of a petty demigod as its President, amalgamated with the rampant ungodliness globally the Third World War is nearing sooner rather than later. This is not a new phenomenon. The word of God says that **there is nothing new under the sun in Ecclesiastes 1:9.** Forest fires start with the combustion of the smallest ember of heat upon dormant, brittle dry grass before scorching millions of plush acres of vegetation of arable land. America's enemies laugh hysterically because they cannot believe how easy it actually is to "win Trump over" by just saying something "nice" about him. Simply because his fragile, egotistical, eggshell soft, greedy, self-absorbed, shallow, overly inflated pea brain will not tolerate anything else and he declares you his ally! Tragically, his base supporters ignore this coward's (cadet bone spur, draft dodging bully) colossal, shameful ignorance. His lack of sophistication, his deep well of non-intellectual acumen.

Remember God sets up ***the basest of men*** to govern as we just saw in Daniel words. Possession or acquisition of inherited wealth does not equate or enhance IQ, intelligence quotient. President Trump dips his bucket from the bottom of his reservoir of immaturity, insecurity, imbecilic, infantile, ill-adjusted childish antics, or malevolent social traits as he spews uncontrollable toxic venom, being extremely angry of his demonic character/ideology or third grade epithets with political or personal opponents/critics sideswiping his shortcomings. Artificially hiding his flaws. All the while, prais-ing his ineptitude as he is simultaneously jeopardizing the genuine safety and security of America. Because of his inability to govern the Nation, while applauding his artificial, hypnotizing, expanding pep rally style, barnyard cheerleader events as they wear with pride their Red MAGA hats. Euphorically chanting "Build The Wall" against **unarmed civilians** while turning a "blind eye" to **well-armed nuclear powers** including Russia, China and North Korea **_all_ who are point-ing some form of Nuclear Weapon of Mass Destruction including** Hypersonic-**Nuclear** tipped missiles **directly at the United States of America right now!** The well-armed enemies of America don't care if you "build a wall" their missiles, rockets, bombs, drones and aircraft will fly over it, right through it or completely destroy it. One of Russia's newest and most powerful nuclear missiles aimed at the United States right now is named… **SATAN**! Do you honestly think that is a coincidence or not? I certainly do not. However, I respect your thoughts either way. Russian nuclear submarines, sophisticated fast attack aircraft, capable of carrying highly explosive, nuclear mis-siles and biochemical, warfare munition agents, make daily routine incursions via international waters and airspace over Alaska, Canada and the "Northern Border" of the United States. Russia consistently performs these aggressive acts to probe our defenses—i.e., 12 miles off the coast of America daily and have enough firepower to burn America within 1 hour! Could this prophecy also be referring to America in addition to its original meaning? Remember some proph-ecies have (double application as did Daniel's) including within the last days. See **Revelation 18:3–10** below that reads:

> *For all the nations have drunk of the wine of the wrath of her fornication, the kings of the earth have committed fornication with her and the merchants of the earth have become rich through the 'abundance of her luxury.' And I heard another voice from heaven saying come out of her my people, lest you share in her sins*

and lest you receive of her plagues. For her sins have reached to heaven and God has remembered her iniquities render to her just as she rendered to you. And repay her double according to her works in the cup which she has mixed, mix double for her, in the measure that she glorified herself and live luxuriously in the same measure give her torment and sorrow. For she says in her heart. I sit as a queen, am no widow, and will not see sorrow. Therefore, her plagues will come in one day—death and mourning, famine, and she will utterly be burned with fire. For strong is the Lord God who judges her. The kings of the earth who committed fornication and lived luxuriously with her will weep and lament for her when they see the smoke of her burning. Standing at a distance for fear of her torment saying alas, alas, that great city Babylon that mighty city for in one hour judgment has come!

Review here, what the Lord God says when describing how he will destroy all of the people on the earth, in the Last Days coming against Israel. **Zechariah 14:12** listed here, **"And this shall be the plague with which the Lord will strike all the people who 'fought against Jerusalem.' Their flesh shall dissolve while "they stand on their feet." Their eyes shall dissolve in their sockets and their tongues shall dissolve in their mouths.** My Lord! The total body including all of its facial parts incineration and disseverment *before* the body even hits the ground!

PS: This gruesome above-mentioned scenario is exactly what happens to all flesh man and animals during a nuclear weapon explosion! **Just for those who are unaware or may not know the detonation of Nuclear Weapons is the dividing of the atom, which is the smallest molecule or basic building block of all matter/**

element of life. Which is caused by extreme, unbearable <u>fire and heat</u>, additionally, this unbearable heat is followed by monstrous *shock waves* capable of flattening synthetic structures within seconds immediately for miles around or near the epicenter of the heat blast radius, followed by massive amounts of unbreathable nuclear radiation dust formed by "mushroom clouds" which will kill millions within seconds of detonation. Now, again I sincerely apologize for testing your patience with the digression on Trump. Nevertheless, it had to be included in the body of literature for I talked candidly about Russia, China, North Korea and other nations and it would be hypocritical not to talk about our Nation flaws too. **I am an Honorably Discharged United States Marine Veteran who has faithfully served my country with honor and distinction and I love my country as an American Patriot.** However, that said, the Marine Corps taught us God, Country and Corps in that immutable sequence or order no exceptions! Furthermore, I hold no alliance to any man neither have I ever feared any man. **I emphatically, boldly proclaim my alliance as a Christian Believer in Jesus Christ supersedes that of my alliance to America. This should be true of all professed Christians. Christ first then America. I am a Servant of Jesus Christ only!** Unfortunately, it appears that some believers are compromising their faith and choosing Trump *over* Christ. This is not an accusation more so than it is an observation. Therefore, I ask that you do not read or imply no more into this statement other than the intent and spirit it is proffered.

There are people wearing T shirts that read Trump is my President-Jesus is my Savior. They simply do not understand what they are advertising due to deception by Satan. They are advocating two different alliances as servants that are diametrically opposed to one another. No one can serve Trump and Jesus simultaneously. Although I recognize Trump as America's President I do not serve him, I have never voted, voting opposes faith in God. I will show you why in an upcoming book. Trump may be America's president but I only serve Jesus Christ as My King! Like Joshua, for me and my house, I will only serve the Lord. (Read Joshua 24:15). Therefore, Donald got trumped by a King! Almighty God has opposed every evil ruler from Nimrod, (see Genesis 11:1–9) unto the present day. What makes anyone believe that God is not going to eventually oppose Trump who is a lying, maniacal, racist, divisive, tyrannical, vulgar, shallow, delusional, egotistical, petty, incompetent, evil president…simply because he is a modern day corrupt American politician? Really? Anyone who believes that doesn't know the Holy God of Israel at all. Jesus said in Matthew 22:29 "you are in error because you neither know the scriptures nor the power of God." Jesus said in **Matthew 6:24** no **one can serve two Masters for either he will hate the one and love the other or else he will be loyal to the one and despise the other you cannot serve God and mammon. Paul declares in 2 Corinthians 6:14, "Do not be unequally yoked with unbelievers for what do righteousness and wickedness have in common or what fellowship does light have with darkness."** Additionally**,** I recall Paul words here in **Galatians 4:16, "Have I therefore become your enemy for telling you the truth?"** However, I refocus your attention back to the topic at hand—i.e., the Roman Catholic Church.

Summarily, I surmise that the Roman Catholic Church and its emersion in pagan rituals, mutinously, deceitfully as well as meticulously woven or amalgamated clandestinely, surreptitiously within the quilt of *Christian' precepts*, thus deceptive, will cause many to worship the devil. The Chief Designer of "Luciferian worship" the False Prophet, will use his role on the international stage as the cheerleader for the Antichrist and will lead the orchestra of unrepentant humanity into satanic worship. Logically, a reasonable conclusion in this matter is that the actual False Prophet will probably more likely than not be the Last Pope on earth to the Vatican. This is logical because the ten (10) nation confederacy will arise from the European Union (which currently has 12 nations while Britain is trying to exit/ Brexit thus making it 11). I believe Spain will break away next to get it to 10 Nations as the Bible declares due to separatist movement there)—i.e., the Revised Roman Empire (Daniel's 10 toes prophecy) to challenge the world for leadership during Armageddon. These are the **ten toes** in Daniel's prophetic vision of the image of a man who was struck down by a rock made without hands.

See **Daniel 2:41–45**. Denoted here that says, **"And whereas you saw the feet and toes part of potters clay and part of iron. The kingdom shall be divided, but yet the strength of the iron shall be in it shall be in just as you saw the iron mixed with ceramic clay and as the toes were partly of iron and partly of clay so the kingdom shall be partly strong and partly fragile, as you saw the iron mixed with ceramic clay. They will mingle with the seed of men but they will not adhere to one another just as iron does not mix with clay and in the days of these kings. The God of heaven will set up a kingdom. Which shall never be destroyed and the kingdom shall not be left to other people. It shall break in pieces and consume all these kingdoms. And it shall stand forever inasmuch as you saw the stone was cut out of the mountain without hands and that it broke in pieces the bronze the clay, the silver and the gold—the great God has made known to the king what will come to pass after this the dream is certain and its interpretation is sure."**

Naturally, given the history of Europa on the world stage for conquest and battles they will certainly play a vital role in the battle that engulfs the entire world. No doubt, the Vatican Church will be right by their side as always cheering "the good guys" on all in the name of "god" yes but which God? It certainly will not be the God of Israel. Who created heaven and earth and all therein is in them for his own pleasure and his sovereign might with his Son Yeshua (Jesus) Christ. Review **Colossians 1:15–16** verses for proof. For it **says, "He Yeshua (Jesus) is the image of the invisible God, the firstborn of all creation. For he created all things that are in heaven and that are upon the earth visible and invisible whether thrones or dominions or principalities or powers. All things were created through him and for him."** Many people including believers in Christ as Lord are unaware that centuries ago the "Kings of the West" (Europe) reported to the authority of the **Roman Catholic Church** as the religious overseer of secular authority! The cessation of this ecclesiastical authority of the Roman Catholic Church, over the Kings of Europe especially that of England occurred when King Henry VIII wanted to divorce his first wife Catherine of Aragon.

Due to her inability to produce a *male heir* (preference) to his throne upon his death mandated by virtue of the British Constitution in the Order of Succession. He set his lofty eyes upon Anne Boleyn with whom he had already been having intimate, clandestine liaisons with already.

However, Anne was ambitious and clever she wanted more than to be a mistress hiding behind the veil of secrecy while satisfying the King's appetite for forbidden affection. Anne wanted to be Queen. King Henry VIII requested that Pope Clement the VII grant him a divorce from Catherine so that he could marry Anne. The Pope quickly declined to do so because the imperial troops of the Vatican were already in mutiny and seeking his life as he hid while escaping via secret tunnels within the Vatican Walls. King Henry VIII devised another plot to secure his desire. He appealed to the "Protestant" wing of the faith that had no problem granting him his desire—i.e., allowing him to divorce Catherine. Furthermore, by granting King Henry VIII his divorce form Catherine of Aragon, they empowered him vicariously via enshrinement as the Supreme Head of the Church of England. Now he ruled over the Roman Catholic Church and thereby absorbed all of its monasteries, rectories and coffers instantly within his newfound orbit of power, which he dutifully accepted.

Subsequently, he confiscated all its property redistributed all of this newfound wealth upon those who helped succor his plan to divorce Catherine including his chancellors, ministers and vassals. Later he married Anne Boleyn and she became Queen. However, she too had a daughter and he dutifully divorced her under the guise of adultery, which he alleged, promptly had her beheaded and married his third wife who provided him with a male heir. The Roman Catholic Church has never forgotten, nor forgiven this heinous treachery and are just awaiting the opportunity that will soon come for it to regain hegemony over its "lost sheep." Once attained, one can rest assured, the Roman Catholic Church isn't about to relinquish that ecclesiastical hegemony role voluntarily again not even in the End Time until it is destroyed by the Antichrist and his cohorts who receive power one hour to declare obeisance or allegiance to the Antichrist. Contrastingly, he will use it to assume his false leadership over many people but then he will have it burned with fire. See the entire seventeenth **chapter of Revelation** that I have placed here below for your convenience. The symbolic language in prophecy is explained to the believer John the Revelator, by the angel of the Lord then its actual interpretation and meaning immediately thereafter. Afterward, I will attempt to narrowly, summarize or abbreviate it for newcomers and those believers who are unfamiliar with analysis of biblical symbolism.

Then one of the seven angels who had the seven bowls came and talked with me. Saying to me. Come and see and I will show you the judgment of the great harlot who sits on many waters with whom the kings of the earth have committed fornication and the inhabitants of the earth have been made drunk with the wine of her fornication. So he carried me away in the spirit into the wilderness and I saw a woman sitting on a scarlet colored beast, which was full of names of blasphemy having seven heads and ten horns. The woman was arrayed in purple and scarlet and adorned with gold and precious stones and pearls having in her hand a golden cup full of the abominations and filthiness of her fornication and on her forehead a name written MYSTERY BABYLON THE GREAT, 'THE MOTHER OF HARLOTS' AND OF THE ABOMINATIONS OF THE EARTH. I saw the woman drunk with the blood of the saints and with the martyrs of Jesus and when I saw her, I marveled with great amazement. But the angel said to me why did you marvel? I will tell you the mystery of the woman and of the beast that carries her which has the seven heeds and the ten horns. The beast that you saw was, and is not and will ascend out of the bottomless pit and go to perdition. And those who dwell on the earth will marvel whose names are not written in the book of Life from the foundation of the world when they see the beast that was and is not and yet is. Here is the mind that has wisdom. The seven heads are seven mountains on which the woman sits. There are seven kings five have fallen. One is, the other has not yet come, and when he comes, he must continue a short time. The beast that was and is not is himself also the eighth, is of the seven, and is going to perdition. The ten horns, which you saw, are ten kings who have received no kingdom yet. But they will receive authority for one hour as kings of the beast. They are of one mind, and they will give their power and authority to the beast. These will make war with the lamb and the Lamb will overcome them. For he is the Lord of Lords and King of kings, and those who are with him are called chosen and faithful. Then he said to me the water that you saw where the harlot sits are people, multitudes, nations and tongues. And the ten horns, which you saw on the beast these will hate the harlot, make her desolate and naked, eat her flesh and burn her with fire. For God has put into in their hearts to fulfill his purpose to be of one mind and to give their kingdom to the beast until the words of God are fulfilled and the woman which you saw is that great city which reigns over the kings of the earth.

Obviously, there is a lot of symbolism and substitutionary names to explain this to the John the Revelator by the angel who informed him of the End Time Prophecy scenario of events. This was intentionally encrypted via the symbolism used and done by the Lord to preserve the meaning until the End Time just as God would not let Daniel the prophet fully understand the end time prophecy that he was told by the angel Gabriel. See **Daniel 12:4 and 8–9** versus denoted here: **But you Daniel shut up the words and seal the book *until the time of the end* many shall run to and from and knowledge shall be increased. Although I heard, I did not understand. Then I said my lord what shall be the end of these things? And he said go your way Daniel for the words are closed up <u>till the time of the end</u>.**" The Lord does the exact same thing with John in terms of encryption via symbolism. However, with some minor differences which relates to the need for the Body of Christ (The Worldwide Church of believers in Jesus) need for spiritual growth and understanding. Nevertheless, clearly one can readily see that the Roman Catholic Church is "the woman" who sits upon many waters (people, languages, nations and tongues) via its global ministry who *reigned <u>from the city</u>* that ruled over the kings of the earth. There is only One City that ever did that none other than Rome in antiquity and in times of historical and biblical significance, viva le Roma…and now Vatican, City. I now direct our focus to the next topic regarding this transitional war on earth from heaven to ascertain how Satan will force man to accept his authority as "god on earth."

CHAPTER XVI

Mark Of The Beast

Make no mistake, Satan will use any and every trick of deception, intimidation and outright violence in his arsenal to get man to worship or accept his Anti-Christ (himself in the flesh) as lord on earth. Yet, one might logically ask how? One of the ways or means he is going to employ his agenda is by forcing his mark upon all in order for them to buy or sell anything. Review **Revelation 13:16–17** that states, "**And he causes all small and great, rich and poor, free and bond to receive a *mark in their right hand or in their foreheads* and that no man might buy or sell save he <u>that had the mark </u>or the name of the beast, or the number of his name**." Well superficially, this seems like an innocuous proposition until you understand exactly what it means and how God Almighty will pour out his wrath upon **any individual** who accepts the "Mark of The Beast" because of what it signifies. Currently, today young people do not realize that they are being progressively *enticed* to do so and accept this vile, demonic mark. Let me show you a couple of ways this is happening without them realizing that they are being "groomed" to accept artificial markings, injections and chip implantations to their temples (bodies) before I delve into this subject matter with more detail analysis.

The Millennial generation aka, Generation X, Y, or Z, I am not sure what alphabet collectively they are being referred to right now, are already tattooing their bodies from head to toe. They look more alike as human art canvases and billboards than they do Homo sapiens due to their massive tattoos and portraits all over their bodies including their faces. Professional athletes in all sporting venues basketball, football, boxing, MMA, etc., even actresses and actors, models, etc., are getting in on "the crave" of tattoos. They call it body art. God actually forbids this in the book of **Leviticus 19:28**, which reads, "**You _shall not_ make any cutting in your flesh for the dead: Nor tattoo 'any' marks on you: I am the Lord.**" Furthermore, they are micro chipping themselves for expediency and security to gain access to corporate offices, cash from ATMs, Amazon shop and go, etc., without having to use cash, wallets or identification cards of any type. In fact, Amazon just released a new concept they refer to as "**Amazon Hand**" where all one needs to do is _wave their hand_ with its technology at the pay scanner to pay for purchases altogether. **Wait a minute WHAT**! This is clearly a foreshadowing of Revelation prophecy regarding the mark of the beast in the hand! This is no coincidence by any stretch of the imagination. Additionally, these generations along with older ones copying them have forgotten what King David said when referring to his body from the Lord as it is originally. Stated unflinchingly, **I am fearfully and wonderfully made (Psalms 119:14) no tattoos included**.

God is the Creator if he wanted us to have markings or tattoos on our bodies, he would have put them there during the birth process no doubt. If you do not believe me just ask some people who have noticeable "birthmarks" somewhere on their bodies. Maybe some of the readers of this book have a distinguishing "birthmark" yourself. Therefore, you know exactly what I am talking about relating to birthmarks. Nevertheless, continuing with the narrative, a question that hypothetically has probative merit or value if asked is why God does not want us to have any artificial or fabricated marking on our bodies. I will answer that here in both short hand and long hand form if you will. Simply put, artificial markings declare ownership. (Shorthand). Now the longhand answer. I will provide a brief secular example before reverting to the WOG for biblical support. Cowhands, ranchers as well as cowboys on the cattle drive on the open plain are very familiar with the "branding" process. This historical process of branding animals or livestock made an indel-ible or unalterable "mark" as utilized on various animals including horses, cattle, sheep and other livestock. Different ranch owners, cattle breeders, and sheep owners on wide-open ranges use this pro-cess to identify their specific animals. Therefore, if they are ever sto-len, lost or strayed away from the main herd the owner only has to show their logo or branding iron to the Sheriff, then match that with the one "marked on" the animal then the wrongful possessor can be charged with theft and or return the livestock to the claimant. Originally, this was a brutal, old fashion way of taking a hot iron from the fire afterward placing the heated-burning, branding iron of the logo directly onto the animals body. There was no anesthesia applied. This was proof of ownership undoubtedly. African slaves in America were "branded" in this same fashion too among the many other brutal physical atrocities afflicted upon them against their will. Now, let me demonstrate biblical support from the Holy Scriptures.

I direct the readers' attention to the book of the prophet **Ezekiel 8 and 9** specifically, with an explanation of the background of this storyline. God has an angel of the Lord grab Ezekiel by the lock of his hair to take him to view a vision to see the abominations that the elders and priests of the house of Judah were committing against him. God tells Ezekiel that he will not pity these people as he has become angered with/by their sin and send cherubs (remember them? No baby angels) or angels with swords drawn, to kill these wicked ser-vants. However, before God commands the attack in Jerusalem. He directs the Cherub with the inkhorn in **Ezekiel 9:4 to go through-out the city and "place a mark" on the foreheads of every one of the men who cried and sighed for the abominations that had occurred in the city.** God in other words, told the six angels to kill all those who did not have the **mark of God in their foreheads** and for the angels not to spare anyone young or old, male or female, which did not have the mark **verse 5–6** *but prohibited* them from killing *those with* the mark. God was "claiming ownership" of those people with the *angelic mark* thereby sparing them his judgment from the angels of death as they marched around the city of Jerusalem killing all **who did not** have the mark. Satan is a counterfeiter and he wants to duplicate everything God does to *show himself* that "he is god" as enunciated in here **2 Thessalonians 2:3–4**. That says, "**Let no one deceive you by any means. For that day will, not come unless the falling away comes first and that man of sin is revealed. The son of perdition who <u>opposes</u> and exalts '<u>himself above</u>' <u>all that is called God</u> or that is worshipped <u>*so that he sits as God in the temple of God showing himself that he is God*</u>.**"

This is another reason why he wants people to have the Mark of the Beast. This mark identifies them as ***satanic worshipers*** as opposed to worshippers of the Only and True God, The Lord God of Hosts of Israel and his Son, Jesus Christ! Here is one example whereby Satan is counterfeiting God's kingdom although there are tons more of Lucifer counterfeiting God exemplified throughout the words of the Lord. The Holy Trinity deities of God the Father, Jehovah, God the Son, Jesus Christ and God the Holy Spirit exemplify the Godhead. Satan's counterfeit answer to this is, the Unholy Trinity, the Antichrist, the False Prophet and the Beast. I remand back to the topic at hand regarding the Mark of the Beast. I invite the readers back to read within the Book of Genesis after Adam and Eve's eviction from the Garden of Eden. They had two sons originally before the birth of Seth. These sons were Cain and Abel. The word of God tells us that Cain became angry after God accepted his brother's sacrifice and his sacrifice of grain was not accepted. Initially as a new, convert believing by faith in Christ as a Christian for the salvation of my soul. I didn't understand why Cain's sacrifice of grain was unaccepted and Abel's sacrifice unto the Lord was accepted. It did not mean that God loved Abel more than God loved Cain or that Cain was accursed of God. It simply had to do with God's requirement for the shedding of innocent blood for the sins of the guilty.

Specifically documented requirement here in Hebrews **9:22, and according to the law, almost all things are purified with blood and without the shedding of blood, there is no remission or forgiveness**. However the most glaring example of this had I thought about it many years ago at that time, Jesus Christ (innocent blood) paid for my sins (guilty party) as he did for the sins of the whole world! Now back to the topic at hand. Afterward, Cain used some deception as he talked with his brother in the field. This distraction got Abel to relax his guard then Cain killed him (**Genesis 4:8**). Later God asks Cain where is his brother Abel, Cain lies as most murderers do. I do not know. Then Cain sarcastically asks God, am I my brother's keeper? God tells Cain that his brother's blood is crying out to God for justice. Furthermore, God tells Cain that from that day forward Cain will be a vagabond and a fugitive on the earth. Additionally, the ground that Cain worked as a tiller would no longer provide him with the necessary yield of its strength. Now watch this, Cain cries that his punishment is more than he can bear and he is afraid that whoever sees him will want to kill him. Therefore, God issues a decree that whoever kills Cain vengeance will be taken upon that person sevenfold (7 times worse) or completely… And the Lord "**set a mark**" on **Cain's forehead** lest anyone finding him should kill him (**Genesis 4:15**).

This *mark signified* that Cain was the property of God Almighty who would exact vengeance upon Cain for killing his brother Abel. **No man** was to attack or kill him unless he would incur God's sevenfold judgment upon himself. Read here **Romans 12:19, "Beloved do not avenge yourselves but rather give place unto wrath for it is written Vengeance is mine says the Lord I will repay!"** For those readers who want to review or read the entire scenario or sequence of events of God's conversation with Cain, the aftermath and implementation of actions from The Lord. After Cain killed his brother Abel later at your own convenience that I summarized. This story can be located in **Genesis 4:1–16.**

Naturally marking is so imperative to God that he replicates this again in the Book of Revelation. See **Revelation 7:1–4** listed here: "**After, these things I saw four angels standing at the four corners of the earth holding the four winds of the earth that the winds of the earth should not blow on the earth, on the sea, or on any tree. Then I saw another angel ascending from the east, having the 'seal of the living God' and he cried with a loud voice to the four angels to whom it was granted to harm the earth and the sea. Saying do not harm the earth, the sea, or the trees till we have sealed the servants of our God on their foreheads. And**

I heard the number of them, which were sealed and there were sealed an hundred and forty and four thousands of all the tribes of the children of Israel." Actually, this should read **Revelation 7:1–8** but I abbreviated this section in the interest of time. I can write the background here for brevity, the rest you can read at your own leisure. The first verse in the seventh chapter of Revelation tells us that four angel angels of God are standing at the four corners of the earth holding the four winds of the earth. I surmise this would be North, West, East and South corners so that the winds would not blow on the earth, sea or any tree. John the Revelator tells us that in the second verse of this chapter, that he then saw another angel flying from the East. Who cried in a loud voice to the other four angels who had power to harm the earth and sea that they "hold back" or refrain from doing so until we have 'sealed' the servants of our God on their foreheads which were of all the tribes of the descendants of Israel totaling 144,000! Twelve thousand times twelve tribes for the 144,000 **(Revelation 7:4).** Naturally, this seal is a mark indicating to spare that person from assault by God's decree from heaven indicated by the mark on the Hebrew Nationals!

However, God doesn't stop here to demonstrate that markings declare ownership with another example illustrated when the demonic angelic attack during the Great Tribulation Period occurs upon mankind is prohibited upon select persons who have been "sealed" or "marked" by God. Review **Revelation 9:3–5.** Denoted here: **"Then out of the smoke locusts came upon the earth and to them was given power as the scorpions of the earth have power. They _were commanded not to harm_ the grass of the earth or any green thing or any tree but _only those men_ who _do not_ have the _seal of God_ on their foreheads and they were not given authority to kill them but to torment them for five months."** These grotesque creatures from Hades had a demonic leader guiding or leading them in this horrific attack upon unrepentant mankind who is identified as the King of the Bottomless pit (Abaddon/Apollyon) who is to lead this demonic horde to sting men with the stinger of scorpions for five months by divine decree. Yet, they could sting or hurt all men without harming **any** green grass, or tree with the exception being... **Only** those men who **have** the ***seal/mark of God*** in their foreheads according to **Revelation 9:4**. Conclusively, we can see via specific aforementioned examples that have been included in this section from Genesis to Revelation how and why God used markings to establish ownership. Thus, the mark of the beast, if anyone accepts it tells God that you have another owner and are the property of the devil. Let me briefly redirect our attention or focus to some of the methodologies that will be implemented by Satan and his troops including technologies to gain, maintain, dispense and control people on earth via surveillance, control, intimidation and manipulation of the people of the earth during the Great Tribulation period just before Christ's return to the earth.

Here, I will identify another subtext within the Mark of the Beast query to identify some new emerging technologies that will assist the devil/antichrist quickly with the capability of physically locating anyone who refuses to accept his mark or his name so that they can be killed. I will list some of them here with a brief description of their capabilities. The user should keep in mind these are just some of the sophisticated tools, there are many more emerging technologies that are coming online that will enhance Satan's ability to control people just before, during and after by the time the Great Tribulation Period occurs on the earth.

- **GPS**: Global Positioning Satellites nearly all new technologies in use today have some form of these systems inside of it or attached to it, including **your iPhone**. This simply works by emitting a radio signal to the global positioning system then returns via radio wave the coordinates of the device for accuracy in real time location for tracking.
- **AI, Artificial Intelligence:** Here is one of the biggest evil demonic devices of them all so to speak. This is *computer generated thinking* that will control; dictate "think" manage and govern actions predicated upon altruistic thinking by computers for man-OMG this technology uses algorithms in sequential format in a constant evolution of self-analysis with a liberal program database. Simply put

computer robots designed to think for itself without being programmed what to think. Man has embarked on the terminal phase of his existence with machines thinking for themselves.

- **Facial recognition software**: This technology will allow the end user to quickly identify the person. By using pixels in the facial features to "map out" recognized features in a database or frame via digital imaging. The methodology implores by comparing selected facial features from the preloaded images or pictures from driver licenses, identification cards, passports, etc., within the database to any person under current governmental surveillance. All of this data is already stored in computer servers of automobile driver licenses offices, passport branches databases, etc.

- **Voice recognition software:** This is the field of computational linguistics that enable the user to recognize with specificity the identify of tone, speech, pitch, etc., of the user. It has a specific marker fingerprint or voiceprint to specify your voice out of millions. Be careful next time you ask Alexa, SIRI or any other voice generated application, not only is it responding to your voice it may or could record it as well.

- **Microchips ID:** This simply is a packaged condensed computer circuitry usually referred to as an intergraded circuit that is made from material such as silicon usually the size of a rice grain with a RFID (radio frequency technology) that can be scanned for identification purposes of both pets and humans after implantation beneath the surface of the skin.

- **ALPR, Automated License Plate Reader:** These are networks of highly fast computers attached to camera networks worldwide in first world nations. That capture and track in real time movement of automobiles, trucks, motorcycles, etc., and locations of vehicles when they are/have traveled-data sent to its database for retrieval or storage and review by any law enforcement or government agency for any level of surveillance monitoring without search warrants or court ordered surveillance. Key point: roads, high-ways or bridges are public space, places and domains there-fore no warrant is required to monitor such areas for safety security or general observation all in the interest of public safety. thus no warrant is required by law to maintain sur-veillance of such areas.

- **Cell phones, iPhone, Mobile Phones,** etc., already comes with built in GPS satellite equipment. There is a ton of per-sonal data including pictures, bank accounts, credit cards, Medical data and other personal data stored on the hard drives of these **devices forever**. Even if you "delete or trash" it from your ability to recover it. Skilled forensic computer technicians will always have access unto any or all of it. This includes text messages, calls made or received emails to and from various persons that are time date stamped.

- **Reconnaissance Drones:** These types of drones are air-borne UAV (unmanned aerial vehicles) that can stay afloat indefinitely in real time to specifically surveillance, track and watch residences, people, animals or any other item or thing chosen by the operator

- **AI, Artificial Intelligence Robots:** This is advanced tech-nology far beyond simplistic AI mentioned above-these are robots which are given human software for e.g. sensitivity and mimicking, mark, record, transmit and convey human emotions or traits that will track your every interaction with it. They will replace store mannequins as they record, document and track your behavior twenty-four hours a day.

- **AH, Amazon Hand:** Precursor to biblical recorded pro-phetic evil to come pertaining to tattoo of hand. Supposedly the US Patent Office has received application from Amazon Incorporated pending patent for technology to facilitate transactions without cashiers or phone application. that will allow it to manufacture with cutting edge precise tech-nology to make EFT electronic funds transfer in use today with debit or credit cards or applications on phones or computers to withdraw funds from your account directly to anyone or commercial entity you are purchasing items from in real time. This technology will allow end-users, the general public to make purchases by **scanning their hands** for specific patterns of veins or wrinkles in tones hands hmmm evil epitomized sounds like the mark of the beast is a lot closer than we were aware.

- **Ring Door Bells:** Types of home security cameras that allow you to "surveil your home on your iPhone." Well if you can do this so can it allow government and hackers to do the same
- **Black Boxes:** Every motor vehicle has one right now these are computer data bases that store every interaction with the road weather occupants and other related matter in your vehicle including speed, location idling, mileage, etc., currently requires court order to download data that is stored in perpetuity.

Albeit, these are not the only new technologies that will assist the Anti-Christ in identifying, tracking, locating, surveillance, capturing or eavesdropping on people. Truly, these devices let us know we are living in an Orwellian Time stay tuned for further governmental intrusion and erosion of your proclaimed rights of privacy. Whether people are at home or at their locations outside them in public domains. These are just some of the more prominent ways. Trust me there are many technologies that are highly classified, that allow the United States Government and potential hackers know exactly where you are at all times. Essentially, there will be nowhere to hide from Satan or his deviant henchman as they carry out this all-out war on earth. Although this war emanated from within God's Living Room in the third heaven it will be ferociously concluded here on earth in the first heaven's (our earth) domain.

Our next step in the journey will be to ascertain how the False Prophet, Antichrist and The Beast will kill those who refuse his mark; name or number. Simply put he will utilize a very brutal form of death—i.e., to silence permanently this side of the heavenly equator those who worship Christ or the Tribulation Saints and anyone who rejects him as god. The specific method of how the Anti-Christ will bring about the death to all persons refusing to accept the Mark of the Beast is astounding to say the least. One reason why the Antichrist specifically deployed this methodology is to intimidate and cause fear. The second is it has another entire spiritual dimensional aspect. It is vitally imperative the person's death occurs or happens in a specified manner according to Revelation for many reasons. Although I was familiar with the specific method after reading the word of God for years.

(Personally, I accepted Christ as my personal Savior/Redeemer forty-three years ago). I still did not understand why the person had to die in a definitive manner. I remained stymied by the specified method as opposed to any other manner e.g. shooting, drowning, electrocution, etc. I continued misunderstanding the rationale for many more years until I began writing this short book. Afterward, during the writing of this book as I began researching the specific issue. I still did not comprehend why. Nevertheless, God's Holy Spirit, I believe revealed the reason to me, as I will narrate it here for you. It floored me right out of my seat for the answer was there all along I just did not recognize it.

I will began by reviewing the specific scripture first then apply the body of the text as we proceed. The scripture as told by John the Revelator is **Revelation 20:4,** which reads, "**And I saw thrones** (during the revelation of Christ) **and they sat on them and judgment was committed to them. Then I saw the souls of them who had been _beheaded (Tribulation Saints rapture has already occurred)_ for their witness to Jesus and for the word of God _who had not worshipped_ the beast or his image, and _had not received_ his mark on their foreheads or their hands and they lived and reigned with Christ for a thousand years.**" The key point I want to focus on is the _specific manner_ in which they _killed them or died_—i.e., "**beheading**" as identified in this scripture. The significance of this is amazing. Let me illustrate how this is such an imperative issue. I will begin by referring you back then bringing you forward if you will by the story of Herodias's daughter and King Herod. The background of this story will set the stage up for us here.

Essentially, the storyline is as follows, King Herod was having an affair with his brother's Phillip wife, Herodias. His brother Phillip was tetrarch/governor of two of the four provinces of Rome in the region, specifically Ituraea and the region of Trachonitis that were far away from where his brother Herod was tetrarch/governor reigning in Jerusalem with Philip's wife. Unfortunately, Herod actually married his brother's wife. See **Mark 6:17, "For Herod himself had sent forth, and laid hold upon John and bound him in prison for Herodias sake, _his brother, and Phillip's wife_ for he had married her."**

Additionally, **Luke 3:1** denoted here reads, **"Now in the fifteenth year of the reign of Tiberius Caesar, Pontius Pilate being governor of Judea and 'Herod' being tetrarch of Galilee and his brother Phillip tetrarch of Ituraea and of the region of Trachonitis and Lysanias the tetrarch of Abilene."**

John the Baptist told both of them—i.e., Herod and Herodias, there their relationship was unlawful in the eyes of God. Review here **Mark 6:18–19, "Because John had said that to Herod it is not lawful for you to have your brother's wife. Therefore, Herodias held it against him and _wanted to kill_ him but she could not."** Herodias wanted to kill him immediately on the spot but could not (**Mark 6:19).** However, this practice of marrying one's brother wife was permissible with one **mandatory requirement**. The brother _must be dead_ already. See **Genesis 38:7–9** here; **Then Judah took a wife for Er his firstborn and her name was Tamar. But Er, Judah's firstborn was wicked in the sight of the Lord and the Lord killed him. And Judah said to Onan, Go in to your brother's wife and marry her and raise up an heir to your brother.** Eventually, Herod puts John the Baptist in prison. However, Herod would not harm him because he regarded him as a prophet, a just and holy man. **Mark 6:20**, cited here **for Herod feared John knowing that he was a just and holy man and _he protected him_. And when he heard him, he did many things and heard him gladly**. Nevertheless, sometime later, on another day Herod was so excited about his life at that time, things were going pretty much as he planned contemporaneously. Herod decides to have a feast in his own honor as he invited his lords, chamberlains and captains to a lavish banquet in honor of his birthday. During this banquet Rachel (Herod's niece) Herodias daughter, presumably by her husband Phillip, began to dance for Herod in front of all of his invited guests and dignitaries. Her dance was so mesmerizing that Herod told her to ask whatever she wanted of him and he would give it to her immediately even up to and including half (50 percent) of his Kingdom. If he gives her 50 percent of his kingdom that makes her Governess. Sounds like he wanted the daughter too now as a mistress. Hmmmm.

Nevertheless, the young girl was so astonished and overwhelmed that she went to her mother, Herodias to ask her what should I say and tell him mother. Herodias's answer was swift and to the point. **Ask for <u>the head</u> (beheading) of John the Baptist on a platter!** The entire narration found in the following set of scriptures (**Mark 6:21–26**). However, I will specifically zero in on **Mark 6:24–25** that says, **"So she went out and said to her mother what shall I ask? And she said the head of John the Baptist! Immediately she came into the King and asked saying I want you to give me at once the head of John the Baptist on a platter!"**

Herod was saddened or sorry that he made such an over-arching promise to the young girl in front of so many witnesses. He had absolutely no idea that she would ask him to kill this just and holy man so publicly in front of his distinguished guests. Nevertheless, because all of his lords, vice-lords, regents and vassals were present he had to keep his word, to save face, so he immediately dispatched an executioner to enter into the prison and **_behead_** John the Baptist. Read **Mark 6:27** listed here, **"Immediately the king sent an executioner and commanded his head to be brought. And he went and behead him in prison."** Afterward, the executioner put the decapitated head on a platter gave it to the girl who in turn gave it to her mother, Herodias. Upon hearing of this horrific act, the disciples of John came to retrieve his body, which was separated from the head to lay the remains in a tomb. Review **Mark 6:29 here, "When his disciples heard of it they came, took away his corpse (without the**

head), and laid it in a tomb." Remember Herodias still has John's head that she received from her daughter Rachel as a reward from Herod. Now the act of beheading is extremely violent, brutal, personal and degrading for many reasons.

Among them, the victim must kneel on their knees, bend over in a submissive, fetal like fashion, or be underneath a guillotine or executioner. Next, the person is alive and attempting to anticipate the actual blow of the sword, axe, knife, saw or blade that is about to strike their neck with extreme physical force while alive. Finally, the resulting subliminal messages of this intentional, horrendous action causes extreme pain as it humiliates the victim and intimidates others who witness this gruesome spectacle. Now John the Baptist was not just any old prophet. He was also *the cousin of Jesus Christ* in the flesh. His reputation held high esteem by the people of Judea because he was a modest and humble man who ate locusts and wild honey. See **Mark 1:6** here, **"Now John was clothed with camels hair and with a leather belt around his waist and he ate locusts and wild honey."** See how many preachers today will do this. However, more importantly, was the fact that John the Baptist constantly, publicly and bravely scolded Herod and Herodias for their illicit, adulterous relationship without fear of reprisal. The word of God says that the righteous are brave as a lion. See **Proverbs 28:1** here, **"The wicked flee though no one pursues, <u>but the righteous are as bold as a lion</u>."**

Subsequently, as we saw above this proclamation cost him his life as he testified via faith about the violation of God's law by the two of them. I have been informing the readers up to this point about the manner of death that John Baptist suffered with the goal of showing why this is a major issue in Christendom. However, more importantly, how the Antichrist will use this method preferably over all others to kill anyone who rejects his authority. Now, I want to elaborate further about a couple of other deaths then compare and contrast them with beheading to illustrate the perspective clearly. Here I will start by discussing the death of Lazarus, then the death of the Shunamite woman's son from the OT—i.e., Old Testament.

Afterward, I will compare all of them with the act of death by beheading of John the Baptist and its significance.

Lazarus was a disciple of Christ who had two sisters, Martha and Mary of Bethany. All three wanted to serve Jesus Christ faithfully in their own right. Due to their belief in Christ as being the Son of God, as all believers must come to believe by faith that Christ brings salvation to as many as are willing to believe or accept this truism. However, there came a day when Lazarus was sick but his sickness in the initial stage seemed to be non-fatal. Others informed Jesus about Lazarus illness via messengers from his two sisters while they requested Jesus to come soon to heal him or Lazarus might die. Christ did not leave his ministry. Jesus stayed *two additional days* in the place where he was when he received the message regarding Lazarus' fate. Instead of retuning with them, Christ tells the messengers to return because this event (Lazarus sickness) purposely designed to bring glory to God through Christ. See **John 11:1–4**, that reads, **"Now a certain man was sick Lazarus of Bethany the town of Mary and her sister Martha it was that Mary who had anointed the Lord with fragrant oil and wiped his feet with her hair whose brother Lazarus was sick. Therefore, the sisters sent to him saying; Lord, he whom you love is sick. When Jesus heard that he said this sickness is not unto death but for the glory of God that the Son of God may be glorified through it."**

The WOG tells us that Christ loved all three of them—i.e., Lazarus and his two sisters Martha and Mary review **John 11:5** cited here, **"Now Jesus loved Martha and her sister and Lazarus."** Christ tells his disciples upon the completion of the two days that they will return to Judea even though the religious sects including Pharisees and Sadducees of Jews there wanted to kill him because of his miracles and proclamation that he was the Son of God. Jesus tells his disciples that we will go visit our friend Lazarus because he is sleep and he would wake him up. They did not understand that Jesus was actually foretelling them that Lazarus was dead and he would resurrect him again to life. One key point is even before his arrival; Naturally Christ as the Son of God already knew that Lazarus was dead *without updated* information from messengers or by anyone actually at the scene of his demise. Subsequently, Jesus tells them after their reply that Lazarus will get well by recovering from his sickness. Christ companions assumed that Lazarus was literally sleeping, as a result of his sickness which they thought was a good idea to help him heal rapidly. Jesus tells them pointedly that Lazarus is already dead! Look at the verbal discourse in **John 11:12–15** that reads, **"These things He said and after that, He said to them, our friend Lazarus sleeps, but I go that I may wake him up. The disciples said Lord if he sleeps then he will get well. However, <u>Jesus spoke of his death</u> but they thought that he was speaking about taking rest in sleep. Then Jesus said to them plainly <u>Lazarus is dead</u>."**

The distance between Jerusalem and Bethany was about two miles as Christ's entourage approached the city limits. Upon arrival, Christ discovered that Lazarus lay inside of the tomb four days to that point. Martha hears about Jesus's arrival then sprints to go meet him but Mary remained in the house with the other mourners. Martha tells Christ that had he been there at the first stage of the onset of Lazarus's illness, translation (came when initially requested) Lazarus her brother would not be dead. Jesus gives her a startling reply. However, Martha misinterpreted or did not fully comprehend Christ point as she was in mourning about the death of her brother. **Jesus says to her "your brother will rise again" (John 11:23).** Martha says, I know that he will rise in the resurrection at the last day (implying) that I don't want to wait until then. However, Martha displays her faith in Christ by stating **"even *now"* I know that whatever *you ask* of God he will give you (John 11:22).** This exchange of words between the two of them leads to a discourse that naturally has the crowd around them awaiting the summation of its intensity. Nevertheless, the dialogue continues see **John 11:25–27**; whereby Christ tells Martha that **"I Am the resurrection and the life he who believes in me though he may die he shall live and whoever lives and believes in me shall never die."**

Purposefully, Jesus asks Martha; do you believe this? Martha expresses to Christ that she does believe that he is the Christ, the Son of God who has come into the world. Afterward, Martha goes to get her sister Mary inside their home and tells her that Christ is seeking her presence. Mary immediately leaves the house crying and goes to the locale where Christ is, since he did not actually enter inside the city limits still at this point. Once Mary sees Jesus, she says the exact same thing to him that her sister did—i.e., Lord had you been here my brother would not had died. She cries. Jesus wept. **John 11:33–35.** Jesus asks Mary, where have you laid him? They escorted Christ inside of the city of Bethany to the tomb of Lazarus; Christ began groaning in his spirit. **John 11:33. Therefore, when Jesus saw her weeping and the Jews who came with her weeping <u>he groaned</u> in his spirit.** Christ groaning is attributable to a couple of reasons predicated upon my observation of the context in which it occurs. One might have been that Christ knew that some of the other persons who were following them (were doubters no doubt) and they were about to witness the power of God. Doubt's presence is problematic regardless who has it, because it is the *opposite of faith,* which God requires of all of us to have, display and use when it comes to him **no exceptions**!

Review God's requirement of faith for all denoted in **Hebrews 11:6, "But <u>without faith</u> it is impossible to please him for he who comes to God <u>must believe</u> that he is and that he is a rewarder of those who diligently seek him."** Doubt can hinder prayer and all kinds of blessings because it actually says that "I don't believe" God. That is narrowly close to implying that God is a liar! We all should know that God could not lie! Review **Numbers 23:19, "For God is not a man that he should lie nor the son of man that he should repent has he said and shall he not do it or has he spoken and shall he not make it good."** Ironically, God has faith in us that we will have faith in him, what an awesome God we worship! The second reason could be that Christ was experiencing some of the anguish of pain that Lazarus sisters were feeling for their departed brother. After arriving to Lazarus's tomb Christ discovers that a rock was over the entrance to this cave. Christ requests removal of the rock from the entry access pathway. Martha reminds Christ that due to the length of time Lazarus body laid inside the tomb that the stench of this decaying corpse would be strong emanating a powerful unpleasant odor.

Jesus reminds Martha what he told her earlier in their conversation *that if* she believed she would see the glory of God. Afterward, Christ immediately prays unto his Heavenly Father, and then shouts in a loud voice "Lazarus come forth." Lazarus spirit returns to his body and he gets up with the wrappings of grave clothes on and starts walking out of his tomb. Jesus commands that they untie him from these bindings to let him go. This is my first example of *a dead person returning to life* before detailing the power of the manner in which he died contrasted with the specific style of death for those who reject the mark of the beast.

I now shift the illustration to an example from the OT-Old Testament of a dead person retuning to life, as Lazarus's death is an example of a person retuning to life from the dead from the NT-New Testament. This story can be found in the **2 Kings 4:17–37**. I encourage you to read this powerful story at your own pleasure or leisure for veracity. However, I have taken the liberty to list below the specific storyline here for you regarding the death of the child of the Shunamite woman. Afterward, I analyze it apart from the separated context block below:

> *But the woman conceived and bore a son when the appointed time had come of which Elisha had told her and the child grew. Now it happened one day he went out to his father and to the reapers. And he said to his father my head; my head so he said to a servant carry him to his mother. When he had taken him and brought him to his mother, he sat on her knees till noon and then died. And she went up and laid him on the bed of the man of God. Shut the door upon him and went out then she called to her husband. Please send me one of the young men and one of the donkeys that I may run to the man of God and come back. So he said why are you going to him today? It is neither, the New Moon or the Sabbath and she said it is well. Then she saddled the donkey*

*and said to her servant drive and go forward do not slacken the pace for me unless I tell you. And so she departed and went to the man of God at Mount Caramel so it was when the man of God saw her afar off that he said to his servant Gehazi 'look' the Shumnamite woman. Please run now to meet her and say to her is it well with you? Is it well with your husband? Is it well with the child? And she answered it is well. Now when she came to the man of God at the hill she caught him by the feet but Gehazi came near to push her away. But the man of God said let her alone for her soul is in deep distress and the Lord has hidden it from me and has not told me. So she said did I ask a son of my Lord? Did I not say do not deceive me? Then he said to Gehazi, get yourself ready and take my staff in your hand and be on your way. If you meet anyone, do not greet him and if anyone greets you do not answer him. But lay my staff on the face of the child and the mother of the child said as the Lord lives and as your soul lives, **I will not leave you.** So he arouse and followed her now Ghazi went on ahead of them and laid the staff on the face of the child but there was neither voice nor hearing. Therefore, he went back to meet them and told him saying the child has not awakened. When Elisha came in to the house **there was the child lying dead on the bed**. He went in therefore shut the door behind the two of them and **prayed to the Lord**. And he went and lay on the child and put his mouth on his mouth his eyes on his eyes and his hands on his hands and stretched himself out on the child. And the flesh of the child became warm he returned and walked back and forth in the house. And again went up and stretched himself out on him the child sneezed seven times and the child opened his eyes and he called Gehazi and said call* *the Shunamite woman. So he called her and when she came into him he said pick up your son so she went in fell at his feet and bowed to the ground, then she picked up her son and went out.*

Essentially, the narrative is as follows; the prophet Elisha who was the understudy of Elijah the man of God, who has now been raptured into heaven by God passes continuously by the home of this Shunamite woman as he conducts God's work throughout the region of Shunem (**2 Kings 4:8).** She tells her husband one day after several occasions of feeding Elisha and now his understudy Gehazi food. That she is aware that he is a man of God and she would like her husband to build a small room on the wall of the house so periodically during their travels in the region that they could go stay there to refresh themselves on their journeys. Her husband acquiesces, then builds the room and places a bed, chair and a lamp inside of this new addition to their home for the prophet Elisha and Gehazi (**2 Kings 4:9–12).**

Subsequently, Elisha is so pleased with the woman's hospitality that he tells Gehazi to summon the woman to ascertain if he could do anything on her behalf to demonstrate his appreciation for her generosity to them. Upon the woman's arrival, Elsisha inquires if he could speak to the King or the commander of the army for anything that they could do or assist her to make her life better (**2 Kings 4:12–13).** The woman refuses such an invitation by declaring that she dwells among her own people. Elisha is dumbfounded then asks Gehazi in despair if there is anything that can be done for her? Gehazi informed Elisha that the woman has no son and that her husband is an old man. Therefore, Elisha decides to bless her by telling her that this time next year she would have a son. Women in the OT time era that were childless or had old husbands whose natural life expectancy would soon expire had a difficult time of earning or making a living in Patriarchal dominated communities then similar to some places even now. Naturally, the woman disbelieves Elisha because her husband is an old man and back then there was no such thing as any of the modern day artificial male stimulant supplements for virility stimulation/reproduction such as Viagra, Levitra, Cialis—i.e., male assistance reproduction (enhancement) pills, etc. The woman adamantly asks the prophet not to deceive her by saying something that he thought she wanted to hear especially if it was untrue. Nevertheless, just as Elisha told her when the time did arrive the next year, she does have a child and the child grows up to be a young boy. However, one day while out in the field with his father (the storyline aforementioned above) the child is struck in the head due to an accident of some kind and is rushed to his mother's care by one of the fathers' reapers. Shortly thereafter, he dies in his mother's lap.

She lays his body in the room that she had set aside for Elisha and tells one of her husband's servants quickly escort her to Mount Caramel where the prophet Elisha was (**2 Kings 4:17–25**). Upon arrival Elisha and Gehazi meet with her then she tells Elisha what has happened to the boy and that he is dead. Elisha quickly dispatches Gehazi to the home in Shunem with very specific instructions not to greet or speak with anyone enroute to the home and lay his staff upon the child's face. Gehazi departs immediately. However, the woman refuses to let Elisha go and tells him that she will go everywhere he does unless he comes to the home too. This steadfastness is similar to that of Ruth with her mother in law Naomi. Gehazi does exactly as directed but returns to them as he meets them on their way to the home. Afterward, Gehazi informs Elisha that the child has not awakened—i.e., revived to life. Elisha continues on the journey then arrives to the residence as he goes inside the room he closes the door behind him then lays face to face upon the child. Elisha does this twice after walking back and forth in the house suddenly the child opens his eyes, sneezes seven times after resurrecting back to life (**2 Kings 4:29–37**) that is afore-noted in the previous section. Elisha returns the resurrected boy back to his mother alive and well. These are two examples that have provided the readers with specific instances of _**returning to life**_ embedded in the WOG to make a vivid point now. Both of these illustrations depict that the person(s) died in a non-brutal or non-dramatic fashion. The purposes for displaying these two examples is to demonstrate a key point, which simply is, a distinction between these two deaths and that of John the Baptist. I want to show you via contrast and comparison why the word of God tells us about *the manner of death* in which those who *reject the mark of the beast* is so imperative.

I request that you recall John the Baptists' manner of death. Remember he was **beheaded** at the request of Rachel, Herodias's daughter upon the order of King Herod's decree for her reward of her mesmerizing, seductive, enchanting dance at his birthday banquet. Now contrast John's manner of death with the two illustrations I have just narrated above for you, one from the NT-New Testament and the other from the OT-Old Testament—i.e., Lazarus (**John 11:12–15**) and the Shunamite woman's son (**2 Kings 4:19–20**). Do you recognize the theme? The issue is extremely important! Ok I will let you know here without further suspense. Both of the other two persons could be ***resurrected or revived*** to life here on earth, ***after death***. Yet, John the Baptist **did not** resurrect to life this side of the eternal divide! In addition, if you will recall, I mentioned that the prescribed manner of death for those who reject the mark of the beast initially puzzled or befuddled me for years. I could not understand why the person must die in such a fashion via beheading, during the regime of the Antichrist on earth. Until what I believe was the Holy Spirit of God's revelation to me that there was **NO ONE EVER** from Genesis to Malachi of the OT or Matthew to Revelation of the NT has ever been **"resurrected back to life"** on earth who was **beheaded!** Bam! This is the reason why the Antichrist, False-Prophet and the Beast will behead all those who reject the mark of the beast in this specific manner. Satan knows this as well that no one ever resurrected back to life after beheading. The Devil knew this long before I did. They do not want them **ever to come back** on this side of the eternal hemisphere. Not even for a moment to attest of God's power to resurrect from the dead. No not anyone! Even though they are keenly aware that those persons will receive eternal life with Christ in heaven, they reason among themselves that is ok, as long as they do not ***return here*** to give others hope.

If a person retuned from the dead by divine resurrection that would diminish some of the horror of the Antichrist reign of terror here on earth during the Great Tribulation Period. Satan knows the war that he originated in heaven (God's Living Room specifically) which has now cascaded down to the earth is in its final stages. Consequently, he is about to unleash "hell on earth" at an unprecedented level ever known to occur this side of the eternal chasm. Furthermore, since Satan and his cohorts permanently banned now from even accessing the second heaven, yet alone the third heaven during this specific period. He has absolutely *no idea exactly* what is going on in the divine dimension of Christ's sovereign kingdom now. Consequently, as a direct result of non-believers who become believers in Christ after the rapture of the church (current believers) called "Tribulation Saints" have ascended to heaven. During an updated version of "Satan's Inquisition" contrasted or diverse from the Spanish Inquisition reign of horror differentiating themselves from others who are terrorized into accepting the mark of the beast or the name of his number. These repentant non-believers convert to Christianity and refuse to accept his number, mark or name so they promptly behead all of them. They will receive a special award directly from Christ for their faithfulness unto death.

See **Revelation 20:4**, that reads, **"And I saw thrones, they sat on them, and judgment was committed to them. *Then* I saw the souls of those who *had been beheaded* (Tribulation Saints) for their witness to Jesus and for the word of God, who had not 'worshipped the beast or his image' and had not received his mark on their foreheads or on their hands and they lived and reigned with Christ for a thousand years."** Yes, these brave heavenly battlefield Christian patriots will reign and live with Jesus Christ the Son of God for one thousand years as a reward for their steadfastness, ability to resist the devil and his unholy alliance marks, tattoos or blasphemous name or numbers. It is imperative that No One accept the Mark of The Beast from God's perspective! Let us see why from God's perspective following!

However, there are additional reasons why one should not want to accept the mark of the beast. The consequences of doing so are horrendous directly from God himself! The word of God suggests among them is the level of punishment from God's divine hand because it is stupendous or unbearable. See **Revelation 14:9–11** *v which reads;* **a third angel followed with a loud voice; 'If anyone worships the beast and his image and receives his mark on his forehead or on his hand <u>he himself shall also drink of the wine of the wrath of God</u> which is poured out <u>full strength</u> into the cup of his indignation. He shall be tormented with fire, brimstone in the presence of the holy angels and in the presence of the Lamb and the smoke of their torment ascends forever and ever, they have no rest day or night who worship the beast and his image, and whoever receives his mark or his name. In addition, review Revelation 16:1 that reads Then I heard a loud voice from the temple, saying to the seven angels. Go pour out the bowls of the wrath of God on the earth. So the first went out and poured his bowl upon the earth and a foul and loathsome sore <u>came upon the men who had the mark of the beast and those who worshipped his image</u>.**

Furthermore, an additional reason why God does not want anyone to accept the mark of the beast or the name of his number on their forehead is that God himself **needs that exact space** to write "three significant names" on your body reserved **exclusively** for him. Let us see what these names are that God is going to place on your forehead. God is going to place his name Jehovah ***on their foreheads.*** However, God is not going to stop there he is going to add two other imperative names let us see what these are here. See **Revelation 3:12** and **Revelation 22:4**. Jesus Christ the Son of God said: **"he who overcomes, I will make a pillar in the temple of my God, and he shall go out no more,** _**I will write on him the**_**:**

1. **Name of My God**
2. **Name of the city of My God**—i.e., **New Jerusalem**
3. **My New name**

Therefore, these are the three names Christ will write upon the forehead of each individual who accounts worthy by obedience accepted into the kingdom of Jehovah. Wow what a powerful way to claim ownership! There is no need for any license, identification card, passport, government picture, biometric identification, fingerprints, social security card, etc., or anything else of that nature. Your identification is on your forehead for all heaven to see. My Lord! Now these are the only tattoos I will ever want anywhere on my body and these will I seek after until I die. Now I understand what King David aka the Psalmist meant in **Psalms 27:4** that reads, **"One thing have I desired of the Lord, <u>That will I seek after</u> That I may dwell in the house of the Lord all the days of my life to behold the beauty of the Lord and to inquire in his temple."** In addition, we can clearly see that this would be confusing or would be a reason why a person has to choose who they will allow to mark them. Remember Jesus said, **"No man can serve 'two masters' he will love one and hate the other or cling unto one and despise the other"** **(Matthew 6:24).** You cannot have God's name and Satan's mark on your forehead simultaneously. Can you imagine a NFL player wearing a Dallas Cowboy Star helmet along with the pants and jersey of the Washington Redskins at the same time on to the field of play during a competitive game between Dallas and Washington? Which team is he on the crowd would ask? To which team is his loyalty? You cannot be the property of God and the property of Lucifer simultaneously. Period! Jesus said no man can serve two masters **he will love one or hate the other** or he will hold to one while despising the other! Repeated again for emphasis as well as clarity **Matthew 6:24**.

Additional Methods Used to Gain Global Command and Control of Mankind Miracles, Signs, and Wonders

Another tactic utilized by this unholy alliance will be miracles, signs and wonders. This will be a key trick that this group will use because this is what appeals most to people when considering examples or authentication for "god like" qualities or another world special power. We can review the word of God for numerous miracles to ascertain their importance in Christendom general and worldwide in particular. Jesus <u>began</u> his public ministry by "performing miracles" among them were; he turned water into wine, raised the following persons from the dead; Lazarus, the widow of Nain's son, the daughter of Jairus the synagogue ruler. Furthermore, Jesus walked on the sea, calmed the winds that were violently blowing against the boat he traveled in while sleeping and released via divine exorcisms the lunatic who had been possessed by a legion of demons inside of his body. Christ even turned five loaves of bread into hundreds to feed those who came to hear him preach the gospel. These are just a few of the miracles that Christ did. Therefore, the Antichrist will not be outdone. He has some counterfeit miracles he wants to perform before he exits stage left forever to deceive as many people as possible. Remember, earlier I stated that the devil is a counterfeiter and he attempts to duplicate anything Christ or Jehovah did to verify he is a god. Paul tells us not to be fooled or deceived for the *"devil himself transforms"* himself into an "angel of light" (2 Corinthians 11:44).

One of the more powerful signs or miracles that the Antichrist will do is cause fire to come down from heaven in the sight of men. **Revelation 13:13–14** denoted here, **"He performs <u>great signs</u> so that he even <u>makes fire come down</u> <u>from heaven</u> on the earth in the sight of men. And <u>he deceives</u> those who dwell on the earth *by those signs,* which he was granted to do in the sight of the beast telling those who dwell on the earth to make an image to the beast who was wounded by the sword and lived."**

See also, **Revelation 16:14** that reads **for these are the "*spirits of demons*" <u>performing signs.</u> Which go out to the kings of the earth and of <u>the whole world</u> to gather them to the battle of that great day of God Almighty**. He does so without the aid or assistance of a "magician's trick." This is a key act because Elijah the Prophet of God performed this feat when he confronted the 450 prophets of Jezebel who worshipped the false god Baal at Mount Caramel. Elijah did this feat as he challenged doubters of God to a spiritual duel. This duel is reviewable in the specific narrative located in **1 Kings 18:37–38. Hear me; O Lord hear me, that this people may know that you are the Lord God and that you have turned their hearts back to you again. The fire of the Lord fell, and consumed the burnt sacrifice and the wood and the stones and the dust and it licked up the water that was in the trench** Elijah also did this miracle when he killed the 102 soldiers, *<u>by fire from heaven</u>* when they came to arrest him on the order of King Ahab. If the readers will recall from earlier narrative illustration in this book. The word of God says the Antichrist by these acts or signs and miracles which he was granted to do in the sight of the beast, telling those who dwell on the earth that they should make an image (statue) to the beast that was wounded by the sword (violence) via head wound.

Look at **Revelation 13:3** listed here, **"And I saw one of his heads as if it had been wounded, and '*his deadly*' wound was healed. And all the world marveled and followed the beast."**

Revelation 13:14 cited here, **"And he deceives those who dwell on the earth by *<u>those signs</u>* which he was granted to do in the sight of the beast telling those who dwell on the earth to make an image to the beast who was wounded by the sword and lived."** This monumental deception will serve to deceive those who dwell on the earth as they follow, worship and adore the enemy of God Almighty to save their lives here on earth. Jesus said *<u>he who seeks to save his life shall lose</u>* it and he who **"loses his life for my sake or the gospels sake" the same shall <u>save</u> it (Luke 9:24).** This feat of fire falling from the sky exponentially duplicated to another degree in the NT (New Testament), by the "two witnesses" of Jehovah in the Last Days during the Great Tribulation period. Anyone who attempts to attack, injure or kill them during their specific ministry must die by fire. See **Revelation 11:3–6**, denoted here, which reads, "**And I will give power to my two witnesses. And they will prophesy one thousand two-hundred and sixty days. (Tribulation saints believe their ministry during this period) clothed in sackcloth. These are the two olive trees and the two lampstands standing before the God of the earth and if anyone wants to harm them, _fire proceeds out of their mouth_ and devours their enemies and if anyone wants to harm them, _he must be killed in this manner._**"

However, this event is different in one critical aspect the "fire will proceed out of their mouth" as opposed to the sky, to kill anyone who attempts to harm them before their ministry is complete. God demands that anyone who harms or attempts to harm this **must be killed** in this manner. Unfortunately, later upon completion of their ministry to the world they will be killed, but not by human hands. They will be killed by the demonic/angel King Abaddon/Apollyon upon their completion of their ministry on earth to a dying world of people. Read **Revelation 9:11** cited here, "**And they had as king over them the angel of the bottomless pit whose name in Hebrew is Abaddon but in Greek, he has the name Apollyon.**"

See **Revelation 11:7** listed here that states, "**When they finish their testimony, the beast that ascends out of the bottomless pit will make war against them, overcome them and kill them.**"

False Resurrection

False resurrection, this is another means whereby the enemy of God will deceive the world Vis a Vis a false resurrection. Let me describe what I am referring to by making such a dramatic statement. Let us talk briefly about the resurrection of Christ to illustrate the point here more clearly. After Jesus's crucifixion, then burial inside the tomb of Joseph of Arimathea, a wealthy, secret believer, who like Nicodemus, wanted to worship Jesus as the Son of God. However, they were afraid of friends, relatives and the religious leaders of the Sanhedrin Council, Pharisees and Sadducees. The word of God tells us that after Christ's body was laying in repose within this tomb on the third day Jesus "rose" resurrected from the dead by the power of the Holy Spirit. Afterward, ascended into heaven and is seated at the right hand of his Father where he has been ever since including right now!

Review **Acts 1:9**, "**Now when he had spoken these things, while they watched <u>he was taken up and a cloud received</u> him out of their sight.**"

Actually, Mary Magdalene wanted to touch Christ after he appeared unto her after arising from the dead and Jesus told her "**touch me not**" **for I have not yet** *ascended* **to my Father. John 20:16–17.** Resurrecting or coming back to life after being dead will cause many people to believe definitively that somehow you relate, connect to or that God Almighty sent you. Resurrection requires the approval and permission of God. No one just resurrects on demand at will on their own with family or friends approval. Otherwise, everyone would resurrect himself or herself back to life and would never "die" this side of the eternal chasm. Resurrection means that one actually **died** then "came back" to life. Resurrection of any kind is not something that is done on a regular basis. Nevertheless, God usually reserves this for special occasions where he knows doubters are in large numbers. Furthermore, God does it for people who have served God faithfully for eons or when God is having mercy upon a particular family for whatever reason, he chooses. Remember God said **I will have mercy upon who I will have mercy and I will pity whom I will pity (Romans 9:15).**

Christ's rising from the dead or resurrection will serve as our foundational explanation or aspect of resurrection per se. Resurrection, or arising from the dead simply is, the process of <u>reunifying</u> or putting (**back into**) "the spirit" inside "the body," whereas *death* is the "exiting of the spirit" *from* the body. See **Genesis 2:7**, which says, "**God formed man from the dust of the ground (his body) and breathed *into* his nostrils the *<u>breath of life</u>* (his spirit).**" Furthermore, **Ecclesiastes 12:7** says, "**And the dust shall *<u>return to the earth</u>* as it was and the *<u>spirit shall return to God</u>* who gave it!** Wow! Here is how the vilest being on earth will attempt to replicate Christ's signature ascension from the dead to acquire power over the people on earth. Look at **Revelation 13:3–4**; it reads, "**And I saw one of his heads** (political leader's person/physical body) **as it were wounded to death and his deadly wound was healed and all the world wondered** (captivated, enraptured, followed, mesmerized, influenced by) **after the beast.**" Continuing verse 4 **and they worshipped the dragon** (symbolic name for **Satan/Lucifer, as in Revelation 20:2) saying, "who is like the beast?"** (Via fictitious miraculous recovery) from a fatal head wound "**Who is able to make war with him?**"

Therefore, the enemy of Christ knows that he **does not have power or authority to grant life again to anyone** ever. Additionally, since Satan is the *angel of death* he would not do it anyway because Satan brings *death not life* which resurrection does. It brings life back to the deceased person. However, Satan desires to counterfeit this feat of Christ so that he can appear unto the world to be all-powerful with "*god" like* qualities or capabilities. Furthermore, keep in mind that every supernatural action that God has done on the earth with Jesus and the Holy Spirit Lucifer has counterfeited. That will be my next book. Simply entitled counterfeit. Essentially, what happens here is that the actual man (world political leader) at the time of this event (attempt to kill him) sustains a fatal head wound that will cause *his actual* death. The political leader actually dies but Satan will quickly *substitute his spirit* for that of the departing human spirit by entering into or inside of his body to set up residency (falsely asserting his wound healed). Read here **Revelation 13:3, "And I saw one of his heads as it had been wounded and _his deadly would was healed_ and all the world marveled and followed the beast." This is a "false resurrection."** The **only purpose** for his **deadly** "wound being healed" via Satan's trickery by embodying his body, is to cause the whole world **to *marvel*** and ***follow*** after the beast as *divine through deceit* as enumerated in **Revelation 13:3.**

The purposes for the ascension of Jesus Christ as he actually "rose" from the dead was to give him his life back that he laid down for man. Read **John 10:17–18** here Jesus said, "**Therefore My Father loves me because I lay down my life that I may** (resurrect his life) **take it again. No one _takes it_ from me, I lay it down _of myself._ I** *have power* to lay it down and I *have power to take it* again. This command I have received of My Father." *Bam!* This is truly powerful. Furthermore, Christ resurrection was so that he could return to his glorified position for reunification with his Father and ours as he always had been before the beginning of the creation of all things. Let me digress just a moment here to elaborate on Christ's powerful statement regarding power to take his life back again after laying it down. Earlier in this book approximately a paragraph or so prior to this one, I mentioned no one had the power to take their own life back. **I was wrong**! Jesus statement says so by declaring that *I lay my life down and I have power* to (resurrect it) **take it again**. My God, My God. Jesus Christ is truly the King of all Kings! Christ tells us that his Father who sent him granted him the power to take his life back on earth and in heaven. I am about to shout now saints of the Most High God of Israel and to any others whom are reading this book. Hallelujah! Now back to the narrative.

Therefore, another purpose for Christ resurrection was so that he could return to God who sent him where he currently sits or is seated at the right hand of God where he was before as our High Priest and Intercessor with God the Father. Read **Ephesians 1:19–21** here, **"And what is the exceeding greatness of his power toward us who believe according to the working of his mighty power. Which he worked in Christ when he raised him from the dead** (resurrection) **and seated him at his right hand in the heavenly places far above all principality, power, might, dominion, and every name that is named not only in this age but also in that which is to come."**

Also, read **Hebrews 4:14–15** here, **"Seeing then that we have a great High Priest who has *passed through the heavens*** (i.e., T1 and T2 enroute to T3) **Jesus the Son of God let us hold fast our confession. For we do not have a High Priest who cannot sympathize with our weaknesses, but was in all points tempted like as we were yet without sin.** Consequently, Satan keeping true to his evil scheme "rises" from the dead though this *artificial* takeover of the mortally wounded political leader person's body. Satan now actually has a body to which he can govern the world, whereby he can receive worship that he always coveted and carry out the most heinous, sinister, diabolical systematic butchering of people known to humanity since the dawning of the world! Remember, Jesus said that he (the devil) **is a thief, killer and a liar who seeks to destroy (John 10:10).** Additionally, The Apostle Peter said in **1 Peter 5:8, "Because your adversary the devil, as a roaring lion, walks about seeking whom he may devour."** He is a thief who steals possession of this body to carry out his diabolical plan to be worshipped which was one of his original five Satanic *I wills*, if the reader will recall from earlier discussion on this specific topic. Review section of Satan's fall from heaven for the itemized "I wills" of Satan.

Satan wants to live "in the flesh" inside a human body just as Jesus Christ did "live in the flesh" (another example of his counterfeiting acts) inside an actual human body to carry out his Holy Commission from his and Our Heavenly Father. The human (world leader) from the Revived Roman aka European Union Empire (Daniel's 10 toes interpretation of Nebuchadnezzar's dream) whomever he is that originally inhabits the actual Antichrist body, prior to Satan, begins to go through the portal of death (i.e., his spirit begins to exit his body) and return to God who gave it as we just saw. Look at **Ecclesiastes 12:7** recited again that says, **"Then shall the dust return to the earth as it was (God made Adam from the dust of the earth Genesis 2:7)** *and the spirit* **shall return to God who gave it (God breathed) into Adam's nostrils the breath of life and man became a living being."** The political leader's death occurs because of the mortal head wound—i.e., his physical "body" has fallen to the ground will be *inhabited* by none other than Lucifer or the Devil himself.

This is the transformative power of his "false resurrection." Satan has to do this because he cannot inhabit or obtain a human body "in the manner" like Christ did because Jesus Christ <u>was born/ created</u> in the womb of the Virgin Mary by the power of the Holy Spirit. He cannot duplicate this one feat even though he is the Master Counterfeiter. Therefore, Satan has to find an "alternate route" to gain possession with his limited power of transformation. Remember back in the Garden of Eden how Lucifer *slipped into* the <u>*body of the serpent*</u> to beguile Eve **(Genesis 3:13–15)**. Noted here, **"And the**

Lord God said to the woman what is this you have done? The woman said the serpent deceived me and I ate. So, the Lord God said to the serpent. Because you have done this, you are cursed more than all the cattle, and more than every beast of the field. On your belly, you shall go and you shall eat dust all the days of your life and, I will put enmity between you and the woman and between your seed and her seed he shall bruise your head and you shall bruise his heel." Furthermore, the devil fought with Michael the Archangel, when contending (attempting to take possession of) about the body of Moses when he died.

Review here **Jude 1:9. "Yet, Michael the Archangel when contending with the devil *about the body of Moses* dared not bring against him a railing accusation but said the Lord rebuke you."** Imagine the irreversible damage Satan would have caused the tiny, little struggling nation of Israel in its embryonic stages of development on its quest to enter into the Promised Land. If he would have been able to deceive the State of Israel by pretending or masquerading around as though he was, Moses had Satan gotten possession of Moses's body. The Nation of Israel would have been in a crisis then and now, the Hebrews would have been thoroughly deceived, and would have never inherited the land that God promised to give the descendants of Abraham the Father of many nations.

During our next inquiry through the word of God, we will seek to understand how this war terminates as well as see how the victory of God and Christ proclamation for all eternity occurs throughout the cosmos within all T3 levels of heaven.

CHAPTER XVII

Victory Proclaimed

The War on earth has to end just as the War in God's Living Room ended from the principle or initial locale where it originated inside God's Temple, but wars on via various stages of the battle as it has now descended to the earth or first heaven. Albeit this is the Final Stage of this unfortunate travesty in the galaxy. Therefore, in a sense, this is just a continuation of the original battle that has its genesis or beginning in heaven as it transitioned to another realm of the battlefield area at a different phase of the war. This is the **only rea-son** why there are **_wars on earth_**, it **_started in heaven_** and it **_has descended_** to the earth! God did not "allow war" in heaven then neither does he allow war on earth now. Evidentiary proof is that God took direct and immediate action against Lucifer and his demonic co-conspirators by banning them from his holy kingdom forever. God will conclude the war on earth during the final phase of the war aptly termed "Armageddon." Therefore, the answer to our initial query that began back on page thirteen (13) during the introduction of the book's purpose and intent, I have answered why, who, where as well as when wars started as well as why God seemed to be silent on this matter. Although in actuality, God was never silent on this or any other matter relating to the governance of his kingdom. Since man did not know or understand God, man has misinterpreted the events on earth as God's silence. When in fact, God has never nor will he ever be silent regarding his divine Kingdom, character, persona, ways or purposes for doing things sovereignly as he so chooses. Humanity just needs to know where to look and how to seek God's will and ways to understand what his position or thoughts are regarding manufactured crises. Regardless whether they happen because of heavenly or earthly rebellion by angels or humanity against the will of the Living God of Israel!

Read **Psalm 53:2** here, "**God looks down from heaven upon the children of men to see if there were any who *understand or who seeks* God**." Now I turn to a brief recap. This is a brief marker or point where I want to highlight for all readers the answers to the initial questions for this mini book's designation, purpose or intent to answer. Recap. I have copied for your convenience here the actual sentence from page thirteen (13) in red font typing enclosed by bold face brackets {**The purpose and intent of this book is to explore why, where, how, whom and when wars originated and why does God "seem" to be silent on the matter.**} Lucifer caused this war, this will answer **who** because he desired to do a hostile takeover of the very Kingdom of God Almighty in his lust for adoration, praise and worship. Predicated upon his excessively, maniacal egomania exuberant perspective of his heavenly beauty and celestial wisdom that he deemed "superior" over his angelic peers in heaven. This war occurred in heaven—i.e., God's Living Room, this would answer **the where**. The first combatants and casualties in the war fought ferociously in the very presence of God Almighty. Tsk, tsk, tsk. Imagine how daringly diabolical, sinister with reptilian cold-bloodedness calculation of unabated, unashamed evil Satan caused with his gall and nerve of such rebellion he displayed in God's Holy presence.

This will explain how it started in God's Temple in heaven between angels originally. Now the celestial war has become a hybrid of both terrestrial and celestial violence unheard of in the annals of eternity fought among or between all of God's creation in heaven and earth. This answers **the how**. Finally, this war began approximately shortly before or immediately after the creation of man on earth to the best of our finite knowledge and understanding according to scriptural documentation within God's word. This will be sufficient for us to approximate **the when** for we do not know with 100 percent accuracy. However, we do have a strong lexicon of biblical background to support the premises thus proffered—i.e., either just before or immediately after the creation of man. Therefore, this answers **when this war** occurred within God's Living Room. Lucifer instigated it, while God is *not silent* on this paramount issue. God is simply allowing it to run its course. This is analogous to you or I, periodically, when we have or whom may have been temporarily infected with a "twenty-four-hour bug" to let it *run its course* without interference via artificial means of ingesting antibiotics, medicines or treatments to suppress it. We simply let **nature take its course** because we know that soon it will be gone! God Almighty knows that soon this war will be over forever and gone never to be remembered again, **the former things have passed away**.

Review **Revelation 21:4** cited here, "**And God shall wipe away every tear from their eyes there shall be no more death, nor sorrow, nor crying, there shall be no more pain for the 'former things' have passed away**." Every war has three phases; they are initial, middle and terminal. This war is now transitioning to the terminal phase of the battle on earth. The Final Phase referred to as the Battle of Armageddon. Review **Revelation 16:16** cited here, "**And they gathered them together to the place called in Hebrew Armageddon**." This is somewhat mystifying because this battle as we have seen thus far originated in heaven yet terminates on earth. The fight started in God's Living Room in heaven and ends in our Living Rooms on earth. Euphemistically speaking that is, as a matter fact the earth is an extension of God's Living Room from heaven. Read **Psalm 24:1** that says, "**For _the earth_ is the Lord's and the fullness thereof, _the world_ _and they_ that dwell therein**."

Technically speaking then it terminates in **_God's Living Room on Earth too_** (annex section of God's Living Room) since it belongs to him as well. We are simply guests occupying God's space allotted to us temporally as stewards. Consequently, what should readily be seen now is the battles' constant degradation and downward movement in a constantly, descending spiral format emanating from the third heaven to the second heaven now down to the first heaven—i.e., earth of this battle's conclusion for Lucifer and his evil demons! After the conclusion of this battle on earth in which Satan will ultimately lose as well. He will continue to descend and go down to hell and forever be in a free-fall descent, spiraling downward as he is burning away from God's Holy presence. **Isaiah 14:15–20,** listed here that says, **"Yet you shall be brought down to Sheol (hell) to the lowest depths of the pit. Those who see you will gaze at you and consider you saying is this the man that made the earth to tremble who shook kingdoms. Who made the world as a wilderness and destroyed cities who did not open the house of his prisoners. All the kings of the nations all of them sleep in glory everyone in his own house, but you are cast out of your grave like an abominable branch like the garment of those who are slain thrust through with a sword. Who go down to the stones of the pit like a corpse trodden under foot? You will not be joined with them in burial because you have destroyed your land and slain your people the brood of evildoers shall never be named."**

Also, review **Revelation 20:10** that says, **"The devil who deceived them was cast into the lake of fire and brimstone where the beast and the false prophet are and they will be tormented day and night forever and ever."** God wants Satan constantly to have this feeling of downward separation from him in the bottomless pit of hell as he is descending into the depths of Hades. Falling, descending or stumbling signifies loss of control in addition to the constant burning of his body while doing so. All of us have fallen down some time or another in our lives either accidentally, playing sports, stumbling or involved in a fight of some kind or another. Therefore, we can recognize one of the worst things associated with "free falling" is a sense of loss of control, the inability to right one's self as the fall gives the eerie feeling of equilibrium imbalance. We panic in a sense of desperation while trying to control our rate of descent before we make impact with whatever surface lies underneath us. However, Satan will not, be accorded any such luxury as he makes his Last Stand just as Custer made his Last Stand.

Satan's falling downwardly will be eternal, swift, as well as violent. Once Lucifer's capture by Michael and his angels occurs upon the conclusion of the Battle of Armageddon. They throw him into the *lake of fire* after the battle that is taking its last gasps while being fought on earth. See **Revelation 20:10** afore-cited above. Satan's fall will be constant in the bottomless pit. He will never ever make contact with any bottom per se. His descent is everlasting with no end whatsoever! However, someone may inquire why must or will the last battle on earth be fought at Armageddon. Well let me see if I can provide some biblical clues as to the reasons why. Armageddon itself is a Greek term that describes the area of Palestine along the southern basin of the Plain of Esdraelon. Historically, this was an area or crossroad for trade and various victories and defeats for the Israelites. Furthermore, the last temple on earth is to be built (by man) in Israel, symbolizing God's Living Room in heaven being attacked on earth as it was attacked in heaven. Therefore, this battle in that sense is no different. This epic final battle fought at the crossroad of the navel epicenter of earth or world wherein we dwell. This war symbolizes the victories and defeats of all humankind fighting against the wicked angel Lucifer and his horde of rebellious fallen angels. However, it is Israel's last battle against Anti-Semanticists of heaven and earth. The plain of Armageddon itself is a picturesque, flat, open terrain that allows swift movement of vast military units and equipment engaging in open battle. The intensity of this battle will be so bloody that the WOG—i.e., words of God states that the blood spilled on this plateau will reach the bridle of horses' gait.

Review **Revelation 14:20** cited here says, "**And the winepress was trampled outside the city and blood came out of the winepress up to the horses' bridles for one thousand six-hundred furlongs**." This is the equivalent of **two hundred miles**! This will be the amalgamated total blood of human combatants, soldiers and civilians, horses and any other animals involved in the horrendous battle that emerges on the horizon of life. However, the majority of the blood will come from humans killed in this fantastic melee. Contextually, the amount of blood spilled by humans will cover the landscape as the battle reaches its crescendo or crest. Relatively speaking, the *average* human being's body only has approximately ten to twelve pints of blood predicated upon size, mass or gender. Therefore, some may contain nine pints just a little bit lower than the average while others may have thirteen pints—i.e., just a fraction above the normal. However, this war wages on in locations globally upon earth's surface violently. The colossal War of Wars among nations fighting is unsurpassed given the modern technological capabilities of nations to wage war simultaneously in space, in the air, on land and seas including underwater. Some of these nations will be loyal to the Antichrist and some will not. However, this specific region is the central theme of the fierce gladiatorial battle or the Matriarch of all Battles on earth. The reason attributable to the fact that Christ will return to earth in Israel and this is where the Antichrist will fight his final campaign. Review **Zechariah 12:2** here where "**God said that he would make Jerusalem a cup of trembling to all nations about her.**" Furthermore, God declares that... **All who burden themselves _against it_ _shall be cut_ in pieces, although _all the people of the earth_ are _gathered together_ against it (Zechariah 12:3).**

We will began with the first battle then progressively move via the various battles leading up to the climaxing termination of war on earth forever! The battle begins in Israel because once the Jewish People recognize the Antichrist (False Messiah) for whom he is, then they will revolt against his authority and leadership and appeasement for allowing them to worship in the rebuilt temple in Jerusalem to the true God of Heaven and earth. Nevertheless, before we delve too deep into the various stages of battle let us see how the Antichrist will gain influence over various people and societies besides those we reviewed earlier in this narrative. Deception is one of Lucifer's main strategies and tactics that worked back in heaven when he first started all of this evil activity originally. Satan's thoughts are something along the line that it worked on holy angels in heaven why certainly it will work on mere sinful humans on earth. I will show you one example from the OT (Old Testament) how he deceived a very influential King then how he will do the same thing again in contemporary times toward the end. Thereby deceiving millions of people to follow his evil anarchy. The story of King Jehoshaphat is a very interesting one simply because he wanted to serve God honestly but somehow he became mixed up with the "wrong crowd" if you will. Here is the background narrative concerning this gullible but likeable king. The nation of Israel during his reign involved the divided or separated kingdoms of Israel, between Israel and Judah—i.e., northern and southern Israel. Similar to America during the Civil War of North and South. Notwithstanding though, King Ahab was the King of Israel (northern partition) while Judah's King was Jehoshaphat (southern partition). The complete story of the divided kingdom and why it was shortly divided is narrated within both books of the Kings and the 1 and 2 books of the Prophet Samuel. There was peace for approximately three years between the Syrians and Israel.

Afterward, King Jehoshaphat—i.e., King of "Southern" Israel, decided to go visit King Ahab—i.e., King of "Northern" Israel and discuss various diplomatic deals whereby they could agree to stabilize their respective divided yet related monarchies. Upon his arrival during this State visit, King Ahab mentioned that Ramoth in Gilead belonged to him but his army had not yet taken it because the Syrians by implication intimidated them just a little. See **1 King 22:2–3** that reads, **"Then it came to pass in the third year that Jehoshaphat King of Judah went down to visit the king of Israel and the king said to his servants do you know that Ramoth Gilead is ours but we 'hesitate' to take it out of the hand of the king of Syria?"** I am inserting an imperative diversion from the text here to inform or remind those who are unfamiliar or who may have forgotten the _divine history_ of the Hebrew State that God promised the Hebrews vast land that **_was not_** originally theirs because he choose them to be his people. Review **Joshua 24:2–8** and **1 Peter 2:9–10** cited below here:

And Joshua said to all the people this says the Lord God of Israel your fathers including Terah the father of Abraham and the father of Nahor dwelt on the other side of the river in old times and they served other gods. Then I took your father Abraham from the other side of the river led him throughout all the land of Canaan and multiplied his descendants and gave him Isaac. To Isaac I gave Jacob and Esau, to

*Esau I gave the mountains of Seir but Jacob and his children went down into Egypt. Also, I sent Moses, Aaron, and I plagued Egypt according to what I did among them. Afterward, I brought you out then I brought your fathers out of Egypt and you came to the sea and the Egyptians pursued your fathers with chariots and horsemen to the Red Sea. So they cried out to the Lord and he put darkness between you and the Egyptians, brought the sea upon them and covered them and your eyes saw what I did in Egypt. Then you dwelt in the wilderness for a long time, and I brought you into the land of the Amorites who dwelt on the other side of the Jordan and they fought with you. But I gave them into your hand that you **might possess their land** and I destroyed them before you. In addition, **1 Peter 2:9–10**. But you are a chosen generation, a royal priesthood, a holy nation **his own special people** that you may proclaim the praises of him who called you out of darkness into his marvelous light <u>who once were not a people</u> but are now the **people of God** who had not obtained mercy but now have obtained mercy.*

Now back to the main narrative, Ahab asked King Jehoshaphat if he would unite with him in battle against the Syrians to take Ramoth. King Jehoshaphat gladly obliged and said we are relatives by lineage in terms of ethnicity and identity as Hebrews; I will go with you with *only one precondition*, which I ask you grant me upon royal request. King Ahab was excited now upon hearing this news so he readily agreed. However, Jehoshaphat's request quickly tempered his happiness because it involved **seeking God's leadership** in battle before deciding to attack Syria. Look at **1 Kings 22:5** here, **"Also Jehoshaphat said to the king of Israel 'Please inquire for the word of the Lord today.'"** Ahab was not expecting such a request of this nature. Therefore, Ahab had to quickly scheme and devise an impromptu idea to offset such an ignoble, astonishing request. Ahab's plan to counter this request involved a brash but cunning solution. King Ahab rashly assembled 400 of his wife's (Jezebel) prophets all who would lie at the drop of a dime to agree with him to further his wicked agenda.

Jehoshaphat heard all four hundred prophets of Queen Jezebel, Ahab's evil wife tell him that God would give the battle to these two Kings representing the divided monarchy of Israel/Judah so they should start the battle in earnest. Unfortunately, the four hundred prophets of Baal that Jehoshaphat knew did not serve the Lord Jehovah did not convince Jehoshaphat. Therefore, he inquired if there was any prophet at all who did worship Jehovah the Lord God of Israel whom they could ask that did serve the God of Jerusalem. Therefore, he kindly asked Ahab if they could speak to such a man of God first prior to finalizing battle plans. Well Ahab replied there is **_one_**, but I hate him because he is always telling of my impending doom whenever he prophesies about me. Wow 400 to 1 odds, all of the veteran Las Vegas gamblers or odds makers would not take that bet! Jehoshaphat requested that the "one" prophet who King Ahab referred to which was Micaiah be brought before them to discuss this imperative dilemma. Now, while Micaiah was in prison for previous foretelling of doom regarding King Ahab Incorporated, the jailer told him to go out there and say what is politically correct—i.e. (lie) so that the King would receive favor in Jehoshaphat eyes. Micaiah replied, **I will only say what the Lord says to me (1 Kings 22:14).**

Translation decrypted no lies whatsoever. Literally, the interpretation here is I am not going to lie for your King even if it costs me my freedom and ultimately my life no matter what physical or psychological harm you people do to me. The Judgment hall lay pristine as it set both Kings attired in their royal regalia. The soldiers are standing tall, erect with pensive looks upon their faces. The audience nearby comprised of lords, bishops, generals, soldiers and the public. Today's equivalent of the Israeli Knesset (Supreme Court) or America's State of the Union attendees including all three branches of government united for assembly, etc. The crowd is stoic, resolute in listening, standing attentively without slouching down or around waiting to see and hear the outcome of what this true prophet of the true God has to say. They have always listened unto these lying prophets so that was no big deal, but to hear a true prophet of God this is a matter of importance all together for their very lives hinged upon what God Almighty had to say from heaven! Furthermore, Micaiah has already promised to speak only what God says is going to occur. So all of them listened intently. All of them knew their very lives, fortune or misfortune was certain either way. Therefore, what Micaiah had to say certainly mattered! Suddenly, the doorway to the royal hall at the threshing floor to the gate of Samaria opens wide then meanders in a shackled, disheveled, tired, and worn out little man whom is a meager shell of a man. Micaiah the prophet of God, is bound hand and foot, dirty with disoriented clothing on as he is escorted into the hall where these two well attired, clean and "noble" kings regally surrounded by strong, attentive, armed soldiers.

The entire escorting garrison of troops who were physically manhandling him as they escorted him before these two puffed up kings (1 **Kings 22:10)**. Solemnly, King Ahab asks the prophet Micaiah shall we go to war against Syria or not, what says the Lord in this matter? Initially Micaiah lies and goes along with this ruse and tells them go up to battle for the Lord will deliver them into your hands (**1 Kings 22:15)**. Actually, he did not lie in a sense _on God_ for he **_never_** said, "The **_Lord said_** he will deliver the Syrians into your hands he just lied on himself. Micaiah did not lie on the Lord. Lies masquerading as sarcasm knows no limits or heights when used to convey any such untruth regardless to the author or audience."

King Ahab knows from experience during interrogations of Micaiah that this is not a true answer from God. Historically, without fail all of Micaiah's prophecies regarding him have been negative. Therefore, this turnabout of positive prophecy does not resonate or sits well with him. Consequently, **King Ahab tells the man of God how many times I have to tell you only tell me the truth of what the Lord says (1 Kings 22:16)**. This is an oxymoronic or paradoxical idea that a man bent on distortion, telling lies as a deceitful worker of falsehoods who had four hundred of his prophets tell King Jehoshaphat lies wants the prophet of God to tell him the truth. Well

Micaiah replied since you want me to tell you what the Lord says here it is: **there I saw all of Israel scattered on the mountains as sheep that have no shepherd and the Lord said these have no master let every man return to his own home in peace (1 Kings 22:17).** King Ahab became enraged then tells King Jehoshaphat **did not I tell you he only has negative prophecies regarding me (1 Kings 22:18).** Micaiah continues his narration by saying **Hear the word of the Lord, I saw the Lord sitting high on His throne and the host of heaven standing by on his right and on his left hand. The Lord said who will persuade Ahab that he may go up that he may fall (die) at Ramoth Gilead? Each (angelic being) said I would do this or that to convince him one in this manner and another in that manner, back and forth till each had their turn speaking (1 Kings 22:19).** Now just who do you suppose was going to win this debate to convince the Lord that he could *deceive* King Ahab?

Exactly right, if you guessed it was **Lucifer the Father of Lying (John 10:10).** However, at this point the Lord is unconvinced that any of those that have already spoken would actually be successful in deceiving him via outright strategy. Now watch this, in **1 Kings 22:20;** it reads, **"Then a spirit came forward and stood before the Lord and said I will persuade him." The Lord asks, in what way?** So he replied, **I will go out and be a _lying_ spirit in the mouth of all his prophets'** the lord replied **"you shall persuade him"** and also **prevail.** Go out and do so! **(1 Kings 22:23).** Why take another guess who that was that spoke to the Lord. Well, if you guessed Satan you are correct again. This specific being tells the Lord that he will be a **lying spirit** in the mouth of Ahab's prophets. Remember what Jesus said about Lucifer in **John 8:44, "The devil is _a liar_ and _the Father_ of it!"** Therefore, we see how Lucifer goes to deceive King Ahab to battle the Syrians for Ramoth where he will actually die.

Consequently, Ahab and Jehoshaphat go to battle the Syrians and just as Micaiah prophesied, Ahab dies by an arrow shot at him by one of the Syrian archers who chased his chariot fiercely in battle. This narrative specifically written with the express purpose being to demonstrate how Lucifer will deceive the whole world in the End Time just as he did King Ahab and Jehoshaphat. Summarily, one of the prominent tactics the Antichrist, the False Prophet and the Beast will use will be deception. Now once Satan has convinced the world that he is *"god on earth"* he demands universal worship of himself. Satan will be successful for a time—i.e., 42 months that equates to 3.5 years. He will resolve food shortages, trade disputes, economic, political, military skirmishes and other world crises See **Revelation 13:5** the Antichrist will blaspheme and blame everyone in heaven to speak horrendous blasphemy against God, Christ and the Holy Spirit and all who dwell in the third heaven. I will outline in bullet format the five stages of the battles then highlight with more detail in paragraph form some key points of the battle for the readers here as follows. The five stages of this battle outlined sequentially in Daniel 11:35–45 and Revelation 16:16 below

---

*The five stages of this battle outlined methodically in **Daniel 11:35–45** and **Revelation 16:16** below.*

- Phase 1 The King of the South Egypt and its allies attack the Antichrist but will be losing see Daniel 11:42.
- Phase 2 The King of the North Syria and the Russians out of the North push south toward Israel (Daniel 11:40)
- Phase 3 He will hear tidings (news) the Kings of the East-China moving toward him Daniel 11:44, Revelation 16:12
- Phase 4 The Antichrist destroys his attackers from North and South-revised Roman Empire, NATO, European Union, Daniel 11:44
- Phase 5 Armies of the world fight in Armageddon Revelation 16:16 for world hegemony. Christ comes (Dan. 11:45)

Phase 1 above outlined here **Ezekiel 30:22–23, "Therefore, thus says the Lord God. Surely, I am against Pharaoh King of Egypt and will break <u>his arms both the strong one and the one</u>**

that was broken." (Refers to Current state of Egyptian rule as a Nation-State with small strength and the Egyptian Empire of antiquity when it was dominant force on earth as one of seven empires to rule world per God's decree) **And I will make the sword fall out of his hand verse 26. I will scatter the Egyptian among the nations and disperse them throughout the countries.** See also **Daniel 11:40–42, "And at the time of the end. Shall the king of the south push at him. And the king of the north shall come against him like a whirlwind with chariots with horsemen and with many ships and he shall enter into the countries and shall overflow and pass over it. He shall enter into the glorious land and many countries shall be overflown but these shall escape out of his hand. Even Edom and Moab and the chief of the children of Amon, but he shall have power over the treasures of gold and of silver and over all the precious things of Egypt and the Libyans and the Ethiopians shall be at his steps."**

Phase 2 from above outlined here. **"The King of the North Russia, also Persia (Iran) Ethiopia and Libyan allies push toward Israel."** Read entire chapter of Ezekiel 38. Listed here: **"And the word of the Lord came unto me saying son of man set your face against Gog. The land of Magog the chief prince of Meshach and Tubal. And prophesy against him and saying thus says the Lord God. Behold I am against you O Gog. The chief prince of Meshach and Tubal and I will turn you back and put hooks into your jaws, and I will bring you forth and all of your army, horses and horsemen. All of them clothed with all sorts of armor even a great company with bucklers and shields all of them handling swords Persia, Ethiopia and Libya with them all of them with shield and helmet. Gomer and all of his bands the house of Togarmah of the north quarters and all his bands and many people with you. Be thou prepared and prepare for yourself and all thy company that are assembled with you and be thou a guard unto them. After many days, you shalt be visited in the latter years you 'shall come into the land' that is brought back from the sword and is gathered out of many people against the mountains of Israel which have always been laid waste. But it is brought forth out of the nations**

and they shall dwell safely all of them. Thou shall ascend and come like a storm. Thou shall be like a cloud to cover the land. Thou, all your bands, and many people with thee. Thus says the Lord God, it shall also come to pass that at the same time shall things come into your mind and you shall think an evil thought. And thou shall say I will go up to the land of unwalled villages. I will go to them that are at rest that dwell safely. All of them dwelling without walls and having neither bars nor gates to take a spoil and to take a prey to turn hand upon the desolate places that are now inhabited and upon the people that are gathered out of the nations. Which have gotten cattle and goods that dwell in the midst of the land. Sheba, Dedan, and the merchants of Tarshish with all the young lions thereof shall say unto you art you come to take a spoil? Hast you gathered your company to take a prey? To carry away silver and gold to take away cattle and goods to take a great spoil? Therefore, son of man prophesy and say unto Gog, this says the Lord God in that day when my people of Israel dwell safely shall you not know it? And you shall come from your place *out of the north parts* you and many people with you. All of them riding upon horses, a great company and *a mighty army and you shall come up against my people Israel as a cloud* to cover the land. It shall be *in the latter days* and I will bring you against my land, that the heathen may know me when I shall be sanctified in you, O Gog before their eyes. This says the Lord God, art you he of whom I have spoken in in old time by my servants the prophets of Israel. Which prophesized in those days many years that I would bring you against them? And it shall come to pass at that same time when Gog, shall come against the land of Israel says the Lord God that *my fury shall come up in my face*. For in my jealousy and in the fire of my wrath have I spoken? Surely, in that day, there shall be a great shaking in the land of Israel. So that the fishes of the sea, and the fowls of heaven, and the beasts of the field, and all creeping things that creep upon the earth. And all the men that are upon the face of the earth shall shake at my presence and the mountains shall be thrown down and the steep places shall fall and every wall shall fall to the ground. And

I will call for a sword against him throughout all my mountains says the Lord God. Every man's sword shall be against his brother and I will bring him to judgment with pestilence and bloodshed I will rain down on him, on his troops and on the many people who are with him. Flooding rain, great hailstones, fire and brimstone. Thus, I will magnify myself and sanctify myself and I will be known in the eyes of many nations <u>then they shall know that I am the Lord</u>."

Now Ezekiel 39:1: Now this requires little further translation because modern readers don't know what the meaning of the names such as, Tubal or Togarmah as it relates to Russia attacking Israel in the future war to come. I will illustrate a little more in detail to bridge the gap of these words for their understanding to shed some light on this subject matter. Also, let me decipher this prophecy in contemporary terms for the readers whom may be unfamiliar with how "Russia" along with its confederacy come against Israel. Including all of the hostile Nations moving toward Israel has been identified as the nation to the *north of Israel* with its mighty army. Whom will attack Israel in the latter days or time (wherein we live) as foretold by the prophet Ezekiel by the God of Israel. Ezekiel described this futuristic battle just as God directed him to describe the scene so vividly in certain details in its description. However, Russia and its allies decimation by the God of Israel without mercy as a direct result of this attack upon his people and his land. Specifically, Russia is not spelled out definitively in contemporary language as it is denoted on the current maps in usage today. Therefore, a neophyte, new, or unfamiliar reader regarding the historical origins of the country's heritage may not readily understand it's identity in prophetic events to come are readily noticeable to the average reader as he or she reads the passages regarding Russian involvement and subsequent attack upon the nation of Israel in the Last Days. I will attempt to modify some of this verbiage to make it simpler. Again, because of the enormity of volume or scope of work of biblical passages involved. I will attempt to abbreviate the contents in summary format. Narrowing it down to key points for the readers whom may be or are new comers to the Holy Scriptures without compromising syntax or important materials. Essentially, I will attempt to summarize key scriptures via bullet points while deciphering this lengthy chapter's applicability to End Time events upon our world but Israel specifically while analyzing their impact upon the foretold prophecy concerning Russia's move toward Israel during the last days. There is _only one country_ in "the world to the utmost North" of Israel with a mighty army that can fulfill prophecy—i.e., Russia.

Reminder: **THE "LAST DAYS" OR "END TIMES" OCCURS JUST BEFORE THE RETURN OF CHRIST TO OUR WORLD**

Ezekiel entire thirty-eight chapter cited above in Phase 2 simplified, divided for easier understanding or comprehension

- **Ezekiel 38:1–3:** The prophet Ezekiel tells us that God directs him to identify Israel's enemy-the land of Gog and Magog
- History of Russia: Gog was a descendant of Noah's Son Japheth, who settled in the "North Country" or Northern Europe
- Ezekiel was to specifically prophesy to the chief prince of Meshach and Tubal—i.e., Moscow and Toblosk, both in Russia
- **Ezekiel 38:4–5**: God says that _he will turn_ the "Russian army back" with hooks and **bring them** upon the land of Israel
- 'Turning back' Refers to _toward the South_ from current habitation _in the North-allied with Persia/Iran, Ethiopia and Libya_
- **Ezekiel 38:6–7**: Identifies Gomer united with Togarmah, additional relatives of Noah's son Japheth—i.e., Turkey-Armenians
- **Ezekiel 38:7–8**: God tells them to be ready for war and equip all of your allies for this Great End Time day of battle

- **Ezekiel 38:9–10**: The Russians and her confederacy of rogues will descend like a mighty storm upon Israel while she is at peace
- **Ezekiel 38:11–13**: Russians with evil thoughts will decide to attack land of unwalled villages to take a spoil in Israel
- **Ezekiel 38:14–16**: Israel lies securely as Russians with a mighty, united, army attack from the north with intent to conquer
- **Ezekiel 38:17–19**: God fights for Israel himself due to his fury, jealousy and anger regarding the unprovoked Russian attack upon Israel
- **Ezekiel 38:20–21**: All life forms tremble at **the presence of God Almighty** who fights on Israel's side and decimates Russia
- **Ezekiel 38:22–23:** God is magnified as he destroys Russia and her Allies with great hailstones, fire, brimstone and rain

Phase 3: The Antichrist hears news about the Kings of the East—China, its proxy allies, as well it hordes and the Russians from the North too are coming toward his position rushing toward Israel.

How do we know that China will attack the Anti-Christ from such a long distance someone may logically ask? Furthermore, how will they accomplish such a monumental feat that covers vast land topography from such a great geographical distance that is approximately 4,433 miles anyway? We can review **Revelation 16:12** verse here to ascertain some of our answers. For it reads: **and the sixth angel poured out his vial upon the great river Euphrates and the water thereof was dried up that the way of the "kings of the east" might be prepared**. There exists two critical facts embedded in this significant descriptive scripture. First, *the river* that will become a major *land bridge* for rapid troop movement identified as the Euphrates River dries up. Therefore, it is no longer a water barrier. It is dry ground for rapid movement of gargantuan military assets and personnel. Secondly, it identifies the most colossal, formidable, dreadful military forces ever assembled by any nation this side of the eternal divide that will fight in this epic End-Time battle as the *kings* *of the east*. What nation possibly best description fits the title as the "kings of the east"? Alternately, we could ask it another way, which would say something to the effect what nation best meets the criteria for bearing the title "kings" of the east? However, before discovering this imperative truth, let us decipher the importance of identifying the Euphrates River.

What is the big deal someone may inquire or ask about identifying the river? What is the significance of the Euphrates River? I am glad that these hypothetical questions present themselves in the context of our quest. Well to answer these questions one must understand the historical origins and importance of the Euphrates River itself. We will do a quick review or recap from the book of Genesis to grasp a more complete analysis of the Euphrates River. The original paradise of God when he created the earth was Eden, as we all know. The Garden of Eden we all should know should I say was God's Paradise on earth as it were when God originally created Eden. However, the Bible tells us that there was a great river, which flowed out of Eden to water the garden. This majestic river had four riverheads or ingress/egress points of flowing water sprouts. These riverheads were/are Pishon, Gihon, Hiddekel and ***the Euphrates*** look at **Genesis 2:10–14** listed here: **"Now a great river went out of Eden and became four riverheads the name of the first is Pishon, it is the one which skirts the whole land of Havilah where there is gold and the gold of that land is good. Bdellium and the onyx stone are there. The name of the second river is Gihon. It is the one that goes around the whole land of Cush. The name of the third river is Hiddekel, it is the one that goes toward the east of Assyria. The fourth river is Euphrates."** Ahh now we see why the Euphrates River is so imperative! It was one of the original rivers of the earth when God Almighty created the world.

Actually, it flowed directly from the Garden of Eden! Keep in mind that God told Daniel the entire vision "twice" in a double prophetic message that is to be unsealed during the End Time. As outlined in **Daniel 12:4** listed here; **But you oh Daniel *"shut up the words and seal the book"* until the <u>time of the end</u> many shall run to and from and *knowledge* shall be increased.** No one should or could reasonably doubt that we are in the End Times or the time of the end. That the angel Gabriel foretold Daniel regarding the secular, humanistic, man's rule upon earth as it takes its final bow. The self-governance of man upon the earth has resulted in nothing but wars, terrorism, corruption, misery, death, racism, murders, kidnappings, modern day slavery-human trafficking, starvation, hatred, jealously, greed that is exponentially exploding around us before our very eyes daily. These events collectively have set the stage for the man of the hour's ascendancy to his earthly throne. However, others will challenge his hegemony. Especially the Kings of the East China and her allies. The Antichrist upon hearing the news of the approaching Kings of the East, becomes furious, retaliates and kills many people.

See **Daniel 11:44** that says, "**Therefore, he shall go out with great fury to destroy and annihilate many**." However, the next verse, i.e., **Daniel 11:45** sets his doom denoted here it says "**and he shall plant the tents of his palace between the seas and the glorious mountain yet he shall come to his end and no one will help him.**" This is astounding. He goes from everyone helping or assisting him to no one will help him. The Chinese have morphed into a mighty world power now able to challenge the United States on every conceivable level. These include but are not limited to militarily, politically, economically and has reached its Communist tentacles to all corners of the earth vying for influence in geopolitical matters. Meanwhile, the United States withdraws or shrinks from influence, respect, sphere of power, due to stupidity, ignorance and plain incompetence of its current administration under Donald Trump's blatant intolerant racism for all non-European whites in America. Trumps incendiary race-baiting, rhetoric causing divisiveness, goofiness and isolationist, cocoon, tribalism and petty meanness. Trump is in way over his level of intellect due to his inability to govern a nation. He is intentionally dividing America via his childish tweets and vulgar name-calling with outlandish, incomprehensible, disgraceful lying untold in the history of the galaxy daily!

See Christ words in **Matthew 12:25, "Every kingdom divided against itself is brought to desolation and every city-divided against itself will not stand."** Trump admires dictatorial autocrat killers such as Putin of Russia, Kim Jong Un of North Korea and Chairman Xi of China because he wants to be a dictator just like them—i.e., unanswerable to any power on earth other than their own Satanic influenced little devious minds. The Kings of the East, the Chinese move with blitzkrieg speed toward Israel to fight against the Antichrist and his armies. The Chinese have declared they are siding with the Pakistanis in their current war of words and threats and battles with India while the United States allies itself with India. Well the reason is simple the Chinese **must move through** Pakistan land peninsulas enroute through India to reach Israel which is approximately five thousand miles away. The resupply line for arming, equipping, refueling, mobilizing, feeding and hydrating its millions of ungodly troops from mainland China toward the Battle must be unbroken for the army's needs are vast. The enormity of the size of its military forces who will invade will dwarf the ability to loot or pillage its way successfully along the way among countries that lie between them as they march to conquer the holy land. The word of God says the army is composed of **200 million men**.

See Revelation 9:16 and the number of the army of the horsemen were (200,000,000) two hundred thousand thousand and I heard the number of them. It is so many it is almost like "human locusts" descending upon the world. Currently, China has the largest standing military force in the entire world bar none! It has the second largest annual military budget expenditures in the world second only to the America. China has the largest population of people in the world living under the auspices and governance of its Communist dictatorial system of government. The People's Liberation Army as the Communist, Maoist Regime calls its military or refer their army as or unto, has only the United States of America as it closest competitor. However, that may change to their favor within the next five years or so if America does not purge itself of the debilitating paralysis of stupor or ineptitude here very soon and get itself together. Which it will not because of its divisiveness and date with destiny. Furthermore, to complicate matters China and Pakistan have collaboration on many levels.

Here are just a few of things that the Chinese and Pakistan authoritarian governments have partnered together with or have done in preparation for the great day of battle to assist themselves in getting ready or prepared to travel and fight in the Middle East Theater or Area of Operations.

- China and Pakistan have just completed the world's largest highway from China to Pakistan: **Karakoram Highway**
- China and Pakistan constructed the largest difficult trans railway bridge in the world est. value **$60 billion** land/sea projects
- China and Pakistan have formed the China/Pakistan Economic Corridor current estimate in US dollar est. above total **50 billion dollars**
- China and Pakistan Intelligence Agencies share Regional, National and International secrets among their Intel Community
- China and Pakistan complete joint military maneuvers some openly some clandestinely together regularly

Pakistan is absolutely critical or crucial to China's ability to move its gargantuan army to Israel to join in the Revelation battle. simply because Pakistan is the land bridge that connects Far East Asia to the Middle East Asian continent. However, they are not aimlessly wandering or drifting adroit to Israel with no leadership or demonic purpose make no mistake about it. Evil spiritual principalities of demons spearhead or drive China to their date with divine destiny! We find our rationale for such a premise in the word of the Lord God Almighty of Israel. Their purpose is specific as is their goal, which is to fight for control of the world's most sacred spot on earth Jerusalem, Israel. Keep in mind an often being repeated theme from this point onward that Jerusalem is the only city in the entire world that exists in Heaven and on earth simultaneously. Just as there was a fight for Jerusalem's Living Room in Heaven there will be a fight for Jerusalem's Living Room here on earth. In addition, Jerusalem is **the only** city that God promises and does make new again in the kingdom of God. See **Revelation 21:1–2** that says, **"And I saw a new heaven and a new earth for the first heaven and the first earth were passed away and there was no more sea"** and I John saw <u>the holy city, New Jerusalem coming down from God out of heaven</u> **prepared as a bride adorned for her husband. Good God Almighty!** What such a splendid blessing to read these words and yet how much more it will be blessed to **see** the New Jerusalem coming down from heaven from God if one is to witness this sight in the future!

Consequently, spirits of demons go out together to assemble all the armies of the world to Armageddon in Northern Israel to determine world hegemony where they intend to defeat the Antichrist. **Revelation 16:13–16** *reads, "And I saw three unclean spirits like frogs (each* one was able to spew one demonic spirit from his throat) *coming out of the mouth of the dragon, out of the mouth of the beast and out of the mouth of the false prophet. For they are the spirits of demons, performing signs which go out to the kings of the whole world to gather them to the battle of that great day of God Almighty and they gathered them together to the place called in Hebrew Armageddon."* The battle rages fiercely. After all sides the Americans, Chinese, Russians, Anti-Christ forces comprised of the, Arabs-Israelis, European Union, and NATO and all military forces on earth who are military units from or of the vast numerous fractured Muslim desert kingdoms of ancient warrior empires of the Middle East, attempt to take control of the Holy Land of Israel. By attempting to annihilate each other to rule the world for supremacy from Israel. Then suddenly, unexpectedly, the heavens open, Christ appears on a white horse and the armies of heaven are behind him; See **Revelation 19:11–20,** which reads,

> *Now I saw heaven opened, and behold a white horse and he that sat on him was called Faithful and True and in righteousness, he judges and makes war. His eyes were like a flame of fire and on his head were many crowns. He had a name written*

that no man knew except himself. He was clothed with a robe dipped in blood and his name is called the word of God. And the armies in heaven clothed in fine linen white and clean followed him on white horses. Out of his mouth goes a sharp two-edged sword and with it he shall strike the nations. And he himself shall rule them with a rod of iron. He himself treads the winepress of the fierceness and wrath of Almighty God. And he had on his robe and on his thigh a name written KING of KINGS AND LORD OF LORDS. Then I saw an angel standing in the sun and he cried with a loud voice. Saying to all the birds come and gather together for the supper of the great God. That you may eat the flesh of Kings, the flesh of captains, the flesh of horses and of those who sit on them. And the flesh of all people free and slave both small and great. I saw the beast and the kings of earth and their armies gathered together to make war against him who sat on the horse and against his army.

Revelation 1:7 tells us, **"Behold he is coming with the clouds and <u>every eye will see</u> him 'even they who pierced' him and all the tribes of the earth shall mourn because of him even so amen!"** Pay close attention to this if you will for the revelation of Jesus Christ from heaven is so stupendous that even those ***Roman Centurions who pierced Christ's side with a spear in Jerusalem two thousand years ago although dead will see Christ too*** as he descends from the T3 heaven! His revelation is so powerful that it penetrates all layers of the T3 Heavens and even to hell itself. So that all may witness the glorious, triumphant return of the Son of God! God wants every eye of man or angel ever created regardless to whether they are on earth, in heaven or in hell itself to witness the triumphant return of his Holy Son, Jesus Christ to see him in his entire divine splendor, majesty, glory and honor that he always had with his Father. My Lord what an awesome spectacle this will be!

Christ makes his move toward earth, while mounted majestically upon his white stallion, as all eyes shall see him in splendorous glory revealed from the majestic kingdom of Almighty God's Living Room that has retained him since his Ascension into heaven at his tortuous crucifixion. Christ is seated far above all power, principality, dominion and authority on both sides of the heavens eternal divide with the only exception being he is subservient to his and Our Heavenly Father. Christ is gloriously, mounted and highly atop his steed surveying all the mourning tribes of the earth as he triumphantly gallops seamlessly toward earth exalted as the Archangel blows the heavenly shofar announcing his return to the earth. See **2 Thessalonians 1:7–9,** which reads, "**Rest with us when the Lord Jesus shall be revealed from heaven, with his mighty angels in flaming fire, taking vengeance on them that know not God. And that obey not the gospel of our Lord Jesus Christ who shall be punished with everlasting destruction from the presence of the Lord and from the glory of his power.**" These kings as well as their armies will stop fighting against the Anti-Christ and or each other in an attempt to join the Antichrist and his minions to fiercely and futilely unite their armies against the King of King, Jesus Christ, accompanied by the armies of heaven both holy angels and redeemed mankind.

This turn of events to fight against Christ and the armies of heaven, occur for two reasons. Primarily, because the Lord has surprised and caught all demons and people off guard since they were not expecting his sudden majestic arrival when he comes from heaven. Astonishingly, when the heavens scroll back like a banana peel, all lose their mind, bewildered by this heavenly intervention. Secondly, they are just trying to stay alive for they now know that the end of times has arrived. In their exasperation, some will even call upon rocks for cover. See **Revelation 6:14–16** here, "**Then the sky receded as a scroll when it is rolled up and every mountain and island was moved out of its place. And the kings of the earth, the great men, the rich men, the commanders, the mighty men and every slave** and every free man hid themselves in caves and in the rocks and mountains. And said to the mountains and rocks fall on us and hide us from the face of him who sits on the throne and from the wrath of the Lamb for the great day of his wrath has come and who is able to stand?" Especially Satan and his fallen angels they know exactly what time it is for them. Remember Satan no longer has any access to heaven at all. Therefore, even he is unaware of the exact time of the return of Christ since banished from all access to the third or second heavens to the first heaven or earth realm.

Review **Matterhew 24:36, "But of that day and hour knows 'no man, no not the angels' of heaven but my _Father only_."** Also see, **2 Peter 3:10** that reads; **_but the day of the Lord will come as a thief in the night in which the heavens will pass away with a great noise and the elements shall melt with fervent heat. The earth also and the works that are herein shall be burned up_**. The fugitives from heavenly justice are quickly being rounded up and their armies defeated. See **Revelation 20:10** that reads; **the devil is cast into the lake of fire** (delayed sentence enforced) **where the beast and false prophet** (who proceeded him for their punishment) **are and shall be tormented day and night.** Judgment immediately begins for all fallen humanity who have rejected Christ.

See **Revelation _20:12_** _that says, "**And I saw the dead small and great stand before God and 'the books were opened' and another book was opened which is 'the book of life' and the dead were judged out of those things which were written in the books according to their works.**"_ _Summarily, all renegades against God Almighty whether they are angels or man are doomed forever. Afterward, God prepares for the eternal blissful transition via the creation of a new world with redeemed human beings, holy angels, animals, etc., who are very devoted to worshipping him and Jesus Christ voluntarily. See_ **Isaiah _65:17–25_** _cited here that states,_ **"For behold I create new heavens and a new earth. And the former shall not be remembered or come to mind. For behold I create Jerusalem as a rejoicing and her people a joy. And I will rejoice in Jerusalem and joy in my people. The voice of weeping shall no longer be heard in her, no more shall an infant from there live but a few days. Nor an old** man who has not fulfilled his days, for the child shall die one hundred years old. But the sinner being one hundred years old shall be accursed. They shall build houses and inhabit them they shall plant vineyards and eat their fruit. They shall not build and another inhabit. They shall not plant and another eat for, as the days of a tree so shall be the days of my people. And my elect shall long enjoy the work of their hands. They shall not labor in vain nor bring forth children for trouble. For they shall be the descendants of the blessed of the Lord, and their offspring with them. It shall come to pass before they call I will answer. And while they are still speaking, I will hear. <u>The wolf and the lamb shall feed together. The lion shall eat straw like the ox and dust shall be the serpent's food. They shall not hurt nor destroy in all my holy mountain says the Lord.</u>"

In addition, review **Revelation 21:1**, "Now I saw a new heaven and a new earth for the first heaven and the first earth had passed away. Also there was no more sea. Then I John saw the holy city <u>New Jerusalem coming down out of heaven from God</u> prepared as a bride adorned for her husband."

This is the **<u>very first time</u>** since man's creation and the existence and of the foundation of the created heavens, the worlds or seas or the creation of man upon the earth, whereby **God actually <u>*lives*</u> with man.** On the other hand, shall I more aptly say, God allows **man to live** with and **be physically near the holy presence of the Divine God** of all creation! I presume that had Adam fully understood that God Almighty <u>always wanted man</u> to be with him in paradise <u>maybe</u> just maybe Adam would not have sinned. Then again, you know that I could just simply be dead wrong on this issue. Man of all of God's created being has a special favor eternally with his Creator. Man does not fully appreciate or understand the depths that God was willing to go through to save man's soul from eternal damnation in spite of our willful disobedience. God spared no expense whatsoever. Actually, he gave the ultimate sacrifice any Father could ever do...he gave *his only begotten, Holy, Son Jesus Christ as our eternal atoning sacrifice to die for our sins*! The first world God drowned or destroyed all life by water. The second one God will destroy by fire. Review here **2**

Peter 3:10–13 but the day of the Lord will come as a thief in the night in which the heavens will pass away with a great noise and the elements will melt with fervent heat. both <u>the earth and the works that are in it will be burned up.</u> Therefore, since all these things will be dissolved what manner of persons ought you to be in holy conduct looking for and hastening the coming of the day of God. Because of which <u>the heavens will be dissolved being on fire and</u> <u>the elements will melt with fervent heat.</u> Nevertheless, we according to his promise look for new heavens and a new earth in which righteousness dwells. Finally, now God has created a new heaven and a new earth.

Revelation 21:5 cited here, "**Then he that sat upon the throne said 'Behold I make <u>all things</u> new." And he said unto me write for these words are true and faithful**. I have had numerous conversations with others including friends, family or acquaintances who have always said I am going to cry when I am in heaven. I quickly would reply then you are not going to heaven (joking *sarcastically while using a sincere tone*) they would reply why would you say that I am not going to heaven? I would tell them go back and read the scriptures. Subsequently, my response to their reply to support my assertions was the word of God says that **he will wipe away all tears** and **there is <u>no crying, no death, no night</u>, <u>no sorrow</u>, <u>no more suffering,</u>** etc., inside of heaven. I informed them that there was biblical support for my statement that says in **Revelation 21:4, "And God shall wipe away all tears from their eyes, and there shall be no more death, neither sorrow, *nor crying* neither shall there be <u>any more pain</u> for the former things are passed away."**

Therefore, I would tell them, how are you going to cry when God wipes away your tears and the tear duct that enables you to cry personally? This act of God wiping away ones tears from believers' faces is reminiscent to me when Jesus personally washed the disciples' feet. Review **John 13:3–7,** listed here that says, "**Jesus knowing that the Father had given all things into his hands and that he had come from God. And was going to God, after that rose from supper and laid aside his garments, took a towel and girded himself after that he poured water into a basin and *began to wash the*** *disciples' feet* **and to wipe them with the towel with which he was girded."** Christ was symbolically demonstrating that one's sins were washed away forever by the fact that he was washing their feet (not them washing his feet) in an act of utmost heavenly display of God's humility that would ever be displayed. Remember Jesus said in **Mark 10:45, "For even the Son of Man** (Christ himself) **did not come to be served, but to serve and give his life a ransom for many."** God humbling himself for man by either wiping away tears, saving his soul or washing his feet. The level of humility that God and Christ consistently display is unfathomable! Other acts include but are not limited to, the Lord merely walked with Adam in the cool of the day *he did not live with him* in the Garden of Eden.

God talked with Moses atop Mount Sinai where he gave him the Holy Commandments to tell man how to live upon the earth. God Almighty had Holy angels usher Isaiah the prophet into his divine presence as he described the transgressions of Israel to him when he asked the rhetorical question who will go for us to warn Israel of its ways. The Prophet Isaiah promptly replied here I am Lord send me. The Lord God of Israel was with Daniel the prophet in the Lion's den. Just as he accompanied the other three wise men of Israel—i.e., Meshach, Shadrach, and Abednego in the fiery furnace as he protected them from the flame, heat and smoke because they refused to bow down or serve other gods other than the Lord God of Jerusalem. I Am that I Am, walked alongside Joshua as he marched the armies of the Lord with swords around Jericho seven times before he flattened the walls thereby allowing the Hebrew armies to attack the enemy inside of this fortress from all sides simultaneously. Yahweh instilled courage into the heart of a young boy, who later, as a man became King David, as he fought against an adult man, who just happened to be a mammoth of a man inside of his giant body (possibly a Nephilim) remember them from earlier discourse? The Holy Redeeming God of Jerusalem, allowed his Holy Spirit to appear in the shape of a dove to descend from heaven atop the shoulder of his Holy begotten Son, Jesus Christ, to confirm to those around him Christ's divine heritage of the Lord forever! The Invisible God of Israel spoke to the disciples upon Mount Tabor—i.e., the Mount of Transfiguration whereby Christ was "transfigured" which is to say seen in all his holy glory by Peter, James and John talking *with Moses and Elijah who were already dead* and from a by gone era in the Old Testament were alive with Jesus there.

Summarily, The Lord God of Hosts humbled himself to save his image…humanity from eternal death. This is something rarely if ever mentioned to parishioners as they fill the houses of worship globally each week to acknowledge God Almighty in unison. I am referring to the fact *by saving man*… *God saved his own image*. For man was created in the image of God. Read **Genesis 1:26, "So God created man in his own image, in the image of God he created him male and female he created them."** The Living God of Jerusalem turned away toward the hill of Golgotha so that God Almighty's face would not witness the King of all Kings agonizing, brutal, slow crucifixion death of his Son for the sins of the whole world. Afterward, the Lord God of Hosts of Israel displayed his majestic, mighty power from heaven raising his Son Jesus from the dead to atone for *our* sins. Thereby granting us the opportunity to live with and among God in paradise forever! Essentially, we must understand that The Lord Our God until this futuristic event occurs in the time of promise to come. Never previously at any other time in the dateless past, to the current dated present, this side of the chasm of heaven and earth has **ever lived** with man in heaven or earth ever. **God has lived with angels in heaven above but he has never lived with man until he does so in the future.** However, God has always *wanted man to live* with him inside of his living room. Now let us discover or find the scriptures together that support this amazing revelation here.

CHAPTER XVIII

Living With God And Christ
Inside God's Living Room

Coincidentally or by divine design (I believe it is the latter). It is only befitting and poetic justice that we conclude this journey from where it all originated. Since wars actually started in heaven before they cascaded by celestial gravity and divine jurisprudence to the earth. We come back full circle to end this narrative returning to the place or the origin of all life, visible and invisible directly inside of the sanctuary of God's Living Room. This is anaolgous to the salmon that swims "*upstream*" *against* the treacherous currents, predators and other dangers to return to where life began for them in the shallow ponds of the vastness of the Alaskan rivers to give birth to the next generation of salmon. Adam completely misinterpreted God's original intent for humanity when God created him upon the earth. Adam merely supposed that God wanted him to toil in labor in the Garden of Eden, while in it, keep it, dress it, manicure it, eat from it, live with his wife Eve inside it, bare children within it, sacrifice animals to God out of it, worship God from it, then die upon it. Afterward, that is it.

Nothing could have been further from the truth. We must all resist or fight the natural inclination or temptation to be judgmental, sanctimonious, pompous, having a holier than thou feeling or self-righteous smug attitude my friends regarding Adam/

Eve actions within the Garden of Eden. Because we probably more likely than not, would not have done any better than Adam and Eve, had we been in it! Proof being, all we have to do is just look at how we are living now upon the earth before God, hmmmmm. Need I say more? Now we are going to go back to where we started for a moment to explore this premise. Return if you will back to the opening stanza of the book where I began discussing the origin. Now that we are in the Origin section of this book (pages 6–7). I want to direct your attention to the third paragraph whereby God makes a decision about creating other life forms that he can share his glory as well as love with as all the universe lies silently before him in its grand splendor. God has to decide among many things; about these newly created beings e.g. *__where will these beings live__, how will they forage, what will they do, how can they after their creation know, act or be in relation to me?* Et cetera. Watch closely now if you will. Herein is a subliminal message that I want to unravel which simply is that God "wanted" Adam to **live with him** or **where he was living all along**. Translation God **wanted them (humanity) to live with him** inside of his living room from the very start as he contemplated our creation. For biblical proof, See **Colossians 1:13, 16, and 20**. Cited here **that says He has delivered us from the power of darkness and conveyed us into the kingdom of the Son of his love. For he created all things that are in heaven and that are on the earth visible and invisible whether thrones or principalities or powers. __All things__ were created through him and __for him__ for it pleased the Father that in him all the fullness should dwell and by him "__to reconcile all things to himself__" by him __whether things on earth or things in heaven__ having made peace through the blood of his cross**. Adam simply did not understand __why__ God created him. Neither did he comprehend the purposes of him being in God's paradise garden although he presumed it was simply work it for God. Question, why would God want to create beings *in __his own image__* then want or have them reside or *__live somewhere else__* "other than" where he was apart or away from him? Simply put that would be illogical. This lacks sound reasoning period. Further scriptural proof documented for all to see in **Revelation 21:3** that reads:

> *And I heard a great voice saying behold the <u>tabernacle of God is with men and 'he will dwell' with them</u> and they shall be his people and '<u>God himself shall be with them</u>' and be their God.*

Cheer up saints of the Most High God! Your redemption draws near. You have the down payment—i.e., the earnest pledge by the indwelling of your body of the Holy Spirit of Jesus Christ who is Lord forever! You are closer to being with Christ today than you were this same time yesterday! God had obstacles to overcome with man's character who voluntarily sinned against him in the Garden of Eden, in order to have man *live among* his holy personage, although he always wanted man to reside with him. God is Holy. **Leviticus 19:2** says, "**Speak unto all the congregation of the children of Israel and say, you shall be holy for I the Lord 'your God am holy.'**"

Revelation 4:8 states, "**And the four beasts each of them had six wings about him and they were full of eyes within and they <u>rest not</u> <u>day or night</u> saying *Holy, holy, holy* Lord God Almighty which is, which was which are to come. Also, see Leviticus 11:44** that reads, **For I am the Lord your God. You shall therefore sanctify yourselves and you shall be holy. <u>For I am Holy</u> neither shall you defile yourselves with any manner of unclean things.**"

Moreover, **Isaiah 6:3** listed here, that says, "**And one cried unto the other and said <u>holy, holy, holy</u> is the Lord of host the whole earth is full of his glory.**" Consequently, anyone or anything that is near, around or that approaches God <u>**must**</u> be holy too. **Absolutely no exceptions!** The Bible declares, <u>**without holiness**</u> no man shall see the Lord! See **Hebrews 12:14** that reads, "**Make every effort to live in peace with everyone and <u>be holy</u> for <u>without holiness</u> no one will see the Lord.**" Man <u>**was not**</u> holy in the Garden of Eden.

Adam was in a "neutral estate" of being so to speak. Originally without sin while possessing the possibility or capability to sin which later he did. Subsequently, he moved from a neutral status to a sinful estate of existence. This truism involving the high proclivity to sin DNA/RNA strand is in the bloodline of every person born in this world as a direct result of the physiological, biological and metaphysical inheritance of this transition from neutrality to sinful activism inherited from Adam and Eve. God is omniscient, meaning that he knows everything from the beginning. Therefore, because he foreknew (God via Omniscience) that Satan would cause an insurrection within his living room...

Nevertheless, just as importantly, God knew (in advance) that Adam and Eve would disobey him as well. Thereby forfeiting their right to live in harmony with God in blissful paradise eternally—i.e., within (God's Living Room in heaven) not just within the Garden of Eden on earth temporarily. Which simply was an image of paradise in heaven, God acted on our behalf by providing himself a satisfying substitutionary propitiation, atoning, sacrificial lamb. Worthy of his forgiveness/acceptance so that we could be allowed to live with him via eternal pardoning in Christ's death. God's scapegoat through his eternal sacrifice yielded through his broken, tattered, tortured, spat upon, mocked, ridiculed, speared, bloodied, forsaken, beaten, abused and crucified body of his Only Begotten Son, Jesus Christ to save our souls from the same eternal fate as Lucifer! God planted the Garden of Eden, strategically within the naval or situated epicenter of the earth, as such, it was a pristine testing laboratory for Adam/Eve to ascertain if they would develop or exhibit Pavlov's theory of classical conditioning from God's perspective.

Ivan Pavlov's theory of classical conditioning behavioral conceptually/theoretically predicates action/reward based upon interaction with the milieu or environment. Essentially Pavlov theorizes when one receives an award for a particular action within a specific environment one repeats the action to receive additional "rewards" whatever that may be, causing one's behavior to become easily predictable based upon the action/reward principle. Simply put, when Adam and Eve saw the tree initially it did not bother them. They were obedient to God for they ate from all of the other trees that were present. However, once the tempter told them it could make them "like God" they began salivating for its forbidden fruit. Alternatively when thy received the "reward" of knowledge, wisdom or awareness of sin (being like God who was aware of Satan's sin in heaven) within the garden by disobedience they continued to sin (act) against God desiring more rewards—i.e., knowledge in the future based upon their errant behavior. Well, I guess we all know how those scientific hypothesis results turned out. Thereby Adam/Eve's actions mandated that God due to his holy nature had to either punish sin or develop a process for remission to forgive sin. If sin went unforgiven or unaccounted for then or now the cosmos would explode because God would had been tempted so to speak, not literally to wink at this rebellion, which is virtually impossible! God cannot be tempted with evil at all ever!

See **James 1:13–15** that reads, "***Let no man say that when he is tempted 'I am tempted of God' for God cannot be tempted by evil nor does he himself tempt anyone. But each one is tempted when he is drawn away of his own lusts and enticed then when lusts has conceived it gives birth to sin and sin when it is full grown brings for death.***" Temptation only comes from four sources. **None of them emanate or originate from God Almighty**! One of them is the devil, who is aka the tempter. Remember when he tempted Christ three times, one was to worship him. Another was to turn the stones into bread after his forty day–forty night fast. The third or final temptation of Christ was when he tempted Christ to leap from the pinnacle of the temple to prove that he was the Son of God because the angels of God would swoop down less Christ foot would dash upon a stone. (Review **Matthew 4:1–11** for the three temptations of Christ by Satan.) I recited them here in paragraph form for your convenience. Naturally all can readers can peruse it in your own Bible (different versions) at your choosing or now if you so desire.

Then was Jesus was led up of the spirit into the wilderness <u>to be tempted of the devil</u>. And when he *had fasted forty days and forty nights afterward, he was hungry. Now when the tempter came to him he said if you are the Son of God command that these stones become bread. But he answered and said it is written that man shall not live by bread alone but by every word that proceeds out of the mouth of God (first temptation). The devil took him up to the holy city, set him on the pinnacle of the temple and said to him if you are the son of God throw yourself down, for it is written he shall give his angels charge over you and in their hands they shall bear you up lest you dash your foot against a stone. Jesus said to him it is written you shall not tempt the Lord thy God (second temptation.) Again, the devil took him to an exceedingly high mountain and showed him all the kingdoms of the world and their glory. And he said unto him all these things I will give you if you will fall down and worship me. Then Jesus said to him away with you Satan, for it is written you shall worship the Lord your God and him only shall you serve (third temptation.) Then the devil left him and behold angels came and ministered unto him.*

The other three sources of temptation besides the devil are the world, the flesh and one's own lusts or sensual desires of evil thoughts are the remaining other three sources of temptation for man. God's holiness caused him to ultimately send his only begotten Son Christ Jesus to be a sacrificial lamb and become sin for us (**for he who knew no sin became sin for us 2 Corinthians 5:21**) for without the atoning death of Jesus Christ humanity would be forever lost away from the love and mercy of God period. God had to go create an eternal sacrifice, forgive man, redeem man, and clean man up to prepare man to live in unison with or near God's Divine and Holy presence inside the tabernacle of God's Living Room. Adam was not holy but God created him pure. Adam/Eve's willful disobedience of their actions transitioned them to an unholy level of existence worthy of the holy punishment of God that we all inherited and deserve. Holiness **can't be** tainted with evil but *purity* can be contaminated with impurities. Whenever contamination occurs, it alters eternally the purity of the substance or being (in this case humanity) thus transforming it to an impure estate from its original status. Consequently, it can't be used for the original intended purpose for its existence. Subsequently, this is attributable unto the existence of the impurities, which makes it unusable or unreliable. If it is used at all, everything that it is amalgamated with will be contaminated or impure due to the existence that it now contains because of the mixture of the contaminated ingredients that exist inside the holistic body of the main substance in this case...mankind. However, God wasn't about to abandon his plans for man to live with him because of Lucifer's evil tirade in heaven and Adam's fall from grace on earth. God via Christ...**works all things according to the counsel of his own will (Ephesians 1:11).**

Subsequently, God's will was (still is) to have man live with him that caused God to enact Plan B... God entitled Plan B as **Operation Salvation** via Jesus Christ. Jesus mentions Gods will to them. Jesus tells his disciples something that stirs up the spirit within them when he is giving account of his life as he is about to die for the sins of the world. We pick up the story here in **Matthew 14:2–3** where Jesus tells them: *I go to prepare a place for you for within my Father's house. There are many mansions (God's Living Room) and if I go and "prepare a place" for you. I will come again and receive you to myself that **where I am there you may be also**! Here is where the Son of God explains to man the intention of God's will from the very beginning—i.e., **where I am you may be also**.* God desired man's friendship, companionship and presence to be with him in Paradise the entire time. *This is something that alluded Adam's ability to understand or comprehend initially.* My Lord! This was the mysterious, unrevealed original intent that God always wanted to have with man (Adam) who did not recognize what God really wanted. Some may be skeptical or still unconvinced. Ok that is fine. Let me show you what the Apostle Paul had to say regarding this subject matter. Look at **Ephesians 1:9–10** verses I have highlighted below for all readers.

> ***Ephesian 1:9–10*** *states that having made known unto us the* ***"mystery of his will"*** *according to his good pleasure. Which he purposed within himself verse 10; that in the dispensation of the fullness of times (end of the age)—i.e. (the natural progression of generational culmination, conclusion, passing or extinguishment of man's time on earth)* **"he might gather together" all things** *in Christ both* **which are in heaven and which are on earth**-*in him!*

The Apostle Paul goes on to inform us in **1 Corinthians 2:9**. "*That eye has not seen, nor ear heard, neither have entered into the heart of man the things which God has prepared for them that love him.*" All of these things whatever they are God the Father, via Christ will give **to all those inside of his living room** once they are there in eternal bliss with him! Predicated upon this scripture, man lacks the mental or spiritual acumen to fully ascertain, contemplate or imagine the things that God has actually prepared for those who love him and his Holy Son Jesus Christ the Lord. Continuing with this theme, **1 Corinthians 2:11** says, "*Even so, no one knows the things of God except the Spirit of God.*" However, we can see some of them listed in **Revelation 21 and 22**, and these include but are not limited to no death, no pain, no sorrow, no crying, no fear, no threat, no lies and no deceit. However, I think the most awesome thing of all **is being in the very presence of God Almighty** and **his Son, Jesus Christ** gives me goosebumps now as I think about this. Seeing God and Christ face to face there can be no comparison at all with nothing this world can ever offer. See **Revelation 22:4** that states, "**And they shall see his face and his name shall be in their foreheads.**" **Absolutely** nothing can ever be more breathtaking than this! The ability to be up close and personal with God who is the epitome of divine love, mercy, truth, holiness, righteousness, purity, serenity, peace, power, omnipotence, omniscience, omniscient with tranquil grace **My God, My God, Oh My God!**

The word of the Lord says that there will be no night. This is intriguing because the human experience has always been associated in some way with resting which usually occurs at night. Currently our body's biological clock begins releasing chemicals within the brain during nighttime hours to assist the body and person with sleeping to prepare for the next day. Now imagine there is no night thus there are no need for chemicals to alter the state of mind anticipating sleep. There is no sun, no moon or no stars in heaven… Review **Revelation 21:22–23** cited here: "**And I saw no temple therein for the Lord God Almighty and the Lamb are the temple of it. And the city had no need of the sun neither of the moon to shine in it for the glory of God did lighten it and the Lamb is the light of it…**" just like it was *before God created* them for seasons, signs and years to measure time for man to live thereby them. In addition, the word of the Lord talks about the conduct of animals inside of his living room too. Interestingly, it describes or illustrates animals who were mortal enemies on the previous earth will not be enemies there in heaven. Once upon a time, some of these animals fought to death. One as predator and the other as prey with each other. Here in heaven they will no longer have any more animosity. All animals become eternal instant vegetarians.

See **Isaiah 65:25** it *reads, "The wolf and the lamb shall feed together and the lion shall eat straw like the bullock and the dust shall be the serpent's meat they shall not hurt nor destroy in all my holy mountain."* Wow! Try that now at Sea World, Wild Kingdom or any other animal shelter or sanctuary and witness the violent carnage that would occur. God not only dwells with man, God has gathered all of his creation in one place to enjoy all of the blessings that he originally intended for man to have after he created him upon the earth. Man's pilgrimage to the eternal kingdom of God has been a long and painful journey because of man's willful disobedience and Satan's cascading catastrophic instigation of war in heaven (God's

Living Room) that transcended down to the earth. Yet, God always had a plan, which has made our suffering pilgrimage all more the worthwhile. See Paul's word's in **Romans 8:18, for I consider that the suffering of this present time _are not worthy_ to be compared with the glory, which shall be revealed in us.** We will be able to see the Lord, Jesus Christ in all his regal glory that he originally had with his Holy Father God in divine splendor before the world began! See **John 17:1, 4–5** and **verse 24** combined here where Jesus says, "*Father the hour has come Glorify your Son that your Son may also glorify you. I have glorified you on the earth. I have finished the work, which you have given me. And now O Father, glorify me together with yourself with "the glory that I had" with you before the world began. Father, I desire that they also whom you gave me be with me where I am that they may behold my glory which you have given me for you loved me before the foundation of the world! Get ready saints of the Most High God of heaven and earth for your redemption draws nigh.*"

*Paul Revere warned the colonists that the British are coming as he rode throughout the towns of the emerging nation that later became the United States of America that all of us as American patriots who love our country and have served her defense as proof of our devotion. However, I am sounding the clarion alarm in the spirit of Paul Revere and John the Baptist who declared to say that **Jesus Christ the Son of the Most High God of Israel is coming. Ready or Not, Christ the King is on his way! Even so, Come Lord Jesus come! Amen***

THE END

POST COMMENTS

The Apostle Paul said in **2 Timothy 4:7**, "**I have fought the good fight**, *I have finished the race*, **I have kept the faith**." Therefore, along with the theme initiated by the Son of God and repeated by the Apostle Paul, I say that **I *have finished a short book*** that the Lord gave me to do. I pray earnestly, dear readers, that this book has truly been a blessing and joy for you to read, as it has been a blessing and joy for me to write. I have done so with the express purpose of glorifying the One, True, Only, and Holy God.

The Lord God of Hosts of Israel and his Holy Begotten Son, Our Lord and Savior, Jesus Christ who loves and accepts us just as we are with all our faults and shortcomings of his holy glory unconditionally. May the Lord God of Abraham, Isaac, and Jacob watch between you and me as we go about our life on this journey toward his Living Room. I pray that The Holy, Invisible, Eternal God of Israel who never slumbers or sleeps keeps all of us and will cause his holy face to shine upon us. For God alone through Christ and the power of his Holy Spirit keeps a watchful eye as the Guardian over Jerusalem, Israel. The day is rapidly approaching when we will we meet God Almighty and his Holy Son, Jesus Christ, face-to-face.

Until then, may the true King of all kings and Lord of all lords, be with each one of us and all as we pray for the peace of Jerusalem. For it is the City of the Great King. I humbly ask that our God unite our prayers with that of all those who are in heaven now and guide us to the door of his Living Room and grant us a heartwarming "Well done, you good and faithful servants." Welcome to your eternal home. Enter into the joy of your Lord with his divine love ushering our entrance while we are escorted to our seats by holy angels at the Lord's Table inside his Living Room. My prayer is that God will grant all those who believe that Jesus Christ was sent from God get the eternal privilege to live with Christ Inside of God's Living Room and inquire within his temple to behold the beauty of the Lord and see him just as he is in his entire Majestic Glory world without end. I repeat some familiar words shouted by the Colonial Rider, Paul Revere, with a different variation of his rallying cry. Just as Paul Revere proclaimed, "The *British are coming.*" I echo John the Baptist and Paul Revere by proclaiming Jesus Christ is coming soon! Amen! Maranatha.

Marine Bootcamp Summer 1980

Author Larry K. Thompson (R) with BFFL
Military Police Academy Fall 1980

CPL. Larry K. Thompson
Marine Ball 1982

SELECTED BIBLIOGRAPHY

HOLY BIBLE, KJV AND NKJV
OLD SCOFIELD STUDY SYSTEM
The Destruction of Black Civilization
David Walker's Appeal
ORIGIN OF THE SPECIES by CHARLES DARWIN
HEBREWS TO NEGROES
The Age of Voltaire
A Higher Loyalty
Late Great Planet Earth
The Antichrist and a Cup of Tea
The Complete Apocrypha
The Book of Giants
Biblical World
The Spanish Inquisition
Earth's Last Empire
A Colony in a Nation
Bible Almanac
Hebrew to Greek Study Bible
Post Traumatic Slave Syndrome
Unhinged
Expository Dictionary of New Testament Words
Bible Prophecy and Trump

ABOUT THE AUTHOR

The author holds a Bachelor's of Science degree in Criminal Justice from Wayne State University in Detroit, Michigan and attended Law School in Houston, Texas. Also, he is an Honorably Discharged United States Marine. The author holds two certifications in Emergency Management, one from (IAEM) i.e. International Association of Emergency Managers and the other from (TDEM) Texas Division of Emergency Management. Furthermore, he is certified by FEMA as a Master Continuity Practitioner. Mr. Thompson retired from The Office of Homeland Security after 24 years as Division Chief, Critical Infrastructure Asset Protection. Responsibilities included instructional delivery for Multiple-Hazard emergency protocols and responses specializing in Active Shooter Countermeasures. The author is currently a private consultant specializing in Active Shooter Offensive/Defensive Countermeasures tactics to enhance survival training for non-law enforcement personnel. He has one adult son, Jason. Mr. Thompson currently resides in Las Colinas, a suburb just outside of Dallas, Texas.

CPSIA information can be obtained
at www.ICGtesting.com
Printed in the USA
LVHW041009131120
671368LV00001B/38